EIGHTH EDITION

MARKETING MISTAKES AND SUCCESSES

Robert F. Hartley
Cleveland State University

JOHN WILEY & SONS, INC.

New York • Chichester • Weinheim
Brisbane • Toronto • Singapore

Acquisition Editor	Brent Gordon
Marketing Manager	Jessica Garcia
Senior Production Editor	Patricia McFadden
Illustration Editor	Gene Aiello
Production Management	Hermitage Publishing Services

This book was set in New Caledonia by Hermitage Publishing Services, and printed and bound by Courier Companies. The cover was printed by Lehigh Press.

This book is printed on acid-free paper. ∞

Library of Congress Cataloging in Publication Data

Hartley, Robert F.
 Marketing mistakes / Robert F. Hartley. — 8th ed.
  p.   cm
 Includes bibliographical references.
 ISBN 0-471-37060-6 (pbk. : alk. paper)
 1. Marketing—United States—Case studies.   I. Title.
HF5415.1.H37 2000
658.8'00973—dc21   00-038172

Printed in the United States of America

10   9   8   7   6   5   4

PREFACE

This edition marks the twenty-fifth anniversary of *Marketing Mistakes and Successes*. Who would have thought that interest in mistakes would have been so enduring?

I know of one person, Michael Pearson, of Loyola University, New Orleans who has used all of the editions. If anyone else has, going back to 1976, I would really like to hear from you. I know that many of you are past users, though, and I hope you will find this eighth edition with its new and updated cases a worthy change from earlier editions. It is always difficult to abandon interesting cases that have stimulated student discussions and provided good learning experiences. But newer case possibilities are ever competing for inclusion. Examples of good and bad handling of problems and opportunities are always emerging.

For new users, I hope the book will meet your full expectations and be an effective instructional tool. Although case books abound, you and your students may find this somewhat unique and very readable, a book that can help transform dry and rather remote concepts into practical reality, and lead to lively class discussions, and even debates amid the arena of decision making.

NEW TO THIS EDITION

In contrast to the early editions, which examined only notable mistakes, and based on your favorable comments about recent editions, I have again included some well-known successes. While mistakes provide valuable learning insights, we can also learn from successes, and we can learn by comparing the unsuccessful with the successful.

New to this edition is Marketing Wars, where the moves and countermoves of four pairs of direct competitors are examined. Another new section is Crisis Management, with its examples of how firms have mishandled or handled well their major crises. Again, we have included cases dealing with great comebacks, the truly inspiring examples of firms coming back from adversity. We have also tried where appropriate to present in Late-Breaking News sections the most recent developments as we go to publication.

Some of you have asked that I identify which cases would be appropriate for the traditional coverage of topics as organized in most marketing texts. With many cases it is not possible to truly compartmentalize the mistake or success strictly according to each topic. The patterns of success or failure tend to be more pervasive. Still, I think you will find the following classification of cases by subject matter to be helpful. I thank those of you who made this and other suggestions.

TABLE 1. Classification of Cases by Major Marketing Topics

Topics	Most Relevant Cases
Marketing research and consumer analysis	Coca-Cola, Disney, McDonald's, Maytag, Johnson & Johnson
Product	Nike, Coca-Cola, McDonald's, Boeing, Disney, Southwest Air, Vanguard, Coors, Rubbermaid, Perrier, Maytag
Distribution	Nike/Reebok, Coca-Cola/Pepsi, Borden, Coors, Rubbermaid, Wal-Mart, Tobacco
Promotion	Nike, Pepsi/Coca-Cola, Maytag, Southwest, Burger King/McDonald's, Boston Chicken/Planet Hollywood, Borden, Coors, Vanguard
Price	IBM, Borden, Disney, Vanguard, Southwest, Wal-Mart, Toys "Я" Us, Airbus/Boeing, McDonald's, ADM, Tobacco
International	Pepsi/Coca-Cola, Nike, Disney, Maytag, Airbus/Boeing, Wal-Mart, Tobacco
Customer relations	Rubbermaid, Vanguard, Southwest, Wal-Mart, Tobacco
Non-Profit/Non-Product	United Way, Disney, Airlines
Social and ethical	United Way, Met Life, ADM, Tobacco, Johnson & Johnson

TARGETED COURSES

As a supplemental text, this book can be used in a variety of courses, both under-graduate and graduate, ranging from introduction to marketing to marketing management or strategic marketing. Even retailing, entrepreneurship, and ethics courses could use a number of these cases and their learning insights.

TEACHING AIDS

As in the previous editions, this edition contains a number of teaching aids within and at the end of each chapter. Some of these will be common to several cases, and illustrate that certain successful and unsuccessful practices tend to cross company lines.

Information Boxes and Issue Boxes are included within each chapter to highlight relevant concepts and issues. Learning insights help students see how certain practices—both errors and successes—cross company lines and are prone to be either traps for the unwary or success modes. Discussion Questions and Hands-On Exercises encourage and stimulate student involvement. A recent pedagogical feature is the Team Debate Exercises, in which formal issues and options can be debated for each case. Invitation to Research suggestions allow students to take the cases a step further, to investigate what has happened since the case was written. In the final chapter, the various learning insights are summarized and classified into general conclusions.

An Instructor's Manual accompanies this text to provide possible answers and considerations for the pedagogical material within and at the ends of chapters.

ACKNOWLEDGMENTS

In this anniversary edition it seems fitting to acknowledge all those who have provided encouragement, information, advice, and constructive criticism through the years since the first edition of these *Mistakes* books. I hope you all are well and successful as we come into the new millennium, and I truly appreciate your contributions.

Beverlee Anderson; Y. H. Furuhashi, Notre Dame; Bob R. Ferguson, Virginia Commonwealth; Robert E. Moore, Colorado at Denver; James R. Ogden, Kutztown; T. N. Somasundaram, San Diego; Roderick C. Henry, Bemidji State; Allen H. Vargas, South Dakota; Elizabeth Cooper Martin, Georgetown; Barbara Coe, North Texas; Vernon R. Stauble, California State Polytechnic; Donna Giertz, Parkland; Don Hantula, St. Joseph's; William O'Donnell, Phoenix; Milton J. Alexander, Auburn; James F. Cashman, Alabama; H. Lee Meadow, Northern Illinois; Gregory Gundlach, Notre Dame; Eldon Little, Indiana; Allan Reddy, Valdosta State; Neal Pruchansky, Keene State; Donna Giertz, Parkland; Richard Cooley, Cal State Chico; Don Johnson, Oregon State; John Gottko, Hampston; Ken Mayer, Nebraska, William Rice, Cal State Fresno; Douglas Wozniak, Ferris State; Greg Bach, Bismark State; Glenna Dod, Wesleyan; Anthony McGann, Wyoming; Robert D. Nale, Coastal Carolina; Robert H. Votaw, Amber; Don Fagan, Daniel Webster; Peter Schneider, Seton Hall; Paula Saunders, Wright State; Curt Dommeyer, California State Northridge; Andrew J. Deile, Mercer; Samuel Hazen, Tarleton State; Michael B. McCormick, Jacksonville State; Charles Martin, Wichita State University; Debra Cartwright, Truman State University; Karen L. Stewart, Stockton College; Michael M. Pearson, Loyola University New Orleans; Larry Goldstein, Iona College; Lori Lohman, Augsburg College; Maria Sanella, Boston College.

Barnett Helzberg, Jr. of the Shirley and Barnett Helzberg Foundation.

My colleagues at Cleveland State: Donald Scotton, Ram Rao, Sanford Jacobs, Andrew Gross, and Benoy Joseph.

Richard Blander, Tim Kent, Ellen Ford, and Brent Gordon at Wiley.

Robert F. Hartley
James J. Nance College of Business Administration
Cleveland State University
Cleveland, Ohio 44115

CONTENTS

Chapter 1   Introduction   1

PART I   **MARKETING WARS**   **9**

Chapter 2   Cola Wars: Pepsi vs. Coca-Cola   11
Chapter 3   Sneaker Wars: Reebok vs. Nike   28
Chapter 4   Airliner Wars: Airbus vs. Boeing   42
Chapter 5   Hamburger Wars: Burger King vs. McDonald's   59

PART II   **GREAT COMEBACKS**   **79**

Chapter 6   Continental Airlines—From the Ashes   81
Chapter 7   IBM—A Fading Giant Rejuvenates   94

PART III   **CRISIS MANAGEMENT**   **113**

Chapter 8   Met Life—Underresponding to a Crisis   115
Chapter 9   Perrier—Overresponding to a Crisis   127
Chapter 10   United Way—A Not-for-Profit Tries to Cope with Image Destruction   138
Chapter 11   Johnson & Johnson—The Classic Masterpiece for Handling a Major Crisis   152

PART IV   **MARKETING MANAGEMENT MISTAKES**   **169**

Chapter 12   Toys "Я" Us—A Category Killer Falters   171
Chapter 13   Boston Chicken and Planet Hollywood—It Takes More Than Hype   184
Chapter 14   Borden—Letting Brands Wither   196
Chapter 15   Disney—Euro Disney and Other Stumbles   209
Chapter 16   Coors—What's Wrong with Being Number Three?   226
Chapter 17   Maytag—Bungling a Promotion in England   243
Chapter 18   Rubbermaid—Perils of Not Satisfying a Major Customer   257

PART V   **NOTABLE MARKETING SUCCESSES**   **269**

Chapter 19   Vanguard—Success with Minimal Marketing   271

Chapter 20   Southwest Airlines—"Try to Match Our Prices"   283

Chapter 21   Wal-Mart—The Unstoppable   299

PART VI   ETHICAL MISTAKES   315

Chapter 22   ADM—Price Fixing and Political Cronyism   317

Chapter 23   Tobacco—An Industry Beleaguered   329

Chapter 24   Conclusions: What Can Be Learned?   344

CHAPTER ONE

Introduction

$\mathbf{A}$s I write this, *Marketing Mistakes and Successes* is approaching its twenty-fifth anniversary. The first edition was 147 pages and included such long-forgotten cases as Korvette, W. T. Grant, Edsel, Corfam, Gilbert, and the Midi.

In this eighth edition, we have dropped ten cases from the seventh edition, and added nine. Other cases have been revamped and updated, and in some instances reclassified. New to this eighth edition is the section on Marketing Wars, in which major competitors are examined and compared, and four of these subcases are also new. Many of the cases are as recent as today's headlines; some have still not come to complete resolution.

In accordance with your expressed preferences, we have continued the format of the last two editions by examining not only notable mistakes but also some notable successes. We continue to seek what can be learned—insights that are transferable to other firms, other times, and other situations. What key factors brought monumental mistakes for some firms and resounding successes for others? Through such evaluations and studies of contrasts, we may learn to improve the "batting average" in the intriguing, ever-challenging art of decision making.

We will encounter examples of the phenomenon of organizational life cycles, with an organization growing and prospering, then failing (just as humans do), but occasionally resurging. Success rarely lasts forever, but even the most serious mistakes can be (but are not always) overcome.

As in previous editions, a variety of firms, industries, mistakes, and successes are presented. You will be familiar with most of the organizations, although probably not with the details of their situations.

We are always on the lookout for particular cases that bring out certain points or caveats in the art of marketing decision making, and that give a balanced view of the spectrum of marketing problems. We have sought to present examples that provide somewhat different learning experiences, where at least some aspect of the mistake or success is unique. Still, we see similar mistakes occurring time and again. The prevalence of some of these mistakes makes us wonder how much decision making has really improved over the decades.

Let us then consider what learning insights we can gain, with the benefit of hindsight, from examining these examples of successful and unsuccessful marketing practices.

LEARNING INSIGHTS

Analyzing Mistakes

In looking at sick companies, or even healthy ones that have experienced difficulties with certain parts of their operations, we are tempted to be unduly critical. It is easy to criticize with the benefit of hindsight. Mistakes are inevitable, given the present state of the art of decision making and the dynamic environment facing organizations.

Mistakes can be categorized as errors of omission and of commission. *Mistakes of omission* are those in which no action was taken and the status quo was contentedly embraced amid a changing environment. Such errors, which often characterize conservative or stodgy management, are not as obvious as the other category of mistakes. They seldom involve tumultuous upheaval; rather, the company's fortunes and competitive position slowly fade, until management at last realizes that mistakes having monumental impact have been allowed to happen. The firm's fortunes often never regain their former luster. But sometimes they do, and this leads us to the intriguing cases of Part II, Great Comebacks, showing how IBM and Continental Airlines fought back successfully from adversity.

Mistakes of commission are more spectacular. They involve bad decisions, wrong actions taken, misspent or misdirected expansion, and the like. Although the costs of the erosion of competitive position coming from errors of omission are difficult to calculate precisely, the costs of errors of commission are often fully evident. For example, the costs associated with the misdirected efforts of Met Life in fines and restitution totaled nearly two billion dollars. With Euro Disney, in 1993 alone the loss was $960 million; it improved in 1994 with only a $366 million loss. With Maytag's overseas Hoover Division, the costs of an incredibly bungled sales promotion were more than $200 million, and still counting.

Although they may make mistakes, organizations with alert and aggressive managements show certain actions or reactions when reviewing their own problem situations:

1. Looming problems or present mistakes are quickly recognized.
2. The causes of the problem(s) are carefully determined.
3. Alternative corrective actions are evaluated in view of the company's resources and constraints.
4. Corrective action is prompt. Sometimes this requires a ruthless axing of the product, the division, or whatever is at fault.
5. Mistakes provide learning experiences. The same mistakes are not repeated, and future operations are consequently strengthened.

Slowness to recognize emerging problems leads us to think that management is lethargic and incompetent or that controls have not been established to provide prompt feedback at strategic control points. For example, a declining competitive position in one or a few geographical areas should be a red flag to management that something is amiss. To wait months before investigating or taking action may mean a permanent loss of business. Admittedly, signals sometimes get mixed, and complete information may be lacking, but procrastination cannot be easily defended.

Just as problems should be quickly recognized, the causes of these problems—the "why" of the unexpected results—must be determined as quickly as possible. It is premature, and rash, to take action before knowing where the problems really lie. To go back to the previous example, the loss of competitive position in one or a few markets may reflect circumstances beyond the firm's immediate control, such as an aggressive new competitor who is drastically cutting prices to "buy sales." In this situation, all competing firms will likely lose market share, and little can be done except to stay as competitive as possible with prices and servicing. However, closer investigation may reveal that the erosion of business was due to unreliable deliveries, poor quality control, uncompetitive prices, or incompetent sales staff.

With the cause(s) of the problem defined, various alternatives for dealing with it should be identified and evaluated. This may require further research, such as obtaining feedback from customers or from field personnel. Finally, the decision to correct the situation should be made as objectively and prudently as possible. If drastic action is needed, there usually is little rationale for delaying. Serious problems do not go away by themselves: They tend to fester and become worse.

Finally, some learning experience should result from the misadventure. A vice president of one successful firm told me,

> I try to give my subordinates as much decision-making experience as possible. Perhaps I err on the side of delegating too much. In any case, I expect some mistakes to be made, some decisions that were not for the best. I don't come down too hard usually. This is part of the learning experience. But God help them if they make the same mistake again. There has been no learning experience, and I question their competence for higher executive positions.

Analyzing Successes

Successes deserve as much analysis as mistakes, although admittedly the urgency is less than with an emerging problem that requires remedial action lest it spread.

Any analysis of success should seek answers to at least the following questions:

Why were such actions successful?
> Was it because of the nature of the environment, and if so, how?
> Was it because of particular research, and if so, what and how?
> Was it because of particular engineering and/or production efforts, and if so, can these be adapted to other aspects of our operations?
> Was it because of any particular element of the strategy—such as service, promotional activities, or distribution methods—and if so, how?
> Was it because of the specific elements of the strategy meshing well together, and if so, how was this achieved?

Was the situation unique and unlikely to be encountered again?
> If not unique to the situation, how can we use these successful techniques in the future or in other operations at the present time?

ORGANIZATION OF THE BOOK

In this eighth edition we have modified the classification of cases somewhat from earlier editions. As mentioned earlier, Part I, Marketing Wars, examines the actions and countermoves of arch rivals in a hotly competitive arena. In Part II we have continued a feature introduced in the sixth edition that many of you approved of: Great Comebacks. The learning insights where great adversity was finally turned to success seemed too fertile to abandon. Another new section is Crisis Management, where we examine four firms that faced major crises and handled them either effectively or poorly. Next, we have categorized cases under traditional marketing mistakes and notable marketing successes. Finally, of course, we can hardly ignore social and ethical concerns in the closer scrutiny of business practices today.

Marketing Wars

Pepsi and Coca-Cola for decades have competed in the lucrative international arena. Usually Coca-Cola has won out, but it can never let its guard down, and it recently did in Europe.

Reebok and Nike are major competitors in the athletic footwear and apparel market. Nike was overtaken by Reebok in the late 1980s, but then Nike surged far ahead. What happened, and how did Nike do this?

Boeing long dominated the worldwide commercial aircraft market, with the European Airbus only a minor player. A series of Boeing miscalculations, however, coupled with an aggressive Airbus brought the war close to parity with the momentum now with Airbus.

McDonald's dominated the hamburger fast-food market for four decades, with Burger King only a distant second. Today, while McDonald's is hardly challenged in foreign markets, its share of the U.S. fast-food market has become so vulnerable that it is exploring radical changes in its menu to try to bring back domestic growth and fight off Burger King and other panting competitors.

Great Comebacks

The comeback of Continental Airlines from extreme adversity and devastated employee morale to become one of the best airlines in the country is an achievement of no small moment. New CEO Gordon Bethune brought marketing and human relations skills to one of the most rapid turnarounds ever, overcoming a decade of raucous adversarial labor relations and a reputation in the pits.

In an earlier edition, I classified IBM as a prime example of a giant firm that had failed to cope with changing technology. Along with many other analysts, I thought the behemoth could never rouse itself enough to again be a major player. But we were wrong, and IBM resurrected itself to become a premier growth company again.

Crisis Management

Met Life, the huge insurance firm, whether through loose controls or tacit approval, permitted an agent to use deceptive selling tactics on a grand scale, and enrich himself and the company in the process. Investigations of several state attorneys general brought a crisis situation to the firm that it was slow to react to. Eventually, fines and lawsuits totaled almost $2 billion. The costs of a damaged reputation could not be calculated.

Perrier, the bottled-water firm, encountered adversity when traces of benzene were found in some of its product. Responsibly, it ordered a sweeping recall of all bottles in North America and a few days later in the rest of the world while it tried to correct the problem. For five months Perrier kept the product off the market, thereby allowing competitors an unparalleled windfall. Worse was public recognition that the claims regarding the purity of its product were false.

United Way of America is a not-for-profit organization. The man who led it to prominence as the nation's largest charity came to perceive himself as virtually beyond authority. Exorbitant spending, favoritism, conflicts of interest—these went uncontrolled and uncriticized until investigative reporters from the *Washington Post* brought to light the scandalous conduct. Amid the hue and cry, charitable contributions drastically declined as the organization desperately tried to rectify the situation and cope with image destruction.

Johnson & Johnson (J&J) exemplifies a superb example of crisis management under the most severe circumstances: loss of life directly connected to its flagship product, Tylenol. J&J became a role model on how to "keep the faith" with its customers, putting their best interests ahead of the firm's and in the process enhancing a public image as a responsive and caring firm. Of late, however, the steadfastness of this philosophy is in question.

Marketing Management Mistakes

A major category-killer retail chain, Toys "Я" Us, found its past successful strategy eroding. It failed to keep in the vanguard with inventory control, state-of-the-art stores, and enhanced customer service.

The next case describes two concept restaurant chains: Boston Chicken and Planet Hollywood. Both went public with great publicity and hype, and the offering prices were quickly bid up. Unfortunately, their popularity with customers, and with investors, proved short-lived, with their viability even in question. How could those entrepreneurs and investors who bought into the hype of their initial public offerings (IPOs) have been so mistaken?

Borden, with its enduring symbol, Elsie the Cow, was the country's largest producer of dairy products. In the 1980s, through a host of acquisitions it became a diversified food processor and marketer, and a $7 billion company. But Borden allowed consumer acceptance of its many brands to wither through unrealistic pricing and ineffective advertising and an unwieldy organization.

In April 1992 just outside Paris, Disney opened its first theme park in Europe. It had high expectations and supreme self-confidence (critics would say this confidence was really arrogance). The earlier Disney parks in California, Florida, and, more recently, Japan were all spectacular successes. But the rosy expectations were soon revealed to be a delusion as a variety of marketing strategy miscues finally showed

Disney that Europeans, and particularly the French, were not necessarily carbon copies of visitors elsewhere.

The Coors case shows how a great image can be lost through inattention. It is an object lesson on how important marketing really is. Coasting on a mystique that its brand had somehow developed, Coors enjoyed great success. But this mystique faded. With virtually no advertising, a disregard for basic marketing ideas, and cool public and employee relations, the company's fortunes faltered badly. It eventually embraced marketing, but still finds itself a distant third in the industry.

The problems of Maytag's Hoover subsidiary in the United Kingdom almost defy reason and logic. The subsidiary planned a promotional campaign so generous that the company was overwhelmed with takers; it was unable either to supply the products or to grant the prizes. In a marketing miscue of multimillion-dollar consequences, Maytag had to foot the bill while trying to appease irate customers.

Rubbermaid also miscalculated the staying power of its brand name, and let customer service slip in its dealings with behemoth retail chains. In 1999 it was acquired by Newell, a successful consumer products marketer to these chains. But the problems of Rubbermaid were not easily corrected and it negatively impacted the fortunes of Newell as well.

Notable Marketing Successes

Vanguard, the second-largest mutual fund company, will soon become number one as it rapidly closes on Fidelity. Vanguard's strategy is to downplay marketing, shunning the heavy advertising and overhead of its competitors. It provides investors with better returns through far lower expense ratios, and relies on word of mouth and unpaid publicity to gain new customers, while old customers continue to pour money in. And its momentum is ever increasing.

In somewhat similar fashion, Southwest Airlines found a strategic window of opportunity as the lowest-cost and lowest-price carrier between certain cities. And how it milked this opportunity! Now it threatens major airlines in many of their domestic routes.

Our last success in this section is also about a firm that dominates its industry through offering customers the lowest prices. Wal-Mart now is by far the largest retailer in the world, and its invasion of Europe is traumatizing retailers there. Its founder, Sam Walton, believed in frugality and a lean but efficient organization. The story of one man's rise to the pinnacle of his chosen field in just a few decades is inspiring. Despite his wealth and prestige, his was the common touch.

Ethical Mistakes

ADM presents a paradox: It was a highly successful firm, but its success was tarnished by unethical practices and even illegal price-fixing. A dictatorial CEO also fostered political cronyism.

The tobacco industry continued to be beleaguered but defiant as it pursued its profit-maximizing strategy. A November 1998 deal with state attorneys general in which it would pay some $200 billion over 25 years seemed to give relief from lawsuits, but also forced significant price increases for cigarettes. Yet, in late-breaking news the Justice Department filed another multibillion-dollar lawsuit against the industry.

GENERAL WRAP-UP

Where possible, we have depicted the major personalities involved in these cases. Imagine yourself in their positions, confronting the problems and facing choices at their points of crisis or just-recognized opportunities. What would you have done differently, and why? We invite you to participate in the discussion questions, the hands-on exercises, and, yes, the debates appearing at the ends of chapters. There are also discussion questions for the various boxes within chapters. We urge you to consider the pros and cons of alternative actions.

In so doing you may feel the excitement and challenge of decision making under conditions of uncertainty. Perhaps you may even become a better future executive and decision maker.

QUESTIONS

1. Do you agree that it is impossible for a firm to avoid mistakes? Why or why not?

2. How can a firm speed up its awareness of emerging problems so that it can take corrective action? Be as specific as you can.

3. Large firms tend to err on the side of conservatism and are slower to take corrective action than smaller ones. Why do you suppose this is so?

4. Which do you think is likely to be more costly to a firm, errors of omission or errors of commission? Why?

5. So often we see the successful firm eventually losing its pattern of success. Why is success not more enduring?

MARKETING WARS

CHAPTER TWO

Cola Wars:
Pepsi vs. Coca-Cola

*I*ntense competition between Pepsi and Coca-Cola has characterized the soft-drink industry for decades. If anything could be called "war" outside of actual bloodshed, this was it. Despite strong challenges from Pepsi, however, Coca-Cola ruled the soft-drink market throughout the 1950s, 1960s, and early 1970s. It outsold Pepsi by two to one. But this was to change.

EARLY BATTLES, LEADING TO NEW COKE FIASCO

Pepsi Inroads, 1970s and 1980s

By the mid-1970s, the Coca-Cola Company was a lumbering giant. Performance reflected this. Between 1976 and 1978, the growth rate of Coca-Cola soft drinks dropped from 13 percent annually to a meager 2 percent. As the giant stumbled, Pepsi Cola was finding heady triumphs. First came the "Pepsi Generation." This advertising campaign captured the imagination of the baby boomers with its idealism and youth. This association with youth and vitality greatly enhanced the image of Pepsi and firmly associated it with the largest consumer market for soft drinks.

Then came another management coup, the "Pepsi Challenge," in which comparative taste tests with consumers showed a clear preference for Pepsi. This campaign led to a rapid increase in Pepsi's market share, from 6 to 14 percent of total U.S. soft-drink sales.

Coca-Cola, in defense, conducted its own taste tests. Alas, these tests had the same result—people liked the taste of Pepsi better, and market share changes reflected this. As Table 2.1 shows, by 1979 Pepsi had closed the gap on Coca-Cola, having 17.9 percent of the soft-drink market, to Coke's 23.9 percent. By the end of 1984, Coke had only a 2.9 percent lead, while in the grocery store market it was now trailing by 1.7 percent. Further indication of the diminishing position of Coke relative to Pepsi was a study done by Coca-Cola's own marketing research department. This showed that in 1972, 18 percent of soft-drink users drank Coke exclusively, while only 4 percent drank only Pepsi. In 10 years the picture had changed greatly: Only 12 percent now claimed loyalty to Coke, while the number of exclusive Pepsi drinkers almost matched, with 11 percent. Figure 2.1 shows this graphically.

TABLE 2.1. Coke and Pepsi Shares of Total Soft-Drink Market, 1950s–1984

	Mid-1950s Lead	1975		1979		1984	
		% of Market	Lead	% of Market	Lead	% of Market	Lead
Coke	Better than 2 to 1	24.2	6.8	23.9	6.0	21.7	2.9
Pepsi		17.4		17.9		18.8	

Source: Thomas Oliver, *The Real Coke, The Real Story* (New York: Random House, 1986), pp. 21, 50; "Two Cokes Really Are Better Than One—For Now," *Business Week*, September 9, 1985, p. 38.

What made the deteriorating comparative performance of Coke all the more worrisome and frustrating to Coca-Cola was that it was outspending Pepsi in advertising by $100 million. It had twice as many vending machines, dominated fountains, had more shelf space, and was competitively priced. Why was it losing market share? The advertising undoubtedly was not as effective as that of Pepsi, despite vastly more money spent. And this raises the question: How can we measure the effectiveness of advertising? See the following information box for a discussion.

Coca-Cola Tries to Battle Back

Changing of the Guard at Coke

J. Paul Austin, chairman of Coca-Cola, was nearing retirement in 1980. Donald Keough, president for the American group, was expected to succeed him. But a new name, Roberto Goizueta, suddenly emerged.

Goizueta's background was far different from that of the typical Coca-Cola executive. He was not from Georgia, was not even southern. Rather, he was the son of a

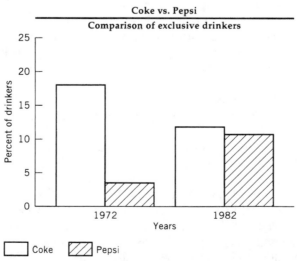

Figure 2.1. Coke versus Pepsi: Comparison of exclusive drinkers, 1972 and 1982.

INFORMATION BOX

HOW DO WE MEASURE THE EFFECTIVENESS OF ADVERTISING?

A firm can spend millions of dollars for advertising, and it is only natural to want some feedback of the results of such an expenditure: To what extent did the advertising really pay off? Yet, many problems confront the firm trying to measure this.

Most methods for measuring effectiveness focus not on sales changes but on how well the communication is remembered, recognized, or recalled. Most evaluative methods simply tell which ad is the best among those being appraised. But even though one ad may be found to be more memorable or to create more attention than another, that fact alone gives no assurance of relationship to sales success. A classic example of the dire consequences that can befall advertising people as a result of the inability to directly measure the impact of ads on sales occurred in December 1970.

In 1970, the Doyle Dane Bernbach advertising agency created memorable TV commercials for Alka-Seltzer, such as the "spicy meatball man," and the "poached oyster bride." These won professional awards as the best commercials of the year and received high marks for humor and audience recall. But in December the $22 million account was abruptly switched to another agency. The reason? Alka-Seltzer's sales had dropped somewhat. Of course, no one will ever know whether the drop might have been much worse without these notable commercials.

So, how do we measure the value of millions of dollars spent for advertising? Not well; nor can we determine what is the right amount to spend, what is too much or too little.

Can a business succeed without advertising? Why or why not?

wealthy Havana sugar plantation owner. He came to the United States at age 16 speaking virtually no English. By using the dictionary and watching movies, he quickly learned the language and graduated from Yale in 1955 with a degree in chemical engineering. Returning to Cuba, he went to work in Coke's Cuban research lab.

Goizueta's complacent life was to change in 1959 when Fidel Castro seized power. With his wife and three children he fled to the United States, arriving with $20. At Coca-Cola he became known as a brilliant administrator and in 1968 was brought to company headquarters, and became chairman of the board thirteen years later in 1981. Donald Keough had to settle for being president.

In the new era of change, the sacredness of the commitment to the original Coke formula became tenuous and the ground was laid for the first flavor change in 99 years.

Introducing a New Flavor for Coke

With the market share erosion of the late 1970s and early 1980s, despite strong advertising and superior distribution, the company began to look at the product itself. Taste was suspected as the chief culprit in Coke's decline, and marketing research seemed to confirm this. In September 1984 the technical division developed a sweeter flavor that, in perhaps the biggest taste test ever, costing $4 million, 191,000 people approved by 55 percent over both the original formula of Coke and Pepsi. The decision was unanimously made by top executives to change the taste and take the old Coke off the market.

The results flabbergasted company executives. While some protests were expected, they quickly mushroomed and by mid-May calls were coming in at the rate of 5,000 a day, in addition to a barrage of angry letters. People were speaking of Coke as an American symbol and as a longtime friend that had suddenly betrayed them.

Anger spread across the country, fueled by media publicity. Fiddling with the formula for the 99-year-old beverage became an affront to patriotic pride. Even Goizueta's father spoke out against the switch and jokingly threatened to disown his son. By now the company began to worry about a consumer boycott against the product.

On July 11, 1985, company officials capitulated to the outcry, apologizing to the public and bringing back the original taste of Coke.

Roger Enrico, president of Pepsi-Cola, USA, gloated, "Clearly this is the Edsel of the 80s. This was a terrible mistake. Coke's got a lemon on its hands and now they're trying to make lemonade." Other critics labeled this the "marketing blunder of the decade."[1]

Unfortunately for Pepsi, the euphoria of a major blunder by Coca-Cola was shortlived. The two-cola strategy of Coca-Cola—it still kept the new flavor in addition to bringing back the old classic—seemed to be stimulating sales far more than ever expected. While Coke Classic was outselling new Coke by better than 2 to 1 nationwide, for the full year of 1985, sales from all operations rose 10 percent and profits 9 percent. Coca-Cola's fortunes continued to improve steadily. By 1988 it was producing five of the top 10 top-selling soft drinks in the country, and now had a total of 40 percent of the domestic market to 31 percent for Pepsi.[2]

BATTLE SHIFTS TO INTERNATIONAL ARENA

Pepsi's Troubles in Brazil

Early in 1994, PepsiCo began an ambitious assault on the soft-drink market in Brazil. Making this invasion even more tempting was the opportunity to combat arch-rival Coca-Cola, already entrenched in this third-largest soft-drink market in the world, behind only the United States and Mexico.

The robust market of Brazil had attracted Pepsi before. Its hot weather and a growing teen population positioned Brazil to become one of the world's fastest-growing soft-drink markets, along with China, India, and Southeast Asia. But the potential still had barely been tapped. Brazilian consumers averaged only 264 eight-ounce servings of soft drinks a year, far below the U.S. average of about 800.[3]

---

[1] John Greenwald, "Coca-Cola's Big Fizzle," *Time,* July 22, 1985, pp. 48–49.

[2] "Some Things Don't Go Better with Coke," *Forbes,* March 21, 1988, pp. 34–35.

[3] Robert Frank and Jonathan Friedland, "How Pepsi's Charge into Brazil Fell Short of Its Ambitious Goals," *The Wall Street Journal,* August 30, 1996, p. A1.

Three times before over the previous 25 years, Pepsi had attempted to enter this market with splashy promotional campaigns and different bottlers. Each of these efforts proved disappointing and Pepsi had given up after a short time. Now it planned a much more aggressive and enduring push.

A Superbottler, Baesa, and Charles Beach

Buenos Aires Embotelladora SA, or Baesa, was to be the key to Pepsi's rejuvenated entry into Brazil. Baesa would be Pepsi's "superbottler," one that would buy small bottlers across Latin America, expand their marketing and distribution, and be the fulcrum in the drive against Coca-Cola. Charles Beach, the CEO of Baesa, was the person Pepsi planned its strategy around.

Beach, 61, was a passionate, driven man, a veteran of the cola wars, but his was a checkered past. He had been manager for a Carolina Coca-Cola bottler, but left to buy Pepsi's small Puerto Rican franchise in 1987. He was indicted by a federal grand jury on charges of price fixing and received a $100,000 fine and a suspended prison sentence.

Then in 1989 he acquired the exclusive Pepsi franchise for Buenos Aires, Argentina, one of the most important bottling franchises outside the United States, and by discounting and launching new products and packages, he caught Coke by surprise. In only three years he had increased Pepsi's market share in the Buenos Aires metro area from almost zero to 34 percent.[4]

With Pepsi's blessing, Beach expanded vigorously, borrowing heavily to do so. He bought major Pepsi franchises in Chile, Uruguay, and most importantly, Brazil, where he built four giant bottling plants. Pepsi worked closely with Baesa's expansion, providing funds to facilitate it.

However, they underestimated the aggressiveness of Coca-Cola. Their rival spent heavily on marketing and cold drink equipment for its choice customers. As a result Baesa was shut out of small retail outlets, those most profitable for bottlers. Goizueta, CEO of Coca-Cola, used his Latin American background to influence the Argentine president to reduce an onerous 24 percent tax on cola to 4 percent. This move strengthened Coke's position against Baesa, which was earning most of its profits from non-cola drinks in contrast to Coca-Cola.

By early 1996, Baesa's expansion plans, and Pepsi's dream, were foundering. The new Brazilian plants were running at only a third of capacity. Baesa lost $300 million for the first half of 1996, and PepsiCo injected another $40 million into Baesa.

On May 9, Beach was relieved of his position. Allegations now surfaced that Beach might have tampered with Baesa's books.[5] But PepsiCo's troubles did not end with the debacle in Brazil.

Intrigue in Venezuela

Brazil was only symptomatic of other overseas problems for Pepsi. Roger Enrico, now CEO, had reasons to shake his head and wonder at how the gods seemed against him.

---

[4] Patrica Sellers, "How Coke Is Kicking Pepsi's Can," *Fortune*, October 28, 1996, p. 78.

[5] Sellers, p. 79.

But it was not the gods, it was Coca-Cola. Enrico had been on Coke's blacklist since he had gloated a decade before about the New Coke debacle in his memoir, *The Other Guy Blinked: How Pepsi Won the Cola Wars.* Goizueta was soon to gloat, "It appears that the company that claimed to have won the cola wars is now raising the white flag."[6]

The person Enrico thought was his close friend, Oswaldo Cisneros, head of one of Pepsi's oldest and largest foreign bottling franchises, suddenly abandoned Pepsi for Coca-Cola. Essentially, this took Pepsi out of the Venezuela market.

Despite the close ties of the Cisneroses with the Enricos, little things led to the chasm. The closeness had developed when Enrico headed the international operations of PepsiCo. After Enrico left this position for higher offices at corporate headquarters, Oswaldo Cisneros felt that Pepsi management paid scant attention to Venezuela: "That showed I wasn't an important player in their future," he said.[7] As Cisneros was growing older, he wanted to sell the bottling operation, but Pepsi was only willing to acquire 10 percent.

Coca-Cola wooed the Cisneroses with red carpet treatment and frequent meetings with its highest executives. Eventually, Coca-Cola agreed to pay an estimated $500 million to buy 50 percent of the business.

Pepsi's Problems Elsewhere in the International Arena

Pepsi's problems in South America mirrored its problems worldwide. It had lost its initial lead in Russia, Eastern Europe, and parts of Southeast Asia. While it had a head start in India, this was being eroded by a hard-driving Coca-Cola. Even in Mexico its main bottler reported a loss of $15 million in 1995.

The contrast with Coca-Cola was significant. Pepsi still generated more than 70 percent of its beverage profits from the United States; Coca-Cola got 80 percent from overseas.[8]

Table 2.2 shows the top ten markets for Coke and Pepsi in 1996. In the total world market, Coke had a 49 percent market share while Pepsi's was only 17 percent, despite its investment of more than $2 billion since 1990 to straighten out its overseas bottling operations and improve its image.[9] With its careful investment in bottlers and increased financial resources to plow into marketing, Coke continued to gain greater control of the global soft-drink industry.

If there was any consolation for PepsiCo, it was that its overseas business had always been far less important to it than to Coca-Cola, but this was slim comfort in view of the huge potential this market represented. Most of Pepsi's revenues were in the U.S. beverage, snack food, and restaurant businesses, with such well-known brands as Frito-Lay chips and Taco Bell, Pizza Hut and KFC restaurants. But as a former Pepsi CEO was fond of stating, "We're proud of the U.S. business. But 95 per-

---

[6] Sellers, p. 72.

[7] Sellers, p. 75.

[8] Frank and Friedland, p. A1.

[9] Robert Frank, "Pepsi Losing Overseas Fizz to Coca-Cola," *The Wall Street Journal,* August 22, 1996, p. C2.

TABLE 2.2. Coke and Pepsi Shares of Total Soft-Drink Sales, Top 10 Markets, 1996

Markets	Market Shares	
	Coke	Pepsi
United States	42%	31%
Mexico	61	21
Japan	34	5
Brazil	51	10
East-Central Europe	40	21
Germany	56	5
Canada	37	34
Middle East	23	38
China	20	10
Britain	32	12

Source: Company annual reports, and Patricia Sellers, "How Coke Is Kicking Pepsi's Can," *Fortune,* October 28, 1996, p. 82.

Commentary: These market share comparisons show the extent of Pepsi's ineptitude in its international markets. In only one of these top 10 overseas markets is it ahead of Coke, and in some, such as Japan, Germany, and Brazil, it is practically a nonplayer.

cent of the world doesn't live here."[10] And Pepsi seemed unable to hold its own against Coke in this world market.

COKE TRAVAILS IN EUROPE, 1999

The Trials of Douglas Ivester

In early 1998, Douglas Ivester took over as chairman and chief executive of Coca-Cola. Things seemed to mostly go downhill from then on, but it was not entirely his fault. The first quarter of 1999 witnessed a sharp slowdown in Coca-Cola's North American business, at least partly because of price increases designed to overcome weakness overseas due to economic woes. While most analysts thought the sticker shock of higher prices would be temporary, some thought the company needed to be more innovative, needed to do more than offer supersize drinks.[11] Other problems emanated from a racial-discrimination lawsuit, as well as Mr. Ivester's "brassy" attempts to make acquisitions such as Orangina and Cadbury Schweppes that angered overseas regulators and perhaps motivated them to make life difficult for Coke.

Such concerns paled before what was to come.

[10] Frank, p. C2.

[11] Nikhil Deogun, "Coke's Slower Sales Are Blamed on Price Increases," *The Wall Street Journal,* March 31, 1999, pp. A3 and A4.

Contamination Scares

On June 8, a few dozen Belgian schoolchildren began throwing up after drinking Cokes. This was to result in one of the most serious crises in Coca-Cola's 113-year history. An early warning was seemingly ignored when in mid-May a bar owner of a pub near Antwerp complained of four people becoming sick from drinking bad-smelling Coke. The company claimed to have investigated but found no problems.

The contamination news could not have hit at a worse time. Belgium was still reeling from a dioxin-contamination food scare in Belgian poultry and other foods, and European agencies were coming under fire for a breakdown in their watchdog responsibilities. Officials were inclined to be overzealous in their dealings with this big U.S. firm.

The problems worsened. Coca-Cola officials were meeting with Belgium's health minister, seeking to placate him, telling him that their analyses "show that it is about a deviation in taste and color" that might cause headaches and other symptoms but "does not threaten the health of your child." In the middle of this meeting news came that another 15 students at another school had gotten sick.[12]

It was thought that the contamination came from bottling plants in Antwerp, Ghent, and from the Dunkirk plant that produced cans for the Belgium market. European newspapers were speculating that Coke cans were contaminated with rat poison.

Soon hundreds of people in France were sick and blaming their illnesses on Coke, and France banned products from the Dunkirk plant. These two countries rebuffed Coca-Cola's urgent efforts to lift the ban, and scolded the company for not supplying enough information as to the cause of the problem. The setback left Coke out of the market in parts of Europe as it badly underestimated how much explanation governments would demand before letting it back in business.

Not until June 17 did Belgium and France lift restrictions, and then only on some products as bans were continued on Coca-Cola's Coke, Sprite, and Fanta. Now the Netherlands, Luxembourg, and Switzerland also imposed selective bans until health risks could be evaluated. Some 14 million cases of Coke products eventually were recalled in the five countries, and estimates were that Coke was losing $3.4 million per day in revenues. Case volume for the European division was expected to fall 6 to 7 percent from the year earlier.[13] The peak soft-drink summer season was here, and the timing of the scare could not have been worse.

The European Union requested further study as the health scare spread. At the same time, Coca-Cola and its local distributors launched an advertising campaign defending the quality of their products. The company blamed defective carbon dioxide, used for fizz, for problems at Antwerp. It also said the outside of cans made in Dunkirk were contaminated with a wood preservative during shipping. One company-commissioned study suggested that health problems were in the victim's heads.

---

[12] "Anatomy of a Recall: How Coke's Controls Fizzled Out in Europe," *The Wall Street Journal*, June 29, 1999, p. A6.

[13] Will Edwards, "Coke Chairman Tries to Assure Europeans," *Cleveland Plain Dealer*, June 19, 1999, pp. 1–C and 3–C; and Nikhil Deogun, "Coke Estimates European Volume Plunged 6% to 7% in 2nd Quarter," *The Wall Street Journal*, July 1, 1999, p. A4.

Meanwhile, the Ivory Coast seized 50,000 cans of Coke imported from Europe as a precautionary measure, though there was no evidence that anyone in the Ivory Coast had become ill by drinking imported Coke.

Problems continued to spread. All glass bottles of Bonaqua, a bottled-water brand of Coca-Cola, were recalled in Poland because about 1,500 bottles were found to contain mold. This recall in Poland soon spread to glass bottles of Coke. Company officials believed the mold was caused by inadequate washing of returnable bottles. Barely a week later, the company recalled 180,000 plastic bottles of Bonaqua after discovering nonhazardous bacteria. Coca-Cola also had to recall some soft drinks in Portugal because of small bits of charcoal from a filtration system found in some cans.

Coca-Cola Finally Acts Aggressively

In the initial contamination episodes, Coca-Cola was accused of dragging its feet. Part of the problem in ameliorating the situation was the absence of any high-level Coca-Cola officials explaining what happened. Ivester was criticized for this delay as he finally made an appearance in Brussels on June 18, ten days after the initial scare. He visited Brussels again four days later, meeting with the prime minister. Now strenuous efforts were started to improve the image and public relations.

Ivester in a major advertising campaign apologized to Belgian consumers and explained "how the company allowed two breakdowns to occur." The ads had his photograph along with these opening remarks, "My apologies to the consumers of Belgium; I should have spoken with you earlier." He further promised to buy every Belgian household a Coke. A special consumer hotline was established, and 50 officials from the Atlanta headquarters including several top executives were temporarily shifted to Brussels.

Five thousand delivery people now fanned out across the country offering a free 1.5-liter bottle of Coke's main brands to 4.37 million households. Around Belgium, Coke trucks and displays proclaimed, "Your Coca-Cola is coming back." In newspaper ads, the company explained its problems, and noted it was destroying old products and using fresh ingredients for new drinks. A similar marketing strategy was planned for Poland with two million free beverages distributed to consumers.

Pepsi's Competitive Maneuvers on the Brink of the New Millennium

Pepsi's Role in Coke's European Problems

Some thought that Coca-Cola's problems should have been Pepsi's gain. Yet, Pepsi did nothing to exacerbate the situation, did not gloat, did not increase advertising for its brand. Worldwide, there were some temporary gains in sales for Pepsi, most surprisingly in countries far removed from the scare, such as China. A Pepsi bottler in Eastern Europe probably expressed the prevailing company attitude when he observed that people were buying bottled water and juices instead of soda pop: "That's why we don't wish this stuff on anyone," he said, referring to the health scare.[14]

But Pepsi was not idle in Europe.

---

[14] Nikhil Deogun and James R. Hagerty, "Coke Scandal Could Boost Rivals, But Also Could Hurt Soft Drinks," *The Wall Street Journal,* June 23, 1999, p. A4.

Pepsi's Antitrust Initiations Against Coca-Cola

In late July 1999, European Union officials raided offices of Coca-Cola and its bottlers in four countries in Europe—Germany, Austria, Denmark, and Britain—on suspicions that the company used a dominant market position to shut out competitors. Coming at a time when Coca-Cola was still trying to recover from the contamination problems this was a cruel blow. All the more so since such alleged noncompetitive activities impacted on its plans to acquire some additional businesses in Europe.

The raids were expected to lead to a full-blown antitrust action against Coke. The major suspicion was that Coke was illegally using rebates to enhance its market share. The several types of rebates under investigation were rebates on sales that boosted Coke's market share at the expense of rivals, as well as rebates given to distributors who agreed to sell the full range of Coke products or else stop buying from competitors.

Coca-Cola's huge market share in most countries of Europe fed the concern. See Table 2.3 for Coke's market shares of the total soft-drink market in selected countries in Europe.

While the huge market share of Coke was under scrutiny from European antitrust officials, the investigation was sparked by a complaint filed by Pepsi that Coke was illegally trying to force competitors out of the market.

Pepsi also filed a complaint with Italian regulators, and they were quicker to act. A preliminary report found that Coca-Cola and its bottlers violated antitrust laws by abusing a dominant market position through practices such as discounts, bonuses, and exclusive deals with wholesalers and retailers. The Italian regulators also said there was evidence that Coke had a "strategic plan" to remove Pepsi from the Italian market, one of the biggest in Europe, by paying wholesalers to remove Pepsi fountain equipment and replace it with Coke. At about this time, Australian and Chilean officials also began conducting informal inquiries in their markets.

Coca-Cola officials responded to the Italian report as follows: "we believe this is a baseless allegation by Pepsi and we believe that Pepsi's poor performance in Italy is

TABLE 2.3.   Coca-Cola's Market
Share of Soft-Drink Market in
Selected European Countries, 1998

France	59%
Spain	58
Germany	55
Central Europe	47
Italy	45
Nordic and Northern Eurasia	41
Great Britain	35

Source: Company published reports.

Commentary: The dominance of Coke in almost all countries of Europe, not surprisingly, makes it vulnerable to antitrust scrutiny.

due to their lack of commitment and investment there. As a result, they are attempting to compete with us in the courtroom instead of the marketplace."[15]

ANALYSIS

What Went Wrong with the New Coke Decision?

The most convenient scapegoat was the marketing research that preceded the decision. Yet Coca-Cola spent about $4 million and devoted two years to the marketing research. About 200,000 consumers were contacted during this time. The error in judgment was surely not from want of trying. But when we dig deeper into the research, some flaws become apparent.

Flawed Marketing Research

The major design of the marketing research involved taste tests by representative consumers. After all, the decision point was whether to go with a different-flavored Coke, so what could be more logical than to conduct taste tests to determine acceptability of the new flavor, not only versus the old Coke but also versus Pepsi? The results were strongly positive for the new formula, even among Pepsi drinkers. This was a clear "go" signal.

With benefit of hindsight, however, some deficiencies in the research design merited concern. Research participants were not told that by picking one cola they would lose the other. This proved to be a significant distortion: Any addition to the product line would naturally be far more acceptable than would be a complete substitution with the traditional product being eliminated.

While three or four new tastes were tested with almost 200,000 people, only 30,000 to 40,000 of these involved the specific formula for the new Coke. Research was geared more to the idea of a new, sweeter cola than the final formula. In general, a sweeter flavor tends to be preferred in blind taste tests. Particularly is this true with youths, the largest drinkers of sugared colas, the very ones drinking more Pepsi in recent years. Interestingly, preference for sweeter-tasting products tends to diminish with use.[16]

Consumers were asked whether they favored change as a concept, and whether they would likely drink more, less, or the same amount of Coke if there were a change. But such questions could hardly prove the depth of feelings and emotional ties to the product.

Symbolic Value

The symbolic value of Coke was the sleeper. Perhaps this should have been foreseen. Perhaps the marketing research should have considered this possibility and designed the research to map it and determine the strength and durability of these values— that is, would they have a major effect on any substitution of a new flavor?

---

[15] Betsy McKay, "Coke, Bottlers Violated Antitrust Laws in Italy, a Preliminary Report States," *The Wall Street Journal*, August 13, 1999, p. A4.

[16] "New Cola Wins Round 1, But Can It Go the Distance?" *Business Week*, June 24, 1985, p. 48.

Admittedly, when we get into symbolic value and emotional involvement, any researcher is dealing with vague and nebulous attitudes. But various attitudinal measures have been developed that can measure the strength or degree of emotional involvement.

Herd Instinct

Here we see a natural human phenomenon, the herd instinct, the tendency of people to follow an idea, a slogan, a concept, to "jump on the bandwagon." At first, acceptance of new Coke appeared to be reasonably satisfactory. But as more and more outcries were raised—fanned by the media—about the betrayal of the old tradition (somehow this became identified with motherhood, apple pie, and the flag), public attitudes shifted strongly against the perceived unworthy substitute. The bandwagon syndrome was fully activated. It is doubtful that by July 1985 Coca-Cola could have done anything to reverse the unfavorable tide. To wait for it to die down was fraught with danger—for who would be brave enough to predict the durability and possible heights of such a protest movement?

Could, or should, such a tide have been predicted? Perhaps not, at least as to the full strength of the movement. Coca-Cola expected some protests. But perhaps it should have been more cautious, and have considered a worst-case scenario in addition to what seemed the more probable, and been well prepared to react to such a contingency.

Pepsi's, and Later Coca-Cola's, International Problems

Pepsi's Defeats in South America

With hindsight we can identify many of the mistakes Pepsi made. It tried to expand too quickly in Argentina and Brazil, imprudently putting all its chips on a distributor with a checkered past, instead of building up relationships more slowly and carefully. It did not monitor foreign operations closely enough or soon enough to prevent rash expansion of facilities and burdensome debt accumulations by affiliates. It did not listen closely enough to old distributors and their changing wants, and so lost Venezuela to Coca-Cola. Pepsi apparently did not learn from its past mistakes: For example, three times before it had tried to enter Brazil and had failed. Why the failures? Why did it not use more care to prevent failure this time?

Finally, we can speculate that maybe Pepsi was not so bad, but rather, that its major competitor was so good. Coca-Cola had slowly built up close relationships with foreign bottlers over decades. It was aggressive in defending its turf. Perhaps not the least of its strengths, especially in the lucrative Latin American markets, was a CEO who was also a Latino, who could speak Spanish and share the concerns and build on the egos of its local bottlers. In selling, this is known as a dyadic relationship, and it is discussed further in the following information box. After all, why can't a CEO do a selling job on a distributor and capitalize on a dyadic relationship?

Coca-Cola's Problems in Europe

Could Coca-Cola have handled the Belgian crisis better? With hindsight we see a flawed initial reaction. Still, the first incident of twenty-four schoolchildren getting ill

---

INFORMATION BOX

THE DYADIC RELATIONSHIP

Sellers are now recognizing the importance of the buyer–seller interaction, *a dyadic relationship.* A transaction, negotiation, or relationship can often be helped by certain characteristics of the buyer and seller in the particular encounter. Research suggests that salespeople tend to be more successful if they have characteristics similar to their customers in age, size, and other demographic, social, and ethnic variables.

Of course, in the selling situation this suggests that selecting and hiring sales applicants most likely to be successful might require careful study of the characteristics of the firm's customers. Turning to the Pepsi/Coke confrontation in Brazil and Venezuela, the same concepts should apply and give a decided advantage to Coca-Cola and Roberto Goizueta in influencing government officials and local distributors. After all, even a CEO in interacting with customers and affiliates needs to be persuasive in presenting ideas as well as handling problems and objections.

Can you think of any situations where the dyadic theory may not work?

---

and throwing up after drinking Coke seemed hardly a major crisis at the time. But crises often start slowly with only minor indications, and then mushroom to even catastrophic proportions. Eventually hundreds of people reported real or imagined illnesses from drinking the various Coca-Cola products.

The mistakes of Coca-Cola in handling the situation were (1) not taking the initial episodes seriously enough, (2) not realizing the intense involvement and skepticism of governmental officials, who demanded complete explanations of the cause(s) and were reluctant to lift bans, and (3) not involving Coke chairman Douglas Ivester and other high-level executives soon enough. Ten days before his personal intervention was a long time to allow problems to fester. Add to this the fact that quality-control lapses should not have been allowed to occur in the first place.

Eventually, Ivester and Coke acted aggressively in restoring Coca-Cola, but lost revenues could not be fully recovered.

Of interest in the environment of cola wars was Pepsi's restraint in not trying to take advantage of Coke's problems. This was not altruism but fear that the whole soft-drink industry would face decreased demand, so don't aggravate the situation. Anyway, Pepsi saved its competitive thrusts for antitrust challenges.

With its great size and market-dominance visibility in country after country, Coca-Cola was vulnerable to regulatory scrutiny and antitrust allegations, especially when stimulated by its number-one competitor, PepsiCo. Does this mean that it is dangerous for a firm to become too big? In certain environments, such as that facing a foreign firm in some European countries, this may well be the case. The firm then needs to tread carefully, tone down inclinations toward arrogance, and be subtle and patient in seeking acquisitions on foreign turf.

LATE-BREAKING NEWS

Coca-Cola's problems in Europe spread to Russia by Fall 1999. Sales had fallen 60 percent, with depleted consumer spending power being blamed. Not only were major cuts in production necessary, but some of Coca-Cola's $750 million investment in Russia was in danger of being written off.

In October 1999, news surfaced that Coca-Cola, taking full advantage of the law of supply and demand, was quietly testing a vending machine that would automatically raise prices for its drinks in hot weather. This would essentially extend to the soft-drink industry what has become the practice for airlines and other companies that sell consumer products and services. Pepsi said it was considering no similar innovation, and condemned this "exploitation" of consumers.

PepsiCo has found soft-drink success in the United States in its marketing of Mountain Dew, a direct competitor of Coca-Cola's Sprite. By late 1999 Dew was the nation's fourth most popular drink and also the fastest growing. The success came from repositioning the brand. In the 1980s, Pepsi had pitched Mountain Dew as a hillbilly drink, with dubious results. Finally, it began to target young males with commercials of men in action, and the drink took off. Now the ads also include young women.

Question: How do you personally feel about raising soft-drink prices during hot weather?

Sources: Compiled from Betsy McKay, "Coke Staff Cuts in Russia," *The Wall Street Journal,* September 30, 1999, p. B20; Constance L. Hays, "Prices Go Up Better With Coke When It Gets Hot," *New York Times,* reported in *Cleveland Plain Dealer,* October 28, 1999, p. 14-A; and Greg Johnson, "Today's 'Pepsi Generation' Digs its Dew," *Los Angeles Times,* reported in *Cleveland Plain Dealer,* October 31, 1999, p. 6H.

WHAT CAN BE LEARNED?

The inconstancy of taste. Taste tests are commonly used in marketing research, but I have always been skeptical of their validity. Take beer, for example. I know of few people—despite their strenuous claims—who can in blind taste tests unerringly identify which is which among three or four disguised brands of beer. We know that people tend to favor the sweeter in taste tests. But does this mean that a sweeter flavor will always win out in the marketplace? Hardly; something else is operating with consumer preference other than the fleeting essence of a taste—unless the flavor difference is extreme.

Brand image usually is a more powerful sales stimulant. Advertisers consistently have been more successful in cultivating a desirable image or personality for their brands or the types of people who use them, than by such vague statements as "better tasting."

Don't tamper with tradition. Not many firms have a 100-year-old tradition to be concerned with, or even 25 years, or even 10 years. Most products have much shorter life cycles. No other product has been so widely used and so deeply entrenched in societal values and culture as Coke.

The psychological components of the great Coke protest make interesting speculation. Perhaps in an era of rapid change, many people wish to hang on to the one symbol of security or constancy in their lives—even if this is only the traditional Coke flavor. Perhaps many people found this protest to be an interesting way to escape the humdrum, by "making waves" in a rather harmless way, and in the process to see if a big corporation might be forced to cry "uncle."

One is left to wonder how many consumers would even have been aware of any change in flavor had the new formula been quietly introduced without fanfare. But, of course, the advertising siren call of "New!" would have been muted.

So, do we dare tamper with tradition? In Coke's case the answer is probably not, unless done very quietly, but then Coke is unique.

Don't try to fix something that isn't broken. Conventional wisdom may advocate that changes are best made in response to problems, that when things are going smoothly the success pattern or strategy should not be tampered with. Perhaps. But perhaps not.

Actually, things were not going all that well for Coke by early 1985. Market share had steadily been lost to Pepsi for some years. So it was certainly worth considering a change, and the obvious one was a different flavor. I do not subscribe to the philosophy of "don't rock the boat." But Coke had another option.

Don't burn your bridges. Coke could have introduced the new Coke, but kept the old one. Goizueta was concerned about dealer resentment at having to stock an additional product in the same limited space. Furthermore, he feared Pepsi emerging as the number-one soft drink due to two competing Cokes. This is flawed rationale.

The power of the media. Press and broadcast media are powerful influencers of public opinion. With new Coke, the media exacerbated the herd instinct by publicizing the protests. News seems to be spiciest when someone or something can be criticized or found wanting. We saw this fanning of protests in Coke's contamination problems in Europe, to the extent that some people came up with psychosomatic illnesses after drinking Coca-Cola products. The power of the media should be recognized and be one of the factors considered in decisions that may affect the public image of an organization.

International growth requires tight controls. In Pepsi's problems with Baesa we saw the risks of placing too much trust in a distributor. One could question the selection of Charles Beach to spearhead the Pepsi invasion of Coke strongholds in South America. Prudence would dictate close monitoring of plans and performance, with major changes—in expansion planning, marketing strategy, financial commitments—approved by corporate headquarters. In international dealings, the tendency is to loosen controls due to the distances, different customs and bureaucratic procedures, as well as unfamiliar cultures. We will see an extreme example of this in the Maytag case.

The human factor may be more important in international dealings. Rapport with associates and customers may be even more important in the international environment than domestically. The distances involved usually necessitate more decentralization and therefore more autonomy. If confidence and trust in foreign associates is misplaced, serious problems can result. Customers and affiliates may need a closer relationship with corporate management if they are not to be wooed away. Furthermore, in some countries the political climate is such that the major people in power must be catered to by the large firm wanting to do business in that country.

Sound crisis management requires top management's prompt participation. The chief executive is both an expediter and a public relations figure in crises, particularly in foreign environments. The delay of Ivester in rushing to Belgium may have delayed resolution of the crisis for several weeks, and cost Coca-Cola millions in lost revenues. No other person is as well suited to handle serious crises. Some sensitive foreign officials see an affront to their country without top management involvement and are likely to express their displeasure in regulatory delays, calls for more investigations, and bad publicity toward a foreign firm. In the case of Coca-Cola, even though Ivester eventually made a conciliatory appearance, some countries were receptive to antitrust allegations made by Pepsi against Coca-Cola.

CONSIDER

Can you think of other learning insights?

QUESTIONS

1. In the new Coke fiasco, how could Coca-Cola's marketing research have been improved? Be a specific as you can.

2. When a firm faces a negative press, as Coca-Cola did with the new Coke, and again almost 15 years later in Europe, what recourse does a firm have? Support your conclusions.

3. "If it's not broken, don't fix it." Evaluate this statement.

4. Do you think Coca-Cola engineered the whole scenario with the new Coke, including fanning initial protests, in order to get a bonanza of free publicity? Defend your position.

5. Critique Pepsi's handling of Baesa. Could it have prevented the South American disaster? If so, how?

6. With hindsight, how might Enrico, CEO of PepsiCo, have kept Cisneros, his principal bottler in Venezuela, in the fold instead of defecting to Coke?

7. How could Coca-Cola have lessened the chances of antitrust and regulatory scrutiny in Europe?

8. Do you think Pepsi can ever make big inroads in Coke's market share in Europe? Why or why not?

9. A big stockholder complains, "All this fuss over a few kids getting sick to their stomach. The media have blown this all out of proportion." Discuss.

HANDS-ON EXERCISES

1. Assume that you are Roberto Goizueta and that you are facing increased pressure in early July 1985 to abandon the new Coke and bring back the old formula. However, your latest marketing research suggests that only a small group of agitators are making all the fuss. Evaluate your options and support your recommendations to the board.

2. As a market analyst for PepsiCo, you have been asked to present recommendations to Roger Enrico, CEO, and the executive board, for the invasion of Brazil's soft-drink market. The major bottler, Baesa, is already in place and waiting for Pepsi's final plans and objectives. You are to design a planning blueprint for the "invasion," complete with an estimated timetable.

3. You are a staff assistant to Ivester. It is 1998, and he has just assumed the top executive job with Coca-Cola. One of his first major decisions concerns raising soft-drink prices 5 percent to improve operating margins and make up for diminished revenues in a depressed European market. He wants you to provide pro and con information on this important decision.

TEAM-DEBATE EXERCISES

1. "There is no way Pepsi can ever win the war with Coca-Cola. We are better off to try to hang on to what we have with soft drinks, and devote our efforts to diversify outside the soft-drink industry."
   Debate this issue: Should Pepsi essentially leave the battlefield to Coke and diversify, or should it continue to focus on the soft-drink core and try to win the cola war?

2. Debate the plan of Ivester to distribute millions of free bottles of Coke products to people in Belgium and Poland. In particular, debate the cost/benefit of this marketing strategy. Are the benefits likely to be worth the substantial cost?

INVITATION TO RESEARCH

What is the newest in the Cola wars? Has Coke lost market share in Europe? Has Pepsi been able to make any inroads in Latin America? How do the two firms stack up in profitability?

CHAPTER THREE

Sneaker Wars: Reebok vs. Nike

*B*y the late 1970s and early 1980s, Nike had wrested first place in the athletic shoe industry from Adidas, the firm that had been supreme since the 1936 Olympics when Jesse Owens wearing Adidas shoes won his medals in front of Hitler, the German nation, and the world.

In the early 1980s, Reebok emerged as Nike's major competitor, showing a tremendous growth and becoming number one in this industry by 1987. But Nike fought back, and three years later had regained the top-dog position. And it has decisively pulled away at the beginning of the new millennium. How did Reebok fight its way to the top? Why did it permit Nike to dislodge it so soon? Or did Nike use some inspired marketing strategy to do so?

REEBOK

History

The ancestor to Reebok goes back to the 1890s when Joseph William Foster made himself the first known running shoes with spikes. By 1895, he was handmaking shoes for top runners. Soon, the fledgling company, J.W. Foster & Sons, was furnishing shoes for distinguished athletes around the world.

In 1958, two of the founder's grandsons started a companion company, which they named—fittingly, they thought—after an African gazelle: Reebok. This company eventually absorbed J.W. Foster & Sons.

In 1979, Paul Fireman, a partner in an outdoor sporting goods distributorship, saw Reebok shoes at an international trade show. He negotiated for the North American distribution license and introduced three running shoes in the United States that year. It was the height of the running boom. These were at the time the most expensive running shoes on the market, retailing for $60. But no matter, demand burgeoned, outpacing the plant's capacity, and production facilities were established in Korea.

In 1981, sales were $1.5 million. But a breakthrough came the next year. Reebok introduced the first athletic shoe designed especially for women. It was a shoe for aerobic dance exercise, and was called the Freestyle. Whether accidentally or with brilliant foresight, Reebok anticipated three major trends that were to transform the athletic footwear industry: (1) the aerobic exercise movement, (2) women's great embracing of sports and exercise, and (3) the transference of athletic footwear to street and casual wear.

Sales exploded from $13 million in 1983 to $307 million in 1985. Almost unbelievably, sales tripled in 1986 to $919 million and by 1991 reached $2.7 billion.

A company publication in 1993, said: "For more than a decade, the semi-official corporate motto has called for the company, its products and its people to always strive to 'make a difference'; and one of the company's business objectives is to become 'the best, most innovative and exciting sporting goods company in the world.'"[1]

Shifting Competitive Picture for Reebok

In 1987, Reebok's share of the U.S. athletic footwear market surpassed arch-rival Nike's as it racked up sales of $1.4 billion against Nike's plateauing sales of $900 million. Somehow, Reebok's sales growth then slowed, and in 1990 Nike overtook it, with $2,235,244,000 in sales to Reebok's $2,159,243,000. The margin widened as Reebok began to lose ground, not sporadically but steadily. Its meteoric sales increases of a few years before were no more, and stock market valuations and investor enthusiasm reflected this.

Part of the shift of competitive position could be attributed to Nike's savvy advertising and to its two well-paid athlete endorsers: Michael Jordan and Pete Sampras. But perhaps Reebok could blame itself more for the change in its fortunes. Certainly as the 1990s moved toward mid-decade, the flaws of Reebok were becoming more obvious and self-destructing.

Paul Fireman had purchased Reebok in 1984 and led it to more than a tenfold increase in sales in only five years. But with such growth, directors felt they needed an executive with experience running a big operation. Fireman, who owned 20 percent of the company's stock, didn't object. He maintained that he was glad to give up day-to-day responsibilities. While he still retained the titles of chairman and CEO, he turned his attentions to private pursuits, including building a golf course on Cape Cod.

The new management was to prove inept. Amid unimproving performance, Reebok went through three different top executives in the next five years, the last being John Duerden, formerly with Xerox. Nothing seemed to stem losing ground against Nike. Finally, in August 1992, Fireman again took active charge and he wasted little time bringing in a new management team. At the same time, he introduced aggressive plans for the company to regain its competitive position.

Aggressive Thrusts of Reebok

Fireman first attacked Nike in the basketball arena. Nike's share of basketball shoes was almost 50 percent, against Reebok's 15 percent. But about this time, Michael

---

[1] *Reebok International, Ltd. Corporate Background,* January 1993, pp. 13–14.

Jordan retired from basketball to try baseball. "Nike's success has become their albatross," Fireman exulted. "Jordan is no longer on the radar screen."[2] He signed up Shaquille O'Neal, "the next enduring superstar," and planned to destroy the market dominance of Nike.

The pressure was stepped up on Nike at the NBA All-Star game in February 1994, when Reebok launched a national ad campaign for its Instapump. This was a sneaker that had no laces, but instead was inflated with CO_2 to fit the foot. It was pricey, retailing for $130, but seemed on the cutting edge. Fireman expected this innovation to account for 10 percent of all Reebok's sales in three years.

He also attacked another Nike stronghold, the $250 million market for cleated shoes. Nike had 80 percent of this. In January 1993 Reebok introduced a new line of cleated shoes aimed at high-school athletes. Fireman predicted that these sales should triple by 1994 to $45 million. In 1994 he also aimed an offensive into the outdoor hiking and mountaineering market, with 12 new shoes that he predicted would produce $100 million in new sales.

During the years Fireman was not at the helm, Reebok had tried a number of advertising slogans, such as "UBU" and "Physics Behind Physique." None of these was notably effective—not like the "Just Do It" theme of Nike. Fireman now approved a new unifying theme for all ads, "Planet Reebok."

Fireman also did an about-face with his endorsement promotions. Despite Nike's heavy use of endorsements in its advertising, Reebok always had been reluctant to do much, thinking the huge sums celebrity athletes demanded were unreasonable. Suddenly he signed O'Neal in 1992 for $3 million, and then went on to sign endorsement deals with some 400 football, baseball, and soccer stars. The brand logo was also changed to an inverted "V" with a slash through it that he hoped consumers would identify with high performance. "We'll be the market leader by the end of 1995," Fireman predicted.[3]

Consequences

Unfortunately, the aggressive efforts of Fireman to rejuvenate the company and win back market leadership from Nike continued to sputter. Some flaws were coming to light. For example, with Shaquille O'Neal, the Shaq Attaq shoe seemed a sure thing for teens. But it bombed. The problems: The shoes were white with light-blue trim, and they cost $130. But now black shoes were the hot look, and how many teens could afford $130? In the first six months of 1993, sales of Reebok basketball shoes fell 20 percent, despite the Shaq.

By 1995, operating costs were surging, up to 32.7 percent of sales compared with 24.4 percent in 1991. They also exceeded the industry average of 27 percent. Reebok admitted that the increased costs were partly due to its aggressive pursuit of endorsement contracts with athletes as well as sporting-event sponsorships. For example, it had signed up 3,000 athletes to wear Reebok shoes and apparel at the 1996 Olympics in Atlanta, up from 400 four years before. It had also bought endorsements from the

---

[2] Geoffrey Smith, "Can Reebok Regain Its Balance?" *Business Week*, December 20, 1993, p. 109.

[3] Ibid., p. 108.

San Francisco 49ers and other NFL teams, as well as basketball star Rebecca Lobo, to wear its products.

Some of the prior endorsements had not worked out well: Tennis pro Michael Chang had a $15-million endorsement contract, but Sampras and Agassi, both Nike endorsers, had eclipsed Chang. And Shaquille O'Neal became unhappy with his $3 million Reebok contract and began looking around for bigger money.

Reebok's costs also were increased by investments aimed at fixing distribution snags and opening a new facility in Memphis.

Other Reebok problems stemmed from the management turmoil, the departures and resignations of top executives. Some shareholders questioned whether Fireman was too difficult a boss: "How do you attract first-rate talent when there's been a history of turnover at the top?"[4]

Adding to Reebok's difficulties were price-fixing charges brought by the Federal Trade Commission. The government contended that Reebok had told retailers their supplies would be cut off if they discounted Reebok shoes too much. In May 1995, Reebok agreed to pay $9.5 million to settle the price-fixing charges, saying that while no evidence of wrongdoing was established, still it settled to avoid costly litigation.

But the major Reebok problem seemed to lie in its relations with the major retailer player in the athletic footwear industry.

The Struggle to Win Foot Locker

By 1995, Woolworth's Foot Locker, a chain of some 2,800 stores, had become the biggest seller of athletic footwear. It and related Woolworth units accounted for $1.5 billion of the $6.5 billion U.S. sales, this being some 23 percent. Nike had a winning relationship with this behemoth customer. In 1993, Nike's sales in Foot Lockers were $300 million, while Reebok was slightly behind, with $228 million. Two years later, Nike's Foot Locker sales had risen to $750 million, while Reebok's dropped to $122 million.[5]

The decline of Reebok's fortunes with Foot Locker can be attributed to poor handling by top management of this very important relationship. Fireman seemed to resent the demands of Foot Locker almost from the beginning. For example, in the 1980s when Reebok's aerobics shoes were facing robust demand, Foot Locker wanted exclusivity, that is, special lines solely for itself. The retailer saw exclusive lines as one of its major weapons against discounters, and was getting such protection from other manufacturers. But not from Reebok, which persisted in selling its shoes to anybody, including discounters near Foot Locker stores.

In contrast, Nike had been working with Foot Locker for some years, and by 1995 had a dozen items sold only by the chain, including Flights 65 and 67, high-priced basketball shoes. While Fireman began belatedly trying to fix the relationship, little had apparently been accomplished by the end of 1995.[6]

Adding to Reebok's troubles in cracking this major chain, Foot Locker's customers were mainly teens and generation-X customers willing to pay $80 to $90 for

---

[4] Joseph Pereira, "In Reebok-Nike War, Big Woolworth Chain Is a Major Battlefield," *The Wall Street Journal*, September 22, 1995, p. A6.

[5] Ibid., p. A1.

[6] Ibid., p. 6A.

shoes. But Reebok had given up that high-end niche with most of its products. Reebok's primary customer base was older people and pre-teens unwilling or unable to pay the high prices.

Aggravating the poor relationship with Foot Locker was Reebok's carelessness in providing samples on time to Foot Locker buyers. Because of the chain's size, buying decisions had to be made early in the season. Late-arriving samples, or no samples, virtually guaranteed that such new items would not be purchased in any appreciable quantity. See the following information box for a discussion of the importance of major customers.

NIKE

History

Phil Knight was a miler of modest accomplishments. His best time was a 4:13, hardly in the same class as the below-4:00 world-class runners. But he had trained under the renowned coach Bill Bowerman at the University of Oregon in the late 1950s. Bowerman had put Eugene, Oregon on the map when year after year he turned out world-record-setting long-distance runners. Bowerman was constantly experimenting with shoes: He had a theory that an ounce off a running shoe might make enough difference to win a race.

INFORMATION BOX

IMPORTANCE OF MAJOR ACCOUNT MANAGEMENT

Recognizing the importance of major customers has come belatedly to some sellers, probably none more belatedly than Reebok. These very large customers often represent a major part of a firm's total sales volume, and satisfying them in an increasingly competitive environment requires special treatment. Major account management should be geared to developing long-term relationships. Service becomes increasingly important in cementing such relations. To this end, understanding and catering to customer needs and wants is a must. If this means giving such important customers exclusivity, and the absolute first opportunity to see new goods and samples, this ought to be done unhesitatingly.

Such account management has resulted in changes in many organizations. Separate sales forces are often developed, such as "account managers," who devote all their time to one or a few major customers, while the rest of the sales force calls on smaller customers in the normal fashion. For a customer the size of Foot Locker, senior executives, even the president of the firm, need to become part of this relationship.

Given that you think the demands of a major retailer are completely unreasonable, what would you do if you were Mr. Fireman: give in completely, hold to your principles, negotiate, or what?

In the process of completing his MBA at Stanford University, Phil wrote a research paper based on the theory that the Japanese could do for athletic shoes what they were doing for cameras. After receiving his degree in 1960, Knight went to Japan to seek an American distributorship from the Onitsuka Company for Tiger shoes. Returning home, he took samples of the shoes to Bowerman.

In 1964 Knight and Bowerman went into business. They each put up $500 and formed the Blue Ribbon Shoe Company, sole distributor in the United States for Tiger running shoes. They put the inventory in Knight's father-in-law's basement, and they sold $8,000 worth of these imported shoes that first year. Knight worked by days as a Coopers & Lybrand accountant, while at night and on weekends he peddled these shoes mostly to high school athletic teams.

Knight and Bowerman finally developed their own shoe in 1972 and decided to manufacture it themselves. They contracted the work out to Asian factories where labor was cheap. They named the shoe Nike after the Greek goddess of victory. At that time they also developed the "swoosh" logo, which was highly distinctive and subsequently was placed on every Nike product. The Nike shoe's first appearance in competition came during the 1972 Olympic trials in Eugene, Oregon. Marathon runners persuaded to wear the new shoes placed fourth through seventh, whereas Adidas wearers finished first, second, and third in the trials.

On a Sunday morning in 1975, Bowerman began tinkering with a waffle iron and some urethane rubber, and he fashioned a new type of sole, a "waffle" sole whose tiny rubber studs made it more springy than those of other shoes currently on the market. This product improvement—seemingly so simple—gave Knight and Bowerman an initial impetus, and brought 1976 sales to $14 million, up from $8.3 million the year before, and from only $2 million in 1972.

Now Nike was off and running. It was to stay in the forefront of the industry with its careful research and development of new models. By the end of the decade Nike was employing almost 100 people in the research and development section of the company. Over 140 different models were offered, many of these the most innovative and technologically advanced on the market. Such diversity came from models designed for different foot types, body weights, running speeds, training schedules, sexes, and levels of skill. By 1981, Nike led all athletic shoe makers with approximately 50 percent of the total market. Adidas, the decades-long market leader, had seen its share of the market fall well below that of Nike.

In 1980 Nike went public, and Knight became an instant multimillionaire, reaching the coveted *Forbes* Richest Four Hundred Americans with a net worth estimated at just under $300 million.[7] Bowerman, at age 70, had sold most of his stock earlier and owned only 2 percent of the company, worth a mere $9.5 million.

In the January 4, 1982 edition of *Forbes*, in the "Annual Report on American Industry," Nike was rated number one in profitability over the previous five years, ahead of all other firms in all other industries.[8]

---

[7] "The Richest, People in America—The *Forbes Four Hundred*," *Forbes*, Fall 1983, p. 104.

[8] *Forbes*, January 4, 1982, p. 246.

But by the latter 1980s, Reebok had emerged as Nike's greatest competitor, and threatened its dynasty. A good part of the reason for this was Nike's underestimation of an opportunity. Consequently, it was late into the fast-growing market for shoes worn for the aerobic dancing that was sweeping the country, fueled by best-selling books by Jane Fonda and others. Reebok was there with the first athletic shoe designed especially for women: a shoe for aerobic dance exercise.

Figure 3.1 shows the sales growth of Reebok and Nike from their beginnings to 1995. Of particular note is the great growth of Reebok in the mid-1980s, in only a few years surpassing Nike, which had plateaued as it missed the new fitness opportunity. Then, as can be graphically seen, Reebok began slowing down, a slowdown it was unable to turn-around through the mid-1990s, while Nike again surged. Table 3.1 shows the net income comparisons. Both firms had somewhat erratic incomes, but the early income growth promise of Reebok relative to Nike, as with sales, could not be sustained. This is confirmed with the latest revenue and income figures from 1995 to 1998 shown in Table 3.2.

Nike's Rejuvenation

The recharge of Nike, after letting its guard down to the wildly charging Reebok, has to be a significant success story. Usually when a front runner loses momentum, the trend is difficult to reverse. But Phil Knight and Nike were not to be denied.

Still, in 1993, Nike did not look very much a winner, even though it had wrested market dominance from Reebok. From the high eighties in February of that year, share prices had plummeted to the mid-fifties. The reason? Nike's sales were up only 15 percent and earnings just 11 percent, nothing outstanding for a once-hot stock. So

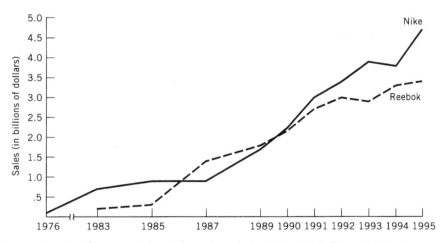

Figure 3.1. Sneaker wars: Sales, Nike and Reebok 1976–1995 (billions of dollars).

Source: Company annual reports.

Commentary: Here we can graphically see the charge of Reebok in the late 1980s that for a few years surpassed Nike, but then faltered by 1990 as Nike surged ever farther ahead.

TABLE 3.1.   Sneaker Wars: Net Income Comparisons, Nike and Reebok 1985–1994 (billions of dollars)

	Nike	Reebok
1985	$10.3	$39.0
1986	59.2	132.1
1987	35.9	165.2
1988	101.7	137.0
1989	167.0	175.0
1990	243.0	176.6
1991	287.0	234.7
1992	329.2	114.8
1993	365.0	223.4
1994	298.8	254.5

Source: Company annual reports.

Commentary: Note how much more profitable Reebok was than Nike in the late 1980s. In one year, 1987, it was almost five times more profitable. But then in 1990 the tide swung strongly in Nike's favor. Note also that Nike's profitability was far more steady than Reebok's during this period.

TABLE 3.2.   Nike versus Reebok Comparative Operating Statistics, 1995–1998

	Nike	Reebok	Nike % of Total
Revenues (million $):			
1995	$4,761	$3,481	57.8%
1996	6,471	3,478	65.0
1997	9,187	3,644	71.6
1998	9,553	3,225	74.8
Net Income (million $):			
1995	400	165	70.8
1996	553	139	79.9
1997	796	135	85.5
1998	400	24	82.2

Source: Calculated from company reports.

Commentary: In this comparative analysis, the further widening of the gap between Nike and Reebok is clearly evident. In revenues, Nike's market share against Reebok has grown from 57.8 percent to 74.8 percent in these four years, a truly awesome increase in market dominance. In net income, Nike's comparative performance is even more impressive, despite the poor 1998 profit performance partly due to sorry economic conditions in the Asian markets: Nike's profits were down, but not nearly as much as Reebok's.

Wall Street began questioning how many pairs of sneakers does the world need? (Critics had once assailed McDonald's under the same rationale: How many hamburgers can the world eat?)

Knight's response was that the Nike mystique could sell other kinds of goods, such as outdoor footwear, from sandals to hiking boots, and apparel lines, such as uniforms, for top-ranked college football and basketball teams—from pants and jerseys to warmup jackets and practice gear—with these same products eagerly sought by the general public. Could it be that an athletic shoe company still faced a growth industry? Apparently so, through wise diversifications within the larger athletic goods industry. See the following issue box for a discussion of how a business should define itself.

In his quest to remain the dominant player, Knight recalled what he learned from his old coach and Nike cofounder, Bill Bowerman: "Play by the rules, but be ferocious."[9]

But Knight and Nike were not ferocious to their customers. They pampered them, as we have seen in their relations with Foot Locker. And by the end of 1995, Nike's sales lead over Reebok was 38 percent.

Handling Adversity

In the summer of 1996, Nike as well as many other U.S. manufacturers came under fire for farming production out to "sweatshops" in poor countries of the world as they sought to reduce manufacturing costs. Nike became the major target for critics of these "abuses."

ISSUE BOX

HOW SHOULD WE DEFINE OUR BUSINESS?

Nike has developed its business horizons through the following sequence:

running shoes → athletic shoes → athletic clothing → athletic goods

In so doing, it has greatly expanded its growth potential. This idea of expanding perception of one's business was first put down on paper by Theodore Levitt in a seminal article, "Marketing Myopia," in the *Harvard Business Review* in July–August 1960. He suggested that it was shortsighted for railroads to consider themselves only in the railroad business, and not in the much larger transportation business. Similarly, petroleum companies should consider themselves in the energy business, and plan their strategies accordingly.

Can such expanding of a firm's business definition go too far? Even in Levitt's day, could a railroad really have the expertise to run an airline? Looking to Nike today, and its expanding views of tapping into the athletic goods market, do you think golf clubs and bags would be a viable expansion opportunity? football equipment? fishing tackle?

---

[9] Fleming Meeks, "Be Ferocious," *Forbes*, August 2, 1993, p. 41.

Then in April 1997 came another blow to Nike's image. Thirty-nine members of the Heaven's Gate cult committed suicide, *all* wearing Nikes with the swoosh logo readily visible. The "Just Do It" slogan of Nike was trumpeted as being entirely apt, and some even spoofed that Nike's slogan should be changed to "Just Did It."

Environmental factors, by no means unique to Nike, also tormented it. Demand in Asia was drastically reduced due to deep recession there. Another troubling portent was the public's growing disenchantment with athletes. Fan interest seemed to be dropping, perhaps reflecting a growing tide of resentment at overpriced athletes proving to be selfish, arrogant, and decadent—the very role models that Nike, Reebok, and other firms spent millions to enlist.

Knight had to wonder at another disturbing possibility: Had Nike grown too big? Was its logo, the swoosh, too pervasive, to the point that it turned some people off? Even the tag line, "Just Do It," was this becoming counterproductive?

Concerned about such questions, Nike began reassessing. A new advertising campaign had the softer tag line, "I can." Nike even began toning down its use of the swoosh, removing it from corporate letterheads and most advertising, and substituting a lowercase, "nike."

Most Recent Developments

At the beginning of the new millennium, Nike's dominant position seems to be strengthening. Changing fashion trends, new products, cost cutting, and an Asian revival are aiding Nike. It found that with the public's growing disenchantment with athlete endorsers it could shave its marketing budget by $100 million. Furthermore, prospects for 2000 have to be optimistic. Athletic gear sales peak in Olympic years, and the summer games in Sydney, Australia should stimulate a big buying spree in merchandise where Nike has a 35 percent share.[10]

ANALYSIS

The case shows the whipsawing of the two major competitors in what was once merely the athletic shoe industry, an industry now expanding far beyond its original focus. Nike originally had outgunned the old, entrenched Adidas, only to find Reebok surpassing it in the mid-1980s as it failed to recognize soon enough a new opportunity. Somehow Nike came back stronger than ever. The explanation lies in both the mistakes of Reebok and the luck and aggressiveness of Nike after its brief hiccup.

The most controllable factor in the divergent success patterns of the competitors had to be customer relations. Nike cultivated its customers, especially the larger dealers such as Foot Locker, while Reebok was surprisingly nonchalant and even arrogant in such dealings. It is a major mistake for a maker of seemingly high-demand goods to become arbitrary and dictatorial toward dealers. The temptation is to capitalize on the perceived "king of the hill" position. But the caprice of fashions and fads can quickly destroy this smugness as the winner one year may be left at the gate the next,

---

[10] Leigh Gallagher, "Rebound," *Forbes*, May 3, 1999, p. 60.

as was the case with the Shaq Attaq shoes and the expensive endorsements of the rookie basketball player, O'Neal.

In other aspects of its comeback, Nike may have lucked out. It chose for its endorsing athletes ones who grew to become the dominant figures in their sport, ones lionized by fans. The advertising theme of Nike caught on, "Just do it," with its great appeal to youth. But such home runs in advertising can never be guaranteed.

Can Reebok Pull a Rejuvenation as Nike Did?

The remarkable rejuvenation of Nike resulted from both aggressive actions by Nike and perhaps a misstep by Reebok. The same thing could happen as Reebok strives to overtake Nike. However, as 1998 results are in (see Table 3.2), Reebok's revenues are only 34 percent of Nike's, and net income only 6 percent. That seems an insurmountable lead unless Nike suffers some catastrophe. Still, nothing is for sure.

WHAT CAN BE LEARNED?

No one is immune from mistakes; success does not guarantee continued success. Many executives fool themselves into thinking success begets continued success. It is not so! No firm, market leader or otherwise, can afford to rest on its laurels, to disregard a changing environment and aggressive but smaller competitors. Adidas had as commanding a lead in its industry as IBM once had in computers. But it was overtaken and surpassed by Nike, a rank newcomer and a domestic firm with few resources in an era when foreign brands (of beer, watches, cars) had a mystique and attraction for affluent Americans that few domestic brands could achieve. But Adidas let down its guard at a critical point. Similarly, but to a lesser degree, Nike then lagged against Reebok as it underestimated or was unaware of the growing interest among women in aerobic dancing and other physical activities.

Importance of catering to major customers. A firm should seek to satisfy all its customers, but for the larger ones, the major accounts, the need for catering to their needs and wants is absolutely vital. In few cases is the stark contrast between effective and ineffective dealings with larger customers more obvious than between Nike and Reebok in their relations with the huge Foot Locker retail chain. Even though a manufacturer may resent the demands of a powerful retailer, the alternative is either meeting them or losing part or all of the business to someone else. However, a better course of action is to work closely with the large customer in a spirit of cooperation and mutual interest, not in an adversarial power struggle.

The power of public image. Granted that technological differences in running shoes have narrowed so that any tangible advantage of a brand is practically imperceptible, what makes Nike stand out? Of course it is the image and the "swoosh" that identifies the brand. See the following information box for a discussion of the "swoosh."

INFORMATION BOX

THE NIKE "SWOOSH" LOGO

The Nike "swoosh" is one of the world's best-recognized logos. In the very early days of Nike, a local design student at Portland State University was paid $35 for creating it. The curvy, speedy-looking blur turned out to be highly distinctive and has from then on been placed on all Nike products. Phil Knight even has the swoosh logo tattooed on his left calf. Because it has become so familiar, Nike no longer has to add the name Nike to the logo. (Tiger Woods wears a cap and other clothing with the swoosh logo discretely visible.)

The power of such a well-known logo makes Nike's sponsorship of famous athletes unusually effective as they wear shoes and apparel displaying it in their sports exploits.

In your judgment, do you think Nike could have achieved its present success without this unique but simple logo? What do you think of the Reebok logo?

For something like running shoes and athletic equipment and apparel, their visibility readily stands out. For many youth, the sight of famous and admired athletes actively using the brand is an irresistible lure, and creates the desire to emulate them even if only through wearing the same brand ... and maybe dreaming a little. The popularity of a brand becomes a further attraction: being "cool," belonging to the "in" group.

Is Nike's success in building its image transferable to other firms whose products cannot be identified with use by the famous? Do such firms have any possibilities for developing image-enhancing qualities for their brands? They certainly do.

Consider the long-advertised lonesome Maytag repairman. Maytag has been highly successful in building a reputation, an image, for dependability and assured quality. In so doing it has been able to sustain a higher price advantage over its competitors. A carefully nurtured image of good quality, dependability, reliable service, and being in the forefront of technology or fashion can bring a firm great success in its particular industry.

Is there a point of diminishing returns with celebrity endorsements? One would think so, and public attitudes today seem to bear this out. Athlete celebrities demand big bucks. Are their endorsements worth the price? Perhaps only in moderation, and only with the best of the best. But one cannot always predict with certainty the future exploits of any athlete, even a Michael Jordan. Yet, contracts are binding. While some would criticize Nike for too much emphasis on celebrity advertising, the right role models can pay dividends. But the overkill of Reebok in seeking celebrity endorsements led to burgeoning costs and a mediocre payoff in sales. The message seems clear: Overuse of celebrity endorsements can be a financial drain. Added to this is the always-present risk that the athlete celebrity in contact sports may have a career-ending injury, or be guilty of some nefarious activity that destroys his or her image.

Is a great executive the key? Was the rejuvenation of Nike and the decline of Reebok due mostly to the talents of a Phil Knight versus a Paul Fireman? Does the success of an enterprise depend almost entirely on the ability of its leader? Such questions have long baffled experts.

Several aspects of this issue are worth noting. The incompetent is usually clearly evident and identifiable. The great business leader may also be, but perhaps he or she simply lucked out. In most situations competing executives are reasonably similar in competence: They have vision, the support of their organizations, and reasonable judgment and prudence. What then makes the difference? A good assessment of opportunities, an advertising slogan that really hits, a hunch about competitor vulnerability? Yes; but how much is due just to a fortuitous call, a gamble that paid off?

We know that Phil Knight had a history of great successes. After all, he beat Adidas, and brought Nike from nowhere to the premier athletic footwear firm. Add to this his handling of a great challenge by moving Nike, for a second time, into the heady atmosphere of market leader. Was his ability as a top executive so much greater than that of Fireman? Would his absence destroy the promise of Nike?

Perhaps the basic question is: Can one person make a difference? Perhaps only if that person is infallible. But Phil Knight was not infallible. He had a major perceptual lapse in the mid-1980s. But Fireman's lapses were more serious.

In the final analysis, Knight made a great difference for Nike. Certainly we can identify other leaders who made great differences: Sam Walton of Wal-Mart, Herb Kelleher of Southwest Airlines, Lee Iacocca of Chrysler, Ray Kroc of McDonald's come readily to mind. Sometimes, one person can make a major difference. But they can still make bad decisions, misjudgments. Perhaps their success was in having a higher percentage of good decisions and, yes, having a little luck on their side.

CONSIDER

Can you think of additional learning insights?

QUESTIONS

1. "The success of Nike was strictly fortuitous and had little to do with great decision making." Evaluate this statement.

2. In recent years Nike has moved strongly to develop markets for running shoes in the Far East, particularly in China. Discuss how Nike might go about stimulating such underdeveloped markets.

3. How could anyone criticize Fireman for signing up Shaquille O'Neal to a lucrative endorsement contract? Discuss.

4. Do you think the swoosh logo has become too widespread, that it is turning off many people?

5. Given that all decision makers will sometimes make bad calls, how might their batting averages be improved? Can decision making really be improved?

6. Do you think the athletic goods industry has limited potential? Or is it still a growth industry? Your opinions, and rationale, please.

7. Is there a danger in catering too much to major customers? Discuss.

8. What do you think of the inverted-V-slash logo of Reebok? How would you evaluate it against Nike's swoosh?

HANDS-ON EXERCISES

Before

1. It is 1985. Your production of shoes can hardly meet the burgeoning demand. The future seems unlimited. Design a program for Reebok to build stronger relations with its major customers, including Foot Locker.

After

2. It is 1995. Nike has again achieved market dominance, and its position seems unassailable. Some shareholder critics are calling for your resignation, Mr. Fireman. Design a strategy for again bringing Reebok to victory in this war against Nike. Be as specific as you can, and defend your recommendations.

TEAM DEBATE EXERCISE

Debate the issue of endorsements for athletes. How much is too much? Where do we draw the line? Should we go only for the few famous? Or should we gamble on lesser stars eventually making it big and offer them long-term contracts? Argue the two sides of the issue: aggressive and conservative.

INVITATION TO RESEARCH

How has the battle gone between Reebok and Nike? Has Reebok been able to gain any ground? How are the two firms doing in overseas markets? What is your prognosis for their future competitive positions?

CHAPTER FOUR

Airliner Wars:
Airbus vs. Boeing

*T*he commercial-jet business had long been subject to booms and busts: major demand for new aircraft and then years of little demand. By the second half of the 1990s, demand burgeoned as never before. Boeing, the world's leading producer of commercial airplanes, seemed in the catbird seat amid the worldwide surge of orders. This was an unexpected windfall, spurred by markets greatly expanding in Asia and Latin America at the same time as domestic demand, helped by deregulation and prosperity, boomed. In the midst of these good times, Boeing in 1997 incurred its first loss in 50 years.

During this same period, Airbus (Airbus Industrie), a European aerospace consortium, and an underdog, began climbing toward its long-stated goal of winning 50 percent of the over-100-seat airplane market. The battle was all-out, no-holds-barred, and Boeing was blinking.

BOEING

Background of the Company

Boeing's was a fabled past, being a major factor in the World War II war effort, and in the late 1950s leading the way in producing innovative, state-of-the-art commercial aircraft. It introduced the 707, the world's first commercially viable jetliner. In the late 1960s, it almost bankrupted itself to build a jetliner twice the size of any other then in service, as critics predicted it could never fly profitably. But the 747 dramatically lowered costs and airfares and brought passenger comfort previously undreamed of in flying. In the mid-1990s, Boeing introduced the high-technology 777, the first commercial aircraft designed entirely with the use of computers.

In efforts to reduce the feast-or-famine cycles of the commercial aircraft business, Boeing acquired Rockwell International's defense business in 1996, and in 1997 purchased McDonnell Douglas for $16.3 billion.

In 1997, Boeing's commercial aircraft segment contributed 57 percent of total revenues. This segment ranged from 125-passenger 737s to giant 500-seat 747s. In

1997, Boeing delivered 374 aircraft, up from 269 in 1996. The potential seemed enormous: Over the next twenty years, air passenger traffic worldwide was projected to rise 4.9 percent a year, and airlines were predicted to order 16,160 aircraft to expand their fleets and replace aging planes.[1] As the industry leader, Boeing had 60 percent of this market. At the end of 1997, its order backlog was $94 billion.

Defense and space operations comprised 41 percent of 1997 revenues. This included Airborne Warning and Control Systems (AWACS), helicopters, B-2 bomber subcontract work, and the F-22 fighter, among other products and systems.

Problems with the Commercial Aircraft Business Segment

Production Problems

Boeing proved to be poorly positioned to meet the surge in aircraft orders. Part of this resulted from drastic layoffs it had made of experienced workers during the industry's last slump, in the early 1990s. Though it hired 32,000 new workers over 18 months starting in 1995, the experience gap upped the risk of costly mistakes. Boeing had also cut back its suppliers in strenuous efforts to slash parts inventories and increase cost efficiency.

But Boeing had other problems. Its production systems were a mess. It had somehow evolved some 400 separate computer systems, and these were not linked. Its design system was labor intensive and paper dependent, and very expensive as it tried to cater to customer choices. A $1 billion program had been launched in 1996 to modernize and computerize the production process. But this was too late: The onslaught of orders had already started. (It is something of an anomaly that a firm that had the sophistication to design the 777 entirely by computers was so antiquated in its use of computers otherwise.)

Demands for increased production were further aggravated by unreasonable production goals and too many plane models. Problems first hit with the 747 Jumbo, and then with a new version of the top-selling 737, the so-called next-generation 737NG. Before long, every program was affected: also the 757, 767, and 777. In 1997, while Boeing released over 320 planes to customers for a 50 percent increase over 1996, this was far short of the planned completion rate. For example, by early 1998 a dozen 737NGs had been delivered to airlines, but this was less than one/third of the 40 supposed to have been delivered by then. Yet, the company maintained through September 1997 that everything was going well, that there was only a month's delay in the delivery of some planes.

Soon it became apparent that problems were much greater. In October, the 747 and 737 assembly lines were shut down for nearly a month to allow workers to catch up and ease parts shortages. *The Wall Street Journal* reported horror stories of parts being rushed in by taxicab, of executives spending weekends trying to chase down

---

[1] *Boeing 1997 Annual Report.*

TABLE 4.1.   Boeing's Trend of
Revenues and Income, 1988–1997

	(million $)	
	Revenue	Net Income
1988	16,962	614
1989	20,276	675
1990	27,595	1,385
1991	29,314	1,567
1992	30,184	1,554
1993	25,438	1,244
1994	21,924	856
1995	19,515	393
1996	22,681	1,095
1997	45,800	–177

Source: Boeing annual reports.

Commentary: Note the severity of the decline in revenues and profits during the industry downturn in 1993, 1994, and 1995. It is little wonder that Boeing was so ill-prepared for the deluge of orders starting in 1995. Then in an unbelievable anomaly, the tremendous increase in revenues in 1997 to the highest ever—partly reflecting the acquisitions—was accompanied by a huge loss.

needed parts, of parts needed for new planes being shipped out to replace defective parts on an in-service plane. Overtime pay brought some assembly-line workers incomes over $100,000, while rookie workers muddled by on the line.[2]

Despite its huge order backlog, Boeing took a loss for 1997, the first in over 50 years. See Table 4.1 for the trend in revenues and net income over the last ten years.

The loss mostly resulted from two massive writedowns. One, for $1.4 billion, arose from the McDonnell Douglas acquisition and in particular from its ailing commercial aircraft operation at Long Beach, California. The bigger writeoff, $1.6 billion, reflected production problems, particularly on the new 737NG. Severe price competition with Airbus resulted in not enough profits on existing business to bring the company into the black. Production delays continued, with more writedowns on the horizon.

As Boeing moved into 1998, analysts wondered how much longer it would take to clear up the production snafus. This would be longer than anyone had been led to expect. Unexpectedly, a new problem arose for Boeing. Disastrous economic conditions in Asia now brought major order cancellations.

---

[2] Frederic M. Biddle and John Helyar, "Behind Boeing's Woes: Clunky Assembly Line, Price War with Airbus," *The Wall Street Journal*, April 24, 1998, p. A16.

Customer Relations

Not surprisingly, Boeing's production problems resulting in delayed shipments seriously impacted on customer relations. For example, Southwest Airlines had to temporarily cancel adding service to another city because ordered planes were not ready. Boeing paid Southwest millions of dollars of compensation for the delayed deliveries. Continental also had to wait for five overdue 737s.

Other customers switched to Boeing's only major competitor, Airbus Industrie, of Toulouse, France.

AIRBUS INDUSTRIE

Airbus had to salivate at Boeing's troubles. It was a distant second in market share to the 60 percent of Boeing. Now this was changing and it could see achieving a sustainable 50 percent market share. See the following information box for a discussion of market share.

Background of Airbus

Airbus was founded in 1970 as a consortium that now includes four countries: British Aerospace, DaimlerChrysler Aerospace (Germany), France's Aerospatiale, and

---

INFORMATION BOX

IMPORTANCE OF MARKET SHARE

The desire to surpass a competitor is a common human tendency, whether in sports or business. A measurement of performance relative to competitors encourages this and can be highly motivating for management and employees alike. Furthermore, market share performance is a key indicator in ascertaining how well a firm is doing and in spotting emerging problems, as well as sometimes allaying blame. As an example of the latter, declining sales over the preceding year, along with a constantly improving market share, can suggest that the firm is doing a good job, even though certain factors adversely affected the whole industry.

Market share is usually measured by (1) share of overall sales, and/or (2) share relative to certain competitors, usually the top one or several in the industry. Of particular importance is trend data: Are things getting better or worse? If worse, why is this, and what needs to be done to improve the situation?

Since Boeing and Airbus were the only real competitors in this major industry, relative market shares became critical. The perceived importance of gaining, or not losing, market share led to severe price competition that cut into the profits of both firms, as will be discussed later.

How would you respond to the objection that market share data is not all that useful, since "it doesn't tell us what the problem really is"?

Can emphasizing market share be counterproductive? If so, why?

Spain's Case. Each of the partners supplied components such as wings and fuselages, and underwrote the consortium's capital expenses (sometimes with government loans), and were prepared to cover its operating losses.

The organizational structure seemed seriously flawed. It was politicized, with the partners voting on major issues in proportion to their country's ownership stakes. From this fragmented leadership, public squabbles frequently arose, some very serious. For example, plans to produce a new 107-seat A318 were held up by the French, who thought they were not getting their fair share of the production. Finances were also tangled with components supplied by the various countries charged to Airbus at suspiciously high prices.

The result was that in 1998, Boeing made $1.1 billion on sales of $56.1 billion, while Airbus was losing $204 million on sales of $13.3 billion. Boeing accused Airbus of selling below cost in order to steal business from Boeing, and Airbus blamed Boeing for the low bids.

The competition between the two companies became increasingly bitter after 1996. In that year Boeing and several Airbus partners discussed a joint development of a superjumbo. However, the talks ended when they could not agree on a single design. But Airbus suspected Boeing was not sincerely interested in this collaboration, that its main purpose in the talks was to stall Airbus's plans.

Airbus went ahead with its plans, while Boeing pooh-poohed the idea of such a huge plane.

Airbus Chairman Noel Forgeard

A slightly built Frenchman with a cheery disposition, Noel Forgeard, 52, joined the consortium in 1998 from Matra, a French aerospace manufacturer. He came with several major goals: to centralize decision-making, to impose sensible bookkeeping, and to make Airbus consistently profitable. The task was not easy. For example, plans to build the world's largest airplane, code-named A3XX, were even threatened by disagreements over where it would be assembled. Both France and Germany thought it should be produced in their country. Forgeard stated, "The need for a single corporate entity is well recognized. Everybody here is focused on it."[3] Still, while the need for reorganizing into something like a modern corporation was evident to most executives, the major partners were divided over how to proceed.

The World's Largest Plane

The A3XX was designed as a double-decker plane that could carry 555 passengers comfortably on overseas routes (it could even carry 750 people on routes around Asia where people did not care as much about seating comfort), 137 more than a Boeing 747–400. It is expected to fly by 2004, and prices will start somewhere over $200 million. Development costs could reach $15 billion, so essentially the A3XX is a bet-the-company project with an uncertain outlook, much as was Boeing's 747 thirty years

[3] Alex Taylor II, "Blue Skies for Airbus," *Fortune*, August 2, 1999, p. 103.

before. To pay for these costs, Airbus expects to get 40 percent from suppliers such as Sweden's Saab, 30 percent from government loans arranged by its partners, and the rest from its own resources.

The huge financing needed for this venture can hardly be obtained without a corporate reorganization, one that will provide a mechanism for handling internal disputes among the various partner countries, not the least of which is where the plane will be assembled. So, Forgeard has necessity on his side for reorganizing. But the A3XX faces other issues and concerns.

Should a Plane Like the A3XX Even Be Built?

The publicly expressed opinion of Boeing was that such a plane would never be profitable. "Let them launch it," said one Boeing official, with a hint of malice.[4] The position of Boeing was that consumers want frequent, nonstop flights, such as Southwest Airlines has brought to prominence with its saturation of city-pair routes with frequent flights. An ultra-large aircraft would mean far less frequency.[5]

Airbus, meantime, surveyed big airlines and discerned enough interest in a superjumbo to proceed. It also consulted with more than 60 airports around the world to determine whether such a big plane would be able to take off and land easily. Weight is critical to this, and Airbus pledged that the A3XX would be able to use the same runways as the 747 because of a new light-weight material called Glare, made of aluminum alloy and glass-fiber tape that could be used instead of regular aluminum.

Airbus promised ambitious plans for passenger comfort in this behemoth. It built a full-size 237-foot mockup of the interior to show prospective customers, and enlisted 1,200 frequent flyers to critique the cabin mockup. In order to reduce claustrophobia, it planned a wide staircase between upper and lower decks. Early plans also included exercise rooms and sleeping quarters fitted with bunk beds.

Airbus claimed that the 555-seat A3XX would be 15 percent cheaper to operate per seat-mile than Boeing's 747. Boeing maintained this was wildly optimistic. United Airlines Frederick Brace, vice president of finance, also expressed doubts: "The risk for Airbus is whether there's a market for A3XX. The risk for an airline is: Can we fill it up? We have to be prudent in how we purchase it."[6]

Competitive Position of Airbus

Airbus was well positioned to supply planes to airlines whose needs Boeing couldn't meet near term. Some thought it was even producing better planes than Boeing.

United Airlines chose Airbus's A320 twinjets over Boeing's 737s, saying passengers preferred the Airbus product. Several South American carriers also chose A320s over the 737, placing a $4 billion order with Airbus. For 1997, Airbus hacked out a 45 percent market share, the first time Boeing's 60 percent market share had eroded.

---

[4] Steve Wilhelm, "Plane Speaking," *Puget Sound Business Journal,* June 18, 1999, p. 112.

[5] Ibid.

[6] Taylor, p. 108.

The situation worsened drastically for Boeing in 1998. US Air, which had previously ordered 400 Airbus jets, announced in July that it would buy 30 more. But the biggest defection came in August, when British Airways announced plans to buy 59 Airbus jetliners and take options for 200 more. This broke its long record as a Boeing-loyal customer. The order would be worth as much as $11 billion, the biggest victory of Airbus over Boeing.[7]

Beyond the production delays of Boeing, Airbus had other competitive strengths. While it had less total production capability than Boeing (235 planes vs. Boeing's 550), its production line was efficient and it had done better in trimming its costs. This meant it could go head to head with Boeing on price. And price seemed to be the name of the game in the late 1990s. This contrasted with earlier days when Boeing rose to world leadership with performance, delivery, and technology more important than cost. "They [the customers] do not care what it costs us to make the planes," Boeing chairman and chief executive Philip Condit admitted. With airline design stabilized, he saw the airlines buying planes today as chiefly interested in how much carrying capacity they can buy for a buck.[8]

Today many passengers, and now the media, are grousing about the cramped interiors of planes designed for coast-to-coast trips, and the sparsity of lavatories to accommodate 126 to 189 passengers on long flights. Passenger rage appears to be cropping up more and more. *Forbes* magazine editorialized that "the first carrier that makes an all-out effort to treat passengers as people rather than oversized sardines will be an immense money-maker."[9]

Boeing's new 737-700s and 737-800s give customer comfort low priority. Airbus differentiated itself from Boeing by designing its A320 150-seat workhorse with a fuselage 7 $1/2$ inches wider than Boeing's, thus adding an inch to every seat in a typical six-across configuration.

In the first four months of 1999, Airbus won an amazing 78 percent of orders. US Airways Chairman Stephen Wolf, whose airline has ordered 430 Airbus planes since 1996, said, "Airbus aircraft offer greater flexibility for wider seats, more overhead bin space, and more aisle space—all important in a consumer-conscious business."[10]

A Donnybrook

An interesting marketing brawl occurred in mid-1999 that was indicative of the intensity of this airliner war. Boeing won a $1.9 billion order for ten of its 777 jetliners from Singapore Airlines. This in itself would not have raised eyebrows, but there was more to it. As a condition, Boeing agreed to purchase for resale 17 competing Airbus A340-300 jets from Singapore Airlines, which would allow the airline to phase out these Airbus planes.

---

[7] "British to Order Airbus Airliners," *Cleveland Plain Dealer,* August 25, 1998, p. 6-C.

[8] Howard Banks, "Slow Learner," *Forbes,* May 4, 1998, p. 54.

[9] "Plane Discomfort," *Forbes,* September 6, 1999, p. 32.

[10] Taylor, p. 104.

Airbus officials claimed that Boeing had agreed to unprofitable terms out of desperation to close a 777 sale agreement and that this signaled a new price war involving trade-ins to provide a discount rather than direct price cutting. Boeing crowed that the carrier's decision to eliminate the competing version of the A340 from its fleet was a victory for Boeing.[11]

A month later, still stung by the marketing move of Boeing, and in an effort to thwart it, Airbus announced that it would not provide its standard support services for the jets it sold to Singapore Airlines if Boeing buys and resells them. Such a countermove could prove costly to Boeing. On the other hand, Boeing is likely to offer the jets first to airlines with fleets of the same planes, several of whom had already expressed interest. Refusing to provide support service would put Airbus in the position of denying support for a small number of planes within the fleet of a major customer. Move and countermove.[12]

WHO CAN WE BLAME FOR BOEING'S TROUBLES?

Was it CEO Philip Condit?

Philip Condit became chief executive in 1996, just in time for the emerging problems. He had hardly assumed office before he was deeply involved in the defense industry's merger mania, first buying Rockwell's aerospace operation and then McDonnell Douglas. He later admitted that he probably spent too much time on these acquisitions, and not enough time on watching the commercial part of the operation.[13]

Condit's credentials were good. His association with Boeing began in 1965 when he joined the firm as an aerodynamics engineer. The same year, he obtained a design patent for a flexible wing called the sailwing. Moving through the company's engineering and managerial ranks, he was named CEO in 1996 and chairman in 1997. Along the way, he earned a master's degree in management from the Massachusetts Institute of Technology in 1975, and in 1997 a doctorate in engineering from Science University of Tokyo, where he was the first Westerner to earn such a degree.

Was Condit's pursuit of the Rockwell and McDonnell Douglas mergers a major blunder? While analysts do not agree on this, prevailing opinion is more positive than negative, mostly because these businesses could smooth the cyclical nature of the commercial sector.

Interestingly, in the face of severe adversity, no heads have rolled, as they might have in other firms. See the following issue box for a discussion of management climate during adversity.

---

[11] Jeff Cole, "Airbus Industrie Charges Boeing Is Inciting Price War in Asian Deal," *The Wall Street Journal,* June 21, 1999, p. A4.

[12] Daniel Michaels, "Airbus Won't Provide Support Service for Jets It Sold to Singapore Air if Boeing Resells Them," *The Wall Street Journal,* July 28, 1999, p. A17.

[13] Banks, p. 56.

ISSUE BOX

MANAGEMENT CLIMATE DURING ADVERSITY: WHAT IS BEST FOR MAXIMUM EFFECTIVENESS?

Management shakeups during adversity can range from practically none to widespread head-rolling. In the first scenario, a cooperative board is usually necessary, and it helps if the top executive(s) controls a lot of stock. But the company's problems will probably continue. In the second scenario, at the extreme, wielding a mean ax with excessive worker and management layoffs can wreak havoc on a company's morale and longer-term prospects.

In general, neither extreme—complacency or upheaval—is good. A sick company usually needs drastic changes, but not necessarily widespread bloodletting that leaves the entire organization cringing and sending out resumes. But we need to further define *sick*. At what point is a company so bad off it needs a drastic overhaul? Was Boeing such a sick company? Would a drastic overhaul have quickly changed things? Certainly Boeing management had made some miscalculations, mostly in the area of too much optimism and too much complacency, but these were finally recognized. A major competitor Airbus was finally aggressively attacking, and certainly had something to do with Boeing's problems. Major executive changes and resignations might not have helped.

How do you personally feel about the continuity of management at Boeing during these difficult times? Should some heads have rolled? What criteria would you use in your judgment of whether to roll heads or not?

Were the Problems Mostly Due to Internal Factors?

The unexpected buying binge by airlines that was brought about by worldwide prosperity fueling air travel maybe should have been anticipated. However, probably even the most prescient decision maker would have missed the full extent of this boom. For example, orders jumped from 124 in 1994 to 754 in 1996. With hindsight we know that Boeing made a grievous management mistake in trying to bite off too much, by promising expanded production and deliveries that were wholly unrealistic. We know what triggered such extravagant promises: trying to keep ahead of arch-rival Airbus.

Huge layoffs in the early 1990s contributed to the problems of gearing up for new business. An early retirement plan had been taken up by 9,000 of 13,000 eligible people. This was twice as many as Boeing expected, and it removed a core of production-line workers and managers who had kept a dilapidated system working. New people could not be trained or assimilated quickly enough to match those lost.

Boeing had begun switching to the Japanese practice of lean inventory management that delivers parts and tools to workers precisely as needed so that production costs could be reduced. Partly because of this and also because of the downturn in the early 1990s, Boeing's supplier base changed significantly. Some suppliers quit the aviation business; others had suffered so badly in the slump that their credit was affected and they were unable to boost capacity for the suddenly increased business. The result was serious parts shortages.

Complicating production problems was Boeing's long-standing practice of customizing, thereby permitting customers to choose from a host of options, to fine tune not only for every airline but for every order. For example, it offered the 747's customers 38 different pilot clipboards, and 109 shades of the color white.[14] Such tailoring added significantly to costs and production time. Perhaps this was acceptable when these costs could be easily passed on to customers in a more leisurely production cycle, but it was far from maximizing efficiency. Deregulation-fare wars made extreme customizing archaic. Boeing apparently got the message with the wide-bodied 777, designed entirely by computers. Here, choices of parts were narrowed to standard options, such as carmakers offer in their transmissions, engines, and comfort packages.

Cut-rate pricing between Boeing and Airbus epitomized the situation by the mid-1990s. Now, costs became critical if a firm was to be profitable. In this climate, Boeing was so obsessed with maintaining its 60 percent market share that it fought for each order with whatever price it took. Commercial airline production had somehow become a commodity business, with neither Boeing nor Airbus having products all that unique to sell. Innovation seemed disregarded, with price the only factor in getting an order. So, every order became a battleground, and prices might be slashed 20 percent off list in order to grab all the business possible.[15] And Boeing did not have the low-cost advantage over Airbus.

Such price competition worked to the advantage of the airlines, and they grew skillful at gaining big discounts from Boeing and Airbus by holding out huge contracts and negotiating hard.

The cumbersome production systems of Boeing—cost inefficient—became a burden in this cost-conscious environment. While some of the problems could be attributed to computer technology not well applied to the assembly process, others involved organizational myopia regarding even such simple things as a streamlined organization and common parts. For example, before recent changes the commercial group had five wing-design groups, one for each aircraft program. It now has one. Another example cited in *Forbes* tells of different tools needed in the various plane models to open their wing access hatches.[16] Why not use the same tool?

We see a paradox in Boeing's dilemma. Its 777 was the epitome of high technology and computer design, as well as efficient production planning. Yet, much of the other production was mired in a morass with supplies, parts management, and production inefficiency.

Harry Stonecipher, former CEO of McDonnell Douglas before the acquisition and now president and chief operating officer of Boeing, cited arrogance as the mind-

---

[14] John Greenwald, "Is Boeing Out of Its Spin?" *Time*, July 13, 1998, p. 68.

[15] Biddle and Helyar, pp. A1, A16.

[16] Banks, p. 60.

set behind Boeing's problems. He saw this as coming from a belief that the company could do no wrong, that all its problems came from outside, and that business-as-usual will solve them.[17]

The Role of External Factors

Adding to the production and cost-containment difficulties of Boeing was increased regulatory demands. These came not only from the U.S. Federal Aviation Administration, but also from the European Joint Airworthiness Authority (a loose grouping of regulators from more than 20 European countries). The first major consequence of this increased regulatory climate concerned the new 730NG. Boeing apparently thought it could use the same over-the-wings emergency exits as it had on the older 737. But Europe wanted a redesign. They were concerned that the older type of emergency exits would not permit passengers in the larger version of the plane to evacuate quickly enough. So Boeing had to design two new over-the-wing exits on each side. This was no simple modification since it involved rebuilding the most crucial aspect of the plane. The costly refitting accounted for a major part of the $1.6 billion writedown Boeing took in 1997.

Europe's Airbus Industrie had made no secret of its desire to achieve parity with Boeing and have 50 percent of the international market for commercial jets. This mindset led to the severe price competition of the latter 1990s as Boeing stubbornly tried to maintain its 60 percent market share even at the expense of profits. While its total production capacity was somewhat below that of Boeing, Airbus had already overhauled its manufacturing process, and was better positioned to compete on price. Airbus's competitive advantage seemed stronger with single-aisle planes, those in the 120–200 seat category, mostly 737s of Boeing and A320s of Airbus. But this accounted for 43 percent of the $40 billion expected to be spent on airliners in 1998.[18]

The future was something else. Airbus placed high stakes on a superjumbo successor to the 747, with seating capacity well beyond that of the 747. Such a huge plane would operate from hub airports such as New York City's JFK. Meantime, Boeing staked its future on its own 767s and 777s, which could connect smaller cities around the world without the need for passenger concentration at a few hubs.

Have you ever heard of a firm complaining of too much business? Probably not, were it not for Boeing's immersion in red ink trying to cope with too many orders. However, Boeing's feast of too much business abruptly ended. Financial problems in Asia brought cancellations and postponements of orders and deliveries.

In October 1998, Boeing disclosed that 36 completed aircraft were sitting in company storage areas in the desert, largely because of canceled orders. By

---

[17] Bill Sweetman, "Stonecipher's Boeing Shakeup," *Interavia Business & Technology*, September 1998, p. 15.
[18] Banks, p. 60.

December 1998, Boeing warned that its operations could be hurt by the Asian situation for as long as five years, and it announced that an additional 20,000 jobs would be eliminated and production cut 25 percent.[19] Of course, it didn't help that Airbus was capitalizing on the production difficulties of Boeing to wrest orders from the stable of Boeing's long-term customers and planned a 30 percent production increase for 1999.

WHO WILL WIN THE AIRLINER WAR?

There seems little doubt that Boeing will survive these difficulties and continue to be a major player in the airline, military, and aerospace markets. The acquisitions of Rockwell and McDonnell Douglas should prove long-term advantageous. The Asian crisis will go away, and orders rejuvenate. Competition with Airbus will continue strong and even intensify. The international market has room for two such firms. However, Boeing may have lost its dominant competitive advantage.

Troubling is the time Boeing has taken to cope with its production and efficiency problems. Mistakes opened the way for an aggressive and hungry competitor. Meanwhile, severe price competition played havoc with profitability. Boeing badly needed to get its costs under control and develop some uniqueness in products and service over Airbus. At this point in time, its only advantage is higher production capability than Airbus.

Airbus itself faces a stressful near-future. It has virtually staked the company on the success of its superjumbo jet, the A3XX. Should this be successful, it may well thrust Airbus into the dominant market-share position. It would be prudent for Boeing to hedge its bets, to make preliminary plans for its own 550-seat transport, just in case, and it evidently is doing so, according to an aviation trade magazine published in April 1999 and reported in *Fortune*.[20]

WHAT CAN BE LEARNED?

Beware the "king-of-the-hill" three-C's mindset. Firms that have been well entrenched in their industry and that have dominated for years tend to fall into a particular mindset that leaves them vulnerable to aggressive and innovative competitors.

The "three C's" are detrimental to a frontrunner's continued success:

Complacency

Conservatism

Conceit

[19] Frederick M. Biddle and Andy Pasztor, "Boeing May Be Hurt Up to 5 Years by Asia," *The Wall Street Journal,* December 3, 1998, p. A3.
[20] Taylor, p. 108.

LATE-BREAKING NEWS

Toward the end of 1999, Boeing seemed confronted with nothing but problems. In early November it had to halt some deliveries because of a faulty cockpit shield. The halt came as Boeing was still recovering from several years of production delays that hurt profits, but worse, allowed Airbus to gain market share.

The company also faced the possibility of liabilities from the October 31 crash of an EgyptAir 767. This plane had been built while Boeing workers were considering a strike and complaining of stress from working too much overtime. As if this was not enough, Boeing was also on the defensive from questions raised by governmental officials that it had failed to disclose a 19-year-old study of fuel-tank overheating that might have helped to prevent the crash of a TWA 747 in 1996.

Only a few weeks earlier, a big aerospace merger was announced by Germany and France to challenge Boeing and Lockheed. This European Aeronautic, Defense and Space Co. (EADS) would be the world's third-largest aerospace company. Such streamlining of Europe's aerospace industry was expected to lead to Airbus Industrie transforming itself into a private company that could compete more efficiently against Boeing with greater freedom in pricing and other major decisions.

As 1999 drew to a close, the business press was full of articles about the superjumbo jet, and the risks facing both Airbus and Boeing regarding it. Airbus was still determined, and had already invested $500 million of the $12 billion probable project cost.

For the present, though, Boeing had to confront its eroding market share: Through the first nine months of 1999, Airbus had 358 new aircraft orders to Boeing's 166.

Sources: Compiled from Paul Geitner and the Associated Press, as reported in "Europe Plans Merged Rival to Giants Boeing, Lockheed," *Cleveland Plain Dealer,* October 15, 1999, pp. 1-C and 2-C; Associated Press, as reported in "Boeing Stops Delivery," *Cleveland Plain Dealer,* November 3, 1999, p. 1-C; Jeff Cole, "Airbus Prepared to 'Bet the Company' as It Builds a Huge New Jet," *The Wall Street Journal,* November 3, 1999, pp. A1, A2, and A10.

Complacency is smugness—a complacent firm is self-satisfied, content with the status quo, no longer hungry and eager for innovative growth. *Conservatism,* when excessive, characterizes a management that is wedded to the past, to the traditional, to the way things have always been done. Conservative managers see no need to change because they believe nothing is different today (e.g., "Our 747 jumbo jet is the largest that can be profitably used"). Finally, *conceit* further reinforces the myopia of the mindset: conceit regarding current and potential competitors. The beliefs that "we are the best" and "no one else can touch us" can easily permeate an organization that has dominated its industry for years. Usually the three C's insidiously move in at the highest levels and readily filter down to the rest of the organization.

Stonecipher, former CEO of McDonnell Douglas and then president of Boeing, admitted to company self-confidence bordering on arrogance. The current problems of Boeing should have destroyed any vestiges of the three C's mindset. But the former king-of-the-hill position may be lost.

Growth must be manageable. Boeing certainly showed the fallacy of attempting growth beyond immediate capabilities in a growth-at-any-cost mindset. The rationale for embracing great growth is that we "need to run with the ball" if we ever get that rare opportunity to suddenly double or triple sales. But there are times when a slower, more controlled growth is prudent.

Risks lie on both sides as we reach for these opportunities. When a market begins to boom and a firm is unable to keep up with demand without greatly increasing capacity and resources, it faces a dilemma: (1) stay conservative in fear that the opportunity will be shortlived, but thereby abdicate some of the growing market to competitors, or (2) expand vigorously to take full advantage of the opportunity, but risk being overextended and vulnerable should the potential suddenly fade. Regardless of the commitment to a vision of great growth, a firm must develop an organization and systems and controls to handle it, or find itself in the morass of Boeing, with quality control problems, inability to meet production targets, alienated customers, and costs far out of line—and not the least, having its stock price savaged by Wall Street investors, while its market share tumbles. Growth must not be beyond the ability of the firm to manage it.

Perils of downsizing. Boeing presents a sobering example of the risks of downsizing in this era when downsizing is so much in fashion. With incredibly bad timing, it encouraged many of its most experienced and skilled workers and supervisors to take early retirement, just a few years before the boom began. Boeing found out the hard way that it could replace bodies, but not the skills needed to produce the highly complex planes under severe time pressure for output. It would have been better off to have maintained a core of experienced workers during the downturn, rather than lose them forever. It would have been better to have suffered with higher labor costs during the lean times, disregarding management's typical attitude of paring costs to the bone during such times. Yet, when we look at Table 4.1 and see the severe decreases of revenues and income in 1993, 1994, and lasting well into 1995, we can appreciate the dilemma of Boeing's management.

Problems of competing mostly on price. Price competition almost invariably leads to price cutting and even price wars to win market share. In such an environment, the lowest-cost, most efficient producer wins.

More often, all firms in an industry have rather similar cost structures, and severe price competition hurts the profits of all competitors without bringing much additional business. Any initial pricing advantage is quickly matched by competitors unwilling to lose market share. In this situation, competing on nonprice bases has much to recommend it. Nonprice competition emphasizes uniqueness, perhaps in some aspects of product features and quality, perhaps through service and quicker deliveries or maybe better quality control. A firm's reputation, if good, is a powerful nonprice advantage.

Usually new and rapidly growing industries face price competition as marginal firms are weeded out and more economies of operation are developed. The more mature an industry, the greater the likelihood of nonprice competition since cutthroat pricing causes too much hardship to all competitors.

Certainly the commercial aircraft industry is mature, and much has been made of airlines being chiefly interested in how much passenger-carrying capacity they can buy for the same buck, and of their pitting Airbus and Boeing against each other in bidding wars.[21] Nonprice competition badly needs to be reinstated in this industry. At this point, Airbus appears to be doing a better job of finding uniqueness, with its passenger-friendly planes and its charting new horizons with the A3XX superjumbo.

The synergy of mergers and acquisitions is suspect. The concept of synergy says that a new whole is better than the sum of its parts. In other words, a well-planned merger or acquisition should result in a better enterprise than the two separate entities. Theoretically, this would seem possible since operations can be streamlined for more efficiency and since greater management and staff competence can be brought to bear as more financial and other resources are tapped; or in Boeing's case, since the peaks and valleys of commercial demand could be countered by defense and space business.

Unfortunately, such synergy often is absent, at least in the short and intermediate term. More often such concentrations incur severe digestive problems—problems with people, systems, and procedures—that take time to resolve. Furthermore, greater size does not always beget economies of scale. The opposite may in fact occur: an unwieldy organization, slow to act, and vulnerable to more aggressive, innovative, and agile smaller competitors. The siren call of synergy is often an illusion.

The acquisitions of McDonnell Douglas and Rockwell may yet work out well for Boeing. But their assimilation came at a most troubling time for Boeing. The Long Beach plant of McDonnell Douglas alone led to a massive $1.4 billion writeoff, and contributed significantly to the losses of 1997. Less easily calculated, but certainly a factor, was the management time involved in coping with these new entities.

CONSIDER

Can you think of additional learning insights?

QUESTIONS

1. Do you think Boeing should have anticipated the impact of Asian economic difficulties long before it did?

2. If it had anticipated sooner the drying up of the Asian market for planes, would this have prevented most of the problems now confronting Boeing? Discuss.

---

[21] For example, Banks, p. 54.

3. Do you think top management at Boeing should have been fired after the disastrous miscalculations in the late 1990s? Why or why not?

4. A major stockholder grumbles, "Management worries too much about Airbus, and to hell with the stockholders." Evaluate this statement. Do you think it is valid?

5. What do you see for Boeing three to five years down the road? for Airbus?

6. Do you think it likely that Boeing will have to contend with new competitors over the next ten years? Why or why not?

7. Discuss synergy in mergers. Why does it so often seem to be lacking despite expectations?

8. You are a skilled machinist for Boeing, and had always been quite proud of participating in the building of giant planes. You have just received notice of another lengthy layoff, the second in five years. Discuss your likely attitudes and actions.

9. How wise do you think Airbus's betting the company on the huge A3XX was?

10. Do you think Airbus's more passenger-friendly planes give it a significant competitive advantage? Why or why not? Discuss as many aspects of this as you can.

HANDS-ON EXERCISES

Before

1. You are a management consultant advising top management at Boeing. It is 1993 and the airline industry is in a slump, but early indications are that things will improve greatly in a few years. What would you advise that might have prevented the problems Boeing faced a few years later? Be as specific as you can, and support your recommendations as to practicality and probable effectiveness.

After

2. It is late 1998, and Boeing has had to announce drastic cutbacks, with little improvement likely before five years, and Boeing's stock has collapsed and Airbus is charging ahead. What do you recommend now? (You may need to make some assumptions; if so, state them clearly and keep them reasonable.)

TEAM DEBATE EXERCISES

1. A business columnist writes: Boeing could "have told customers 'no thanks' to more orders than its factories could handle…. It could have done itself a

huge favor by simply building fewer planes and charging more for them."[22] Debate the merits of this suggestion.

2. Debate the controversy of Airbus chairman Forgeard's decision to go for broke with the A3XX superjumbo. Is the risk/reward probability worth such a mighty commitment? Debate as many pros and cons as you can, and also consider how much each should be weighted or given priority consideration.

INVITATION TO RESEARCH

What is the situation with Boeing today? Has it recovered its profitability? How is the competitive position with Airbus?

What is the situation with the A3XX of Airbus? Is it still an ongoing project with delivery scheduled for 2004?

---

[22] Holman W. Jenkins Jr., "Boeing's Trouble: Not Enough Monopolistic Arrogance," *The Wall Street Journal*, December 16, 1998, p. A23.

CHAPTER FIVE

Hamburger Wars:
Burger King vs. McDonald's

Some would see an exaggeration in titling this chapter, "Wars." When one adversary has 13,000 U.S. restaurants and 44 percent of the quick-serve hamburger market and the nearest competitor a mere 7,800 restaurants and 21.9 percent of the market, this suggests an unequal battle more like a sandlotter versus a Super Bowl powerhouse. But Burger King, the underdog, has been improving its number-two position. In 1993, its industry position was 17.9 percent, so its 21.9 percent at the beginning of 1999 was a 22 percent increase in five years. McDonald's was the giant, but it had several lapses during this period. Could it be showing some vulnerability?

BACKGROUNDS OF THE TWO RIVALS

Interestingly, the origins of both Burger King and McDonald's go back to almost the same year. Burger King was founded in 1954 in Miami by James McLamore and David Edgerton. Ray Kroc founded McDonald's one year later. Perhaps because of Kroc's age the media focused on him far more than the attention given to McLamore and Edgerton. Somewhere along the way Kroc became a phenomenon and the others only an underdog competitor.

Ray Kroc's Dream

Ray Kroc faced a serious dilemma. He was 57 years old and all his life had dreamed of becoming rich, and worked hard at it, but real success eluded him. He had played piano with dance bands, then turned to selling paper cups for a firm called Lily-Tulip. He also moonlighted by working for a Chicago radio station, accompanying singers and arranging the music programs. Then he thought he might make his fortune by selling land in a Florida land boom. But this did not work out, and he returned to Chicago a year later almost broke. Lily-Tulip gave him back his old job and he stayed there for more than 10 years.

In 1937 he became intrigued with a new gadget, a simple electrical appliance that could mix six milkshakes at the same time, and he quit Lily-Tulip again and made a deal with the inventor. He soon became the world's exclusive agent for the Prince Castle

TABLE 5.1.   Top Four Fast-Food
Restaurants, 1972 Sales
(thousands of dollars)

McDonald's	$1,032,000
Kentucky Fried Chicken	840,000
International Dairy Queen	510,000
Burger King	270,700

Source: Company records.

Multi-Mixer and for the next twenty years traveled all over the country peddling it. Though he didn't yet know it, at long last he was on the threshhold of his dream.

In 1954 Kroc received an order for eight of the Multi-Mixers from a small hamburger stand in San Bernardino, California. He wondered what wild kind of business sold so many milkshakes. So he decided to go out and see for himself this operation of Maurice and Richard McDonald that needed to make 48 milkshakes at the same time.

When Ray Kroc arrived, he was amazed. It was a self-service hamburger stand, and he saw crowds of people waiting in line under golden arches. He was even more impressed with the speed of service and the cleanliness. Kroc badly wanted in on this business, and hounded the McDonald brothers until they allowed him to start selling franchises. By 1960 he had sold some 200 franchises.

Kroc bought out the McDonald brothers, though he kept their name, and they took their money and quietly retired to their hometown of Bedford, New Hampshire. Now in control, it took Kroc only 17 years to reach the billion-dollar milestone. It gave him great satisfaction to think that IBM needed 46 years to do this. Kroc would boast in his autobiography that the company was responsible for making more than 1,000 millionaires, the franchise holders.[1]

When Kroc retired in 1968, the company had more than 1,200 restaurants, and sales were $400 million. By 1972 the number of outlets had climbed to 2,272 and sales had reached over $1 billion and were accelerating. Table 5.1 shows the sales of McDonald's and its three leading competitors, including Burger King, in 1972.

Burger King's Growth

As can be seen from Table 5.1, Burger King grew far slower than McDonald's, despite being a little older. In 1967, it had 8,000 employees in 274 restaurants when it was acquired by Pillsbury Company for $18 million.

Despite slower growth, Burger King was the first in the industry to introduce dining rooms where patrons could sit inside as they chewed on their burgers and fries. In 1975, it introduced drive-through service, and this came to account for 50 percent of Burger King business. The dining room and drive-through concepts were quickly adopted by McDonald's and other fast-food restaurants.

[1] Ray Kroc and Robert Anderson, *Grinding It Out: The Making of McDonald's* (New York: Berkley Publishing, 1977), p. 200.

In 1988, Grand Metropolitan PLC, an English firm, acquired Pillsbury and its Burger King. In 1997, Grand Metropolitan merged with Guiness to create Diageo, which in addition to owning Burger King also had such well-known consumer brands as Guiness Beer, Pillsbury, Green Giant, Haagen-Dazs, Smirnoff Vodka, and J&B Scotch Whiskey. As of April 1999, Burger King had 10,506 company-owned and franchised restaurants in all 50 states and 54 countries around the world, with sales of $10.3 billion, and employed 300,000 people. It was second only to McDonald's in its industry.

Recent Strategic Moves of Burger King

In April 1999, a prototype for the Burger King restaurant of the future opened in Reno, Nevada. The dated tan-and brick color scheme was dumped in favor of cobalt blue, and the interior was refurbished. Much of the kitchen was left open so that those waiting in line could see flames flickering in the broiler, thus visibly showing the uniqueness of Burger King's "flame-broiled" burgers. A "virtual fun center" provided the usual playground equipment for children, but added electronic kiosks with interactive games.

The company expected that these prototype stores would boost average unit sales to $1.6 million annually from $1.15 million currently. That would surpass the $1.5 million average of McDonald's restaurants. Still, the transformation would be expensive, at least $15,000 more than the current cost of building a new Burger King.

The prototype did not have additional menu items, but with a new cooking system these could be in the offing. In particular, the system featured three computer-controlled broiler chambers that could heat more slowly, allowing for thicker patties. The kitchen upgrade used heated cabinets to keep precooked meat hot and fresh, rather than the old microwaves, heat lamps, and holding chutes. The drive-through counter had its own kitchen to speed up service: "We'll get the food to the window before the car arrives," said the head of research and development to a *The Wall Street Journal* reporter.[2]

The company began converting 40 company-owned restaurants in Orlando, Florida, and planned a full international rollout over the next two to three years. In an ambitious expansion program, Burger King would quadruple its company-owned restaurants to 2,000 from 500, buying some from franchisees and building the rest. It would also help franchisees with their own upgrades.

Burger King might be smaller relative to McDonald's, but it was poised for any lapses by its giant competitor, and McDonald's had some in the 1990s.

THE McDONALD'S GROWTH MACHINE

In its *1995 Annual Report,* McDonald's management was justifiably proud. Sales and profits had continued the long trend upward, and even seemed to be accelerating. See Table 5.2 for sales and profits through 1998. Far from reaching a saturation point, the firm was opening more restaurants than ever, some 2,400 around the world in 1995, up from 1,800 the year before. "We plan to add between 2,500 and 3,200 restaurants in

---

[2] Richard Gibson, "Burger King Seeks New Sizzle," *The Wall Street Journal,* April 14, 1999, p. B6.

TABLE 5.2. Growth in McDonald's Sales and Profits, 1985–1998

	Sales (millions)	Percent Gain	Income (millions)	Percent Gain
1985	$11,011		$ 433	
1986	12,432	12.9	480	12.2
1987	14,330	15.3	549	14.4
1988	16,064	12.1	646	17.7
1989	17,333	7.9	727	12.5
1990	18,759	8.2	802	10.3
1991	19,928	6.2	860	7.2
1992	21,885	9.8	959	11.5
1993	23,587	7.8	1,083	12.9
1994	25,987	10.2	1,224	13.0
1995	29,914	15.1	1,427	16.6
1996	31,812	6.3	1,573	10.2
1997	33,638	5.7	1,642	4.3
1998	35,979	6.9	1,550	−5.6

Source: 1998 Annual Report.

Commentary: Of particular interest is how the new expansion policies brought a burst of revenues and profits in the mid-1990s. But after 1995, growth in sales and earnings slowed. Still, statistically this is a healthy company, and 1999 results should show improving growth.

both 1996 and 1997, with about two thirds outside of the United States. In other words, we opened more than six restaurants per day in 1995; over the next two years, we plan to open eight a day."[3] And, "Our growth opportunities remain significant: on any given day, 99 percent of the world's population does not eat at McDonald's … yet."[4]

Company management extolled the power of the McDonald's brand overseas, and how on opening days lines were sometimes "miles" long. "Often our challenge is to keep up with demand. In China, for example, there are only 62 McDonald's to serve a population of 1.2 billion."[5] By the end of 1995, the company had 7,012 outlets in 89 countries of the world, with Japan alone having 1,482. Table 5.3 shows the top ten countries in 1998 in number of McDonald's units.

Sometimes in marketing its products in different cultures, adjustments had to be made. Nowhere was this more necessary than in Yugoslavia during the NATO bombings in the Kosovo confrontation. The following information box describes the changes McDonald's made there for these turbulent times.

Growth Prospects in the United States

In 1995, with 11,368 of its restaurants in the United States, wasn't McDonald's reaching saturation in its domestic market? Top management vehemently dis-

[3] *McDonald's 1995 Annual Report,* p. 8.
[4] Ibid., p. 7.
[5] Ibid.

TABLE 5.3.   Top Ten Foreign
Markets in Number of McDonald's
Units at Year End, 1998

	Restaurants
Japan	2,852
Canada	1,085
Germany	931
England	810
France	708
Brazil	672
Australia	666
Taiwan	292
China	220
Italy	201

Source: 1998 Annual Report.
Commentary: Is the popularity of McDonald's in
Japan a surprise?

puted this conclusion. Rather, it offered a startling statistical phenomenon to support accelerating expansion. Called Greenberg's law, after newly appointed McDonald's U.S. chairman Jack Greenberg, it maintained that the more stores McDonald's put in a city the more per capita transactions would result. Thus, with two stores in a city there might be 16 transactions per capita per year. Add two or four more stores and the transactions will not only double, or quadruple, but may even do better than that. The hypothesized explanation for this amazing phenomenon seemingly rested on two factors: convenience and market share. With more outlets, McDonald's increased its convenience to consumers, and added to its market share at the expense of competitors. Hence, the justification for the expansion binge.

Aiding this domestic expansion the company had been able to reduce the cost of building a new U.S. traditional restaurant by 26 percent by standardizing building materials and equipment and global sourcing, as well as improving construction methods and building designs. It had also found abundant market opportunities in building satellite restaurants. These were smaller, had lower sales volume, and served simplified menus. This format proved cost efficient in such nontraditional places as zoos, hospitals, airports, museums, and military bases as well as in retail stores such as Wal-Mart, Home Depot, and other major stores. For example, such satellite restaurants were in some 800 Wal-Mart stores by the end of 1995, with more planned. In October 1996, a McDonald's Express opened in an office building in Lansing, Michigan, a harbinger of more such sites to come.

In its eager search for more outlets, McDonald's did something it had never done before. It took over stores from weak competitors. In late summer 1996, it bought 184 company-owned Roy Rogers outlets. "Here was an opportunity that was maybe

---

INFORMATION BOX

McDONALD'S SUCCESSFUL ADVENTURES IN SERBIA, 1999

The NATO air war against Yugoslavia lasted 78 days. At first the 15 McDonald's restaurants in Yugoslavia were closed due to angry mobs bent on vandalizing. Fanned by media attacks on "NATO criminals and aggressors," mobs of youth smashed windows and painted insults. But the restaurants soon reopened, downplaying the U.S. citizenship and presenting McDonald's as a Yugoslav company.

They promoted the McCountry, a domestic pork burger with paprika garnish. (Pork is considered the most Serbian of meats.) To cater to Serbian identity and pride, they brought out posters and lapel buttons showing the golden arches topped with a traditional Serbian cap called the sajkaca. Dragoljub Jakic, the 47-year-old managing director of McDonald's in Yugoslavia, noted that the cap "is a strong, unique Serbian symbol. By adding this symbol of our cultural heritage, we hoped to denote our pride in being a local company."[6] They also handed out free cheeseburgers at anti-NATO rallies. One restaurant's basement in Belgrade even became a bomb shelter.

The result? In spite of falling wages, rising prices, and lingering anger at the United States, the McDonald's restaurants were thronged with Serbs.

Still, McDonald's globally is a prominent symbol of American culture and attracts outbursts of anti-American sentiment. For example, in August 1999, a McDonald's in Belgium was burned down by suspected animal-rights activists. And India has seen militant critics: "They (McDonald's) are the chief killers of cows in the world. We don't need cow killers in India."[7]

Do you think McDonald's in Yugoslavia went too far in downplaying—some would say even denying—its American roots? Did it have any other reasonable option if it were to keep operating?

Should militant activists become more violent about McDonald's "conducting a global conspiracy against cows," do you think McDonald's should abandon the India market? Why or why not?

---

[6] Robert Block, "How Big Mac Kept From Becoming a Serb Archenemy," *The Wall Street Journal*, September 3, 1999, p. B3.
[7] "Delhi Delights in McMutton Burgers," *Cleveland Plain Dealer*, November 6, 1999, p. 3–D.

---

once in a lifetime," Greenberg stated.[8] Earlier the same year, it acquired Burghy's, an 80-store fast-food chain in Italy. And in New Zealand, it added 17 restaurants from the Georgie Pie chain.

The new stores were seldom like the old ones. The drive-through windows generated 55 percent of U.S. sales, and made fewer seats needed inside. This left more space available for gas stations or for indoor playgrounds—"Ronald's Playplaces"—to attract families. McDonald's made joint ventures with Chevron and Amoco to code-

---

[8] Gary Samuels, "Golden Arches Galore," *Forbes*, November 4, 1996, p. 48.

velop properties. It also signed an exclusive marketing deal with Disney for promoting each other's brands.

McDonald's has always spent big for advertising, and this has been effective. Even back in the 1970s, a survey of school children found 96 percent able to identify Ronald McDonald, ranking him second only to Santa Claus.[9] In 1995, advertising and promotional expenditures totaled $1.8 billion, or 6 percent of sales.[10]

Factors in the Invincibility of McDonald's

Through the third quarter of 1996, McDonald's could proudly claim 126 consecutive quarters of record earnings. Since its earliest days, the ingredients of success were simple, but few competitors were able to effectively emulate them. The basic aspects were:

- A brief menu, but having consistent quality over thousands of outlets.
- Strictly enforced and rigorous operational standards controlling service, cleanliness, and all other aspects of the operation.
- Friendly employees, despite a high turnover of personnel because of the monotony of automated food handling.
- Heavy mass media advertising directed mostly at families and children.
- Identification of a fertile target market—the family—and directing the marketing strategy to satisfying it with product, price, promotional efforts, and site locations. (At least in the early years this meant the suburban locations with their high density of families.)

However, by the end of 1996, international operations were the real vehicle of growth, providing 47 percent of the company's $30 billion sales and 54 percent of profits. Of no small concern, the domestic operation had not blossomed accordingly.

STORM CLOUDS FOR THE DOMESTIC OPERATION

Souring Franchisee Relations

In the market-share game, in which McDonald's dominated all its competitors, corporate management concluded that the firm with the most outlets in a given community wins. But as McDonald's unprecedented expansion continued, many franchisees were skeptical of headquarters' claim that no one loses when the company opens more outlets in a community since market share rises proportionately. Many a franchise holder wondered how much his sales would diminish when another McDonald's opened down the street.

The 7,000-member American Franchisee Association, an organization formed to look after franchisees' rights, claimed that McDonald's operators were joining in record numbers.[11] Other franchisees formed a clandestine group called the Consortium, rep-

[9] "The Burger That Conquered the Country," *Time,* September 17, 1973, pp. 84–92.

[10] *McDonald's 1995 Annual Report,* p. 9.

[11] Richard Gibson, "Some Franchisees Say Moves by McDonald's Hurt their Operations," *The Wall Street Journal,* April 17, 1996, pp. A1 and A8.

resenting dissidents who felt present management was unresponsive to their concerns. They remembered a kinder and gentler company. See the following information box for contrasting franchisee views on the high-growth market-share policy.

Other concerns of franchisees were a new set of business practices developed by corporate headquarters, known as Franchising 2000. The company claimed it instituted this as a way to improve standards for quality, service, cleanliness, and value by giving franchisees better "tools." But some saw this as a blatant attempt to gain more power over the franchised operations. One provision revived a controversial A, B, C, and F grading system, with only franchisees who received A's and B's eligible for more restaurants. Furthermore, McDonald's began using Franchising 2000 to enforce a single pricing strategy throughout the chain, so that a Big Mac, for example, would cost the same everywhere. The corporation maintained that such uniformity was necessary for the discounting needed to build market share. Those not complying risked losing their franchise.

INFORMATION BOX

THE CONTENTMENT OF TWO McDONALD'S FRANCHISEES

In 1980, Wayne Kilburn and his wife, Mary Jane, took over the only McDonald's in Ridgecrest, California, a town of 26,000. The Kilburns prospered in the years to come. Then McDonald's instituted its "market-share plan" for Ridgecrest. Late in 1995 it put a company-owned restaurant inside the Wal-Mart. A few months later it built another outlet inside the China Lake Naval Weapons Center. A third company-owned store went up just outside the naval base. "Basically, they killed me," *Forbes* reported Kilburn saying, and he claimed his volume dropped 30 percent.[12]

In its *1995 Annual Report*, corporate headquarters offered another view concerning franchisee contentment. Tom Wolf was a McDonald's franchisee with 15 restaurants in the Huntington, West Virginia and Ashland, Kentucky markets. He opened his first McDonald's in 1974, had eight by the end of 1993, and opened seven more in the last two years, including two McDonald's in Wal-Mart stores and another in an alliance with an oil company; in addition he added indoor Playplaces to two existing restaurants.

Has all this investment in growth made a difference? The *Annual Report* quotes Tom: "I wouldn't change a thing. Sales are up. I'm serving more customers, my market share is up and I'm confident about the future. Customers say that the Playplaces and Wal-Mart units are 'a great idea.' The business is out there. We've got to take these opportunities now, or leave them for someone else to take."[13]

"The high growth, market-share policy should not bother any franchisee. It simply creates opportunities to invest in more restaurants." Evaluate this statement.

---

[12] Samuels, p. 48.
[13] *McDonald's 1995 Annual Report,* p. 32.

TABLE 5.4. **Percent of Franchised to Total Traditional McDonald's Restaurants, Selected Years, 1985–1998**

	1985	1992	1995	1998
Traditional restaurants				
Total	8,901	13,093	16,809	24,800
Operated by franchisees	6,150	9,237	11,240	15,281
Percent franchised to total	69.1%	70.5%	66.9%	61.3%

Source: Calculated from *1998 Annual Report.*

Commentary: Whereas by 1998, the ratio of franchised to total restaurants had dropped, still more than 60 percent are still operated by franchisees. Perhaps this suggests that franchisee concerns ought to receive full consideration by corporate headquarters.

Franchise relations should not be a matter of small concern to McDonald's. Table 5.4 shows the ratio of franchised restaurants to total restaurants both within and outside the United States. As can be seen, franchises comprise by far the largest proportion of restaurants.

Menu Problems

In 1993, domestic per-store sales were increasing at a 4 percent annual rate. By the third quarter of 1996, sales had slumped to a 3 percent decrease, this being the fifth quarter in a row of declining sales. In part this decline was thought to be attributable to older customers drifting away: "Huge numbers of baby-boomers ... want less of the cheap, fattening foods at places like McDonald's. As soon as their kids are old enough, they go elsewhere."[14]

In an attempt to win more business from this customer segment, McDonald's with a $200 million promotional blitz launched its first "grownup taste" sandwich, the Arch Deluxe line of beef, fish, and chicken burgers. It forecast that this would become a $1 billion brand in only its first year. But before long, some were calling this a McFlop. In September 1996, Edward Rensi, head of U.S. operations, tried to minimize the stake in the new sandwich, and sent a memo to 2,700 concerned franchisees, "the Arch Deluxe was never intended to be a silver bullet."[15] On October 8, Rensi was replaced by Jack Greenberg.

McDonald's domestic troubles were not entirely new. As far back as the late 1980s, competitors, including Pizza Hut and Taco Bell, were nibbling at McDonald's market share, and Burger King was more than holding its own. Even the great traditional strength of McDonald's of unsurpassed controlled standards over food, service, and cleanliness seemed to be waning: A 1995 *Restaurants and Institutions Choice in Chains* survey of 2,849 adults gave McDonald's low marks on food quality, value, service, and cleanliness. Top honors instead went to Wendy's.[16]

---

[14] Shelly Branch, "McDonald's Strikes Out With Grownups," *Fortune*, November 11, 1996, p. 158.
[15] Ibid.
[16] Ibid.

In 1991, McDonald's reluctantly tried discounting, with "Extra Value Meals," largely to keep up with Taco Bell's value pricing. But by 1995, price promotions were no longer attracting customers, and per-store sales began slumping. The new, adult-oriented Deluxe line was not only aimed at older adults, but with its prices 20 percent more than regular items, it was expected to parry the discounting.

The company had previously had problems in expanding its menu. The McDLT was notably unsuccessful despite heavy promotion. More recently, the low-fat McLean, an effort to attract weight-conscious adults, was a complete disaster. In fact, this beef-and-seaweed concoction sold so badly that some operators kept only a few frozen patties on hand, while others, as revealed in an embarrassing TV expose, sold fully fatted burgers in McLean boxes to the few customers asking for them.

Some years before, the company had tried but failed to develop an acceptable pizza product. It also was unable to create a dinner menu that would attract evening-hour traffic. Two other experiments were also abandoned: a 1950s-style cafe and a family-type concept called Hearth Express that served chicken, ham, and meatloaf.

THE SITUATION NEAR THE END OF THE MILLENNIUM

In May 1999, McDonald's gave CEO Jack Greenberg the additional title of chairman of the board. He had joined the firm as chief financial officer in 1982, and took over the faltering U.S. operation in 1997, at the time when the domestic business was seeing sagging sales, overexpansion problems, menu and marketing mistakes, quality control lapses, and franchisee discontent. Still, global sales for 1998 reached $36 billion with net income $1.55 billion. There were now 24,800 restaurants in the United States and 114 countries worldwide.

Greenberg began more diversifying within the fast-food industry, buying Donatos Pizza, a Midwestern chain of 143 restaurants. "We would like to make this a growth opportunity for our franchisees," Greenberg said.[17] The company also installed a new cooking system to deliver sandwiches to order, "Made for You," which meant fresher with less waste compared with the old system of holding bins.

Despite concerns about McDonald's future promise and publicity about franchisee worries, franchise applications in the United States were more than ten times the number of outlets available. McDonald's could still be very choosy in selecting franchisees. This popularity of franchises meant that retiring franchisees could count on buyers for their stores, while the difficulty of gaining a franchise assured that only highly motivated people would be finalists.

Financial requirements were not for the marginal. The total price tag for a typical full-size McDonald's was around $500,000, with labor, 8 percent of sales, and rent the major expenses after opening. A prospective franchisee trained at least a year, working in restaurants without pay, even performing such tasks as scrubbing

---

[17] James P. Miller and Richard Gibson, "Did Somebody Say Pizza?" *The Wall Street Journal*, May 1, 1999, p. A4.

TABLE 5.5. Competitive Position of Burger King and McDonald's in Total Sales and Restaurants, 1993–1998

	Total Sales (billions $)					
	1993	1994	1995	1996	1997	1998
McDonald's	23.6	26.0	29.9	31.8	33.6	36.0
Burger King	6.7	7.5	8.4	9.0	9.8	10.3
Percent of McD	28.4%	28.0%	28.1%	28.3%	29.2%	28.0%
	Total Restaurants (hundreds)					
McDonald's	14.2	15.9	18.4	21.0	23.1	24.8
Burger King	7.1	7.5	8.0	8.7	9.4	9.8
Percent of McD	50.0%	47.1%	43.5%	40.0%	40.7%	39.5%

Source: Calculated from company reports.

Commentary: You can see that Burger King has been unable to gain any ground on McDonald's outside of one year, 1997, in total sales. In number of restaurants it has steadily lost ground as McDonald's has opened far more restaurants than Burger King has been able to. This suggests the power position of the firm with greater size and resources.

bathrooms. Usually when an opportunity finally came it involved pulling up stakes and moving.[18]

Despite concerns about domestic business not showing desired sales increases, McDonald's was still on the growth trail. Table 5.5 shows relative comparisons since 1993 of Burger King and McDonald's in worldwide sales and in total restaurants. With McDonald's great growth in number of outlets around the world made possible by the huge advantage in resources, Burger King's ratio of sales and number of restaurants to McDonald's has been steadily declining. The likelihood of Burger King ever posing a serious threat seems remote. However, McDonald's showed no mercy in the burger wars as the following information box suggests.

ANALYSIS

After the many years of uninterrupted growth in sales and profits, and in number of stores opened, McDonald's domestic operation in the latter 1990s showed signs of approaching a crossroads with the enduring growth trend endangered.

The international arena still offered tremendous growth possibilities, despite the more than 8,000 outlets already open. Domestically, however, things were not going as well even though operating statistics looked better than ever. The gains in revenues and income reflected a sharp increase in number of new stores. For example, in 1996 McDonald's opened 2,500 new stores, four times the number of stores opened just

[18] For other information about gaining a McDonald's franchise, see Richard Gibson, "McDonald's Problems in Kitchen Don't Dim the Lure of Franchises," *The Wall Street Journal,* June 3, 1998, pp. A1 and A6.

INFORMATION BOX

McDONALD'S ACCUSES BURGER KING OF UNFAIR COMPETITION

In mid-1999, McDonald's sued Burger King charging unfair competition. It contended that Burger King's "Big Kids Meal" was a copy of a promotion it had launched in Detroit: "The colors and design of the Big Kids Meal logo are strikingly similar to those used by McDonald's." And the name impinged on its trademark application.

Burger King responded that any similarity was because the two companies used similar colors in their logos generally. As for the name "Big Kids Meal," Burger King claimed it is merely a description of a category within the fast-food industry: "Everyone has a kids meal program. You can't own an entire category."[19] Furthermore, Burger King was launching the promotion nationwide, while McDonald's was still only testing the concept in the Detroit area.

Burger King began its kids meal program on June 28, 1999, and McDonald's filed its suit two days later.

Based on this limited information, do you think McDonald's defense of its turf is warranted?

Do you see any significance in this case beyond the almost petty legal maneuverings? or are these petty?

---

[19] Tom Stiebhorst, "McDonald's Accuses Burger King of Unfair Competition," *Knight-Ridder/Tribune Business News,* July 7, 1999.

---

four years before. However, same-store sales dropped 2.5 percent from 1994 to 1995 for its U.S. restaurants—all this despite vigorous discounting and promotional efforts.

Relations with franchisees, formerly best in the industry, deteriorated as corporate management pursued policies more dictatorial and selfish than ever before, policies that signaled the end of the kinder and gentler stance franchisees remembered. In particular, the new expansion policy aimed at increased market share regardless of its effect on established franchisees, portended worsening relations and the start of an adversarial instead of supportive climate.

Of course, the cost/benefit consequences of an aggressive expansion policy can be seen as in the company's best interest, especially with the greater cost efficiencies of recent construction. If total market share could be substantially increased, despite same-store sales declining, the accounting analyses can support more stores. But how much is the franchisee to be considered in this aggressive new strategy of McDonald's outlets competing not so much with Wendy's, Burger King, and Taco Bell as with other McDonald's outlets?

A major domestic challenge for a growth-oriented McDonald's was the menu: how to appeal to adults and expand market potential. This offered another growth alternative, even more so if the dinner market could be tapped. The last successful menu expansion had been the breakfast menu, and that was decades ago.

What menu changes should be made? With a history of past failures, expectations can hardly be robust. Yet, McDonald's, as any chain organization whether fast food or otherwise, can test different prices and strategies or different menus and different atmospheres in just a few outlets, and only if results are favorable expand further.

A potential trouble spot was McDonald's slackening in enforcing the tightest controls of any industry over product quality and services. The rigid standards imposed since the days of Ray Kroc seemed to be eroding. Admittedly, as more and more outlets are added, enforcing tight controls becomes more difficult. Meanwhile, competitors are doing a better job of matching McDonald's in achieving high standards of product quality and services.

To summarize, is McDonald's in jeopardy? Does Burger King threaten McDonald's? The answer is No. Is McDonald's likely to continue its great growth in sales and profits? Probably not domestically; without success in widening the appeal of domestic restaurants, the main engine of growth in future years would be the international operation. Table 5.6 shows the trend in number of restaurants outside the United States compared with those in the United States for selected years since 1985. Table 5.7 compares sales and operating income for U.S. and outside-U.S. operations since 1991. Note in particular that income from outside the United States surpassed domestic by 1995.

Still, the United States is a huge market, and no growth-minded firm would want its luster tarnished here. Whether thousands of new restaurants in the coming years, without some diversification in menus and decor, will fuel the growth needed to continue the trend may be questioned. After all, how many military bases, hospitals, museums, zoos and the like remain untapped? As to outlets in major retail stores, isn't the potential limited here, too?

McDonald's faces a situation that seemingly cries for diversification: perhaps an inspired menu change; maybe a new format to tap different customer segments; perhaps different but related businesses.

What about the prospects for Burger King? Can it be reasonably successful and profitable while only a distant second in its industry? It would seem so, as long as it

TABLE 5.6. Percent of Non-U.S. to Total Traditional McDonald's Restaurants, Selected Years, 1985–1998

	1985	1992	1995	1998
Traditional restaurants				
Total U.S. and non-U.S. restaurants	8,901	13,093	16,809	24,800
Non-U.S. restaurants	1,929	4,134	6,468	12,328
Percent of Total	28.3%	31.6%	38.5%	49.7%

Source: Computed from *1998 Annual Report.*

Commentary: Here we can see the increasing importance of non-U.S. operations in the decade of the 1990s.

TABLE 5.7. Comparison of McDonald's U.S. and Non-U.S. Revenue and Income, 1991–1995

	1991	1992	1993	1994	1995
System wide sales (billions of dollars)	$19.9	21.9	23.6	26.0	29.9
U.S. sales	$12.5	13.2	14.2	14.9	15.9
Non-U.S. sales	7.4	8.6	9.4	11.0	14.0
Operating income (billions of dollars)	1.7	1.9	2.0	2.2	2.6
U.S. income	1.0	1.1	1.1	1.1	1.2
Non-U.S. income	.7	.8	.9	1.1	1.4

Source: Compiled from *1995 Annual Report.*

Commentary: The growing importance of non-U.S. operations compared with McDonald's total sales and income is readily apparent.

stays aggressive and innovative, and not complacent or resigned to being a loser in the burger war. In food, unlike many other industries, there is room for more contenders. We get tired of eating the same thing at the same restaurant. We want some variety. So there should remain profitable niches for firms such as Burger King, Wendy's, Kentucky Fried Chicken, Pizza Hut....

WHAT CAN BE LEARNED?

It is possible to have strong and enduring growth without diversification. For more than four decades, since 1955, McDonald's has grown continuously and substantially. In all this time, the product was essentially the hamburger in its various trappings and accompaniments. Almost all other firms in their quest for growth have diversified, sometimes wisely and synergistically, and other times imprudently and even recklessly. McDonald's has remained undeviatingly focused.

In such a commitment, the product should be something with universal appeal, something frequently consumed, and one having almost unlimited potential. The hamburger probably meets these criteria better than practically any other product, along with beer, soft drinks, and formerly tobacco. And soft drinks, of course, are a natural accompaniment of the hamburger.

But eventually, even the hamburger may not be enough for continued strong growth as the international market becomes saturated and the domestic market oversaturated. Then McDonald's may be forced to seek complementary diversifications or lose the growth mode.

The insight to be gained, however, is that firms in pursuit of growth often jump into acquisitions far too hastily when the better course of action would be to more fully develop market penetration of their existing products.

Beware the reckless drive for market share. A firm can usually "buy" market share, if it is willing to sacrifice profits in so doing. It can step up its advertising

LATE-BREAKING NEWS

The end of the millennium saw major changes in McDonald's domestic operation, and changes were needed as it was averaging only 1 percent same-store sales growth, far behind the 4 percent average of Burger King, as well as Wendy's. After 44 years as one of America's great growth companies, market saturation seemed imminent. The main reason was thought to be a stale menu.

The frenetic growth in outlets of the mid-1990s was over, as many angry franchisees saw their sales decline as much as 20 percent due to cannibalization. In 1999, only 150 new outlets were added, down sharply from the 1,100 of a few years before. In recognition of other franchisee complaints, the new CEO, Jack Greenberg, threw out the Franchise 2000 rulebook with its 80 pages of onerous regulations, and gave franchisees more say in their local menus.

Increasingly he turned his attention to judicious food diversifications. He planned to grow the $70 million purchase of the 143-store regional chain, Donatos Pizza, to a national one of 1,000 stores, and opened 35 new stores in 1999. After buying into Chipotle Mexican Grill, a popular Denver-based chain of 25 Mexican restaurants, 35 more were opened in 1999. The purchase of Aroma, a stylish, coffee-and-sandwich bar in London with 23 outlets, showed perhaps the most promise. In the U.K., the cold-sandwich market was almost double the size of the burger segment and growing twice as fast, appealing to a mostly single, health-conscious and female customer-base, with practically no overlap with the burger crowd—therefore, no cannibalization. Plans were for 150 stores by 2002.

In the major thrust "beyond burgers," more new products were coming out of McDonald's test kitchens than ever before, many of these appealing regionally rather than nationally: for example, the McBrat, a $1.99 sandwich with sauerkraut and onion on the bratwurst, a big hit in Wisconsin and Minnesota; a McLobster Roll in New England; Homestyle Burger with hot mustard in Texas; the Brutus Buckeye Burger for Ohioans; and even bagel breakfast sandwiches, already doing well in 6,000 stores.

Sources: For more information on menu diversifications, see Bruce Upbin, "Beyond Burgers," *Forbes*, November 1, 1999, pp. 218–223; and Dave Carpenter, Associated Press, reported in "McAnalysts Get Taste of How Fast Food Can Be," *Cleveland Plain Dealer*, September 30, 1999, p. 2-C.

---

and sales promotion. It can lower its prices, assuming that lower prices would bring more demand. It can increase its sales staff and motivate them to be more aggressive. And sales and competitive position will usually rise. But costs may increase disproportionately. In other words, the benefits to be gained may not be worth the costs.

McDonald's, as we have seen in its domestic operation, moved to a strategy of aggressively seeking market share by opening thousands of new units. As long as the development costs can be kept sufficiently low to permit these new units good profits and not cannibalize or take too much business away from other McDonald's restaurants, then the strategy is defensible. Still, the costs of damaged franchisee relations, the intangibles of lowered morale and cooperation and festering resentments, are difficult to calculate but can be real indeed.

Maintaining the highest standards requires constant monitoring. McDonald's heritage and its competitive advantage have long been associated with the highest standards and controls in the industry for cleanliness, fast service, dependable quality of food, and friendly and well-groomed employees. The following information box discusses strategy countering by competitors and the great difficulty in matching nonprice strengths.

Alas, in the last few years even McDonald's has apparently let its control of operational standards slip. As mentioned earlier, a 1995 survey of adults gave McDonald's low marks on food quality, value, service, and cleanliness. Wendy's won top honors instead. Why this lapse? Perhaps because the burgeoning international operation became the focus of attention. But maintaining high standards among thousands of units, company-owned as well as franchised, requires constant monitoring and exhortation.

Can controls be too stringent? In a belated attempt to improve standards and tighten up corporate control, McDonald's instituted the controversial Franchising 2000. Among other things this called for grading franchisees, with those receiving the lower grades being penalized. McDonald's also wanted to take away any pric-

INFORMATION BOX

MATCHING A COMPETITOR'S STRATEGY

Some strategies are easily countered or duplicated by competitors. Price cutting is the most easily countered. A price cut can often be matched within minutes. Similarly, a different package or a warranty is easily imitated by competitors.

But some strategies are not so easily duplicated. Most of these involve service, a strong and positive company image, or both. A reputation for quality and dependability is not easily countered, at least in the short run. A good company or brand image is hard to match because it usually results from years of good service and satisfied customers. The great controls of McDonald's with its high standards would seem to be easily imitated, but they proved not to be, as no other firm fully matched the enforced standards of McDonald's until recently.

Somehow it seems that the strategies and operations that are the most difficult to imitate are not the wildly innovative ones, nor the ones that are complex and well researched. Surprisingly, the most difficult to imitate are the simple ones: simply doing a better job in servicing and satisfying customers and in performing even mundane operations cheerfully and efficiently.

What explanation can you give for competitors' inability to match the standards of McDonald's?

ing flexibility for its franchisees: All restaurants now had to charge the same prices, or risk losing their franchise. Not surprisingly, some franchisees were concerned about this new "get-tough" management.

Can controls be too stringent? As with most things, extremes are seldom desirable. All firms need tight controls over far-flung outlets to keep corporate management alert to emerging problems and opportunities and maintain a desired image and standard of performance. In a franchise operation this is all the more necessary since we are dealing with independent entrepreneurs rather than hired managers. However, controls can be so rigid that no room is left for special circumstances and opportunities. If the enforcement is too punitive, the climate becomes more that of a police state than a teamwork relationship with both parties cooperating to their mutual advantages.

This brings us to the next insight for discussion.

Is there room for a kinder, gentler firm in today's hotly competitive environment? Many longtime McDonald's franchisees remembered with sadness a kinder, gentler company. This was an atmosphere nurtured by founder Ray Kroc. To be sure, Kroc insisted that customers be assured of a clean, family atmosphere with quick and cheerful service. To Kroc, this meant strict standards, not only in food preparation but also in care and maintenance of facilities, including toilets. Company auditors closely checked that the standards were adhered to, under Kroc's belief that a weakness in one restaurant could have a detrimental effect on other units in the system. Still, the atmosphere was helpful—the inspectors were "consultants"—rather than adversarial. As mentioned earlier, Kroc was proud that he was responsible for making more than 1,000 millionaires, the franchise holders.[20]

Many franchisees traced the deterioration of franchiser-franchisee relations to the 1992 death of Gerald Newman, McDonald's chief accounting officer. He spent much of his time interacting with franchisees, sometimes encouraging—he had a reputation for a sympathetic ear—sometimes even giving them a financial break.[21]

So, is it possible and desirable to be a kind and gentle company? with franchisees? employees? suppliers? customers? Of course it is. Organizations, and the people who run them, often forget this in the arrogance of power. They excuse this get-tough mindset on the basis of the exigencies of competition and the need to be faithful to their stockholders.

Kind and gentle—is this an anachronism, a throwback to a quieter time, a nostalgia long past its usefulness? Let us hope not.

CONSIDER

Can you add other learning insights?

---

[20] Kroc and Anderson, p. 200.
[21] Gibson, p. A8.

QUESTIONS

1. How do you account for the reluctance of competitors to imitate the successful efforts of another firm in their industry? Under what circumstances is imitation likely to be embraced?

2. To date McDonald's has shunned diversification into other related and unrelated food retailing operations. Discuss the desirability of such diversification efforts.

3. "Eventually—and this may come sooner than most think—there will no longer be any choice locations anywhere in the world for new hamburger outlets. As a McDonald's stockholder, I'm getting worried." Discuss.

4. Does the size of McDonald's give it a powerful advantage over Burger King? Why or why not?

5. What do you think is McDonald's near-term and long-term potential? What makes you think this?

6. Is it likely that McDonald's will ever find a saturated market for its hamburgers?

7. Discuss the importance of market share in the fast-food industry.

8. Discuss the desirability of McDonald's efforts to insist on the same price in all domestic restaurants.

HANDS-ON EXERCISES

1. You have been given the assignment by Edward Rensi in 1993 to instill a recommitment to improved customer service in all domestic operations. Discuss in as much detail as you can how you would go about fostering this among the 10,000 domestic outlets.

2. As a McDonald's senior executive, what long-term expansion mode would you recommend for your company?

3. As a Burger King senior executive, what long-term expansion mode would you recommend for your company? What promises would you make to shareholders?

TEAM DEBATE EXERCISES

1. Debate this issue: McDonald's is reaching the limits of its growth without drastic change. (Note: The side that espouses drastic change should give some attention to the most likely directions for such, and be prepared to defend these expansion possibilities.)

2. Debate the issue of a get-tough attitude of corporate management toward franchisees even if it riles some, versus involving them more in future direc-

tions of the company. In particular, be prepared to address the controversy of unlimited market-share expansion.

3. Debate this contention: Market share is overemphasized in this industry. (Both sides in their debate may want to consider whether this assertion may or may not apply to other industries.)

INVITATION TO RESEARCH

Is McDonald's becoming more vulnerable to competitors today? Does it have any emerging problems? Has it attempted any major diversifications yet? Is the international operation still overshadowing the domestic?

How is the "war" between Burger King and McDonald's progressing?

GREAT COMEBACKS

CHAPTER SIX

Continental Airlines—From the Ashes

Massive marketing and management blunders almost destroyed Continental Airlines. In a remarkable turnaround by new management, in only a few years Continental became a star of the airline industry. The changemaker, CEO Gordon Bethune, wrote a best-selling book on how he turned around the moribund company, titled *From Worst to First.* In this chapter we will look at the scenario leading to the difficulties of Continental, and then examine the ingredients of the great comeback.

THE FRANK LORENZO ERA

Lorenzo was a consummate manipulator, parlaying borrowed funds and little of his own money to build an airline empire. By the end of 1986, he controlled the largest airline network in the non-Communist world: Only Aeroflot, the Soviet airline, was larger. Lorenzo's network was a leveraged amalgam of Continental, People Express, Frontier, and Eastern, with $8.6 billion in sales—all this from a small investment in Texas International Airlines in 1971. In the process of building his network, Lorenzo defeated unions and shrewdly used the bankruptcy courts to further his ends. When he eventually departed, his empire was swimming in red ink, had a terrible reputation, and was burdened with colossal debt and aging planes.

The Start

After getting an MBA from Harvard, Lorenzo's first job was as a financial analyst at Trans World Airlines. In 1966, he and Robert Carney, a buddy from Harvard, formed an airline consulting firm, and in 1969 the two put together $35,000 to form an investment firm, Jet Capital. Through a public stock offering they raised an additional $1.15 million. In 1971 Jet Capital was called in to fix ailing Texas International and wound up buying it for $1.5 million, and Lorenzo became CEO. He restructured the debt as well as the airline's routes, found funds to upgrade the almost obsolete planes, and brought Texas International to profitability.

In 1978, acquisition-minded Lorenzo lost out to Pan Am in a bidding war for National Airlines, but he made $40 million on the National stock he had acquired. In 1980 he created nonunion New York Air and formed Texas Air as a holding company. In 1982 Texas Air bought Continental for $154 million.

Lorenzo's Treatment of Continental

In 1983 Lorenzo took Continental into bankruptcy court, filing for Chapter 11. This permitted the corporation to continue operating but spared its obligation to meet heavy interest payments and certain other contracts while it reorganized as a more viable enterprise. The process nullified the previous union contracts, and this prompted a walkout by many union workers.

Lorenzo earned the lasting enmity of organized labor and the reputation of union-buster as he replaced strikers with nonunion workers at much lower wages. (A few years later, he reinforced this reputation when he used the same tactics with Eastern Airlines.)

In a 1986 acquisition achievement that was to backfire a few years later, Lorenzo struck deals for a weak Eastern Airlines and a failing People Express/Frontier Airlines. That same year Continental emerged out of bankruptcy. Now Continental, with its nonunion workforce making it a low-cost operator, was Lorenzo's shining jewel. The low bid accepted for Eastern reinforced Lorenzo's reputation as a visionary builder.

What kind of executive was Lorenzo? Although he was variously described as a master financier and visionary, his handling of day-to-day problems bordered on the inept.[1] One former executive was quoted as saying, "If he agreed with one thing at 12:15, it would be different by the afternoon.[2] Inconsistent planning and poor execution characterized his lack of good operational strength. Furthermore, his domineering and erratic style alienated talented executives. From 1983 to 1993, nine presidents left Continental.

But Lorenzo's treatment of his unions brought the most controversy. He became the central figure of confrontational labor-management relations to a degree perhaps unmatched by any other person in recent years. Although he won the battle with Continental's unions and later with Eastern's, he was burdened with costly strikes and the residue of ill feeling that impeded any profitable recovery during his time at the helm.

The Demise of Eastern Airlines

In an environment of heavy losses and its own militant unions, Eastern in 1986 accepted the low offer of Lorenzo. With tough contract demands and the stock-

---

[1] For examples, see Todd Vogel, Gail DeGeorge, Pete Engardio, and Aaron Bernstein, "Texas Air Empire in Jeopardy," *Business Week*, March 27, 1989, p. 30.
[2] Mark Ivey and Gail DeGeorge, "Lorenzo May Land a Little Short of the Runway," *Business Week*, February 5, 1990, p. 48.

piling of $1 billion in cash as strike insurance, Lorenzo seemed eager to precipitate a strike that he might crush. He instituted a program of severe downsizing, and in 1989, after 15 months of fruitless talks, some 8,500 machinists and 3,800 pilots went on strike. Lorenzo countered the strike at Eastern by filing for Chapter 11 bankruptcy, and replaced many of the striking pilots and machinists within months.

At first Eastern appeared to be successfully weathering the strike, while Continental benefited with increased business. But soon revenue dropped drastically with Eastern planes flying less than half full amid rising fuel costs. Fares were slashed in order to regain business, and a liquidity crisis loomed. Then, on January 16, 1990, an Eastern jet sheared the top off a private plane in Atlanta. Even though the accident was attributed to air controller error, Eastern's name received the publicity.

Eastern creditors now despaired of Lorenzo's ability to pay them back in full and they pushed for a merger with Continental, which would expose Continental to the bankruptcy process. On December 3, 1990, Continental again tumbled into bankruptcy, burdened with overwhelming debt. In January 1991, Eastern finally went out of business.

CONTINENTAL'S EMERGENCE FROM BANKRUPTCY, AGAIN

Lorenzo was gone. The legacy of Eastern remained, however. Creditors claimed more than $400 million in asset transfers between Eastern and Continental, and Eastern still had $680 million in unfunded pension liabilities. The board brought in Robert Ferguson, veteran of Braniff and Eastern bankruptcies, to make changes. On April 16, 1993, the court approved a reorganization plan for Continental to emerge from bankruptcy, the first airline to have survived two bankruptices. However, creditors got only pennies on the dollar.[3]

Still, despite its long history of travail and a terrible profit picture, Continental in 1992 was the nation's fifth-largest airline, behind American, United, Delta, and Northwest, and it served 193 airports. Table 6.1 shows the revenues and net profits (or losses) of Continental and its major competitors from 1987 through 1991.

The Legacy of Lorenzo

Continental was savaged in its long tenure as a pawn in Lorenzo's dynasty-building efforts. He had saddled it with huge debts, brought it into bankruptcy twice, left it with aging equipment. Perhaps a greater detriment was a ravished corporate culture. The following information box discusses corporate culture and its relationship to public image or reputation.

---

[3] Bridget O'Brian, "Judge Backs Continental Airlines Plan to Regroup, Emerge from Chapter 11," *The Wall Street Journal*, April 19, 1993, p. A4.

TABLE 6.1.   Performance Statistics, Major Airlines, 1987–1991

	1987	1988	1989	1990	1991	Percent 5-Year Gain
Revenues: (millions $)						
American	6,368	7,548	8,670	9,203	9,309	46.0
Delta	5,638	6,684	7,780	7,697	8,268	46.6
United	6,500	7,006	7,463	7,946	7,850	20.8
Northwest	3,328	3,395	3,944	4,298	4,330	30.1
Continental	3,404	3,682	3,896	4,036	4,031	18.4
Income (millions $)						
American	225	450	412	(40)	(253)	
Delta	201	286	467	(119)	(216)	
United	22	426	246	73	(175)	
Continental	(304)	(310)	(56)	(1,218)	(1,550)	

Source: Company annual reports.

Commentary: Note the operating performance of Continental relative to its major competitors during this period. It ranks last in sales gain. It far and away has the worst profit performance, having massive losses during each of the years in contrast to its competitors, who, while incurring some losses, had neither the constancy nor the magnitude of losses of Continental. And the relative losses of Continental are even worse than they at first appear: Continental is the smallest of these major airlines.

A devastated reputation proved to be a major impediment. The reputation of a surly labor force had repercussions far beyond the organization itself. For years Continental had a problem wooing the better-paying business travelers. Being on expense accounts, they wanted quality service rather than cut-rate prices. A reputation for good service is not easily or quickly achieved, especially when the opposite reputation is well entrenched.

On another dimension, Continental's reputation also hindered competitive parity. Surviving two bankruptcies does not engender confidence among investors, creditors, or travel agents.

A Sick Airline Industry

Domestic airlines lost a staggering $8 billion in the years 1990 through 1992. Fare wars and excess planes proved to be albatrosses. Even when planes were filled, discount prices often did not cover overhead.

A lengthy recession drove both firms and individuals to fly more sparingly. Business firms found teleconferencing a viable substitute for business travel, and consumers, facing less discretionary income as well as the threat of eventual layoffs or forced retirements, were hardly optimistic. The airlines suffered.

Part of the blame for the red ink lay directly with the airlines—they were expansion-reckless—yet they did not deserve total blame. In the late 1980s, passenger traffic climbed 10 percent per year, and in response the airlines ordered hundreds of

INFORMATION BOX

IMPORTANCE OF CORPORATE CULTURE

A corporate or organizational culture can be defined as the system of shared beliefs and values that develops within an organization and guides the behavior of its members.[4] Such a culture can be a powerful influence on performance and customer satisfaction:

> If employees know what their company stands for, if they know what standards they are to uphold, then they are much more likely to make decisions that will support those standards. They are also more likely to feel as if they are an important part of the organization. They are motivated because life in the company has meaning for them.[5]

Lorenzo had destroyed the former organizational climate as he beat down the unions. Replacement employees had little reason to develop a positive culture or esprit de corps given the many top management changes, the low pay relative to other airline employees, and the continuous possibility of corporate bankruptcy. They had little to be proud of, and this impacted on the service and consequent reputation among the traveling public.

But this was to change abruptly under new management.

Can a corporate climate be too upbeat? Discuss.

---

[4] Edgar H. Schein, "Organizational Culture," *American Psychologist,* vol. 45 (1990), pp. 109–119.

[5] Terrence E. Deal and Alan A. Kennedy, *Corporate Cultures: The Rites and Rituals of Corporate Life* (Reading, MA: Addison-Wesley, 1982) p. 22.

---

jetliners.[6] The recession arrived just as new planes were being delivered. The airlines greatly increased their debt in these expansion efforts: the big three, for example—American, United, and Delta—doubled their leverage in the four years after 1989, with debt by 1993 at 80 percent of capitalization.[7]

In such a climate, emphasis was on cost-cutting. But how much can be cut without jeopardizing service and even safety? Some airlines found that hubs, heralded as the great strategy of the 1980s, were not as cost-effective as expected. With hub cities, passengers were gathered from outlying "spokes" and then flown to final destinations. Maintaining too many hubs, however, brought costly overheads. While the concept was good, some retrenchment seemed necessary to be cost effective.

Airlines such as Continental with heavy debt and limited liquidity had two major concerns: first, how fast the country could emerge from recession; second, the risk of

---

[6] Andrea Rothman, "Airlines: Still No Wind at Their Backs," *Business Week,* January 11, 1993, p. 96.

[7] Ibid.

fuel price escalation in the coming years. Despite Continental's low operating costs, external conditions impossible to predict or control could affect viability.

THE GREAT COMEBACK UNDER GORDON BETHUNE

In February 1994, Gordon Bethune left Boeing and took the job of president and chief operating officer of Continental. He faced a daunting challenge. While it was the fifth-largest airline, Continental was by far the worst among the nation's 10 biggest, according to these quality indicators of the Department of Transportation:

- In on-time percentage (the percentage of flights that land within 15 minutes of their scheduled arrival)
- In number of mishandled-baggage reports filed per 1,000 passengers
- In number of complaints per 100,000 passengers
- In involuntarily denied boarding (i.e., passengers with tickets who are not allowed to board because of overbooking or other problems)[8]

In late October he became chief executive officer. Now he sat in the pilot's seat.

He made dramatic changes. In 1995, through a "renewed focus on flight schedules and incentive pay," he greatly improved on-time performance, along with lost-baggage claims and customer complaints. Now instead of being dead last in these quality indicators of the Department of Transportation, Continental by 1996 was third best or better in all four categories.

Customers began returning, especially the higher-fare business travelers, climbing from 32.2 percent in 1994 to 42.8 percent of all customers by 1996. In May 1996, based on customer surveys Continental was awarded the J.D. Power Award as the best airline for customer satisfaction on flights of 500 miles or more. It also received the award in 1997, the first airline to win two years in a row. Other honors followed. In January 1997, it was named "Airline of the Year" by *Air Transport World,* the leading industry monthly. In January 1997, *Business Week* named Bethune one of its top managers of 1996.

Bethune had transformed the workforce into a happy one, as measured by these statistics:

- Wages up an average of 25 percent
- Sick leave down more than 29 percent
- Personnel turnover down 45 percent
- Workers compensation down 51 percent
- On-the-job injuries down 54 percent[9]

---

[8] Gordon Bethune, *From Worst to First* (New York: Wiley, 1998) p. 4.

[9] Ibid., pp. 7–8.

Perhaps nothing illustrates the improvement in employee morale as much as this: In 1995, not long after he became top executive, employees were so happy with their new boss's performance that they chipped in to buy him a $22,000 Harley-Davidson.[10]

Naturally such improvement in employee relations and customer service had major impact on revenues and profitability. See Table 6.2 for the trend since 1992.

Gordon Bethune

Bethune's father was a crop duster, and as a teenager Gordon helped him one summer and learned first hand the challenges of responsibility: in this case, preparing a crude landing strip for nightime landings, with any negligence disastrous. He joined the navy at 17, before finishing high school. He graduated second in his class at the Naval Technical School to become an aviation electronics technician, and over 19 years worked his way up to lieutenant. After leaving the navy he joined Braniff, then Western, and later Piedmont Airlines as senior vice president of operations. He finally left Piedmont for Boeing as VP/general manager of customer service. There he became licensed as a 757 and 767 pilot: "An amazing thing happened. All the Boeing pilots suddenly thought I was a great guy," he writes. "I hope I hadn't given them any reason to think otherwise of me before that, but this really got their attention."[11]

How Did He Do It?

Introducing the Human Element

Bethune stressed the human element in guiding the comeback of a lethargic, even bitter, organization. Even by simple things: "On October 24, 1994, I did a very significant thing in the executive suite of Continental Airlines. ... I opened the doors. ... [Before]

TABLE 6.2. **Continental Sales and Profits, Before and After Bethune, 1992–1997**

	Before Bethune			After Bethune		
	1992	1993	1994	1995	1996	1997
Revenues (millions $)	5,494	3,907	5,670	5,825	6,360	7,213
Net income (millions $)	−110	−39	−612	224	325	389
Earnings per share $		−1.17	−11.88	3.60	4.25	5.03

Source: Company annual reports.

Commentary: While the revenue statistics do not show a striking improvement, the net income certainly does. Most important to investors, the earnings per share show a major improvement.

   These statistics suggest the fallacy of a low price strategy at the expense of profitability in the 1992–1994 era. At the same time, we have to realize that the early 1990s were recession years, particularly for the airline industry.

[10] Ibid., frontpiece.

[11] Ibid., p. 268.

The doors to the executive suite were locked, and you needed an ID to get through. Security cameras added to the feeling of relaxed charm. ... So the day I began running the company, I opened the doors. I wasn't afraid of my employees, and I wanted everybody to know it."[12]

Still, he had to entice employees to the twentieth floor of headquarters, and he did this with open houses, supplying food and drink, and personal tours and chat sessions. "I'd take a group of employees into my office, open up the closet, and say, 'You see? Frank's not here.' Frank Lorenzo had left Continental years before; the legacy of cost cutting and infighting of that era was finally gone, and I wanted them to know it."[13]

Of course, the improved employee relations needed tangible elements to cement and sustain it, and to improve the morale. Bethune worked hard to instill a spirit of teamwork. He did this by giving on-time bonuses to all employees, not just pilots. He burned the employee procedure manual that bound them to rigid policies instead of being able to use their best judgments. He even gave the planes a new paint job to provide tangible evidence of a disavowal of the old and an embracing of new policies and practices. This new image impressed both employees and customers.

Better communications was also a key element in improving employee relationships and the spirit of teamwork. Information was shared with employees through newsletters, updates on bulletin boards, e-mail, voice-mail, and electronic signs over worldwide workplaces. To Bethune it was a cardinal sin for any organization if employees first heard of something affecting them through the newspaper or other media.

Marketing Strategy for Winning Back Customers

Now Continental had to win back customers. Instead of the company's old focus on cost savings, efforts were directed to putting out a better product through better service. This meant emphasis on on-time flights, better baggage handling, and the like. By giving employees bonuses for meeting these standards, the incentive was created.

Bethune sought to do a better job of designing routes with good demand, to "fly places people wanted to go." This meant, for example, cutting back on six flights a day between Greensboro, North Carolina and Greenville, South Carolina. It meant not trying to compete with Southwest's Friends Fly Free Fares, which "essentially allowed passengers to fly anywhere within the state of Florida for $24.50.[14] The frequent flyer program was reinstated. Going a step further, the company apologized to travel agents, business partners, and customers and showed them how it planned to do better and earn their business back.

Continental queried travel agents about their biggest clients, the major firms that did the most traveling, asking how could it better serve their customers. As a result, more first-class seats were added, particular destinations were given more attention, discounts for certain volumes were instituted. Travel agents themselves were made members of the team and given special incentives beyond normal airline commissions. The result

---

[12] Ibid., p. 14.

[13] Ibid., p. 32.

[14] Ibid., pp. 51–52.

INFORMATION BOX

IMPORTANCE OF PUBLIC IMAGE

The public image of an organization is its reputation, how it and its output (products, services, or both) are viewed by its various publics: customers, suppliers, employees, stockholders, creditors, the communities in which it dwells, and the various governments, both local and federal. And to these groups must be added the press, which is influenced by the subject's reputation and cannot always be relied upon to deliver objective and unbiased reporting.

In some situations it is impossible to satisfy all the diverse publics: For example, a new, highly automated plant may meet the approval of creditors and investors, but it will undoubtedly find resistance from employees who see jobs threatened. On the other hand, high-quality products and service standards should bring almost complete approval and pride of association—given that operating costs are competitive—while shoddy products, poor service, and false claims would be widely decried.

A firm's public image, if it is good, should be cherished and protected. It is a valuable asset built up from a satisfying relationship with the various publics. If a firm has developed a quality image, this image is not easily countered or imitated by competitors. Such an image may enable a firm to charge higher prices, to woo the best distributors and dealers (or travel agents), to attract the best employees, and to expect the most favorable creditor relationships and the lowest borrowing costs. It should enable a firm's stock to command a higher price-to-earnings ratio than other firms in the same industry that lack such a good image. Herein lies a great competitive advantage.

A bad image, on the other hand, hurts a firm with its various publics. All can turn critical and even litigious. At best, present and potential customers may simply seek alternative sources for goods and services and switch to competitors.

What do you think is the effectiveness of advertising in enhancing the public image?

---

was to greatly improve the public image or reputation of Continental. See the above information box for a discussion of the importance of public image.

This still left financial considerations. Bethune was aggressive in renegotiating loans and poor airplane lease agreements, and in getting supplier financial cooperation. Controls were set up to monitor cash flow and stop waste. Tables 6.3 and 6.4 show the results of Bethune's efforts from the dark days of 1992–94, and how the competitive position of Continental changed. Remember, Bethune joined the firm in February 1994 and did not become the top executive until late October of that year.

WHAT CAN BE LEARNED?

It is possible to quickly turn around an organization. This idea flies in the face of conventional wisdom. How can a firm's bad reputation with employees, customers,

TABLE 6.3. Competitive Position of Continental Before and After Bethune, 1992–1997

	Before Bethune			After Bethune		
	1992	1993	1994	1995	1996	1997
Revenues (millions $):						
AMR (American)	14,396	15,701	16,137	16,910	17,753	18,570
UAL (United)	12,890	14,511	13,950	14,943	16,362	17,378
Delta	10,837	11,997	12,359	12,194	12,455	13,590
Northwest	NA	8,649	9,143	9,085	9,881	10,226
Continental	5,494	3,907	5,670	5,825	6,360	7,213
Continental's Market Share (Percent of total shares of Big Five Airlines):		7.1%	9.9%	9.9%	10.1%	10.8%

Source: Company annual reports.

NA = information not available.

Commentary: Most significant is the gradual increase in market share of Continental over its four major rivals. This is an improving competitive position.

creditors, stockholders, and suppliers be overcome without years of trying to prove that it has changed for the better? This conventional wisdom is usually correct: A great comeback does not often occur easily or quickly. But it sometimes does, with a streetwise leader, and perhaps a bit of luck. Gordon Bethune is proof that negative attitudes can be turned around quickly.

This possibility of a quick turnaround should be inspiring to other organizations mired in adversity.

TABLE 6.4. Profitability Comparison of Big Five Airlines, 1992–1997

	Before Bethune			After Bethune		
	1992	1993	1994	1995	1996	1997
Net Income (millions $):						
AMR	−474	−96	228	196	1,105	985
UAL	−416	−31	77	378	600	958
Delta	−505	−414	−408	294	156	854
Northwest	NA	−114	296	342	536	606
Continental	−110	−39	−696	224	325	389

Source: Company annual reports. NA = information not available.

Commentary: Of interest is how the good and bad times for the airlines seem to move in lockstep. Still, the smallest of the Big Five, Continental, incurred the biggest loss of any airline in 1994. Under Bethune, it has seen a steady increase in profitability, but so have the other airlines, although AMR and Delta have been more erratic.

Still, reputation should be carefully guarded. In most cases, a poor image is difficult to overcome, with trust built up only over time. The prudent firm is careful to safeguard its reputation.

Give employees a sense of pride and a caring management. Bethune proved a master at changing employees' attitudes and their sense of pride. Few top executives ever faced such a negative workforce, reflecting the Lorenzo years. But Bethune changed all this, and in such a short time. His open-door policy and open houses to encourage employees to interact with him and other top executives was such a simple gesture, but so effective, as was his opening wide the channels of communication about company plans. The incentive plans for improving performance, and the encouragement of employee initiatives by abolishing the rigidity of formal policies, were further positives. He engendered an atmosphere of teamwork and a personal image of an appreciative CEO. It is remarkable how quickly such simple actions could turn around the attitudes of a workforce from adversarial with morale in the pits to pride and an eagerness to build an airline.

Contradictory and inconsistent strategies are vulnerable. Lorenzo was often described as mercurial and subject to knee-jerk planning and poor execution.[15] Clearly focused objectives and strategies mark effective firms. They bring stability to an organization and give customers, employees, and investors confidence in undeviating commitments. Admittedly, some objectives and strategies may have to be modified occasionally to meet changing environmental and competitive conditions, but the spirit of the organization should be resolute, provided it is a positive influence and not a negative one.

Try to avoid an adversarial approach to employee relations. Lorenzo used a confrontational and adversarial approach to his organization and the unions. He was seemingly successful in destroying the unions and hiring nonunion replacements at lower pay scales. This resulted in Continental becoming the lowest-cost operator of the major carriers, but there were negatives: service problems, questionable morale, diminished reputation, and devastated profitability.

Bethune used the opposite tack. It is hard to argue against nurturing and supporting an existing organization, avoiding the adversarial mindset of "them or us" if at all possible. Admittedly this may sometimes be difficult—sometimes impossible, at least in the short-run—but it is worth trying. It should result in better morale, motivation, and commitment to the company's best interest.[16]

The dangers of competing mostly on low price. Bethune inherited one of the lowest-cost air carriers, and it was doing badly. He says, "you can make an airline so cheap nobody wants to fly it," [just as] "you can make a pizza so cheap nobody wants to eat it." "Trust me on this—we did it… In fact, it was making us lousy, and people didn't want to buy what we offered."[17]

We might add here that competing strictly on a price basis usually leaves any firm vulnerable. Low prices can easily be matched or countered by competitors if

---

[15] For example, Ivey and DeGeorge, p. 48.

[16] See Chapter 20 for Southwest Airlines' approach to organizational relations.

[17] Bethune, p. 50.

such low prices are attracting enough customers. On the other hand, competition based on such nonprice factors as better service, quality of product, and a good public image or reputation, are not so easily matched, and can be more attractive to many customers.

In Chapter 20, with Southwest Airlines, we find a firm competing ever so successfully with a low-price strategy. But Southwest has operational efficiency unmatched in the industry.

CONSIDER

Can you add any other learning insights?

QUESTIONS

1. Could Lorenzo's confrontation with the unions of Continental have been more constructively handled? How?

2. Do you see any limitations to Bethune's employee relations, especially in the areas of discipline and acceptance of authority?

3. Compare Bethune's handling of employees with that of Kelleher of Southwest Airlines in Chapter 20. Are there commonalities? contrasts?

4. Compare Bethune's management style with that of Lorenzo. What conclusions can you draw?

5. Bethune gave great credit to his open-door policy when he became CEO. Do you think this was a major factor in the turnaround? How about changing the paint of the planes?

6. How do you motivate employees to give a high priority to customer service?

7. Evaluate the causes and the consequences of frequent top executive changes such as Continental experienced in the days of Lorenzo.

8. How can replacement workers—in this case pilots and skilled maintenance people hired at substantially lower salaries than their unionized peers at other airlines—be sufficiently motivated to provide top-notch service and a constructive esprit de corps?

HANDS-ON EXERCISES

1. It is 1994 and Bethune has just taken over. As his staff adviser he has asked you to prepare a report on improving customer service as quickly as possible. He has also asked you to design a program to inform both business and nonbusiness potential customers of this new commitment. Be as specific as possible in your recommendations.

2. You are the leader of the machinists' union at Eastern. It is 1986 and Lorenzo has just acquired your airline. You know full well how he broke the

union at Continental, and rumors are flying that he has similar plans for Eastern. Describe your tactics under two scenarios:

(a) You decide to take a conciliatory stance.

(b) You plan to fight him every step of the way.

How successful do you think you will be in saving your union?

TEAM DEBATE EXERCISE

Bethune was quoted as saying, "You can make an airline so cheap nobody wants to fly it." Debate this issue, and the related issue of how an airline can make itself sufficiently unique that it can command higher prices than competitors.

INVITATION TO RESEARCH

What is the situation with Continental today? Is Bethune still CEO? Whatever happened to Lorenzo?

CHAPTER SEVEN

IBM—A Fading
Giant Rejuvenates

*I*BM exhibited similar roller-coaster fortunes as did Continental Air, with the major difference that it was so much bigger and had so many years of industry domination. The common notion is that the bigger the firm, the more difficult it is to turn it around, just as the grand ship needs far more room to maneuver to avoid catastrophe than a smaller vessel.

THE REALITY AND THE FLAWED ILLUSION

On January 19, 1993, International Business Machines Corporation reported a record $5.46 billion loss for the fourth quarter of 1992, and a deficit for the entire year of $4.97 billion, the biggest annual loss in American corporate history. (General Motors recorded a 1991 loss of $4.45 billion, after huge charges for cutbacks and plant closings. And Ford Motor Company reported a net loss of more than $6 billion for 1992, but that was a non-cash charge to account for the future costs for retiree benefits.) The cost in human lives, as far as employment was concerned, was also consequential, as some 42,900 had been laid off during 1992, with an additional 25,000 planned to go in 1993. In its fifth restructuring, seemingly endless rounds of job cuts and firings had eliminated 100,000 jobs since 1985. Not surprisingly, IBM's share price, which was above $100 in the summer of 1992, closed at an 11-year low of $48.375. Yet IBM had long been the ultimate blue-chip company, reigning supreme in the computer industry. How could its problems have surfaced so suddenly and so violently?

THE ROAD TO INDUSTRY DOMINANCE

"They hired my father to make a go of this company in 1914, the year I was born," said Thomas J. Watson Jr. "To some degree I've been a part of IBM ever since."[1] Watson took over his father's medium-sized company in 1956 and built it into a tech-

---

[1] Michael W. Miller, "IBM's Watson Offers Personal View of the Company's Recent Difficulties," *The Wall Street Journal*, December 21, 1992, p. A3.

nological giant. Retired for almost 19 years by 1992, he now was witnessing the company in the throes of its greatest adversity.

IBM had become the largest computer maker in the world. With its ever-growing revenues since 1946 it had become the bluest of blue-chip companies. It had 350,000 employees worldwide and was one of the largest U.S.-based employers. Its 1991 revenues had approached $67 billion, and while profits had dropped some from the peak of $6.5 billion in 1984, its common stock still commanded a price-earnings ratio of over 100, making it a darling of investors. In 1989, it ranked first among all U.S. firms in market value (the total capitalization of common stock, based on the stock price and the number of shares outstanding), fourth in total sales, and fourth in net profits.[2]

During the days of Watson, IBM was known for its centralized decision making. Decisions affecting product lines were made at the highest levels of management. Even IBM's culture was centralized and standardized, with strict behavioral and dress codes. For example, a blue suit, white shirt, and dark tie was the public uniform, and IBM became widely known as "Big Blue."

One of IBM's greatest assets was its research labs, by far the largest and costliest of their kind in the world, with staffs that included three Nobel Prize winners. IBM treated its research and development function with tender, loving care, regularly budgeting 10 percent of sales for this forward-looking activity: For example, in 1991, the R&D budget was $6.6 billion.

The past success of IBM and the future expectations for the company with a seeming stranglehold over the technology of the future made it esteemed by consultants, analysts, and market researchers. Management theorists, all the way from Peter Drucker to Tom Peters (of *In Search of Excellence* fame), lined up to analyze what made IBM so good. And the business press regularly produced articles of praise and awe of IBM.

Alas, the adulation was to change abruptly by 1992. Somehow, insidiously, IBM had gotten fat and complacent over the years. IBM's problems, however, went deeper, as we will explore in the next section.

CHANGING FORTUNES

Perhaps the causes of the great IBM debacle of 1992 started in the early 1980s with a questionable management decision. Perhaps the problems were more deep-rooted than any single decision; perhaps they were more a consequence of the bureaucracy that often typifies behemoth organizations (Sears and General Motors faced somewhat similar worsening problems), growing layers of policies, and entrenched interests.

In the early 1980s, two little firms, Intel and Microsoft, were upstarts, just emerging in the industry dominated by IBM. Their success by the 1990s can be largely attributed to their nurturing by IBM. Each got a major break when it was "anointed" as a key supplier for IBM's new personal computer (PC). Intel was signed

---

[2] "Ranking the Forbes 500s," *Forbes*, April 30, 1990, p. 306.

on to make the chips and Microsoft the software. The aggressive youngsters proceeded to set standards for successive PC generations, and in the process wrested from IBM control over the PC's future. And the PC was to become the product of the future, shouldering aside the giant mainframe that was IBM's strength.

As IBM began losing ground in one market after another, Intel and Microsoft were gaining dominance. Ten years before, in 1982, the market value of stock of Intel and Microsoft combined amounted to about a tenth of IBM's. By October 1992, their combined stock value surpassed IBM's; by the end of the year, they topped IBM's market value by almost 50 percent. See Table 7.1 for comparative operating statistics of IBM, Intel, and Microsoft. Table 7.2 shows the market valuation of IBM, Intel, and Microsoft from 1989 to 1992, the years before and during the collapse of investor esteem.

Defensive Reactions of IBM

As the problems of IBM became more visible to the entire investment community, chairman John Akers sought to institute reforms to turn the behemoth around. His problem—and need—was to uproot a corporate structure and culture that had developed when IBM had no serious competition.

A cumbersome bureaucracy stymied the company from being innovative in a fast-moving industry. Major commitments still went to high-margin mainframes, but these were no longer necessary in many situations given the computing power of

TABLE 7.1. Growth of IBM and the Upstarts, Microsoft and Intel, 1983–1992 ($ million)

	1983	1985	1987	1989	1991	1992
IBM:						
Revenues	$40,180	$50,056	$54,217	$62,710	$64,792	$67,045
Net income	5,485	6,555	5,258	3,758	(2,827)	(2,784)
% of Revenue	13.6%	13.1%	9.7%	6.0%	—	—
Microsoft:						
Revenues	$50	$140	$346	$804	$1,843	$2,759
Net Income	6	24	72	171	463	708
% of Revenue	12.0%	17.1%	20.8%	21.3%	25.1%	25.7%
Intel:						
Revenues	$1,122	$1,365	$1,907	$3,127	$4,779	$5,192
Net Income	116	2	176	391	819	827
% of Revenue	10.3%	0.1%	9.2%	12.5%	17.1%	15.9%

Source: Company annual statements; 1992 figures are estimates from *Forbes,* "Annual Report of American Industry," January 4, 1993, pp. 115–116.

Commentary: Note the great growth of the "upstarts" in recent years, both in revenues and in profits, compared with IBM. Also note the great performance of Microsoft and Intel in profit as a percent of revenues.

TABLE 7.2. **Market Value and Rank Among all U.S. Companies of IBM and the Upstarts, Microsoft and Intel, 1989 and 1992**

	Rank		Market Value ($mil)	
	1989	1992	1989	1992
IBM	1	13	$60,345	$30,715
Microsoft	92	25	6,018	23,608
Intel	65	22	7,842	24,735

Source: Forbes Annual Directory Issue, "The Forbes Market Value 500," April 13, 1990, pp. 258–259, and April 26, 1993, p. 242. The market value is the per-share price multiplied by the number of shares outstanding for all classes of common stock.

Commentary: The market valuation reflects the stature of the firms in the eyes of investors. Obviously, IBM has lost badly during this period, while Microsoft and Intel have more than tripled their market valuation, almost approaching that of IBM. Yet, IBM's sales were $65.5 million in 1992, against sales of Microsoft of $3.3 and Intel of $5.8.

desktop PCs. IBM had problems getting to market quickly with the technological innovations that were revolutionizing the industry. In 1991, Akers warned an unbelieving group of IBM managers of the coming difficulties. "The business is in crisis."[3]

He attempted to push power downward, to decentralize some of the decision-making that for decades had resided at the top. His more radical proposal was to break up IBM, to divide it into 13 divisions and to give each more autonomy. He sought to expand the services business and make the company more responsive to customer needs. Perhaps most important, he saw a crucial need to pare costs by cutting the fat from the organization.

The need for cost-cutting was evident to all but the entrenched bureaucracy. IBM's total costs grew 12 percent a year in the mid-1980s, while revenues were not keeping up with this growth.[4] Part of the plan for reducing costs involved cutting employees, which violated a cherished tradition dating back to Thomas Watson's father and the beginning of IBM: a promise never to lay off IBM workers for economic reasons.[5] (Most of the downsizing was indeed accomplished by voluntary retirements and attractive severance packages, but eventually outright layoffs became necessary.)

The changes decreed by Akers would leave the unified sales division untouched, but each of the new product group divisions would act as a separate operating unit, with financial reports broken down accordingly. Particularly troubling to Akers was the recent performance of the personal computer (PC) business. At a time when demand, as well as competition, was burgeoning for PCs, this division was languish-

---

[3] David Kirkpatrick, "Breaking up IBM," *Fortune*, July 27, 1992, p. 44.

[4] Ibid., p. 53.

[5] Miller, p. A4.

ing. Early in 1992 Akers tapped James Cannavino to head the $11 billion Personal Systems Division, which also included workstations and software.

IBM PC

PCs had been the rising star of the company, despite the fact that mainframes still accounted for about $20 billion in revenues. But in 1990, market share dropped drastically as new competitors offered PCs at much lower prices than IBM; many experts even claimed that these clones were at least equal to IBM's PCs in quality. Throughout 1992, IBM had been losing market share in an industry price war. Even after it attempted to counter Compaq's price cuts in June, IBM's prices still remained as much as one-third higher than its competitors' prices. Even worse, IBM had announced new fall models, and this development curbed sales of current models. At the upper end of the PC market, firms such as Sun Microsystems and Hewlett-Packard were bringing out more powerful workstations that tied PCs together with mini- and mainframe computers. James Cannavino faced a major challenge in reviving the PC.

Cannavino planned to streamline operations by slicing off a new unit to focus exclusively on developing and manufacturing PC hardware. By so doing, he would cut PCs loose from the rest of Personal Systems and the workstations and software. This, he believed, would create a streamlined organization that could cut prices often, roll out new products several times a year, sell through any kind of store, and provide customers with whatever software they wanted, even if it was not IBM's.[6] Such autonomy was deemed necessary in order to respond quickly to competitors and opportunities, without having to deal with the IBM bureaucracy.

THE CRISIS

On January 25, 1993, John Akers announced that he was stepping down as IBM's chairman and chief executive. He had lost the confidence of the board of directors. Until mid-January, Akers seemed determined to see IBM through its crisis, at least until he would reach IBM's customary retirement age of 60, which would be December 1994. But the horrendous $4.97 billion loss in 1992 changed that, and investor and public pressure mounted for a top management change. The fourth quarter of 1992 was particularly shocking, brought on by weak European sales and a steep decline in sales of minicomputers and mainframes. Now IBM's stock sank to a 17-year low, below 46.

Other aspects of the operation also accentuated IBM's fall from grace: most notably, the jewel of its operation, its mainframe processors and storage systems.

For 25 years IBM had dominated the $50 billion worldwide mainframe industry. In 1992, overall sales of such equipment grew at only 2 percent, but IBM experienced a 10 to 15 percent drop in revenue. At the same time, its major mainframe rivals, Amdahl Corp. and Unisys Corp., had respective sales gains of 48 percent and 10 percent.[7]

---

[6] "Stand Back, Big Blue—And Wish Me Luck," *Business Week*, August 17, 1992, p. 99.

[7] John Verity, "Guess What: IBM Is Losing Out in Mainframes, Too," *Business Week*, February 8, 1993, p. 106.

IBM was clearly lagging in developing new computers that could out-perform the old ones, such as IBM's old System/390. Competitors' models exceeded IBM's old computers not only in absolute power but in prices, selling at prices a tenth or less of IBM's price per unit of computing. For example, with IBM's mainframe computers, customers paid approximately $100,000 for each MIPS, or the capacity to execute 1 million instructions per second, this being the rough gauge of computing power. Hewlett-Packard offered similar capability at a cost of only $12,000 per MIPS, and AT&T's NCR unit could sell a machine for $12.5 million that outperformed IBM's $20 million ES/9000 processor complex.[8]

In a series of full-page advertisements appearing in such business publications as *The Wall Street Journal*, IBM defended the mainframe and attacked the focus on MIPS:

> One issue surrounding mainframes is their cost. It's often compared using dollars per MIPS with the cost of microprocessor systems, and on that basis mainframes lose. But...dollars per MIPS alone is a superficial measurement. The real issue is function. Today's appetite for information demands serious network and systems management, around-the-clock availability, efficient mass storage and genuine data security. MIPS alone provides none of these, but IBM mainframes have them built in, and more fully developed than anything available on microprocessors.[9]

On March 24, 1993, 51-year-old Louis V. Gerstner Jr. was named the new chief executive of IBM. The two-month search for a replacement for Akers had captivated the media, with speculation ranging widely. The choice of an outsider caught many by surprise: Gerstner was chairman and CEO of RJR Nabisco, a food and tobacco giant, but Nabisco was a far cry from a computer company. And IBM had always prided itself on promoting from within, with most IBM executives—for example, John Akers—being lifelong IBM employees. Not all analysts supported the selection of Gerstner. While most did not criticize the board for going outside IBM to find a replacement for Akers, some questioned going outside the computer industry or other high-tech industries. Geoff Lewis, senior editor of *Business Week*, fully supported the choice. He had suggested the desirability of bringing in some outside managers to Akers in 1988:

> Akers seemed shocked—maybe even offended—by my question. After a moment, he answered: "IBM has the best recruitment system anywhere and spends more than anybody on training. Sometimes it might help to seek outsiders with unusual skills, but the company already had the best people in the world.[10]

See the following issue box for a discussion of promotion from within.

---

[8] Ibid.

[9] Taken from advertisement, *The Wall Street Journal*, March 5, 1993, p. B8.

[10] Geoff Lewis, "One Fresh Face at IBM May Not Be Enough," *Business Week*, April 12, 1993, p. 33.

SHOULD WE PROMOTE FROM WITHIN?

A heavy commitment to promoting from within, as had long characterized IBM, is sometimes derisively called "inbreeding." The traditional argument against this stand maintains that an organization with such a policy is not alert to needed changes, that it is enamored with the status quo, "the way we have always done it." Proponents of promotion from within talk about the motivation and great loyalty it engenders, with every employee knowing that he or she has a chance of becoming a high-level executive.

However, the opposite course of action—that is, heavy commitment to placing outsiders in important executive positions—plays havoc with morale of trainees and lower-level executives and destroys the sense of continuity and loyalty. A middle ground seems preferable: filling many executive positions from within, promoting this idea to encourage both the achievement of current executives and the recruiting of trainees, and at the same time bringing the strengths and experiences of outsiders into the organization.

Do you think there are particular circumstances in which one extreme or the other regarding promotion policy might be best? Discuss.

Later in this chapter we will describe and make commentary on the great comeback engineered by Gerstner. But for now, let us examine the factors leading to the decline in IBM's fortunes.

ANALYSIS

In examining the major contributors to IBM's fall from grace, we will analyze the predisposing or underlying factors, resultants, and controversies.

Predisposing Factors

Cumbersome Organization

As IBM grew with its success, it became more and more bureaucratic. One author described it as big and bloated. Another called it "inward-looking culture that kept them from waking up on time."[11] Regardless of phraseology, by the late 1980s IBM could not bring new machines quickly into the market, nor was it able to make the fast pricing and other strategic decisions of its smaller competitors. Too many layers of management, too many vested interests, a tradition-ridden mentality, and a gradually emerging contentment with the status quo shackled it in an industry that some thought to be mature, but which in reality had important sectors still gripped by bur-

---

[11] Jennifer Reese, "The Big and the Bloated: It's Tough Being No. 1," *Fortune*, July 27, 1992, p. 49.

geoning change. As a huge ship requires a considerable time and distance to turn or to stop, so the giant IBM found itself at a competitive disadvantage to smaller, hungrier, more aggressive, and above all, more nimble firms. Impeding all efforts to effect major changes was the typical burden facing all large and mature organizations: resistance to change. The accompanying information box discusses this phenomenon.

Overly Centralized Management Structure

Often related to a cumbersome bureaucratic organization is rigid centralization of authority and decision making. Certain negative consequences may result when all major decisions have to be made at corporate headquarters rather than down the line. Decision making is necessarily slowed, since executives feel they must investigate fully all aspects, and not being personally involved with the recommendation, they may be not only skeptical but critical of new projects and initiatives. More than this, the enthusiasm and creativity of lower-level executives may be curbed by the typical conservatism of a higher-management team divorced from the intimacy of the problem or the opportunity. The motivation and morale needed for a climate of innova-

INFORMATION BOX

RESISTANCE TO CHANGE

People as well as organizations have a natural reluctance to embrace change. Change is disruptive. It can destroy accepted ways of doing things and familiar authority-responsibility relationships. It makes people uneasy because their routines will likely be disrupted; their interpersonal relationships with subordinates, co-workers, and superiors may well be modified. Positions that were deemed important before the change may be downgraded. And persons who view themselves as highly competent in a particular job may be forced to assume unfamiliar duties.

Resistance to change can be combatted by good communication with participants about forthcoming changes. Without such communication, rumors and fears can assume monumental proportions. Acceptance of change can be facilitated if managers involve employees as fully as possible in planning the changes, solicit and welcome their participation, and assure them that positions will not be impaired, only different. Gradual rather than abrupt changes also make a transition smoother, as participants can be initially exposed to the changes without drastic upheavals.

In the final analysis, however, needed changes should not be delayed or canceled because of their possible negative repercussions on the organization. If change is necessary, it should be initiated. Individuals and organizations can adapt to change—although it may take some time.

The worst change an employee may face is layoff. And when no one knows when the next layoff will occur or who will be affected, morale and productivity may both be devastated. Discuss how managers might best handle the necessity of upcoming layoffs.

tion and creativity is stifled under the twin bureaucratic attitudes, "Don't take a chance," and "Don't rock the boat."

The Three C's Mindset of Vulnerability

Firms that have been well entrenched in their industry and that have dominated it for years tend to fall into a particular mindset that leaves them vulnerable to aggressive and innovative competitors. (We first encountered this syndrome in Chapter 4 with Boeing, but it bears repeating.)

The "three C's" that are detrimental to a frontrunner's continued success are:

Complacency

Conservatism

Conceit

Complacency is smugness—a complacent firm is self-satisfied, content with the status quo, no longer hungry and eager for growth. *Conservatism,* when excessive, characterizes a management that is wedded to the past, to the traditional, to the way things have always been done. Conservative managers see no need to change because they believe nothing is different today (e.g., "Mainframe computers are the models of the industry and will always be"). Finally, *conceit* further reinforces the myopia of the mindset: conceit regarding present and potential competitors. The beliefs that "we are the best" and "no one else can touch us" can easily permeate an organization that has enjoyed success for years.

The three C's mindset leaves no incentive to undertake aggressive and innovative actions, and contributes to growing disinterest in such important facets of the business as customer relations, service, and even quality control. Furthermore, it inhibits interest in developing innovative new products that may cannibalize—that is, take business away from—existing products or disrupt entrenched interests. (We will discuss cannibalization in more detail shortly.)

Resultants

Overdependence on High-Margin Mainframes

The mainframe computers had long been the greatest source of market power and profits for IBM. But the conservative and tradition-minded IBM bureaucracy could not accept the reality that computer power was becoming a desktop commodity. Although a market still existed for the massive mainframes, it was limited and had little growth potential; the future belonged to desktop computers and work stations. And here IBM in a lapse of monumental proportions relinquished its dominance. First there were the minicomputers, and these opened up a whole new industry, one with scores of hungry competitors. But the cycle of industry creation and decline started anew by the early 1980s as personal computers began to replace minicomputers in defining new markets and fostering new competitors. While the mainframe was not replaced, its markets became more limited, and cannibalization became the fear. See the following information box.

INFORMATION BOX

CANNIBALIZATION

Cannibalization occurs when a company's new product takes some business away from an existing product. The new product's success consequently does not contribute its full measure to company revenues since some sales will be switched from older products. The amount of cannibalization can range from virtually none to almost total. In this latter case, then, the new product simply replaces the older product, with no real sales gain achieved. If the new product is less profitable than the older one, the impact and the fear of cannibalization becomes all the greater.

For IBM, the PCs and the other equipment smaller than mainframes would not come close to replacing the bigger units. Still, some cannibalizing was likely. And the profits on the lower-price computers were many times less than those of mainframes.

The argument can justifiably be made that if a company does not bring out new products then competitors will, and that it is better to compete with one's own products. Still the threat of cannibalization can cause a hesitation, a blink, in a full-scale effort to rush to market an internally competing product. This reluctance and hesitation needs to be guarded against, lest the firm find itself no longer in the vanguard of innovation.

Assume the role of a vocal and critical stockholder at the annual meeting. What arguments would you introduce for a crash program to rush the PC to market, despite possible cannibalization? What contrary arguments would you expect, and how would you counter them?

Neglect of Software and Service

At a time when software and service had become ever more important, IBM still had a fixation on hardware. In 1992, services made up only 9 percent of IBM's revenue. Criticisms flowed:

> Technology is becoming a commodity, and the difference between winning and losing comes in how you deliver that technology. Service will be the differentiator.
> As a customer, I want a supplier who's going to make all my stuff work together.
> The job is to understand the customer's needs in detail.[12]

In the process of losing touch with customers, the sales force had become reluctant to sell low-margin open systems if it could push proprietary mainframes or minicomputers.

Bloated Costs

As indications of the fat that had insidiously grown in the organization, some 42,900 jobs were cut in 1992, thankfully all through early-retirement programs. An

---

[12] Kirkpatrick, pp. 49, 52.

additional 25,000 people were expected to be laid off in 1993, some without the benefit of early-retirement packages. Health benefits for employees were also scaled down. Manufacturing capacity was reduced 25 percent, and two of three mainframe development labs were closed. But perhaps the greatest bloat was R&D.

Diminishing Payoff of Massive R&D Expenditures

As noted earlier, IBM spent heavily on research and development, often as much as 10 percent of sales (see Table 7.3). Its research labs were by far the largest and costliest of their kind in the world.

And IBM labs were capable of inventing amazing things. For example, they developed the world's smallest transistor, 1/75,000th the width of a human hair.

Somehow, with all these R&D resources and expenditures, IBM lagged in transferring its innovation to the marketplace. The organization lacked the ability to quickly translate laboratory prototypes into commercial triumphs. Commercial R&D is wasted without this.

Controversies

Questionable Decisions

No executive has a perfect batting average of good decisions. Indeed, most executives do well to bat more than 500, that is, to have more good decisions than bad decisions. But, alas, decisions are all relative. Much depends on the importance, the consequences, of these decisions.

IBM made a decision of monumental long-term consequences in the early 1980s. At that time, IBM designated two upstart West Coast companies to be the key suppliers for its new personal computer. Thus, it gave away its chances to control the personal computer industry. Over the next ten years, each of these two firms would develop a near-monopoly—Intel in microprocessors and Microsoft in operating-systems software—by setting standards for successive PC generations. Instead of keeping such developments proprietary (that is, within its own organization) IBM, in an urge to save developmental time, gave these two small firms a golden opportunity,

TABLE 7.3. **IBM Research and Development Expenditures as a Percent of Revenues, 1987–1991**

	1987	1988	1989	1990	1991
Revenues ($million)	$54,217	$59,681	$62,710	$64,792	$67,045
Research, development, and engineeing costs	5,434	5,925	6,827	6,554	6,644
Percent of revenues	10.0%	9.9%	10.9%	10.1%	9.9%

Source: Company annual reports.

Commentary: Where has been the significant contribution from about 10 percent of sales budgeted for R&D?

which both grasped to the fullest. By 1992, Intel and Microsoft had emerged as the computer industry's most dominant firms.

The decision still is controversial. But it saved IBM badly needed time in bringing its PC to market, and as computer technology becomes ever more complex, not even an IBM can be expected to have the ability and resources to go it alone. Linking up with competitors offers better products and services and a faster flow of technology today, and seems the wave of the future.

Former IBM CEO, Thomas Watson Jr., has criticized his successors Frank Cary and John Opel for phasing out rentals and selling the massive mainframe computer outright. Originally, purchasers could only lease the machines, thus giving IBM a dependable cushion of cash each year ("my golden goose," Mr. Watson called it.)[13] Doing away with renting left IBM, and John Akers, a newly volatile business, just as the industry position began worsening. Akers, newly installed as CEO, was thus left with a hostile environment without the cushion or support of steady revenues coming from such rentals, according to Watson's argument. But the counterposition holds that selling brought needed cash quickly into company coffers. Furthermore, it is unlikely, given the more competitive climate that was emerging in the 1980s, that big customers would continue to tolerate the leasing arrangement when they could buy their machines, if not from IBM, then from another supplier whose machines were just as good or better.

Breaking Up IBM

The general consensus of management experts favored the reforms of Akers to break up Big Blue into 13 divisions and give them increasing autonomy—even to the point that shares of some of these new Baby Blues might be distributed to stockholders. The idea is not unlike that of Japan's *keiretsu*, in which alliances of companies with common objectives but with substantial independence seek and develop business individually.

The assumption in favor of such breaking up is that the sum of the parts is greater than the whole, that the autonomy and motivation will bring more total revenues and profits. But these hypothesized benefits are not assured. At issue is whether the good of the whole would be better served by suboptimizing some business units—that is, by reducing the profit maximizing of some units in order to have the highest degree of cordination and cooperation. Giving disparate units of an organization goals of individual profit maximization lays the seeds for intense intramural competition, with cannibalization and infighting likely. Is the whole better served by a less intensely competitive internal environment?

THE COMEBACK UNDER GERSTNER

Louis Gerstner took command in March 1993. The company, as we have seen, was reeling. In a reversal of major proportions, he brought IBM back to record profitability. Table 7.4 shows the statistics of a sensational turnaround. In 1994, the com-

---

[13] Miller, p. A4.

pany earned $3 billion, its first profitable year since 1990. Perhaps of greater signifi-
cance, compared with the previous year this represented a profit swing of $11 billion.
And revenues grew for the first time since 1990. Equally important, 1994 finished
with financial strength: IBM had more than $10 billion in cash and basic debt was
reduced by $3.3 billion.

The winning ways continued. In 1995, record revenues topped $70 billion for the
first time. The rate of growth—12 percent over the previous year—was the best in
more than a decade. And earnings doubled, excluding a onetime charge related to the
acquisition of Lotus Development Corp. Not surprising, the stock market value of
IBM improved nearly $27 billion from the summer of 1993 through year-end 1995,
and continued to improve significantly in 1996.

By all such performance statistics, Gerstner had done an outstanding job of turning the giant around. At first there had been doubters. For the most part, their skepticism was rooted in the notion that Gerstner was not aggressive enough, that he did
not tamper mightily with the organizational structure of IBM. For example, a 1994
Fortune article questioned, "Is He Too Cautious to Save IBM?" The article went on
to say, "After running IBM for more than a year and a half, CEO Lou Gerstner has
revealed himself to be something other than the revolutionary whom the directors of
this battered and demoralized enterprise once seemed to want ... he seems to be
attempting a conventional turnaround: deep-cleaning and redecorating the house
rather than gutting and renovating it."[14]

Before Gerstner took over, IBM was moving toward a breakup into 13 independent units: one for mainframes, one for PCs, one for disk drives, and so on. But he
saw IBM's competitive advantage to be offering customers a complete package, a
one-stop shopping to all those seeking help in solving technological problems: a unified IBM—somehow, an IBM with a single, efficient team.

TABLE 7.4.   IBM's Resurgence Under Gerstner, 1993–1995

	1993	1994	1995
	(millions of dollars)		
Revenue	$62,716	$64,052	$71,940
Net Earnings (loss)	(8,101)	3,021	4,178
Net Earnings (loss) Per Share of Common Stock	(14.22)	5.02	7.23
Working Capital	6,052	12,112	9,043
Total Debt	27,342	22,118	21,629
Number of Employees	256,207	219,839	225,347

Source: Company annual reports.

Commentary: In virtually all measures of performance, IBM has made a significant turnaround from
1993 to 1995. Note in particular the decrease in debt and the great profit turnaround.

---

[14] Allison Rogers, "Is He Too Cautious to save IBM?" *Fortune,* October 3, 1994, p. 78.

The Quiet Revolution

The critics inclined toward revolutionary measures had to be disappointed. "Transforming IBM is not something we can do in one or two years," Gerstner had stated. "The better we are at fixing some of the short-term things, the more time we have to deal with the long-term issues."[15] His efforts were contrasted with those of Albert Dunlap, who overhauled Scott Paper at about the same time. Dunlap replaced 9 of the 11 top executives in the first few days and laid off one-third of the total workforce. Gerstner brought in only eight top executives from outside IBM to sit on the 37-person Worldwide Management Council.

A nontechnical man, Gerstner's strengths were in selling: cookies and cigarettes at RJR, travel services during an 11-year career at American Express Company. Weeks after taking over, he talked to IBM's top 100 customers at a retreat in Chantilly, Virginia. He asked them what IBM was doing right and wrong. They were surprised and delighted: This was the first time the chairman of the 72-year-old company had ever polled its customers. The input was revealing:

> The customers told him IBM was difficult to work with and unresponsive to customers' needs. For example, customers who needed IBM's famed mainframe computers were being told that the machines were dinosaurs and that the company would have to consider getting out of the business.[16]

Gerstner told these customers that IBM was in mainframes to stay, and would aggressively cut prices and focus on helping them set up, manage, and link the systems. And IBM's hardware sales turned around also, rising from $30.6 billion in 1993 to $35.6 billion in 1995.

Perhaps the most obvious change Gerstner instituted was the elimination of a dress code that once kept IBM salespeople in blue suits and white shirts.

By the spring of 1997, *Fortune* highlighted Gerstner on its cover with the feature article, "The Holy Terror Who's Saving IBM."[17] Total company sales for 1996 were $75.947 billion, up 5.6 percent from the previous year, and net profits gained 30 percent over 1995, to $5.429 billion.

The growth continued. Revenues in 1997 were $78.508 billion and net income $6.093 billion. The first three quarters of 1998 showed surprisingly robust sales growth, with practically all the portfolios of businesses contributing to the sparkling performance. For example, third-quarter earnings were up 10 percent, on an unexpectedly healthy sales growth of 8 percent. For the year, IBM shares were one of the leading gainers among the companies that make up the Dow Jones Industrial Average.[18]

Gerstner's turnaround was no fluke.

---

[15] Ibid., p. 78.

[16] "IBM Focuses on Sales," *Cleveland Plain Dealer,* September 10, 1996, p. 6-C.

[17] Betsy Morris, "He's Saving Big Blue," *Fortune,* April 14, 1997, pp. 68–81.

[18] *1998 Annual Report;* and Raju Narisetti, "IBM Profit Rose 10% in 3rd Period, Topping Estimates, Amid Robust Sales," *The Wall Street Journal,* October 21, 1998, p. A3.

LATE-BREAKING NEWS

In late 1999, Louis Gerstner did what to many people, both inside and outside IBM, seemed unthinkable. He decided to sell some of the world's best technology—tiny disk drives, speedy new chips, and much more—to his fiercest rivals. Essentially, Gerstner was putting on sale IBM's renowned research operation, its 2,800 scientists and $5.6 million budget.

The idea of cooperating with your competitors—"coopetition"—is not unique. It started with cross-licensing of patents and has become more common since the 1980s as technology has mushroomed. Still, this unveiling of the secrets of IBM's labs was a major and controversial decision.

IBM stood to gain perhaps $30 billion in sales over seven years from only four customers, this being an important revenue stream. The big risk, however, in selling to competitors is that some of them may outdo the master.

In addition to selling computer parts to former rivals, servicing would be an important additional source of income. An agreement with Dell Computer Corp. would have IBM providing computer installation and repair services for buyers of Dell equipment, this potentially generating $6 billion or more over seven years. For some of these "partners," IBM would even design their new products, flavored with the most advanced technology coming from IBM labs. Essentially, all this boosts potential licensing revenues. Critics proclaimed, "it's what every dying company does in its final moments. Once your businesses start to fail, you try to make money selling pieces." Gerstner saw this as "grasping opportunities."

Sources: William M. Bulkeley and Gary McWilliams, "IBM Broadens Pact With Dell Computer," *The Wall Street Journal*, September 28, 1999, p. B11; and Daniel Lyons, "IBM's Giant Gamble," *Forbes*, October 4, 1999, pp. 91–95.

WHAT CAN BE LEARNED

Beware of the cannibalization phobia. We have just set the parameters of the issue of cannibalization, that is, how far a firm should go in developing products and encouraging intramural competition that will take away sales from other products and other units of the business. The issue is particularly troubling when the part of the business that is likely to suffer is the most profitable in the company. Yet cannibalization should not even be an issue. At stake is the forward-leaning of the company, its embracing of innovation and improved technology, as well as its competitive stance. Unless a firm has an assured monopoly position, it can expect competitors to introduce advances in technology and/or new efficiencies of productivity and customer service.

In general we can conclude that no firm should rest on its laurels, that it must introduce improvements and change as soon as possible, hopefully ahead of competition—all this without regard to any possible impairment of sales and profits of existing products and units.

Need to be "lean and mean" (sometimes called "acting small"). The market-place is uncertain. Especially is this true in high-tech industries. In such environments a larger firm needs to keep the responsiveness and flexibility of smaller firms. It must avoid layers of management, of delimiting policies, and a tradition-bound mindset. Otherwise our big firm is like the behemoth vessel, unable to stop or change course without losing precious time and distance. But how can a big firm keep the maneuverability and innovative-mindedness of a smaller firm? How can it remain lean and mean with increasing size?

We can identify certain conditions or factors of lean-and-mean firms:

1. They have simple organizations. Typically, they are decentralized, with decision-making moved lower in the organization. This discourages the buildup of cumbersome bureaucracy and staff, which tends to add both increasing overhead expenses and the red tape that stultifies fast reaction time.

   With a simple organization comes a relatively flat one, with fewer levels of management than comparable firms. This also has certain desirable consequences. Overhead is greatly reduced because there are fewer executives with their expensive staffs. But communication is also improved, since higher executives are more accessible and directions and feedback are less distorted because of more direct communications channels. Even morale is improved because of the better communication and the accessibility of leaders of the organization.

2. Receptivity and encouragement of new ideas. A major factor in the inertia of large firms are the vested interests who see their power threatened by new ideas and innovative directions. Consequently, real creativity is stymied by not being appreciated; often it is even discouraged.

   A firm that wishes to be lean and mean must seek new ideas. This implies rewards and recognition for creativity but, even more, acting upon worthwhile ideas. Few things are more thwarting to creativity in an organization than pigeon-holing the good ideas of eager employees.

3. Participation in planning should be moved as low in the organization as possible. Important employees and lower-level managers should be involved in decisions concerning their responsibilities, with their ideas receiving reasonable weight in final decisions. Performance goals—and rewards—should be moved as low in the organization as possible. Such an organizational climate encourages innovation, improves motivation and morale, and can lead to the fast-reaction time that so often characterizes small organizations and so seldom the large.

4. A final factor that characterizes some highly successful proactive larger organizations is minimum frills, even austerity at the corporate level. Two of our most successful firms today, Wal-Mart and Southwest Airlines, evince this philosophy to the furthest degree. A no-frills management orientation is the greatest corporate model for curbing frivolous costs throughout an organization.

Beware the "king-of-the hill" three C's mindset. As a firm gains dominance and maturity, a natural mindset evolution can occur, and must be guarded against.

Conservatism, complacency, and conceit insidiously move in. Usually this happens at the highest levels, and readily filters down to the rest of the organization. As discussed earlier, this mindset leaves a firm highly vulnerable to competitors who are smaller and hungrier. And so the king of the hill is toppled.

While top management usually initiates such a mindset, top management can also lead in inhibiting it. The lean-and-mean organization is anathema to the three C's mindset. If we can curb bureaucratic buildup, then the seeds are thwarted. Perhaps most important in preventing this mindset is encouragement of innovative thinking throughout the organization, as well as bringing in fresh blood from outside the organization to fill some positions. A strict adherence to promotion from within is inhibiting.

The power of greater commitment to customers. One of the bigger contributions Gerstner may have made to the turnaround of IBM was his customer focus: putting the needs of customers first and relying on his in-house experts for the technology; asking, not merely talking—finding out what customers wanted, and seeing what could be done to best meet these needs as quickly as possible; at the same time, toning down the arrogance of an "elite" staff of sales representatives. Perhaps the style change from blue suits and white shirts was the visible sign of a change in culture and attitudes.

Many firms profess a great commitment to customers and service. So common are such statements that one wonders how much is mere lip service. It is so easy to say this, and then not really to follow up. In so doing, the opportunity to develop a trusting relationship is lost.

We can overcome adversity! We saw this with Continental Airlines and now with IBM. Such examples should be motivating and inspiring for all organizations and the executives trying to turn them around. Firms and their managers should be capable of learning from mistakes. As such, mistakes should be valuable learning experiences, leading the way to better performance and decisions in the future.

CONSIDER

What additional learning insights do you see emerging from the IBM case?

QUESTIONS

1. Assess the pro and con arguments for the 1982 decision to delegate to Microsoft and Intel a foothold in software and operating systems. (Keep your perspective to that of the early 1980s; don't be biased with the benefit of hindsight.)

2. Do you see any way that IBM could have maintained its nimbleness and technological edge as it grew to a $60 billion company? Reflect on this, and be as creative as you can.

3. "Tradition has no place in corporate thinking today." Discuss this statement.

4. Playing devil's advocate (one who takes an opposing position for the sake of argument), can you defend the position that the problems besetting IBM were not its fault, that they were beyond its control?

5. Would you say that the major problems confronting IBM were marketing rather than organizational? Why or why not?

6. Which of the three C's do you think was most to blame for IBM's problems? Why do you conclude this?

HANDS-ON EXERCISES

1. As the new CEO brought in to turn around IBM in 1993, how would you propose to do so? (State any assumptions you find necessary, but keep them reasonable. And don't be swayed by what actually happened. Perhaps better actions could have been taken.) Be as specific as you can, and also discuss the constraints likely to face your turnaround program.

2. You are a marketing consultant reporting to the CEO in the late 1980s. IBM is still racking up revenue and profit gains. But you detect serious emerging weaknesses. What would you advise management at this time? (Make any assumptions you feel necessary, but state them clearly.) Persuasively explain your rationale.

TEAM DEBATE EXERCISE

At issue; whether to break up the company into 10 to 15 semiautonomous units, or to keep basically the same organization. Debate the opposing views as persuasively as possible.

INVITATION TO RESEARCH

What is the current situation of IBM? Have any new problems arisen for IBM? Is Gerstner still the CEO?

PART THREE

CRISIS MANAGEMENT

CHAPTER EIGHT

Met Life—Underresponding to a Crisis

*I*n August 1993, the state of Florida cracked down on the sales practices of giant Metropolitan Life, a company dating back to 1868 and the country's second-largest insurance firm. Met Life agents based in Tampa, Florida were alleged to have duped customers out of some $11 million. Thousands of these customers were nurses lured by the sales pitch to learn more about "something new, one of the most widely discussed retirement plans in the investment world today."[1] In reality, this was a life-insurance policy in disguise, and what clients were led to think were savings deposits were actually insurance premiums.

As we will see, the growing scandal rocked Met Life, and eventually cost it several billion dollars in fines and restitutions. What was not clear for certain was the full culpability of the company: Was it guilty only of not monitoring agent performance sufficiently to detect unethical and illegal activities, or was it the great encourager of such practices? Regardless, we are also concerned in this chapter with how poorly Met Life reacted to the legal and public relations stigma that enveloped it.

RICK URSO: THE VILLAIN?

The first premonitory rumble that something bad was about to happen came to Rick Urso on Christmas Eve 1993. Home with his family, he received an unexpected call from his boss, the regional sales manager. In disbelief he heard there was a rumor going around the executive suites that he was about to be fired. Now Urso had known that the state of Florida had been investigating and that company auditors had also been looking into sales practices. On September 17, two corporate vice presidents had even shown up to conduct the fourth audit that year, but on leaving they had given him the impression that he was complying with company guidelines.

Urso often reveled in his good fortune and attributed it to his sheer dedication to his work and the company. He had grown up in a working-class neighborhood, the son of an electrician. He had started college, but dropped out before graduating.

[1] Suzanne Woolley and Gail DeGeorge, "Policies of Deception?" *Business Week*, January 17, 1994, p. 24.

115

His sales career started at a John Hancock agency in Tampa, in 1978. Four years later, he was promoted to manager and was credited with building up the agency to number two in the whole company.

He left John Hancock in 1983 for Met Life's Tampa agency. His first job was as trainer. Only three months later he was promoted to branch manager. Now his long hours and overwhelming commitment were beginning to pay off. In a truly inspiring success story, his dedication and his talent as a motivator of people swept the branch from a one-rep office to one of Met Life's largest and most profitable. By 1993 the agency employed 120 reps, seven sales managers, and 30 administrative employees. And he was the head. In 1990 and 1991, Urso's office won the company's Sales Office of the Year award. With such a performance history, the stuff of legends, he became the company's star, a person to look up to and to inspire trainees and other employees.

His was the passion of a TV evangelist: "Most people go through life being told why they can't accomplish something. If they would just believe, then they would be halfway there. That's the way I dream and that's what I expect from my people."[2] He soon became known as the "Master Motivator," and increasingly was the guest speaker at Met Life conferences.

On the Monday after that Christmas, the dire prediction came to pass. He was summoned to the office of William Groggans, the head of Met Life's Southeast territory, and there was handed a letter by the sober-faced Groggans. With trembling hands he opened it and read that he was fired. The reason: engaging in improper conduct.

The Route to Stardom

Unfortunately, the growth of his Tampa office could not be credited to simple motivation of employees. Urso found his vehicle for great growth to be the whole life insurance policy. This was part life insurance and part savings. As such it required high premiums, but only part earned interest and compounded on a tax-deferred basis; the rest went to pay for the life insurance policy. What made this so attractive to company sales reps was the commission: A Met whole life policy paid a 55 percent first-year commission. In contrast, an annuity paid only a 2 percent first-year commission.

Urso found the nurses market to be particularly attractive. Perhaps because of their constant exposure to death, nurses were easily convinced of the need for economic security. He had his salespeople call themselves "nursing representatives," and his Tampa salespeople carried their fake retirement plan beyond Florida, eventually reaching 37 states. A New York client, for example, thought she had bought a retirement annuity. But it turned out to be insurance even though as a single woman she didn't need such coverage.[3]

As the growth of the Tampa agency became phenomenal, Urso's budget for mailing brochures was upped to nearly $1 million in 1992, ten times that of any other Met Life office. This gave him national reach.

---

[2] Weld F. Royal, "Scapegoat or Scoundrel," *Sales & Marketing Management,* January 1995, p. 64.

[3] Jane Bryant Quinn, "Yes, They're Out to Get You," *Newsweek,* January 24, 1994, p. 51.

Urso's own finances increased proportionately as he earned a commission on each policy his reps sold. In 1989, he was paid $270,000. In 1993, as compensation exceeded $1 million, he moved his family to Bay Shore Boulevard, the most expensive area of Tampa.

Early Warnings

A few complaints began surfacing. In 1990, the Texas insurance commissioner warned Met Life to stop its nursing ploy. The company made a token compliance by sending out two rounds of admonitory letters. But apparently nothing changed. See the following information box about the great deficiency of token compliance without follow-up.

An internal Met Life audit in 1991 also raised some questions about Urso's pre-approach letters. The term "nursing representative" was called a "made-up" title. The auditors also questioned the term "retirement savings policy" as not appropriate for the product. However, the report concluded by congratulating the Tampa office for its contribution to the company. Not surprisingly, such mixed signals did not end the use of misleading language at that time.

Allegations Intensify

In the summer of 1993, Florida state regulators began a more in-depth examination of the sales practices of the Urso agency. The crux of the investigation concerned pro-

---

INFORMATION BOX

THE VULNERABILITY OF COMPLIANCE THAT IS ONLY TOKEN

A token effort at compliance with a regulatory complaint or charge tends to have two consequences, neither good in the long run for the company involved:

1. Such tokenism gives a clear message to the organization: "Despite what outsiders say, this is acceptable conduct in this firm." Thus is set the climate for less-than-desirable practices.
2. Vulnerability to harsher measures in the future. With the malpractice continuing, regulators, convinced that the company is stalling and refusing to cooperate, will eventually take more drastic action. Penalties will move beyond warnings to become punitive.

The firm may not have intended to stall, but that is the impression conveyed. If the cause of the seemingly token effort is really faulty controls, one wonders how many other aspects of the operation are also ineptly controlled so that company policies are ignored.

Discuss what kinds of controls Met Life could have imposed in 1990 that would have made compliance actual and not token.

motional material Urso's office was sending to nurses nationwide. From 1989 to 1993, millions of direct mail pieces had been sent out. Charges finally were leveled that this material disguised the product agents were selling. For example, one brochure coming from Urso's office depicted the Peanuts character Lucy in a nurse's uniform. The headline described the product as "Retirement Savings and Security for the Future a Nurse Deserves." Nowhere was insurance even mentioned, and allegations were that nurses across the country unknowingly purchased life insurance when they had thought they were buying retirement savings plans.

As the investigation deepened, a former Urso agent-turned-whistleblower claimed he had been instructed to place his hands over the words "life insurance" on applications during presentations.

As a result of this investigation, Florida Insurance Commissioner Tom Gallagher charged Met Life with violations.

MET LIFE CORRECTIVE ACTIONS, FINALLY

Under investigation by Florida regulators, the company's attitudes changed. At first, Met Life had denied wrongdoing. But eventually it acknowledged problems. Under mounting public pressure, it agreed to pay $20 million in fines to more than 40 states as a result of unethical sales practices of its agents. It further agreed to refund premiums to nearly 92,000 policyholders who bought insurance based on misleading sales information between 1989 and 1993. These refunds were expected to reach $76 million.

Met Life fired or demoted five high-level executives as a result of the scandal. Urso's office was closed, and all seven of his managers and several reps were also discharged. Life insurance sales to individuals were down 25 percent through September 1994 over the same nine-month period in 1993. Standard & Poor's downgraded Met's bond rating based on these alleged improprieties.

Shortly after the fines were announced, the Florida Department of Insurance filed charges against Urso and 86 other Met Life insurance agents, accusing them of fraudulent sales practices. The insurance commissioner said, "This was not a situation where a few agents decided to take advantage of their customers, but a concerted effort by many individuals to dupe customers into buying a life insurance policy disguised as a retirement savings plan."[4]

Now Met Life attempted to improve its public image by instituting a broad overhaul of its compliance procedures. It established a corporate ethics and compliance department to monitor behavior throughout the company and audit personal insurance sales offices. The department was also charged to report any compliance deficiencies to senior management and to follow up to ensure the implementation of corrective actions.

In Met Life's *1994 Annual Report*, Harry Kamen, CEO, and Ted Athanassiades, president, commented on their corrective actions regarding the scandal:

---

[4] Sean Armstrong, "The Good, The Bad and the Industry," *Best's Review, P/C.* June 1994, p. 36.

We created what we think is the most effective compliance system in the industry. Not just for personal insurance, but for all components of the company. We installed systems to coordinate and track the quality and integrity of our sales activities, and we created a new system of sales office auditing.

Also, there were organizational changes. And, for the first time in 22 years, we assembled all of our agency and district managers—about a thousand people—to discuss what we have done and need to do about the problems and where we were going.[5]

Meantime, Rick Urso started a suit against Met Life for defamation of character and for reneging on a $1 million severance agreement. He alleged that Met Life made him the fall guy in the nationwide sales scandal.

The personal ramifications in Urso's life were not inconsequential. More than a year later he was still unemployed. He had looked for another insurance job, but no one would even see him. "There are nights he can't sleep. He lies awake worrying about the impact this will have on his two teenagers." And he laments that his wife cannot go out without people gossiping.[6]

WHERE DOES THE BLAME LIE?

Is Urso really the unscrupulous monster who rose to a million-dollar-a-year man on the foundations of deceit? Or is Met Life mainly to blame for encouraging, and then ignoring for too long, practices aimed at misleading and even deceiving?

The Case Against Met Life

Undeniably Urso did things that smacked of the illegal and unethical. But did the corporation knowingly provide the climate? Was his training such as to promote deceptive practices? Was Met Life completely unaware of his distortions and deceptions in promotional material and sales pitches? There seems to be substantial evidence that the company played a part; it was no innocent and unsuspecting bystander.

At best, Met Life top executives may not have been aware of the full extent of the hard-selling efforts at first emanating from Tampa and then spreading further in the organization. Perhaps they chose to ignore any inkling that things were not completely on the up and up, in the quest for exceptional bottom-line performance. "Don't argue with success" may have become the corporate mindset.

At the worst, the company encouraged and even demanded hard selling and tried to pretend that such could still be accomplished with ethical standards of performance. If such ethical standards were not met, then company top executives could argue that they were not aware of wrongdoing.

There is evidence of company culpability. Take the training program for new agents. Much of it was designed to help new employees overcome the difficulties of selling life insurance. In so doing, they were taught to downplay the life insurance

---

[5] *Met Life 1994 Annual Report*, p. 16.

[6] Royal, p. 65.

aspects of the product. Rather, the savings and tax-deferred growth benefits were to be stressed.

In training new agents to sell insurance over the phone, they were told that people prefer dealing with specialists. It seemed only a small temptation to use the title "nursing representative" rather than "insurance agent."

After the scandal, Met Life admitted that the training might be faulty. Training had been decentralized into five regional centers, and the company believed that this may have led to less standardized and controlled curricula. Met Life has since reorganized, so that many functions, including training and legal matters, are now done at one central location.[7]

The company's control or monitoring was certainly deficient and uncoordinated during the years of misconduct. For example, the marketing department promoted deceptive sales practices while the legal department warned of possible illegality but took no further action to eliminate it.

AN INDUSTRY PROBLEM?

The Met Life revelations focused public and regulatory attention on the entire insurance industry. The Insurance Commissioner of Florida also turned attention to the sales and marketing practices of New York Life and Prudential. The industry itself seemed vulnerable to questionable practices. Millions of transactions, intense competition, and a widespread and rather autonomous sales force afforded opportunity for misrepresentation and other unethical dealings.

For example, just a few months after the Tampa office publicity, Met Life settled an unrelated scandal. Regulators in Pennsylvania fined the company $1.5 million for "churning." This is a practice of agents replacing old policies with new ones, in which additional commissions are charged and policyholders are disadvantaged. Class-action suits alleging churning have also been filed in Pennsylvania against Prudential, New York Life, and John Hancock.

But problems go beyond sales practices. Claims adjusters may attempt to withhold or reduce payments. General agents may place business with bogus or insolvent companies. Even actuaries may create unrealistic policy structures.

With a deteriorating public image, the industry faces further state and federal governmental regulation. But cynics, both within and outside the industry, wonder whether deception and fraud are so much a part of the business that nothing can be done about them.[8]

ANALYSIS

Here we have an apparent lapse in complete feedback to top executives. But maybe they did not want to know. After all, nothing was life-threatening here, no product safety features were being ignored or disguised, nobody was in physical danger.

---

[7] "Trained to Mislead," *Sales & Marketing Management,* January 1995, p. 66.

[8] Armstrong, p. 35.

This raises a key management issue. Can top executives hide from less-than-ethical practices—and even illegal ones—under the guise that they did not know? The answer should be No! See the following information box for a discussion of management accountability.

So, we are left with top management of Met Life grappling with the temptation to tacitly approve the aggressive selling practices of a sales executive so successful as to be the model for the whole organization, even though faint cries from the legal staff suggested that such might be subject to regulatory scrutiny and disapproval.

The harsh appraisal of this situation is that top management cannot be exonerated for the deficiences of subordinates. If controls and monitoring processes are defective, top management is still accountable. The pious platitudes of Met Life management that now we have corrected the situation hardly excuse them for permitting this to have happened in the first place.

Ah, but embracing the temptation is so easy to rationalize. Management can always maintain that there was no solid proof of misdeeds. After all, when do aggressive sales efforts cross the line? When do they become more than simply puffing, and become outright deceptive? See the following information box regarding puffing, and this admittedly gray area of the acceptable. Lacking indisputable evidence of misdeeds, why

INFORMATION BOX

THE ULTIMATE RESPONSIBILITY

In the Maytag case in Chapter 17 we examine a costly snafu brought about by giving executives of a foreign subsidiary too much rein. With Met Life the problem was gradually eroding ethical practices. In both instances, top management still had ultimate responsibility and cannot escape blame for whatever goes wrong in their organization. Decades ago, President Truman coined the phrase, "The buck stops here," meaning that in this highest position rests the ultimate seat of responsibility.

Any manager who delegates to someone else the authority to do something will undoubtedly hold them responsible to do the job properly. Still, the manager must be aware that his or her own responsibility to higher management or to stockholders cannot be delegated away. If the subordinate does the job improperly, the manager is still responsible.

Going back to Met Life, or to any corporation involved with unethical and illegal practices, top executives can try to escape blame by denying that they knew anything about the misdeeds. This should not exonerate them. Even if they knew nothing directly, they still set the climate.

In Japan, the chief executive of an organization involved in a public scandal usually resigns in disgrace. In the United States, top executives often escape full retribution by blaming their subordinates and maintaining that they themselves knew nothing of the misdeed. Is it truly fair to hold a top executive culpable for the shortcomings of some unknown subordinate?

INFORMATION BOX

WHERE DO WE DRAW THE LINE ON PUFFING?

Puffing is generally thought of as mild exaggeration in selling or advertising. It is generally accepted as simple exuberance toward what is being promoted. As such, it is acceptable business conduct. Still, most of us have come to regard promotional communications with some skepticism. "It's New! The Greatest! A Super Value! Gives Whiter Teeth! Whiter Laundry!..." and so on. We have become conditioned to viewing such blandishments with suspicion. But are they dishonest or deceptive? Probably not, as long as the exaggeration stays mild.

But it is a short step from mild exaggeration to outright falsehoods and deceptive claims. Did Met Life's "nursing representatives," "retirement plans," and hiding the reality of life insurance cross the line? Enough people thought so, including state insurance commissioners and the victims themselves.

Do you think all exaggerated claims, even the mild and vague ones known as puffing, should be banned? Why or why not?

should these executives suspect the worst? Especially since their legal departments, not centralized as they were to be later, were timid in their denunciations?

Turning to controls, a major caveat should be posed for all firms: In the presence of strong management demands for performance—with the sometimes imagined pressure to produce at all costs, or else—the ground is laid for less-than-desirable practices by subordinates. After all, career paths and even job longevity depend on meeting these demands.

In a climate of decentralization and laissez-faire, such abuses are more likely to occur. Such a results-oriented environment suggests that it's not how you achieve designated goals, but that you meet them. So, while decentralization on balance is usually desirable, in an environment of top management's laxity in good moral standards it can lead to undesirable practices.

At the least, it leads to opportunistic temptations on the part of lower- and middle-level executives. Perhaps this is the final indictment of Met Life and Rick Urso. The climate was conducive to his ambitious opportunism. For a while it was wonderful. But the abuses of accepted behavior could not be disguised indefinitely.

And wherever possible, top management will repudiate its accountability.

The Handling of the Crisis

Met Life responded slowly to the allegations of misconduct. A classic mode for firms confronted with unethical and/or product liability charges is to deny everything, until evidence becomes overwhelming. Then they are forced to acknowledge problems under mounting public pressure—from regulatory bodies, attorneys, and the media—and have to scramble with damage control to try to undo the threats to pub-

LATE-BREAKING NEWS

On August 18, 1999, Met Life agreed to pay out at least $1.7 billion to settle final lawsuits over its allegedly improper sales practices. In the agreement (in which Met Life admitted no wrongdoing), about six million life insurance policyholders and a million annuity contract holders were involved. Essentially, these customers are expected to get one-to-five years of free term-life insurance coverage.

Met Life has argued for years that it had done nothing wrong. It had previously dispensed with most of its litigation problems by settling rather than going to trial. The incentive for settling these final class-action suits even at the cost of a massive charge, was to clear the way for Met Life's planned conversion to a stockholder-owned company from its current status as a policyholder-owned mutual company. "Clearly it's something they needed to put behind them before they demutualized," or went public.[9]

[9] Deborah Lohse, "Met Life Agrees to Pay out $1.7 Billion or More to Settle Policyholder Lawsuits," *The Wall Street Journal,* August 19, 1999, p. B14.

lic image and finances. In Met Life's case, fines and refunds approached $100 million early on. They would eventually reach almost $2 billion.

Being slow to act, to accept any responsibility, and, for top executives, aloofness until late in the game, are tantamount to inflaming public opinion and regulatory zeal. We saw something similar in the Coca-Cola product-safety crisis in Europe: First there was denial, then grudging admission, then uncoordinated remedial efforts, and only after the crisis had received alarming attention did top management become involved to finally lead massive restorative efforts.

How much better for all involved, victims as well as the organization itself, if initial complaints are promptly followed up and, if serious, given top management attention in a climate of cooperation with any agencies involved as well as the always-interested media. (See the other cases in this section for more bad and good ways of handling crises, including the Johnson & Johnson model for the most extreme crisis, involving loss of life.)

WHAT CAN BE LEARNED?

Beware the ostrich-in-the-sand approach to looming problems or public complaints. Ignoring or giving only token attention to suspected problems and regulatory complaints sets a firm up for a possible massive crisis. Covering one's eyes to malpractices and dangerous situations will not make them go away. They tend to fester and become more serious. Prompt attention, investigation, and action is needed to prevent these problem areas from getting out of hand. Met Life could have saved itself several billion dollars if it had acted on the early complaints of misrepresentation and misleading customers.

Unethical and illegal actions do not go undetected forever. It may take months, it may take years, but a firm's dark side will eventually be uncovered. Its reputation may then be besmirched, it may face loss of customers and competitive position, it may face heavy fines and increased regulation.

The eventual disclosure may come from a disgruntled employee (a whistle-blower). It may originate from a regulatory body or an investigative reporter. Or it may come from revelations emanating from a lawsuit. Eventually, the deviation is uncovered, and retribution follows. Such a scenario should be—but is not always—enough to constrain those individuals tempted to commit unethical and illegal actions.

What made the Met Life deceptive practices particularly troubling is that they were so visible, and yet were so long tolerated. A clear definition of what was acceptable and what was not seemed lacking by much of the sales organization. Something was clearly amiss both in the training and in the controlling of agent personnel.

The control function is best centralized in any organization. Where the department or entity that monitors performance is decentralized, tolerance of bad practices is more likely than when centralized. The reason is rather simple. Where legal or accounting controls are decentralized the persons conducting them are more easily influenced and are likely to be neither as objective nor as critical as when they are more at arm's length. So, reviewers and evaluators should not be close to the people they are examining. And they should report only to top management.

A *strong sales incentive program invites bad practices.* The lucrative commission incentive for the whole life policies—55 percent first-year commission—was almost bound to stimulate abusive sales practices, especially when the rewards for this type of policy were so much greater than for any other. Firms often use various incentive programs and contests to motivate their employees to seek greater efforts. But if some are tempted to cross the line, the end result in public scrutiny and condemnation may not be worth whatever increases in sales might be gained.

Large corporations are particularly vulnerable to public scrutiny. Large firms, especially ones dealing with consumer products, are very visible. This visibility makes them attractive targets for critical scrutiny by activists, politicians, the media, regulatory bodies, and the legal establishment. Such firms ought to be particularly careful in any dealings that might be questioned, even if short-term profits have to be restrained. In Met Life's case, the fines and refunds eventually approached $2 billion. Although the firm in its 1994 annual report maintained that all the bad publicity was behind it, that there were no ill effects, still we can wonder how quickly a besmirched reputation can truly be restored, especially when competitors are eager to grab the opportunity presented. Actually, all the problems were not behind Met Life, as it eventually settled remaining claims for over $1.7 billion in August 1999.

CONSIDER

What additional learning insights do you see?

QUESTIONS

1. Do you think Rick Urso should have been fired? Why or why not?

2. Do you think the Met Life CEO and president should have been fired? Why or why not?

3. Why was the term, "life insurance," seemingly so desirable to avoid? What is wrong with life insurance?

4. Given the widespread publicity about the Met Life scandal, do you think the firm could regain consumer trust in a short time?

5. "This whole critical publicity has been blown way out of proportion. After all, nobody was injured. Not even in their pocketbook. They were sold something they really needed. For their own good." Evaluate.

6. "You have to admire that guy, Urso. He was a real genius. No one else could motivate a sales organization as he did. They should have made him president of the company. Or else he should become an evangelist." Evaluate.

7. Do you think the arguments are compelling that the control function should be centralized rather than decentralized? Why or why not?

HANDS-ON EXERCISES

Before

1. It is early 1990. You are the assistant to the CEO of Met Life. Rumors have been surfacing that life insurance sales efforts are becoming not only too high pressure but also misleading. The CEO has ordered you to investigate. You find that the legal department in the Southeast Territory has some concerns about the efforts coming out of the highly successful Tampa office of Urso. Be as specific as you can about how you would investigate these unproven allegations, and how you would report this to your boss, assuming that some questionable practices seem apparent.

2. It is 1992. Internal investigations have confirmed that Urso and his "magnificent" Tampa office are using deceptive selling techniques in disguising the life insurance aspects of the policies they are selling. As the executive in charge in the Southeast, describe your actions and rationale at this point. (You have to assume that the later consequences are completely unknown as this point.)

After

3. The _____ has hit the fan. The scandal has become well-publicized, especially with such TV programs as "Dateline" and "20/20". What would you do as top executive of Met Life at this point? How would you attempt to save the public image of the company?

TEAM DEBATE EXERCISE

The publicity is widespread about the "misdeeds" of Met Life. Debate how you would react. One position is to defend your company and rationalize what happened and downplay any ill-effects. The other position is to meekly bow to the allegations and admit wrongdoing and be as contrite as possible.

INVITATION TO RESEARCH

How is Met Life faring after this extremely bad publicity? Have sales rebounded? Can you find any information as to whether its image has improved, whether the situation has virtually been forgotten by the general public? Can you find out whether Rick Urso has found another job? Are Kamen and Athanassiades still the top executives of Met Life? What conclusions can you draw from your research?

CHAPTER NINE

Perrier—Overresponding to a Crisis

On a Friday in early February 1990, the first news reached Perrier executive suites that traces of benzene had been found in its bottled water. Ronald Davis, president of the Perrier Group of America, ordered a sweeping recall of all bottles in North America. Just a few days later, Source Perrier S.A., the French parent, expanded the recall to the rest of the world while the company sought to identify the source of the problem and correct it.

Although at first view such a reaction to an unexpected crisis seems zealous and the ultimate in customer concern and social responsibility, a deeper study reveals marketing mistakes of major proportions.

BEFORE

In late 1989, Ronald Davis, 43-year-old president of Perrier's U.S. operations, had reason to be pleased. During his 10-year tenure, Perrier's U.S. sales had risen from $40 million to more than $800 million at retail, which was a significant 25 percent of the company's worldwide sales. He was also proud of his firm being depicted in a May 1989 issue of *Fortune* as one of six companies that compete best. *Fortune* captions: "These are companies you don't want to come up against in your worst nightmare. In the businesses they're in, they amass crushing market share."[1]

A company report in 1987 described the French source, a spring in Vergeze, as follows:

One of Perrier's identifying qualities is its low mineral (particularly sodium) content. This is because the water spends only a short time filtering through minerals. While flowing underground, the water meets gas flowing vertically through porous volcanic rocks. This is how Perrier gets its fizz ... the company assured us that production has never been limited by the source output. The company sells approximately one billion bottles of which 600 million are exported.[2]

---

[1] Bill Saporito, "Companies That Compete Best," *Fortune,* May 22, 1989, pp. 36ff.
[2] B. Facon, *Source Perrier—Company Report,* November 13, 1987, p. 4.

Davis recognized that he was in two businesses, albeit both involved bottled water: (1) sparkling water, in the famous green bottle, which he had been successful in positioning as an adult soft drink with a French mystique, an alternative to soft drinks or alcohol; and (2) still water, a tap-water replacement, with the product delivered to homes and offices and dispensed through watercoolers. This latter business he saw as more resembling package delivery such as UPS and Federal Express, and less akin to pushing soft drinks. Accordingly, he emphasized quality of professional service for his route drivers. While best known for the green-bottled Perrier, a mainstay of most restaurants and bars, the company owned nine other brands of bottled water, including Poland Spring, Great Bear, Calistoga, and Ozarka.

At a price of 300 to 1,200 times that of tap water, bottled water was the fastest growing segment of the U.S. beverage industry (see Table 9.1). Perrier controlled 24 percent of the total U.S. bottled-water business. Of the imported-bottled-water sector, the green bottle dominated with almost 50 percent of the market, although this market share had fallen when more competitors attempted to push into the rapidly growing market. In the 1980s more than 20 firms had taken a run at the green bottle, but without notable success; these included such behemoths as Coca-Cola, PepsiCo, and Anheuser-Busch. Now Davis was more concerned with expanding the category and was trying to shift the brand's image from chic to healthy, so as to make the brand more acceptable to the "masses."

THE CRISIS

The North American Recall

Davis, as he prepared his five-year plan in early 1990, wrote that competing in the 1990s would require not strategic planning, but "flexibility planning."[3] In retrospect, he seemed to be prophetic.

TABLE 9.1. **Average Annual Growth of Beverage Sales, 1985–1989**

Beverage Type	Percent of Growth
Bottled water	+11.1
Soft drinks	+3.2
Milk	+1.5
Tea	+1.2
Beer	+0.4
Coffee	−0.4
Wine	−2.0
Distilled spirits	−2.6

Source: Beverage Marketing Corporation, as reported in *Fortune*, April 23, 1990, p. 277.

---

[3] Patricia Sellers, "Perrier Plots Its Comeback," *Fortune*, April 23, 1990, p. 277.

As he was fine-tuning his plan, the first news trickled in that a lab in North Carolina had discovered traces of benzene, a carcinogen, in some of the bottles. That same day, February 9, he ordered Perrier removed from disribution in North America.

Source Perrier officials were soon to inform reporters that the company believed the contamination occurred because an employee had mistakenly used cleaning fluid containing benzene to clean the production-line machinery that fills bottles for North America. Frederik Zimmer, managing director of Source Perrier, said that the machinery in question had been cleaned and repaired over the weekend. But in another news conference, Davis announced that he expected Perrier to be off the market for 2 to 3 months.

Such a long absence was seen by some marketing observers as potentially devastating to Perrier, despite its being the front-runner of the industry. Al Ries, chairman of a consulting firm and well-known business writer, was quoted in *The Wall Street Journal* article as saying: "If I were Perrier, I would make a desperate effort to reduce that time as much as possible, even if I had to fly it in on 747s from France."[4]

Without doubt, competitors were salivating at a chance to pick up market share of the $2.2 billion annual U.S. sales. Major competitors included Evian and Saratoga, both owned by BSN of France, and San Peligrino, an Italian import. In 1989 PepsiCo had begun test marketing $H_2OH!$, and in January 1990, Adolph Coors Company introduced Coors Rocky Mountain Sparkling Water. The Perrier absence was expected to accelerate their market entry.

Despite competitive glee at the misfortune of Perrier, some in the industry were concerned. They feared that consumers would forsake bottle water altogether, with its purity now being questioned. Would the public be as willing to pay a substantial premium for any bottled brand? See the following information box for a discussion of the relationship between *price and quality.*

Worldwide Recall

A few days later, the other shoe fell. After reports of benzene being found in Perrier bottles in Holland and Denmark, on February 14, Source Perrier expanded its North American recall to the rest of the world and acknowledged that all production lines for its sparkling water had been contaminated in recent months by tiny amounts of benzene.

At a news conference in Paris, company officials acknowledged for the first time that benzene occurs naturally in Perrier water and that the current problem came about because workers failed to replace filters designed to remove it. This was a critical reversal of previous statements that the water was tainted only because an employee mistakenly used cleaning fluid containing benzene to clean machinery. Zimmer even went further, revealing that Perrier water naturally contains several gases, including benzene, that have to be filtered out.

The company insisted that its famous spring was unpolluted. But now questions were being raised about this and other contradictory statements made about the

---

[4] Alix M. Freedman and Thomas R. King, "Perrier's Strategy in the Wake of Recall," *The Wall Street Journal,* February 12, 1990, p. B1.

INFORMATION BOX

IS QUALITY BEST JUDGED BY PRICE?

We as consumers today have difficulty in judging the quality of competing products. With their complex characteristics and hidden ingredients, we cannot rely on our own expertise to determine the best. So, what sources of information can we use? We can rely on our past experiences with the brand; we can be swayed by our friends and neighbors, we might be influenced by advertising and salespeople (but more and more we become skeptical of their claims); we can study *Consumer Reports* and other consumer information publications. But all of these sources are flawed in that the experience and information usually is dated, and is a limited sample—usually of 1—so that we can seriously question how representative the experience is.

Most people judge quality by price: the higher the price, the better the quality. But such a price/quality perception sets us up. While it may be valid, it also may not be. With the publicity about the impurity of Perrier, we are brought to the realization that paying many times the price of tap water gives us no assurance of better quality, as measured by purity.

Is a price/quality misperception limited mostly to bottled water, do you think? How about liquor? Designer clothes? Perfume?

---

problem. For example, how widespread was the contamination? Was benzene a naturally occurring phenomenon, or does it represent man-made pollution? Suspicions were tending toward the man-made origin. While benzene occurs naturally in certain foods, it is more commonly found as a petroleum-based distillate used in many manufacturing processes.

Particularly surprising was the rather nonchalant attitude of Perrier executives. Zimmer, the president, even suggested that "all this publicity helps build the brand's renown."[5]

Ronald Davis was quick to point out that the company did not have to recall its entire 70-million-bottle U.S. inventory. After all, health officials both in the U.S. and France had noted that the benzene levels found in Perrier did not pose any significant health risk. The major risk really was to the image of Perrier: it had gone to great lengths to establish its water as naturally pure. And while not particularly dangerous, it was certainly not naturally pure—as all the world was finding out from the publicity about it. Add to this the undermining of the major attraction of bottled water that it was safer than ordinary tap water, and the recall and subsequent publicity assumed more ominous proportions.

---

[5] Alix M. Freedman and Thomas R. King, "Perrier Expands North American Recall to Rest of globe," *The Wall Street Journal,* February 15, 1990, p. B1.

THE COMEBACK

It took until mid-July before Perrier was again widely available in the United States; this was 5 months rather than the expected 3 months. Still, Davis was confident that Perrier's sales would return to 85 percent of normal by the end of 1991. Actually, he was more worried about short supply than demand. He was not sure the one spring in Vergeze, France, would be able to replace the world's supply before the beginning of 1991.

Davis's confidence in the durability of the demand stemmed from his clout with retailers, where the brand does a majority of its business. He believed the brand's good reputation, coupled with the other brands marketed by Perrier that had replaced some of the supermarket space relinquished by Perrier, would bring quick renewal. To help this, he wrote letters to 550 CEOs of retail firms, pledging heavy promotional spending. The marketing budget was increased from $6 million to $25 million for 1990, with $16 million going into advertising and the rest into promotions and special events. A highly visible discount strategy was instituted, which included a buy-two, get-one-free offer. Supermarket prices had dropped, with bottles now going for $0.89 to $0.99, down from $1.09 to $1.19. To win back restaurant business, a new 52-member sales force supplemented distributor efforts. However, a setback of sorts was the Food and Drug Administration order to drop the words "naturally sparkling" from Perrier labels.

Still, a recent consumer survey indicated that 84 percent of Perrier's U.S. drinkers intended to buy the product again.[6] Davis could also take heart from the less-than-aggressive actions of his competitors during the hiatus. None appeared to have strongly reacted, although most improved their sales considerably. The smaller competitors proved to be short of marketing money and bottling capacity and apparently were fearful that a beleaguered Perrier would negatively affect the overall market. Big competitors, such as PepsiCo and Coors, who were introducing other bottled waters, somehow also appeared reluctant to move in aggressively.

CONSEQUENCES

By the end of 1990, however, it was clear that Perrier was not regaining market position as quickly and completely as Davis had hoped. Now more aggressive competitors were emerging. Some, such as Saratoga, La Croix, and Quibell, had experienced major windfalls in the wake of the recall. Evian, in particular, a nonsparkling water produced by the French firm BSN S.A., was the biggest winner. Through aggressive marketing and advertising it had replaced Perrier by the end of 1990 as the top-selling imported bottled water.

Perrier's sales had reached only 60 percent of prerecall levels, and its share of the imported bottled-water market had sunk to 20.7 percent from the 44.8 percent of one year earlier. While the Perrier Group of America expected to report a sales gain

---

[6] Sellers, p. 278.

for 1990 of 3.7 percent, this was largely because of the strong performance of such domestic brands as Calistoga and Poland Spring.

Particularly worrisome for Davis was the slow return of Perrier to bars and restaurants, which had formerly accounted for about 35 percent of its sales. A sampling of comments of restaurant managers, as reported in such prestigious papers as *The Wall Street Journal* and *Washington Post*, were far from encouraging. For example:

> The manager of the notable Four Seasons restaurant in New York City said his patrons had begun to shift to San Pellegrino: "I think Perrier is finished," he said. "We can write it off."[7]

> The general manager of Spago Restaurant in Los Angeles said: "Now consumers have decided that other brands are better or at least as good, so Perrier no longer holds the monopoly on water." And Spago no longer carries Perrier.[8]

> Le Pavillon restaurant in Washington, D.C., switched to Quibell during the recall, and has not gone back to Perrier. "Customers still ask for Perrier, but it's a generic term like Kleenex, and customers aren't unhappy to get a substitute."[9]

Evian

David Daniel, 34, was Evian's U.S. CEO since June 1988. He joined the company in 1987 as the first director of marketing at a time when the American subsidiary was a two-person operation. By 1990 there were 100 employees.

Daniel came from PepsiCo, and his background was marketing. He saw Evian's sphere to be portable water that is good for you, a position well situated to capitalize on the health movement. He was particularly interested in broadening the distribution of Evian, and he sought out soft-drink and beer distributors, showing them that their basic industries were only growing at 1 to 3 percent a year, while bottled water was growing at over 10 percent per year. In 1989, Evian sales doubled to $65 million, with $100 million in sight for 1990. The attractiveness of such growth to these distributors was of no small moment.

Daniel made Evian the most expensive water on the market. He saw the price as helping Evian occupy a certain slot in the consumer's mind—remember the price/quality perception discussed earlier. For example, at a fancy grocery in New York's West Village, a 1-liter bottle of Evian sold for $2.50; the city charges a fraction of a penny for a gallon of tap water[10]—a lot of perceived quality in that. This type of pricing along with the packaging that made Evian portable—plastic nonbreakable bottles and reusable caps—were seen as keys in the selling of bottled water.

Then, late in 1990, Evian benefited greatly from the Persian Gulf War, with free publicity from several newspapers and from all three national TV networks: GIs were shown gulping water from Evian bottles.

---

[7] Freedman and King, "Perrier's Strategy," p. B3.

[8] Alix M. Freedman, "Perrier Finds Mystique Hard to Restore," *The Wall Street Journal*, December 1, 1990, p. B1.

[9] Lori Silver, "Perrier Crowd Not Taking the Waters," *Washington Post*, July 4, 1990, p. 1.

[10] Seth Lubove, "Perched Between Perrier and Tap," *Forbes*, May 14, 1990, p. 120.

ANALYSIS

Was the massive recall overkill, or was it a prudent necessity? Did it show a concerned corporate citizen, or rather a panicked executive? Were consumers impressed with the responsibleness of the company, or were they more focused on its carelessness? These questions are all directed at the basic impact of the recall and the subsequent actions and admissions: Was it to have favorable, neutral, or unfavorable public reactions?

Perrier did *not* have to recall its product. It was a North Carolina county laboratory that first noticed the excessive amounts of benzene in Perrier and reported its findings to the state authorities. The state agriculture and health departments did not believe that a recall was necessary, but they did insist on issuing a health advisory, warning that Perrier should not be consumed until further tests could be made. It was the state's plan to issue the health advisory that was reported to Davis on the afternoon of the critical day, February 9. He announced the recall later that same day.

ISSUE BOX

ARE BOTTLED WATER CLAIMS BUNK?[11]

The bottled water industry came under serious attack in April 1991. As if the Perrier massive recall was not enough, now a congressional panel with wide media coverage accused the Food and Drug Administration of "inexcusably negligent and complacent oversight of the bottled-water industry." Despite its high price, the panel said, bottled water may be less safe than tap water. The panel noted that although consumers pay 300 to 1,200 times more for bottled water than for tap water, 25 percent of all bottled water comes from public drinking water sources. For example:

> Lithia Springs Water Company touts its "world's finest" bottled mineral water as "naturally pure" and recommends its special Love Water as an "invigorator" before bedtime. Yet, it was found to be tainted with bacteria.

> Artisia Waters, Inc., promotes its "100% pure sparkling Texas Natural Water." But it comes from the same underground source that San Antonio uses for its municipal water supply.

Furthermore, the FDA released a list of 22 bottled-water recalls because of contaminants such as kerosene and mold. For the most part, these went unnoticed by consumers, being overshadowed by the Perrier recall.

At issue: Are we being hoodwinked? Debate two positions: (1) the bottled-water industry really is a throwback to the snake-oil charlatans of the last century; and (2) a few unscrupulous or careless bottlers are denigrating the image of the entire industry, an industry that is primarily focused on health and purity.

---

[11] Examples are taken from Bruce Ingersoll, "FDA Finds Bunk in Bottled-Water Claims," *The Wall Street Journal*, April 10, 1991, p. B1.

We are left to wonder: Perhaps a full and complete recall was not needed. Perhaps things could have been worked out entirely satisfactorily with less drastic measures. Given that a recall meant a 3- to 5-month absence from the marketplace, should it not have been the action of last resort?

But let us consider Davis's thought process on that ill-fated afternoon in February. He did not know the source of the problem; he certainly had no reason to suspect that it emanated from the spring in southern France or that it was a worldwide problem. He probably considered it of less magnitude. Perhaps he thought of the total North American recall as a gesture showing the concerned thinking of the management of this product that had developed such a reputation of health and purity and, yes, status. Only with the experience after the fact do we know the error of this decision: that it was to result in a 5-month absence from the hotly competitive market; that it was to result in revelations of far more serious implications than a simple employee error or even a natural occurrence largely beyond the company's control.

So, perhaps Davis's drastic decision was fully justified and prudent. But it turned out to be confounded by circumstances he did not envision.

A lengthy complete absence from the marketplace is a catastrophe of rather monumental proportions—all the more so for a product that is habitually and frequently consumed, in Perrier's case, sometimes several times daily. Such an absence forces even the most loyal customers to establish new patterns of behavior, in this case switching brands. Once behavior becomes habituated, at least for some people, a change back becomes less likely. This is especially true if the competitive offerings are reasonably similar and acceptable. Anything that Perrier could have done to lessen the time away from the market would have been desirable—regardless of expense.

Perhaps the biggest problem for Perrier concerned the false impressions, and even outright deception, that the company had conveyed regarding the purity of its product. Now, in the wake of this total recall and the accompanying publicity, all was laid bare. Company officials in France had to own up that the contamination had occurred "in recent months," and not suddenly and unexpectedly on February 9.

But more than this, under intense pressure from the media to explain what caused the problem, Source Perrier ultimately conceded that its water does not bubble up pure, already carbonated and ready to drink, from its renowned spring in southern France. Instead, contrary to the image that it had spent tens of millions of dollars to promote, the company extracts the water and carbon dioxide gas separately, and must pipe the gas through charcoal filters before combining it mechanically with the water to give the fizz. Without the filters, Perrier water would contain benzene and, even worse, would taste like rotten eggs.

Finally, the public relations efforts were flawed. Source Perrier officials issued a confusing series of public statements and clarifications. Early on, the company tried to maintain the mystique of Perrier by concealing information about the cause of the contamination and by blaming it on a mistake by cleaning personnel in using an oily rag, which could have contained some benzene, to wipe equipment used for bottles to be shipped to the United States. But the spokespeople knew the problem was more fundamental than that.

INFORMATION BOX

IGNORING POSSIBLE NEGATIVE IMAGE CONSEQUENCES

We can identify several factors that induce a firm to ignore public image considerations until sometimes too late. First, a firm's public image often makes a nonspecific impact on company performance. The cause-and-effect relationship of a deteriorating image is virtually impossible to assess, at least until and unless image problems worsen. Image consequences may be downplayed because management is unable to single out the specific profit impact.

Second, an organization's image is not easily and definitively measured. Although some tools are available for tracking public opinion, they tend to be imprecise and of uncertain validity. Consequently, image studies are often spurned or given short shrift relative to more quantitative measures of performance.

Third, it is difficult to determine the effectiveness of image-building efforts. While firms may spend thousands, and even millions, of dollars for institutional and image-building advertising, measures of the effectiveness of such expenditures are inexact and also of questionable validity. For example, a survey may be taken of attitudes of a group of people before and after the image-building campaign is run. Presumably if a few more people profess to be favorably disposed toward the company after the campaign than before, this is an indication of its success. But an executive can question how much this really translates into sales and profits.

Given the near impossibility of measuring the effectiveness of image-enhancing promotion, how do you account for the prevalence of institutional advertising, even among firms that have no image problems?

An aura of nonchalance was conveyed by corporate executives and reported in the press. This was hardly in keeping with a serious problem having to do with the possible safety of customers. Furthermore, Source Perrier relied mainly on media reports to convey information to consumers. Misinformation and rumors are more likely with this approach to public relations than in a more proactive strategy of direct company advertisement and statements.

The reputation of Perrier was on the ropes. And top management seemed unconcerned about the probability of severe public image damage. The above information box discusses the topic of ignoring possible image damage.

WHAT CAN BE LEARNED?

Exiting a market for several months or more poses critical risks, particularly for a habitually consumed product. To allow new habits to be established and new loyalties to be created not only among consumers but also dealers may be impossible to fully recover from. This is especially true if competing products are comparable, and if competitors are aggressive in seizing the proffered opportunity. Since a front-runner is a target anyway, abandoning the battlefield simply invites competitive takeover.

Deception discovered and grudgingly admitted destroys a mystique. No mystique is forever. Consumer preferences change, competitors become more skilled at countering, or perhaps a firm becomes complacent in its quality control or innovative technology. These conditions act to nibble away at a mystique and eventually destroy it. As in the case of Perrier, where long-believed images of a product, its healthfulness and purity, are suddenly revealed to be false—that the advertising was less than candid and was even deceptive—then any mystique comes tumbling down and is unlikely to ever be regained. This scenario can only be avoided if the publicity about the deception or misdeed is not widespread. But, with a popular product such as Perrier, publicity reaches beyond business journals to the popular press. Such is the fate of large, well-known firms.

A price/quality misperception strongly exists. Without doubt, most consumers judge quality by price: the higher the price, the higher the quality. Is a $2.50 liter of Evian better quality than a gallon of tap water costing a fraction of a cent? Perhaps. But is it a hundred times better? And yet many people embrace the misconception that price is the key indicator of quality, and are consequently taken advantage of every day.

An industry catering to health is particularly vulnerable to a few unscrupulous operators. We, the general public, are particularly vulnerable to claims for better health, beauty, and youthfulness. It is human nature to reach out, hopefully, for the false promises that can be made about such important personal concerns. We become gullible in our desire to find ways to change our condition. And so we have become victims of quacks and snake-oil charmers through the ages. Governmental agencies try to exercise strong monitoring in these areas, but budgets are limited, and all claims cannot be investigated. As recent congressional scrutiny has revealed, the bottled-water industry had long been overlooked by governmental watchdogs. Now this is changing, thanks at least partly to the Perrier recall.

Should an organization have a crisis-management team? Perrier did a poor job in its crisis management. Would a more formal organizational unit devoted to this have handled things better, instead of leaving it to top executives unskilled in handling catastrophes? The issue can hardly be answered simply and all-inclusively. Crises occur rarely; and a serious crisis may never happen to a particular organization. A crisis team then would have to be composed of executives and staff who have other primary responsibilities. And their decisions and actions under fire may be no better than a less formal arrangement. For severe crises—and Perrier's was certainly that—top executives who bear the ultimate responsibility therefore have to be the final decision makers. Some will be cooler under fire than others, but this usually cannot be fully ascertained until the crisis occurs. More desirable for most organizations would seem to be contingency plans, with plans formulated for various occurrences, including the worst scenarios. With such action plans drawn up under more normal conditions, better judgments are likely to result.

CONSIDER

Can you think of other learning insights from this case?

QUESTIONS

1. How could the public relations efforts of Perrier have been better handled?
2. Discuss the desirability of Perrier's price-cutting during its comeback.
3. Whom do you see as the primary customers for Perrier? For Evian? For other bottled waters? Are these segments likely to be enduring in their commitment to bottled water?
4. Why do you think the big firms, such as Coca-Cola, PepsiCo, and Coors, have been so slow and unaggressive in entering the bottled-water market?
5. Are we being hoodwinked by bottled-water claims and images?
6. "The success of bottled water in the United States, unlike the situation in many countries of the world where bottled water is often essential for good health, attests to the power of advertising." Evaluate this statement.
7. Is the consumer appeal of bottled water largely attributable to an image developed of sophistication and status?

HANDS-ON EXERCISES

1. Put yourself in the position of Ronald Davis on the afternoon of February 9, 1990. The first report of benzene found by a Carolina lab has just come in. What would you do? Be as specific as you can, and describe the logic behind your decisions.
2. How would you attempt to build up or resurrect the mystique of Perrier after the recall?

TEAM DEBATE EXERCISE

Debate the issue of extreme measures (a massive recall) undertaken in a product safety situation versus more moderate reactions (a modest recall). Consider as many aspects of this issue as you can, and make educated judgments of various probable consumer and governmental reactions.

INVITATION TO RESEARCH

What is the popularity of bottled water today? Has it increased or lessened since these events described? Has Perrier regained market position? Where are the biggest markets for bottled water?

CHAPTER TEN

United Way—A Not-for-Profit Tries to Cope with Image Destruction

The United Way, the preeminent charitable organization in the United States, celebrated its 100-year anniversary in 1987. It had evolved from local community chests, and its strategy for fund raising had proven highly effective: funding local charities through payroll deductions. The good it did seemed unassailable.

Abruptly in 1992, the image that United Way had created was jolted by revelations from investigative reporters of free spending and other questionable deeds of its greatest builder and president, William Aramony. A major point of public concern was Aramony's salary and uncontrolled perks in a lifestyle that seemed inappropriate for the head of a charitable organization that depended mostly on contributions from working people.

We are left to question the callousness and lack of concern with the public image of such a major charitable and not-for-profit entity. After all, unlike business firms that offer products or services to potential customers, charitable organizations depend on contributions that people give freely out of a desire to help society, with no tangible personal benefits. An image of high integrity and honest dealings without any semblance of corruption or privilege would seem essential for such organizations.

THE STATURE AND ACCOMPLISHMENTS OF THE UNITED WAY

For its 100-year anniversary, then President Ronald Reagan summed up what the United Way stood for (see the following page).

Organizing the United Way as the umbrella charity to fund other local charities through payroll deductions established a most effective means of fund-raising. As a not-for-profit marketer, the United Way became the recipient of 90 percent of all charitable donations. Employers sometimes used extreme pressure to achieve 100 percent participation of employees, which qualified companies for organizational

December 10, 1986

United Way Centennial, 1887–1987
By The President Of The United States Of America
A Proclamation

Since earliest times, we Americans have joined together to help each other and to strengthen our communities. Our deep-roots spirit of caring, of neighbor helping neighbor, has become an American trademark—and an American way of life. Over the years, our generous and inventive people have created an ingenious network of voluntary organizations to help give help where help is needed.

United Way gives that help very well indeed, and truly exemplifies our spirit of voluntarism. United Way has been a helping force in America right from the first community-wide fund-raising campaign in Denver, Colorado, in 1887. Today, more than 2,200 local United Ways across the land raise funds for more than 37,000 voluntary groups that assist millions of people.

The United Way of caring allows volunteers from all walks of life to effectively meet critical needs and solve community problems. At the centennial of the founding of this indispensable voluntary group, it is most fitting that we Americans recognize and commend all the good United Way has done and continues to do.

The congress, by Public Law 99–612, has expressed gratitude to United Way, congratulated it, and applauded and encouraged its fine work and its goals.

NOW, THEREFORE, I, RONALD REAGAN, President of the United States of America, by virtue of the authority vested in me by the Constitution and laws of the United States, do hereby proclaim heartfelt thanks to a century of Americans who have shaped and supported United Way, and encourage the continuation of its efforts.

IN WITNESS WHEREOF, I have hereunto set my hand this tenth day of December, in the year of our Lord nineteen hundred and eighty-six, and of the independence of the United States of America the two hundred and eleventh.

Ronald Reagan

bonuses. Business organizations achieved further cooperation by involving their executives as leaders of annual campaigns, amid widespread publicity. It would consequently cause such an executive acute loss of face if his or her own organization did not go "over the top" in meeting campaign goals. A local United Way executive admitted that "if participation is 100 percent, it means someone has been coerced."[1]

---

[1] Susan Garland, "Keeping a Sharper Eye on Those Who Pass the Hat," *Business Week*, March 16, 1992, p. 39.

For many years, except for some tight-lipped gripes of corporate employees, the organization moved smoothly along, generally increasing local contributions every year, although the needs for charitable contributions invariably increased all the more.

The national organization, United Way of America (UWA), is a separate corporation and has no direct control over the approximately 2,200 local United Ways. But most of the locals voluntarily contributed 1 cent on the dollar of all funds they collected. In return the national organization provided training and promoted local United Way agencies through advertising and other marketing efforts.

Much of the success of the United Way movement in becoming the largest and most respected charity in the United States was due to the 22 years of William Aramony's leadership of the national organization. When he first took over, the United Ways were not operating under a common name. He built a nationwide network of agencies, all operating under the same name and all using the same logo of outstretched hands, which became nationally recognized as the symbol of charitable giving. Unfortunately, in 1992 an expose of Aramony's lavish lifestyle, as well as other questionable dealings, led to his downfall and burdened local United Ways with serious difficulties in fund-raising.

WILLIAM ARAMONY

During Aramony's tenure, United Way contributions increased from $787 million in 1970 to $3 billion in 1990. He increased his headquarters budget from less than $3 million to $29 million in 1991. Of this, $24 million came from the local United Ways, with the rest coming from corporate grants, investment income, and consulting.[2] He built up the headquarters staff to 275 employees. Figure 10.1 shows the organizational chart as of 1987.

Aramony moved comfortably among the most influential people in our society. He attracted a prestigious board of governors, many of these top executives from America's largest corporations, with only 3 of the 37 from not-for-profit organizations. The board was chaired by John Akers, chairman and CEO of IBM. Other board members included Edward A. Brennan, CEO of Sears; James D. Robinson III, CEO of American Express; and Paul J. Tagliabue, commissioner of the National Football League. The presence on the board of such top executives brought prestige to United Way and spurred contributions from some of the largest and most visible organizations in the United States.

Aramony was the highest paid executive in the charity field. In 1992 his compensation package was $463,000—nearly double that of the next highest paid executive in the industry, Dudley H. Hafner of the American Heart Association.[3] The board fully supported Aramony, regularly giving him 6 percent annual raises.[4]

---

[2] Charles E. Shepard, "Perks, Privileges and Power in a Nonprofit World," *Washington Post*, February 16, 1992, p. A38.

[3] Shepard, p. A38; and Charles E. Shepard, "United Way of America President is Urged to Resign," *Washington Post*, February 27, 1992, p. A1.

[4] Joseph Finder, "Charity Case," *New Republic*, May 4, 1992, p. 11.

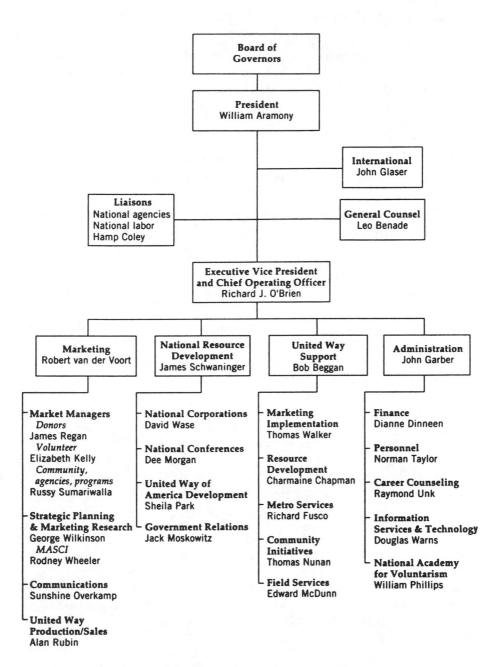

Figure 10.1. Organizational chart, United Way of America, 1987.
Source: E.L. Brilliant, "Appendix B," *United Way: Dilemmas of Organized Charity* (New York: Columbia University Press, 1990) p. 272.

Investigative Disclosures

The *Washington Post* began investigating Aramony's tenure as president of United Way of America in 1991, raising questions about his high salary, travel habits, possible cronyism, and dubious relations with five spinoff companies. In February 1992 it released the following information of Aramony's expense charges:[5]

- Aramony had charged $92,265 in limousine expenses to the charity during the previous five years.
- He had charged $40,762 on airfare for the supersonic Concorde.
- He had charged more than $72,000 on international airfare, which included first class flights for himself, his wife, and others.
- He had charged thousands more for personal trips, gifts, and luxuries.
- He had made 29 trips to Las Vegas between 1988 and 1991.
- He had expensed 49 journeys to Gainesville, Florida, the home of his daughter and a woman with whom he had had a relationship.
- He had allegedly approved a $2 million loan to a firm run by his chief financial officer.
- He had approved the diversion of donors' money to questionable spin-off organizations run by long-time aides and had provided benefits to family members as well.
- He had passed tens of thousands of dollars in consulting contracts from the UWA to friends and associates.

United Way of America's corporate policy prohibited the hiring of family members within the actual organization, but Aramony skirted the direct violation by hiring friends and relatives as consultants within the spin-off companies. The United Way paid hundreds of thousands of dollars in consulting fees, for example, to two aides in vaguely documented and even undocumented business transactions.

The use of spin-off companies provided flexible maneuvering. One of the spin-off companies Aramony created to provide travel and bulk purchasing for United Way chapters purchased a $430,000 condominium in Manhattan and a $125,000 apartment in Coral Gables, Florida, for use by Aramony. Another of the spin-off companies hired Aramony's son, Robert Aramony, as its president. Loans and money transfers between the spin-off companies and the national organization raised questions. No records showed that the board members had been given the opportunity to approve such loans and transfers.[6]

---

[5] Shepard, "Perks, Privileges and Power"; Shepard, "Urged to Resign"; Kathleen Teltsch, "United Way Awaits Inquiry on its President's Practices," *New York Times*, February 24, 1992, p. A12 (L); Charles E. Shepard, "United Way Report Criticizes Ex-Leader's Lavish Lifestyle," *Washington Post*, April 4, 1992, p. A1.

[6] Shepard, "Perks, Privileges and Power," A38.

CONSEQUENCES

When the information about Aramony's salary and expenses became public, reaction was severe. Stanley C. Gault, CEO of Goodyear Tire & Rubber Co., asked, "Where was the board? The outside auditors?"[7] Robert O. Bothwell, executive director of the National Committee for Responsive Philanthropy, said, "I think it is obscene that he is making that kind of salary and asking people who are making $10,000 a year to give 5 percent of their income."[8] At this point, let us examine the issue of executive compensation: Are many executives overpaid? See the following issue box.

ISSUE BOX

EXECUTIVE COMPENSATION: IS IT TOO MUCH?

A controversy is mounting over multimillion-dollar annual compensations of corporate executives. For example, in 1992 the average annual pay of CEOs was $3,842,247; the 20 highest paid ranged from over $11 million to a mind-boggling $127 million (for Thomas F. Frist, Jr., of Hospital Corporation of America).[9]

Activist shareholders, including some large mutual and pension funds, began protesting pay practices, especially for top executives of those firms that were not even doing well. New disclosure rules imposed in 1993 by the Securities & Exchange Commission (SEC) spotlighted questionable executive-pay practices. In the past complacent boards, themselves well paid and often closely aligned with the top executives of the organizations, condoned liberal compensations. Now this may be changing. Still, the major argument supporting high executive compensations is that compared to some entertainers' and athletes', their salaries are modest. And are not their responsibilities far greater than those of any entertainer or athlete?

In light of the for-profit executive compensations, Aramony's salary was modest. And results were on his side: He made $369,000 in basic salary while raising $3 billion; Lee Iacocca, on the other hand, made $3 million while Chrysler lost $795 million. Where is the justice?

Undoubtedly as head of a large for-profit corporation Aramony could have earned several zeros more in compensation and perks, with no raised eyebrows. But is the situation different for a not-for-profit organization? Especially when revenues are derived from donations of millions of people of modest means? This is a real controversy. On one side, shouldn't a charity be willing to pay for the professional competence to run the organization as effectively as possible? But how do revelations of high compensation affect the public image and fund-raising marketing of such not-for-profit organizations?

What is your position regarding Aramony's compensation and perks, relative to the many times greater compensations of for-profit executives?

---

[7] Susan Garland, p. 39.

[8] Felicity Barringer, "United Way Head Is Forced Out In a Furor Over His Lavish Style," *New York Times*, February 28, 1992, p. A1.

[9] John A. Byrne, "Executive Pay: The Party Ain't Over Yet," *Business Week*, April 26, 1993, pp. 56–64.

As a major consequence of the scandal, some United Way locals withheld their funds, at least pending a thorough investigation of the allegations. John Akers, chairman of the board, noted that by March 7, 1992, dues payments were running 20 percent behind those of the previous year, and he admitted, "I don't think this process that the United Way of America is going through, or Mr. Aramony is going through, is a process that's bestowing a lot of honor."[10]

In addition to the decrease in dues payments, UWA was in danger of having its not-for-profit status revoked by the Internal Revenue Service due to the relationship of loans made to the spin-off companies. For example, it loaned $2 million to a spin-off corporation of which UWA's chief financial officer was a director—a violation of not-for-profit corporate law. UWA also guaranteed a bank loan taken out by one of the spin-offs, another violation of not-for-profit corporate law.[11]

The adverse publicity benefitted competing charities, such as Earth Share, an environmental group. United Way, at one time the only major organization to receive contributions through payroll deductions, now found itself losing market share to other charities able to garner contributions in the same manner. All the building that William Aramony had done for the United Way as the primary player in the American charitable industry was now in danger of disintegration owing to his uncontrolled excesses.

On February 28, amid mounting pressure from local chapters threatening to withhold their annual dues, Aramony resigned. In August 1992 the United Way board of directors hired Elaine Chao as Peace Corps director to replace Aramony.

ELAINE CHAO

Chao's story is one of great achievement for one only 39 years old. She is the oldest of six daughters in a family that came to California from Taiwan when Elaine was 8 years old. She did not then know a word of English. Through hard work, the family prospered. "Despite the difficulties ... we had tremendous optimism in the basic goodness of this country, that people are decent here, that we would be given a fair opportunity to demonstrate our abilities," she told an interviewer.[12] Chao's parents instilled in their six daughters the conviction that they could do anything they set their minds to, and the daughters all went to prestigious universities.

Elaine Chao earned an economics degree from Mount Holyoke in 1975, then went on for a Harvard MBA. She was a White House fellow, an international banker, chair of the Federal Maritime Commission, deputy secretary of the U.S. Transportation Department, and director of the Peace Corps before accepting the presidency of the United Way of America.

Chao's salary was $195,000, less than one-half that of Aramony. She cut budgets and staffs: no transatlantic flights on the Concorde, no limousine service, no plush

---

[10] Felicity Barringer, "United Way Head Tries to Restore Trust," *New York Times*, March 7, 1992, p. 8L.

[11] Shepard, "Perks, Privileges and Power," p. A38; Charles E. Shepard, "United Way Chief Says He Will Retire," *Washington Post*, February 28, 1992, p. A1.

[12] "United Way Chief Dedicated," *Cleveland Plain Dealer*, March 28, 1993, p. 24-A.f.

condominiums. She expanded the board of governors to include more local representatives, and she established committees on ethics and finance. Still, she had no illusions about her job: "Trust and confidence once damaged will take a great deal of effort and time to heal."[13] The following information box discusses the particular importance of the public image for not-for-profit agencies.

A Local United Way's Concerns

In April 1993, for the second time in a year, United Way of Greater Lorain County (Ohio) withdrew from the United Way of America. The board of the local chapter was

---

INFORMATION BOX

PUBLIC IMAGE FOR NOT-FOR-PROFIT ORGANIZATIONS

Product-oriented firms ought to be concerned and protective of their public image; even more so not-for-profit organizations such as schools, police departments, hospitals, politicians, and most of all, charitable organizations, should be concerned. Let us consider here the importance of public image for representative not-for-profits.

Large city police departments often have a poor image among important segments of the population. The need to improve this image is hardly less important than for a manufacturer faced with a deteriorating brand image. A police department can develop a "marketing" campaign to win friends; examples of possible activities aimed at creating a better image are promoting tours and open houses of police stations, crime laboratories, police lineups, and cells; speaking at schools; and sponsoring recreation projects, such as a day at the ballpark for youngsters.

Public school systems, faced with taxpayers' revolts against mounting costs and image damage owing to teacher strikes, need conscious effort to improve their image in order to obtain more public support and funds.

Many nonbusiness organizations and institutions, such as hospitals, governmental bodies, even labor unions, have grown self-serving, dominated by a bureaucratic mentality so that perfunctory and callous treatment is the rule and the image is in the pits. Improvement of the image can come only through a greater emphasis on satisfying the public's needs.

Not-for-profits are particularly vulnerable to public image problems because they may depend solely on voluntary support. The need to be untainted by any scandal becomes crucial. In particular, great care should be exerted that contributions are being spent wisely and equitably, that overhead costs are kept reasonable, and that no opportunities exist for fraud and other misdeeds. The threat of investigative reporting must be feared and guarded against.

How can a not-for-profit organization be absolutely assured that moneys are not being misspent and that there are no ripoffs?

---

[13] Ibid.

still concerned about the financial stability and accountability of the national agency. In particular, it was concerned about the retirement settlement for Aramony. A significant "golden parachute" retirement package was being negotiated by the national board and Aramony; it was in the neighborhood of $4 million. Learning of this triggered the decision to again withdraw from UWA.

There were other reasons as well for this decision. The national agency was falling far short of its projected budget, as only 890 of the 1,400 affiliates that had paid membership dues two years before were still paying. Roy Church, president of the Lorain Agency, explained their decision: "Since February … it has become clear that United Way of America's financial stability and ability to assist locals has been put in question. The benefit of being a United Way of America member isn't there at this time for Lorain's United Way."[14]

Elaine Chao's task of resurrecting United Way of America would not be easy.

Chao's Remedial Efforts

As it turned out, Elaine Chao did a fine job. She was hired to restore public faith and confidence in the United Way. And this she did. She oversaw formation of new oversight committees and established policies that would insure "that United Way of America will be accountable and responsive to local United Ways."[15] The board of governors was expanded from 30 to 45 members and included more local representatives.

On May 20, 1996, she announced her resignation effective September 1. "My job is complete," she said.[16] Her plans were to lecture, join a Washington think tank, volunteer for Bob Dole's presidential campaign and work for the re-election of her husband, Sen. Mitch McConnell (R., Ky.).

Still, had United Way recovered completely from the scandal? The enduring aftereffects say not completely. For the nation's leading chapter, Cleveland, donations have slipped considerably from the 1989–90 campaign that raised $52 million. Total contributions in 1995 were only $40 million, and more than $1 million below the goal set at the beginning of the campaign.[17]

The stigma of an abuse to the public image can be enduring. This may especially be true of public service organizations that derive their revenues from voluntary contributions.

See the following information box for a discussion of a related example of nonprofit callousness to its parties.

---

[14] Karen Henderson, "Lorain Agency Cuts Ties with National United Way," *Cleveland Plain Dealer*, April 16, 1993, p. 7C.

[15] Matthew Tungate, "United Way Chief Hails Local Efforts," *Cleveland Plain Dealer*, May 25, 1996, p. 2-B.

[16] "Head of United Way to Leave Her Post Saying Job Is Done," *The Wall Street Journal*, May 20, 1996, p. B8.

[17] Michael K. McIntyre, "United Way Changing Fund Drive Strategies," *Cleveland Plain Dealer*, September 1, 1996, p. 4-B.

INFORMATION BOX

ANOTHER CONTROVERSY: GIRL SCOUTS AND THEIR COOKIES

The main funding source for the nation's 2.6 million Girl Scouts is the annual cookie sale, estimated to generate $400 million in revenue. The practice goes back some 70 years, although in the 1920s the girls sold homemade cookies. Now each regional council negotiates with one or two bakeries that produce the cookies; sets the price per box, which ranges from $2 to $3; and divides the proceeds as it sees fit. Typically, the Girl Scout troops get 10 to 15 percent, the council takes more than 50 percent, and the rest goes to the manufacturer.[18]

Criticisms have emerged and received public attention regarding the dictatorial handling of these funds by the councils. There are 332 regional councils in the United States, each having an office and a paid staff overseen by a volunteer board. Some councils have dozens of employees, with most serving mainly as policy enforcers and supervisors. At the troop level, volunteer leaders, often women with daughters in the troop, guide their units in the true tradition of scouting, giving their time tirelessly. For the cookie drives, the girls are an unpaid sales force—child labor, as critics assail—that supports a huge bureaucratic structure. Little of the cookie revenue comes back to the local troops.

The bureaucracy does not tolerate dissent well. *The Wall Street Journal* cites the case of a West Haven, Connecticut, troop leader, Beth Denton, who protested both the way the Connecticut Trails council apportioned revenue and the $1.6 million in salaries and benefits paid to 42 council employees. After she complained to the state attorney general, the council dismissed her as leader.[19]

Admittedly, the individual salaries in the bureaucracy were not high by corporate standards or even by not-for-profit standards. Council administrators' salaries ranged up to about $90,000. Perhaps more disturbing was that volunteer leaders saw no annual financial statements of their councils' expenditures and activities.[20]

Evaluate the council's position that annual financial records of their council's activities should be entirely confidential and limited to full-time staff.

---

[18] Ellen Graham, "Sprawling Bureaucracy Eats Up Most Profits of Girl Scout Cookies," *The Wall Street Journal,* May 13, 1992, p. A1.

[19] Graham, p. A4.

[20] Ibid.

ANALYSIS

The lack of accountability to the donating public was a major contributor to UWA's problems. Such a loosely run operation, with no one to approve or halt administrators' actions, encouraged questionable practices. It also opened the way for great shock and criticism, come the revelation. The fact that voluntary donations were the

ISSUE BOX

WHAT SHOULD BE THE ROLE OF THE BOARD OF DIRECTORS?

In the past, most boards of directors have tended to be rubber stamps, closely allied with top executives and even composed mostly of corporate officials. In some organizations today this is changing, mostly in response to criticism of board tendencies always to support the status quo and to perpetuate the "establishment."

More and more, opinion is shifting to the idea that boards must assume a more activist role:

> The board can no longer play a passive role in corporate governance. Today, more than ever, the board must assume ... a role that is protective of shareholder rights, sensitive to communities in which the company operates, responsive to the needs of company vendors and customers, and fair to its employees.[21]

Incentives for more active boards have been the increasing risks of liability for board decisions, as well as liability insurance costs. Although the board of directors has long been seen as responsible for establishing corporate objectives, developing broad policies, and selecting top executives, this is no longer viewed as sufficient. Boards must also review management's performance to ensure that the company is well run and that stockholders' interests are furthered. And, today, they must ensure that society's best interests are not disregarded. All of this translates into an active concern for the organization's public image or reputation.

But the issue remains: To whom should the board owe its greatest allegiance—the entrenched bureaucracy or the external publics? Without having board members representative of the many special interests affected by the organization, board members may be inclined to support the interests of the establishment.

Do you think a more representative and active board will prevent a similar scenario for United Way in the future? Why or why not?

---

[21] Lester B. Korn and Richard M. Ferry, *Board of Directors Thirteenth Annual Study* (New York: Korn/Ferry International, February 1986), pp. 1–2.

principal source of revenues made the lack of accountability all the more crucial. The situation was similar for the Girl Scouts. In a for-profit organization, lack of accountability primarily affects stockholders; for a major charitable organization, it affects millions of contributors, who see their money and commitment being squandered.

Where full disclosure and a system of checks and balances is lacking, two consequences tend to prevail, neither one desirable nor totally acceptable. The worst case scenario is outright "white-collar theft," when the unscrupulous see it as an opportunity for personal gain. The absence of sufficient controls and accountability can make even normally honest persons succumb to temptation. Second, insufficient controls tend to promote a mindset of arrogance and allow people to play fast and loose with the system. Aramony seemed to fall into this mindset, with his spending extravagances, cronyism, and other conflict-of-interest activities. (At least some of the Girl Scout Councils, too, perceived themselves as aloof from the dedicated volunteer troop leaders, tolerating no criticism or questioning, dictating and enforcing all policies without consultation or participation, and allowing no scrutiny of their own operation.)

The UWA theoretically had an overseer: the board, similar to the board of directors of business corporations. But when such boards act as rubber stamps, where they are solidly in the camp of the chief executives, they are not really exercising control. This appeared to be the case with United Way of America during the "reign" of Aramony; similarly with the regional councils of the Girl Scouts, many of the volunteer boards appear to have exercised little or no oversight.

Certainly such a situation of a board's failure to fulfill its responsibility is not unique to not-for-profits. Corporate boards have often been notorious for promoting the interests of the incumbent executives. Although this situation is changing today, it still prevails. See the preceding issue box for a discussion of the role of boards of directors.

UPDATE

William Aramony was convicted of defrauding the United Way out of $1 million. He was sentenced to seven years in prison for using the charity's money to finance a lavish lifestyle.

Despite this, a federal judge ruled in late 1998 that the charity must pay its former president more than $2 million in retirement benefits. "A felon, no matter how despised, does not lose his right to enforce a contract," U.S. District Judge Shira Scheindlin in New York ruled.[22]

WHAT CAN BE LEARNED?

Beware the arrogant mindset. A leader's mindset that he or she is so superior to subordinates—and even to concerned outsiders—that other opinions are unacceptable is a formula for disaster, both for an organization and for a society. It promotes dictatorship, intolerance of contrary opinions, and an attitude that "we need answer to no one." The consequences are such as we have seen with William Aramony: moving over the edge of what is deemed by most as acceptable and ethical conduct, assuming the role of the final judge who brooks no questions or criticisms. The absence of real or imagined controls or reviews seems to bring out the worst in humans. We seem to need periodic scrutiny to avoid the trap of arrogant decision making devoid of responsiveness to other concerns. The Girl

---

[22] Reported in *Cleveland Plain Dealer,* October 25, 1998, p. 24–A.

Scout bureaucracy's dealings with its volunteers corroborates the inclination toward arrogance and dictatorship in the absence of objective oversight.

Checks and balances are even more important in not-for-profit and governmental bodies than in corporate entities. For-profit organizations have "bottom-line" performance (i.e., profit and loss statistics) as the ultimate control and standard. Not-for-profit and governmental organizations do not have this control, so they have no ultimate measure of their effectiveness.

Consequently, not-for-profit organizations should be subject to the utmost scrutiny of objective outsiders. Otherwise, abuses seem to be encouraged and perpetuated. Often these not-for-profit organizations are sheltered from competition, which protects them from demands for greater efficiency. Thus, without objective scrutiny, not-for-profits have a tendency to get out of hand, to be run as little dynasties unencumbered by the constraints that face most businesses. Fortunately, investigative reports and increased litigation by allegedly abused parties today act as needed controls for such organizations. In view of the revelations of investigative reporters, we are left to wonder how many other abusive and reprehensible activities have not yet been detected.

Marketing of not-for-profits depends on trust and is particularly vulnerable to bad press. Not-for-profits depend on donations for the bulk of their revenues. They depend on people to give without receiving anything tangible in return (unlike most businesses). And the givers must have trust in the particular organization, trust that the contributions will be well spent, that beneficiaries will receive the maximum benefit, that administrative costs will be held low. Consequently, when publicity surfaces that causes such trust to be questioned, the impact can be devastating. Contributions can quickly dry up or be shunted to other charities.

With governmental bodies, of course, their perpetuation is hardly at stake with bad publicity. However, administrators can be recalled, impeached, or not reelected.

CONSIDER

Can you add to these learning insights?

QUESTIONS

1. How do you feel, as a potential or actual giver to United Way campaigns, about Aramony's "high living"? Would these allegations affect your gift giving? Why or why not?

2. What prescriptions do you have for thwarting arrogance in not-for-profit and/or governmental organizations? Be as specific as you can, and support your recommendations.

3. How do you personally feel about the coercion that some organizations exert for their employees to contribute substantially to the United Way? What implications, if any, emerge from your attitudes about this?

4. Given the information supplied about the dictatorial relationships between Girl Scout councils and the local volunteers—and recognizing that such anecdotal information may not be truly representative—what do you see as the pros and cons of Girl Scout cookie drives? On balance, is this marketing fund-raising effort still desirable, or might other alternatives be better?

5. "Since there is no bottom-line evaluation for performance, not-for-profits have no incentives to control costs and prudently evaluate expenditures." Discuss.

6. How would you feel, as a large contributor to a charity, if you learned that it spent $10 million for advertising? Discuss your rationale for this attitude.

7. Do you think the UWA's action after Aramony left was the best way to salvage the public image? Why or why not? What else might have been done?

HANDS-ON EXERCISES

1. You are an advisor to Elaine Chao, who has taken over the scandal-ridden United Way. What advice do you give her for as quickly as possible restoring the confidence of the American public in the integrity and worthiness of this preeminent national charity organization?

2. You are a member of the board of governors of United Way. Allegations have surfaced about the lavish lifestyle of the highly regarded Aramony. Most of the board members, being corporate executives, see nothing at all wrong with his perks and privileges. You, however, feel otherwise. How do you convince the other board members of the error of condoning Aramony's activities? Be as persuasive as you can in supporting your position.

3. You are the parent of a Girl Scout, who has assiduously worked to sell hundreds of boxes of cookies. You now realize that her efforts and that of thousands of other girls are primarily supporting a bloated central and regional bureaucracy, and not the local troops. You feel strongly that this situation is an unacceptable use of child labor. Describe your proposed efforts to institute change.

TEAM DEBATE EXERCISE

Debate this issue: no not-for-profit organization can ever attain the efficiency of a business firm that always has the bottom line to be concerned about.

INVITATION TO RESEARCH

What is the situation with the United Way today? Are local agencies contributing to the national? Have donations matched or exceeded previous levels? Has Elaine Chao restored public confidence?

CHAPTER ELEVEN

Johnson & Johnson—
The Classic Masterpiece for
Handling a Major Crisis

*I*n one of the greatest examples of superb crisis management, James Burke, CEO of Johnson & Johnson, in 1982 handled a catastrophe that involved loss of life in the criminal and deadly contamination of its flagship product, Tylenol. The company exhibited what has become a model for corporate responsibility to customers, regardless of costs.

Yet in a later day, the company showed a lapse in its customer concern, first with alleged price gouging for one of its cancer drugs, then in not disclosing the risk of liver damage from overusing Tylenol.

PRELUDE

It was September 30, 1982. On the fifth floor of the Johnson & Johnson (J&J) headquarters in New Brunswick, New Jersey, Chairman James E. Burke was having a quiet meeting with President David R. Clair. The two liked to hold such informal meetings every two months to talk over important but non-pressing matters that they usually did not get around to in the normal course of events. That day both men had reason to feel good, for J&J's sales and earnings were up sharply and the trend of business could hardly have been more promising. They even had time to dwell on some nonbusiness matters that sunny September morning.

Their complacency and self-satisfaction did not last long. Arthur Quill, a member of the executive committee, burst into the meeting. Consternation and anguish flooded the room as he brought word of cyanide deaths in Chicago that were connected to J&J's most important and profitable product, Extra-Strength Tylenol capsules.

THE COMPANY

Johnson & Johnson manufactures and markets a broad range of health care products in many countries of the world. Table 11.1 shows the various categories of products and their percent of total corporate sales. In 1981 J&J was number 68 on the *Fortune*

TABLE 11.1.   Contribution to Total Johnson & Johnson Sales of Product Categories, 1983

Product Classification	Sales (millions)	Percent of Total Company Sales
Surgical and First-Aid Supplies	$1,268	21%
Pharmaceuticals	1,200	20
Sanitary Napkins and Tampons	933	16
Baby Products	555	9
Diagnostic Equipment	518	9
Tylenol and Variants	460	8
Other (includes hospital supplies, dental products, contraceptives)	1,039	17
Total	$5,973	100%

Source: "After Its Recovery, New Headaches for Tylenol," *Business Week*, May 14, 1984, p. 137.

500 list of the largest industrial companies in the United States, and it had sales of $5.4 billion. It was organized into four industry categories: professional, pharmaceutical, industrial, and consumer. The professional division included products such as ligatures, sutures, surgical dressings, and other surgery-related items. The pharmaceutical division included prescription drugs, and the industrial area included textile products, industrial tapes, and fine chemicals.

The largest division was the consumer division, consisting of toiletries and hygienic products such as baby care items, first aid products, and nonprescription drugs. These products were marketed primarily to the general public and distributed through wholesalers and directly to independent and chain retail outlets.

Through the years, J&J had assiduously worked to cultivate an image of responsibility and trust. Its products were associated with gentleness and safety—for all customers, from babies to the elderly. The corporate sense of responsibility fully covered the products and actions of any firms that it acquired, such as McNeil Laboratories.

THE PRODUCT

The success of Tylenol, an acetaminophen-based analgesic, in the late 1970s and early 1980s had been sensational. It had been introduced in 1955 by McNeil Laboratories as an alternative drug to aspirin, one that avoided aspirin's side effects. In 1959 Johnson & Johnson had acquired McNeil Laboratories, and the company ran it as an independent subsidiary.

By 1974 Tylenol sales had grown to $50 million at retail, primarily achieved through heavy advertising to physicians. A national consumer advertising campaign, instituted in 1976, proved very effective. By 1979 Tylenol had become the largest selling health and beauty aid in drug and food mass merchandising, breaking the 18-year domination of Procter & Gamble's Crest toothpaste. By 1982 Tylenol had captured 35.3 percent of the over-the-counter analgesic market. This was more than the market shares of Bayer, Bufferin and Anacin combined. Table 11.2 shows the competitive positions of Tylenol and its principal competitors in this analgesic market. Total sales of all Tylenol products went from $115 million in 1976 to $350 million in 1982, a whopping 204 percent increase in a highly competitive market. As such, Tylenol accounted for 7 percent of all J&J sales. More important, it contributed 17 percent of all profits.

Then catastrophe struck.

THE CRISIS

On a Wednesday morning in late September 1982, Adam Janus had a minor chest pain, so he purchased a bottle of Extra-Strength Tylenol capsules. He took one capsule and was dead by midafternoon. Later that same day, Stanley Janus and his wife also took capsules from the same bottle—both were dead by Friday afternoon. By the weekend four more Chicago-area residents had died under similar circumstances. The cause of death was cyanide, a deadly poison that can kill within 15 minutes by disrupting the blood's ability to carry oxygen through the body, thereby affecting the heart, lungs, and brain. The cyanide had been used to contaminate Extra-Strength Tylenol capsules. Dr. Thomas Kim, chief of the critical care unit of Northwest Community Hospital in Arlington Heights, Illinois, noted, "The victims never had a chance. Death was certain within minutes."[1]

Medical examiners retrieved bottles from the victims' homes and found another 10 capsules laced with cyanide. In each case the red half of the capsule was discolored and slightly swollen, and its usual dry white powder had been replaced with a gray substance that had an almond odor. One of the capsules had 65 mg of cyanide—a lethal dose is considered to be 50 mg.

The McNeil executives learned of the poisonings from reporters calling for comment about the tragedy—calls came from all the media, and then from pharmacies, doctors, hospitals, poison control centers, and hundreds of panicky consumers.

TABLE 11.2. **Market Shares of Major Brands—Over-the-Counter Analgesic Market, 1981**

Brand	Percent of Market
Tylenol	35.3
Anacin	13
Bayer	11
Excedrin	10.1
Bufferin	9

Source: "A Death Blow for Tylenol?" *Business Week,* October 18, 1982, p. 151.

[1] Susan Tifft, "Poison Madness in the Midwest," *Time,* October 11, 1982, p. 18.

McNeil quickly gathered information on the victims, causes of deaths, lot numbers on the poisoned Tylenol bottles, outlets where they had been purchased, dates when they had been manufactured, and the route they had taken through the distribution system.

After the deaths were linked to Tylenol, one of the biggest consumer alerts ever took place. Johnson & Johnson recalled batches and advised consumers not to take any Extra-Strength Tylenol capsules until the mystery had been solved. Drugstores and supermarkets across the country pulled Tylenol products from their shelves; it soon became virtually impossible to obtain Tylenol anywhere.

Those tracking down the mysterious contamination quickly determined that the poisoning did not occur in manufacturing, either intentionally or accidentally. The poisoned capsules had come from lots manufactured at both McNeil plants. Therefore, the tampering had to have happened in Chicago, since poisoning at both plants at the same time would have been almost impossible. The FDA suspected that someone unconnected with the manufacturer had bought the Tylenol over the counter, inserted cyanide in some capsules, then returned the bottles to the stores. Otherwise, the contamination would have been widespread, and not only in the Chicago area.

At this point, Johnson & Johnson was virtually cleared of any wrong-doing, but the company was stuck with having one of its major products publicly associated with poison and death, no matter how innocent it was. Perhaps the task of coping with the devastating impact of the tragedy would have been easier for Johnson & Johnson if the perpetrator were conclusively identified and caught. This was not to be, despite a special task force of 100 FBI agents and Illinois investigators who chased down more than 2,000 leads and filed 57 volumes of reports.[2]

COMPANY REACTION

Johnson & Johnson decided to elevate the management of the crisis to the corporate level and a game plan developed that company executives hoped would ensure eventual recovery. The game plan consisted of three phases: Phase I was to figure out what had actually happened; Phase II was to assess and contain the damage; and Phase III was to try to get Tylenol back into the market.

The company that had always tried to keep a low profile now turned to the media to provide it with the most accurate and current information, as well as to help it prevent a panic. Twenty-five public relations specialists were recruited from Johnson & Johnson's other divisions to help McNeil's regular staff of 15. Advertising was suspended at first. All Tylenol capsules were recalled—31 million bottles with a retail value of more than $100 million. Through advertisements promising to exchange tablets for capsules, through 500,000 telegrams to doctors, hospitals, and distributors, and through statements to the media, J&J hoped to demystify the situation.

With proof that the tampering had not occurred in the manufacturing process, the company moved into Phase II. Financially it experienced immediate losses amounting to over $100 million, the bulk coming from the expense of buying unused Tylenol bot-

[2] "Tylenol Comes Back as Case Grows Cold," *Newsweek*, April 25, 1983, p. 16.

tles from retailers and consumers and shipping them to disposal points. The cost of sending the telegrams was estimated at $500,000, and the costs associated with expected product liability suits were expected to run in the millions.

Of more concern to the management was the impact of the poisoning on the brand itself. Many predicted that Tylenol as a brand could no longer survive. Some suggested that Johnson & Johnson reintroduce the product under a new name to give it a fresh start and thus rid itself of the devastated brand image.

Surveys conducted by Johnson & Johnson about a month after the poisonings seemed to buttress the death of Tylenol as a brand name. In one survey 94 percent of the consumers were aware that Tylenol was involved with the poisonings. Although 87 percent of these respondents realized that the maker of Tylenol was not to blame for the deaths, 61 percent said they were not likely to buy Tylenol in the future. Even worse, 50 percent of the consumers said they would not use the Tylenol tablets either. The only promising result from the research was that 49 percent of the *frequent* users answered that they would eventually use Tylenol.[3]

The company found itself in a real dilemma. It wanted so much to keep the Tylenol name; after all, the acceptance had been developed by years of advertising. Now, was it all to be destroyed in a few days of adversity? On the one hand, if J&J brought Tylenol back too soon, before the hysteria had subsided, the product could die on the shelves. On the other hand, if the company waited too long to bring the product back, competitors might well gain an unassailable market share lead. The marketing research results were not entirely acceptable to Johnson & Johnson executives. One manager expressed the company's doubts: "The problem with consumer research is that it reflects attitudes and not behavior. The best way to know what consumers are really going to do is put the product back on the shelves and let them vote with their hands."[4] But what was the right timing?

Johnson & Johnson decided to rebuild the brand by focusing on the frequent users and then to expand to include other consumers. It hoped that a core of loyal users would want the product in both its tablet and capsule forms. In order to regain regular user confidence, J&J ran television commercials informing the public that the company would do everything it could to regain their trust. The commercials featured Dr. Thomas Gates, medical director of McNeil, urging consumers to continue to trust Tylenol: "Tylenol has had the trust of the medical profession and 100 million Americans for over 20 years. We value that trust too much to let any individual tamper with it. We want you to continue to trust Tylenol."[5]

Johnson & Johnson also tried to encourage Tylenol capsule users to switch to tablets, which are more difficult to sabotage. In an advertising campaign it offered to exchange tablets for capsules at no charge. In addition it placed 76 million coupons in Sunday newspaper ads good for $2.50 toward the purchase of Tylenol.

---

[3] Thomas Moore, "The Fight to Save Tylenol," *Fortune*, November 29, 1982, p. 48.

[4] Ibid., p. 49.

[5] Judith B. Gardner, "When a Brand Name Gets Hit by Bad News," *U.S. News & World Report*, November 8, 1982, p. 71.

Finally, it designed a tamper-resistant package to prevent the kind of tragedy that occurred in Chicago. Extra-strength capsules were now sold only in new triple-sealed packages. The flaps of the box were glued shut and were visibly torn apart when opened. The bottle's cap and neck were covered with a tight plastic seal printed with the company name, and the mouth of the bottle was covered with an inner foil seal. Both the box and the bottle were labeled, "Do Not Use If Safety Seals Are Broken." This triple-seal package cost an additional 2.4 cents per bottle, but Johnson & Johnson hoped it would instill consumer confidence in the safety of the product and spur sales. In addition the company offered retailers higher-than-normal discounts—up to 25 percent on orders.

Consumers who said they had thrown away their Tylenol after the scare were given a toll-free number to call, and they received $2.50 in coupons too—in effect, a free bottle, since bottles of 24 capsules or 30 tablets sold for about $2.50.

Over 2,000 salespeople from all Johnson & Johnson domestic subsidiaries were mobilized to persuade doctors and pharmacists to again begin recommending Tylenol tablets to patients and customers. This was similar to the strategy initially used when the product was introduced some 25 years before.

The Outcome

Immediately after the crisis, J&J's market share plunged from 35.3 percent of the pain reliever market to below 7 percent. Competitors were quick to take advantage of the situation. Upjohn Company and American Home Products Corporation were seeking Food and Drug Administration permission to sell an over-the-counter version of ibuprofen, a popular prescription pain reliever. Upjohn also granted marketing rights for its brand, Nuprin, to Bristol-Myers Co., maker of Bufferin, Excedrin, and Datril. Upjohn's prescription brand, Motrin—a stronger formulation than Nuprin—was generating some $200 million in 1982, making Motrin the company's biggest-selling drug. And lurking in the wings was mighty Procter & Gamble Company (P&G), the worlds' heaviest advertiser. P&G was launching national ads for Norwich aspirin and was test-marketing a coated capsule containing aspirin granules.

Yet, there were some encouraging signs for J&J. When *Psychology Today* polled its readers regarding whether Tylenol would survive as a brand name, 92 percent thought Tylenol would survive the incident. This figure corresponded closely with the results of another survey conducted by Leo Shapiro, an independent market researcher, just two weeks after the deaths occurred, in which 91 percent said they would probably buy the product again.

Psychology Today tried to get at the roots of such loyalty and roused comments such as these:

A 23-year old woman wrote that she would continue to use Tylenol because she felt that it was "tried and true."

A 61-year old woman said that the company had been "honest and sincere."

And a young man thought Tylenol was an easy name to say.[6]

---

[6] Carin Rubenstein, "The Tylenol Tradition," *Psychology Today*, April 1983, p. 16.

Such survey results presaged an amazing comeback: J&J's conscientious actions paid off. By May 1983 Tylenol had regained almost all the market share lost the previous September; its market share reached 35 percent, which it held until 1986, when another calamity struck.

New industry safety standards had been developed by the over-the-counter drug industry in concert with the Food and Drug Administration for tamper-resistant packaging. Marketers under law had to select a package "having an indicator or barrier to entry, which if breached or missing, can reasonably be expected to provide visible evidence to the consumer that the package has been tampered with or opened."[7] Despite toughened package standards, in February 1986, a Westchester, New York, woman died from cyanide-laced Extra-Strength Tylenol capsules. The tragedy of $3\frac{1}{2}$ years before was being replayed. J&J immediately removed all Tylenol capsules from the market and offered refunds for capsules consumers had already bought.

Now the company made a major decision. It decided no longer to manufacture any over-the-counter capsules because it could not guarantee their safety from criminal contamination. Henceforth, the company would market only tablets and so-called caplets, which were coated and elongated tablets that are easy to swallow. This decision was expected to cost $150 million. The president explained: "People think of this company as extraordinarily trustworthy and responsible, and we don't want to do anything to damage that."[8]

By July 1986 Tylenol had regained most of the market share lost in February, and it now stood at 32 percent.

THE INGREDIENTS OF CRISIS MANAGEMENT

Johnson & Johnson was truly a management success in its handling of the Tylenol problem. It overcame the worst kind of adversity, that in which human life was lost in using one of its products, and a major product at that. Yet, in only a few months it recouped most of its lost market share and regained its public image of corporate responsibility and trust. What accounted for the success of J&J in overcoming such adversity?

We can identify five significant factors:

1. Keeping communication channels open.
2. Taking quick, corrective action.
3. Keeping faith in the product.
4. Protecting the public image at all costs.
5. Aggressively bringing back the brand.

Effective communication has seldom been better done. Rapport must be gained with the media, to enlist their support and even their sympathy. Alas, this is not eas-

---

[7] "Package Guides Studied," *Advertising Age*, October 18, 1982, p. 82.

[8] Richard W. Stevenson, "Johnson & Johnson's Recovery," *New York Times*, July 5, 1986, pp. 33–34.

ily done, for the press is inclined to sensationalize, criticize, and take sides against the big corporation. Johnson & Johnson gained the needed rapport through corporate openness and cooperation. In the disaster's early days it sought good two-way communication, with the media furnishing information from the field while J&J gave full and honest disclosure of its internal investigation and corrective actions. Important for good rapport, company officials need to be freely available and open to the press. Unfortunately, this goes against most executives' natural bent so that a spirit of antipathy often is fostered.

When product safety is in jeopardy, quick corrective action must be taken, *regardless* of the cost. This usually means immediate recall of the affected product, and this can involve millions of dollars. Even if the fault lies with only an isolated batch of products, a firm may need to recall them all since public perception of the danger likely will transfer to all units of that brand.

Johnson & Johnson kept faith with its product and brand name, despite the counsel of experts who thought the Tylenol name should be abandoned because public trust could never be regained. Of course, the company was not at fault: There was no culpability, no carelessness. The cause was right. Admittedly, in keeping faith with a product there is a thin line between a positive commitment and recalcitrant stubbornness to face up to any problem and accept any blame. But J&J's faith in Tylenol was justified, and without it the company would have had no chance of resurrecting the product and its market share.

Johnson & Johnson strove to protect its public image of being a socially responsible and caring firm. The following information box discusses *social responsibility* and presents the J&J credo regarding this. It is interesting to note that this credo is still prominently positioned in company annual reports ten years later. If there was to be any chance for a fairly quick recovery from adversity, this public image had to be guarded, no matter how beset it was. With the plight of Tylenol well known, with corrective actions prompt and thorough, many people were thus assured that safety was restored. We should note here that for the public image to be regained under adverse circumstances, the corrective actions must be well publicized. Public relations efforts and good communication with the media are essential for this. And, again, it helps when the fault of the catastrophe is clearly not the firm's.

A superb job was done in aggressively bringing back the Tylenol brand. In so doing, coordination was essential. Efforts to safeguard the public image had to be reasonably successful, the cause of the disaster needed to be conclusively established, the likelihood of the event ever happening again had to be seen as virtually impossible. Then aggressive promotional efforts could fuel the recovery.

Johnson & Johnson's efforts to come back necessarily focused on correcting the problem. Initially it designed a tamper-resistant container to prevent the kind of tragedy that had occurred in Chicago. Extra-strength capsules were now to be sold only in new triple-sealed packages. When another death occurred in 1986, the company dropped capsules entirely and offered Tylenol only in tablet form.

With the safety features in place, J&J then used heavy promotion. This included consumer advertising, with the theme of safety assurance and company social responsibility. J&J offered to exchange capsules for tablets at no charge. It

INFORMATION BOX

SOCIAL RESPONSIBILITY AND THE JOHNSON & JOHNSON CREDO REGARDING IT

We can define social responsibility as the sense of responsibility a firm has for the needs of society, over and above its commitment to maximizing profits and stockholders' interests. The following credo of J&J illustrates the wide circle of corporate social responsibility that more and more firms are beginning to accept.

JOHNSON & JOHNSON'S CREDO[9]

We believe our first responsibility is to the doctors, nurses, and patients, to mothers and all others who use our products and services. In meeting their needs everything we do must be of high quality. We must constantly strive to reduce our costs in order to maintain reasonable prices. Customers' orders must be serviced promptly and accurately. Our suppliers and distributors must have an opportunity to make a fair profit.

We are responsible to our employees, the men and women who work with us throughout the world. Everyone must be considered as an individual. We must respect their dignity and recognize their merit. They must have a sense of security in their jobs. Compensation must be fair and adequate, and working conditions clean, orderly, and safe. Employees must feel free to make suggestions and complaints. There must be equal opportunity for employment, development, and advancement for those qualified. We must provide competent management, and their actions must be just and ethical.

We are responsible to the communities in which we live and work and to the world community as well. We must be good citizens—support good works and charities and bear our fair share of taxes. We must encourage civic improvements and better health and education. We must maintain in good order the property we are privileged to use, protecting the environment and natural resources.

Our final responsibility is to our stockholders. Business must make a sound profit. We must experiment with new ideas. Research must be carried on, innovative programs developed and mistakes paid for. New equipment must be purchased, new facilities provided, and new products launched. Reserves must be created to provide for adverse times. When we operate according to these principles, the stockholders should realize a fair return.

"Such statements are only pious platitudes. Social responsibility requires more than lip service." How would you answer this?

[9] From a company recruiting brochure and annual reports.

offered millions of newspaper coupons good for $2.50 toward the purchase of Tylenol. Retailers were also given incentives to back Tylenol through discounts, advertising allowances, and full refunds for recalled capsules with all handling costs paid. These efforts, directed to consumers and retailers alike, bolstered dealer confidence in the resurgence of the brand.

ANOTHER SIDE OF JOHNSON & JOHNSON

Ten years later, the customer empathy of J&J seemed to have changed. First there were malpricing allegations concerning a new drug to treat colon cancer. Then Tylenol itself came under critical scrutiny about side-effect coverups.

Levamisole

In May 1992 publicity surfaced that J&J was guilty of "unconscionable" pricing of levamisole, the drug used to treat colon cancer. The charge came from a distinguished physician and cancer expert, Charles G. Moertel of the Mayo Clinic, at the annual meeting of the American Society of Clinical Oncology. Under J&J's brand name, Ergamisol, levamisole cost patients (or their insurance companies) $1,250 to $1,500 for a year's supply.

The controversy arose not so much from the absolute price of the life-saving drug, but from its price relative to a 30-year-old veterinary version of the drug, which farmers used to treat their sheep for parasites. This version cost only $14. The dispute first came to light when an Illinois farmer being treated for cancer noticed that her pills contained the same active ingredients she used to deworm her sheep.

Under sponsorship of the National Cancer Institute, Dr. Moertel and others found that levamisole, combined with a staple chemotherapy drug, was spectacularly effective in patients with advanced colon cancer. Dr. Moertel lauded it: "We now have a therapy with a national impact. We were specifically promised that it would be marketed at a reasonable price."[10]

Johnson & Johnson doggedly defended its pricing of the consumer version of the drug thus: "The price of the product reflects costly research over decades to determine possible uses in humans for other diseases."[11] J&J also pointed out that sales were less than $15 million a year, a relatively modest amount for a pharmaceutical product. At the same time, the company claimed to have rerun parts of 1,400 studies involving 40,000 patients in seeking new applications of the drug in humans.

Dr. Moertel dismissed J&J's justification for the high prices as being necessary to meet high research and regulatory costs in preparing the drug for human consumption. He maintained that the National Cancer Institute, funded by American taxpayers, sponsored the studies. "The company just supplied the pills, which cost pennies." Moertel raised the question whether a new use for an old drug—a windfall—should justify a price surge. "Just because aspirin was found to improve your risk of heart attack, should you charge more?"[12]

The bad publicity now confronting J&J was not confined to the print media. TV news programs, such as "20/20", soon featured this controversy along with criticisms

---

[10] Marilyn Chase, "Doctor Assails J&J Price Tag on Cancer Drug," *The Wall Street Journal,* May 20, 1992, pp. B1, B8.

[11] Ibid., p. B1.

[12] Ibid., p. B8.

of drug pricing of the entire pharmaceutical industry. Compounding the problem, the spokespersons for J&J and the other pharmaceutical firms did not publicly uphold their positions convincingly.

Unwarned Dangers of Using Tylenol

In January 1998, *Forbes* magazine revealed more questions about J&J's drive for profit-maximization at the expense of customers. It cited specific instances of children and adults being grievously affected by overdosing of Tylenol.

For example, Lucy Keele, 5 years old, had the flu and her mother gave her four extra tablets in one day. The overdose of Tylenol destroyed her liver and within a week she was dead. The bitter irony was that the product's advertising slogan was, "Nothing's safer."[13]

Forbes alleged that hundreds of fatalities and serious liver injuries resulted from acetaminophen, the active ingredient of Tylenol, and that J&J had to pay out millions of dollars in legal settlements, most of these under agreements requiring plaintiffs not to disclose the terms. Children, drinkers, and those undernourished were most at risk, with consequences even life threatening.

Acetaminophen has all of aspirin's effectiveness with fevers and pain, without aspirin's tendency to upset the stomach, or the one-in-a-million chance of aspirin causing Reye's syndrome, a severe nervous system complication for children. Millions of people use Tylenol without ill effects.

The gist of *Forbes'* complaint was that Tylenol labels did not sufficiently spell out liver damage risks. Sure, the labels warned in red letters not to use if the package had been tampered with, a throwback to the cyanide days of 1982. And after cases like Lucy Keele, J&J strengthened the warning label a little at a time. But the severe consequences of overdosing or using if you drank were downplayed. Why was J&J so reluctant to publicize the hazards? Was it due to an innocent oversight, or because it might scare people away?

Finally, after decades of doing little to reveal the hazards of using Tylenol, now perhaps because of the adverse publicity, the company in early July 1998 announced it was redrafting Tylenol labeling. Now it would include a warning that people who consume three or more alcoholic drinks a day should consult a physician before taking the drug, and heavy drinkers "may be at increased risk for liver damage when taking more than the recommended dose."[14]

UPDATE

Johnson & Johnson's is truly a success story, an enduring growth company. Over the last ten years revenues and profits have steadily risen every year. Revenues reached $22.6 billion in 1997, with net income $3.3 billion. The company ranks as the largest

---

[13] Thomas Easton and Stephen Herrera, "J&J's Dirty Little Secret," *Forbes,* January 12, 1998, p. 42.

[14] Thomas Easton and Stephan Herrera, "Better Later Than Never," *Forbes,* August 10, 1998, p. 14.

and most diversified health care company in the world. Its products now range from blockbuster prescription drugs, to professional products such as sutures, surgical accessories, and catheters, to a wide list of consumer products such as Tylenol, bandages, and toiletries.

With this broad product mix, how important is Tylenol to J&J today? It is still very important. Of the company's $22.6 billion revenues for 1997, it is estimated that $1.3 billion or almost 6 percent came from Tylenol. (In 1982, at the time of the contamination, Tylenol contributed 8 percent of the $5.9 billion total company sales.) J&J has heavily promoted Tylenol to maintain this prominence. *Advertising Age* estimated the company's domestic ad budget for Tylenol at $250 million, more than Coca-Cola spent on Coke.[15] In 1997, Tylenol held an overwhelming share of the acetaminophen market, and 30 percent of the combined market for branded cold, headache, and fever remedies.

Consequently, J&J's reluctance to be truly forthright about the dangers is not surprising. As Easton and Herrera of *Forbes* observed, "It's a tricky business to keep your customers from hurting themselves but not scare them away."[16]

But did J&J owe its customers more disclosure? This reluctant warning of the risks of overdosing in any case represents an about-face in concern for customers from the actions taken in 1982 and 1986 in removing all Tylenol capsules from the market without hesitation.

LATE-BREAKING NEWS

On September 23, 1999, *The Wall Street Journal* reported the results of a nationwide survey of 10,830 people conducted on-line the previous month by Harris and the Reputation Institute. It was a public opinion study designed to determine how major U.S. corporations ranked as to reputation and corporate image.

J&J ranked number one. (Coca-Cola, despite the negative headlines in the 1999 scare in Europe about people reporting illnesses when drinking Coke products, came in number two. But Exxon, a decade after the huge oil spill in Alaska, had not shaken the negative image.)

Respondents cited J&J's heritage as the premier maker of baby products, as well as its handling of the Tylenol crises of 1982 and 1986 as influencing their judgment. J&J has apparently weathered well the negative publicity about levamisole and the unwarned dangers of using Tylenol.

Source: Ronald Alsop, "The Best Corporate Reputations in America," *The Wall Street Journal*, September 23, 1999, pp. B1 and B6.

---

[15] Ibid., p. 44.
[16] Ibid.

WHAT CAN BE LEARNED?

Any company's nightmare is having its product linked to death or injury. Such a calamity invariably results in fear and loss of public confidence in the product and the firm. At worst, such disaster can kill a company, as happened with some canned-food firms whose products were contaminated with the deadly botulism toxin. The more optimistic projections would have a firm losing years of time and money it had invested in a brand, with the brand never able to regain its former robustness. In the throes of the catastrophe, J&J executives grappled with the major decision of abandoning the brand at the height of its popularity or keeping it. The decision could have gone either way. Now with hindsight, we know that the decision not to abandon was unmistakably correct, but at the time it was recklessly courageous.

Faced with a catastrophe, a brand may still be saved, but cost might be staggering. J&J successfully brought back Tylenol, but it cost hundreds of millions of dollars. The company's size at the time, over $5 billion in sales from a diversified product line, enabled it to handle the costs without jeopardy. A smaller firm would not have been able to weather this, especially without a broad product line.

Whenever product safety is an issue, the danger of lawsuits must be reckoned with. In the absence of corporate neglect, the swift constructive reaction, and the fact that the company could hardly have anticipated a madman, J&J escaped the worst scenario regarding litigation. Still, hundreds of millions of dollars in lawsuits were filed. Such suits accused J&J of failing to package Tylenol in a tamper-proof container, and the legal expenses of defending were high. The threat of litigation must be a major consideration for any firm. Even if the organization is relatively blameless, legal costs can run into the millions, and no one can predict the decisions of juries.

Copycat crimes are a danger. Although other firms in an industry stand to gain an advantage in a competitor's crisis, they and firms in related industries need to be alert for copycat crimes. By November, a month after the deaths, the Food and Drug Administration had received more than 270 reports of chemicals, pills, poisons, needles, pins, and razor blades in everything from food to drinks to medications. Fortunately, no deaths resulted from these incidents. But FDA Commissioner Hayes worried: "My greatest fear is that because of the notoriety of the case and the financial damage to the company, someone else will take out his or her grudges on a product and do something similar."[17] Actually, the Tylenol case was not the first time products had been deliberately contaminated. Eyedrops, nasal sprays, milk of magnesia, foods, and cosmetics have all been targets of tampering. An Oregon man was sentenced to 20 years in prison for attempting to extort diamonds from grocery chains by putting cyanide in food products on their shelves.

---

[17] "Lessons That Emerge from Tylenol Disaster," *U.S. News & World Report,* October 18, 1982, p. 68.

A firm can come back from extreme adversity with good crisis management. Certainly, one of the major things we can learn from this case is that it is possible to come back from extreme adversity. Before the Tylenol episode, most experts did not realize this. The general opinion was that severe negative publicity resulted in such an image destruction that recovery could take years. The most optimistic predictions were that Tylenol might recover to about a 20 to 21 percent market share in a year; the pessimistic predictions were that the brand would never recover and should be abandoned.[18] Actually, in eight months, Tylenol had regained almost all of its market share, to a satisfactory 35 percent. For such a recovery, a firm has to manifest unselfish concern, quick corrective action, and unsparing spending, and it must have a good public image before the catastrophe.

Contingency planning can aid crisis management. Although not all crisis possibilities can be foreseen, or even imagined, many can be identified. For example, contingency plans for worse-case scenarios can be developed for the possibility of food and medicine tampering or the loss of major executives in an accident of some sort. Sometimes in such planning, precautionary moves may become evident for minimizing the potential dangers. For example, with food and medicine tampering, different containers and sealed bottle tops might virtually eliminate the danger. And with executive accidents, many firms have a policy that key executives not fly on the same flight or ride in the same car.

Behavior may lapse: Good deeds and favorable publicity are not necessarily enduring. Accusations in 1992 of J&J's "unconscionable" drug pricing became widely publicized. Criticisms focused on major price differences for essentially the same drug. Were these the "reasonable prices" that the company credo promised or the best interest of customers that was so superbly manifested ten years before?

The reluctance to fully disclose the risks on Tylenol labels was not as widely publicized as levamisole. J&J was fairly successful in downplaying the accusations and for a while thought it more worthwhile (that is, profitable) to settle matters in the courts rather than risk scaring other customers. Of course, lawsuits did nothing to bring back damaged livers. Under new top management, the evidence suggested that J&J was no longer the customer-responsive firm that it was with CEO James Burke in the traumatic days of 1982.

We always hate to see the best interests of customers subordinated to company profitability. J&J had shown a major commitment to customers in the Tylenol tampering catastrophe, and business schools reveled in case studies of this wonderful paragon of corporate responsibility and crisis management. Now our idol appears tarnished by short-sighted self-interest. The company credo talks about the first responsibility being to those "who use our products and services." One wonders whether J&J in recent years has forgotten that responsibility and manifesto.

---

[18] "J&J Will Pay Dearly to Cure Tylenol," *Business Week*, November 20, 1982, p. 37.

CONSIDER

Can you think of other learning insights?

QUESTIONS

1. Did J&J move too far in recalling all Extra-Strength Tylenol capsules? Would not a sufficient action have been to recall only those in the Chicago area, thus saving millions of dollars? Discuss.

2. How helpful do you think the marketing research results were in the decision on keeping the Tylenol name?

3. "We must assume that someone had a terrible grudge against J&J to have perpetrated such a crime." Discuss.

4. What justification do you think Johnson & Johnson could offer for its levamisole pricing that would be generally acceptable to the press and public opinion?

5. How do you reconcile the great concern of J&J for its customers during the Tylenol scare, and its seeming callousness over levamisole pricing and incomplete warning on labels of Tylenol? On balance, what is your assessment of the company regarding (a) its public image, (b) its concern for customers, (c) its ethical commitment?

6. "The Tylenol episode represents great crisis management. Social responsibility was hardly a factor. The company acted in its own best interest by taking advantage of the situation to cast an aura of great concern for its customers. But the bottom line was still the only concern." Do you agree with this curious statement of company self-interest under the guise of great concern for customers?

HANDS-ON EXERCISES

1. Assume this scenario: It has been established that the fault of the contamination was accidental introduction of cyanide at a company plant. Given this scenario, how will you, as CEO of J&J direct your recovery strategy? Give your rationale.

2. Assume the role of the person responsible for the pricing of levamisole for treatment of colon cancer. What do you advise the executive committee regarding any pricing changes after the negative publicity in May 1992?

3. It is 1998, and publicity has surfaced regarding hundreds of deaths and destroyed livers due to the misuse of Tylenol. Lawyers and other critics are hounding the company for its labeling negligence. A hoard of reporters are besieging company headquarters. Describe your actions as chief representative of the company.

TEAM DEBATE EXERCISES

1. Debate both sides of the burning issue, at the height of the crisis, of keeping the Tylenol name and trying to recoup it, or abandoning it. You must not use the benefit of hindsight for this exercise.

2. Debate this dilemma relative to full disclosure on Tylenol packages of risks from overdosing: To keep customers from hurting themselves but not scare them away.

INVITATION TO RESEARCH

1. What is the situation today with levamisole (or Ergamisole) pricing?

2. How complete is the labeling of Tylenol today in terms of full risk disclosure?

3. Has J&J's selfless image been at all tarnished?

MARKETING MANAGEMENT MISTAKES

CHAPTER TWELVE

Toys "Я" Us—A Category Killer Falters

*C*harles Lazarus was generally regarded as a genius who originated the category-killer concept with his Toys "Я" Us stores. His strategy of offering a huge variety of toys at very good prices, even if service left something to be desired, spawned a host of imitators with other categories of goods. The concept was so potent that it wiped out most other toy stores and even department stores where toys had always been featured at Christmastime. Most department stores gave up their Santas and elves, or else settled for only a few token and hoped-for best-selling items.

With such a powerful concept, how could any non-category-killer stores compete? Yet times were changing.

THE HEADY YEARS

The Beginning

Charles Lazarus, 22 years old, borrowed $2,000 to open a baby furniture store. World War II had ended and a baby boom was beginning. His first store was barely 40 feet by 60 feet. Later, the idea for a toy store came from a customer wanting to buy baby toys.

In 1957, he opened the first toy supermarket. Discount stores were just beginning to emerge on the retail scene and Lazarus's stores brought the discount format to a new category of goods. In the late 1970s, Lazarus took Toys "Я" Us public.

Toys "Я" Us (TRU) became both the largest and fastest-growing toy and children's specialty chain in the world. Its earnings grew an astonishing 40 percent a year between 1978 and 1983. Between 1985 and 1992, TRU opened an average of 43 toy stores each year in the United States, 17 more overseas, and 26 Kids "Я" Us apparel stores. In so doing, it pushed some rivals into bankruptcy and then snapped up their best store sites.

The stores were usually built in uniform dimensions, with this standardization lowering architectural costs, purchasing of fixtures, as well as such other costs as inventory and manpower requirements. Company executives also believed such standardization minimized customer confusion. The stores stocked some 18,000 items throughout the year, in sharp contrast to most competitors who shrunk their toy departments right after Christmas.

171

The year-round commitment of Toys "Я" Us not only generated significant sales volume throughout the year, but also had two further advantages: (1) It secured advantageous terms from toy vendors who quickly saw TRU as the major factor in the market that also provided some leveling of the extreme seasonality, and (2) TRU could determine which toys would be hot sellers in the coming peak Christmas selling season, and order accordingly. The competitive advantage over traditional toy retailers was awesome.

The company gained a whopping 25 percent share of toy retailing in the United States by 1990, and now turned its attention overseas. It pulled off a coup in 1991, breaking into the Japanese market, a market notorious for barriers to entry, especially to discount firms. Japanese consumers flocked to Toys "Я" Us, and in 1992 Michael Goldstein, then vice chairman, predicted that foreign sales would exceed $10 billion by 2000.[1]

The vast buying power of TRU brought prosperity to the major toy manufacturers, in particular, Mattel and Hasbro. For much of the past 15 years, these grew together with TRU. They acquired smaller manufacturers, but cut back on new toy development while funneling more money into movie and TV-licensed products. And they relied on TRU to be the sales engine. In the process, smaller toy departments and stores were spurned.

In these years it seemed that nothing could really compete against the category-killer retailers. See the following information box for more discussion of the category-killer phenomenon.

As 1998 began, TRU operated or franchised 1,454 stores that emphasized products for children. The flagship Toys "Я" Us chain included 698 stores in the United States, and 441 in overseas markets. Its Kids "Я" Us clothing chain had 215 domestic

INFORMATION BOX

CATEGORY-KILLER STORES

A category-killer store is the ultimate in specialty stores. It carries only a limited number of product categories, but offers tremendous choice within those categories. Category killers get their name from the strategy of carrying such a huge assortment of merchandise at good prices in a particular category of goods that they destroy the competition.

For example, Sportmart, a Chicago-based sporting goods chain, offered customers a choice of 70 models of sleeping bags, 265 styles of socks, and 15,000 fishing lures. The huge category-killer bookstores of Borders and Barnes & Noble have some 100,000 book titles in stock. Table 12.1 lists major category specialists.

[1] Paul Klebnikov, "Trouble in Toyland," *Forbes* June 1, 1998, p. 60.

TABLE 12.1 Major Category Specialists, 1996

Company	Sales (millions)	Number of Stores
Home Furnishings:		
Bed, Bath & Beyond	$ 601	80
Linens 'N Things	554	145
IKEA US	511	13
Crafts:		
Michaels	1,295	442
Fabri-Centers	835	936
Books:		
Barnes & Noble	1,349	358
Borders	684	116
Sporting Goods:		
Sports Authority	1,046	136
Sports and Recreation	526	80
Pet Supply:		
PETsMART	1,030	262
Office Supply:		
Office Depot	5,300	504
Staples	3,068	443
OfficeMax	2,543	468
Computers		
CompUSA	2,813	96
Computer City	1,800	99
Consumer Electronics:		
Best Buy	7,200	251
Circuit City	7,030	719

Sources: "DSN Top 200," *Discount Store News* (July 1, 1996), and "State of the Industry," *Chain Store Age Executive* (August 1996), Section 2.

Commentary: Why do you suppose there are no apparel category-killer stores? Or are there?

Do you think the category-killer superstores could result in overkill, in that they offer customers too much variety? Do you see any negative implications for a bookstore offering 100,000 different titles, or a sporting goods store with 70 different sleeping bags?

units. In 1997, the company had purchased a 77-store chain, Baby Superstores. It changed the name to Babies "Я" Us, and grew this to 98 stores, making it the country's largest baby-store chain. It had also opened two megastores called KidsWorld. These combined a toy store, a baby store, a clothing store, a shoe store, a restaurant, a candy store, as well as a kids' hair salon—two acres of floorspace. But these stores were too big for most customers, and no new ones were opened.

Sales for 1997 (actually fiscal year ending Jan. 31, 1998) reached $11 billion, which was an 11 percent increase over the previous year.

CLOUDS ON THE HORIZON

By the early 1990s the environment for toys began to change, a change not recognized very quickly by TRU management.

In 1994, Charles Lazarus, now 74, handed the reins to Michael Goldstein. Gradually the façade of invincibility began to crumble.

Discount chains such as Wal-Mart, Kmart, and Target starting using toys as loss leaders, pricing them at cost or below in order to attract customer traffic. Warehouse clubs like Sam's Club, Costco, and BJ's Wholesale Club began moving into the toy business. At the other end of the market, small chains emphasizing educational toys and interactive shopping for the smaller fry were growing fast; these included Zany Brainy and Noodle Kidoodle.

Suddenly, TRU was being tormented by price competition more severe than it had ever seen. As a double whammy, it was also beset by competitors' service and decor—aimed at making shopping a desirable experience for both parents and kids— beyond anything that its bare-bones boxy stores had even considered. Its big competitive advantage, vast assortments, was still there. But customers began to be drawn by other shopping considerations, not the least of which were avoiding the long waits at TRU cash registers.

At a Wal-Mart, the merchandise assortment may be one 16-inch bicycle instead of the half dozen at TRU. But the bicycle is less expensive, the store is clean and pleasant, and the sales clerks courteous and usually far more knowledgeable than those at TRU, who may be strained to even direct a customer to the right aisle in the cavernous building.

In efforts not to be too badly outpriced by the discounters, the operating margins of TRU slipped from 12 percent to 8 percent over the four years from 1994 to 1998. But still it could not match the prices of Wal-Mart and other discounters.

Michael Goldstein tried to use his market clout to get the big toy manufacturers such as Mattel and Hasbro not to sell to the warehouse clubs. This brought charges of anticompetitive practices by the Federal Trade Commission.

In 1996 Goldstein tried to react to the nicer decor of his new competitors. He instituted Concept 2000, a remodeling plan for the old utilitarian stores. As much as resources would allow, those stores selected were designed to be less cluttered, to be cleaner and brighter with nicer displays and fixtures, and to have better customer service. Books, videogames, Barbie dolls, and Legos were given separate departments. The cost of such rejuvenation averaged $1.5 million per store.

The new concept didn't work. For the money spent, the return on investment was not positive and most sales gains turned out to be disappointing. Eventually only 15 percent of the stores were remodeled; the rest remained the old warehouse-like boxes.

Even the international operations soured. The seeming coup in 1991 of breaking into the Japanese market, leading to the optimism of Goldstein for foreign sales exceeding $10 billion by 2000, was an acute disappointment. For 1997, foreign sales were only $3 billion. What went wrong?

For one thing, the TRU format needed cheap land and big parking lots, conditions hardly met in most foreign environments, whether Far East or Europe. Furthermore, labor laws and regulations were often stifling. TRU found that its operating margins suffered overseas: 6 percent compared to 8 percent in the United States. So this business proved less profitable than expected.[2]

Results

Things came to a head in March 1998. TRU announced earnings of $490 million, or $1.70 a share, for the year ended January 31, way below analysts' expectations. This reflected a loss in market share of toy retailing from 25 percent in 1990 to 20 percent. TRU soon announced inventory cutbacks, store closings, and work force cuts. In so doing, it took a $495 million charge. Efforts to reduce inventories involved another $500 million.[3]

Profitability problems continued into 1998. In the first half of the year, operating profit fell more than 30 percent. In the third quarter, income fell 50 percent.

Losing the Clout

As the largest toy seller, TRU had enjoyed tremendous clout with its suppliers. It was their largest single customer by far. Now this was changing. With the inventory cutbacks announced in 1998, Hasbro and Mattel faced drastic cutbacks in profits themselves. For example, Mattel's second-quarter 1998 sales to TRU were off $72 million, contributing to an 11 percent fall in second-quarter earnings for Mattel.[4]

Not surprising, Mattel expressed a need to reduce its dependency on TRU. For 1998, TRU was expected to account for 15 percent of Mattel's sales, down from 18 percent in 1997, and 22 percent in 1996. Sales to Wal-Mart, on the other hand, were up to 15 percent in 1997 from 12 percent in 1996.[5]

Hasbro's sales to TRU were down even more: $125 million for the first half of 1998, and expected to be down as much as $200 million for the full year.[6]

Such drastic cutbacks brought on by TRU's weaknesses suggested continuing problems for the company as suppliers were driven into the camps of major competitors, most notably Wal-Mart. The deteriorating market share trend of TRU

---

[2] Klebnikov, p. 60.

[3] Joseph Pereira, "Hasbro to Buy Galook, Issues Earnings Warning," *The Wall Street Journal,* September 29, 1998, p. B4.

[4] Lisa Bannon, "Mattel Cuts Forecast for Yearly Profit in Wake of Toys ' Я ' Us Restructuring," *The Wall Street Journal,* September 25, 1998, p. B8.

[5] Ibid.

[6] Pereira, p. B4.

would hardly be easy to turn around for it had lost its momentum to the most aggressive of competitors.

EFFORTS TO REVITALIZE

Two weeks into 1998, Michael Goldstein relinquished operating command to Robert Nakasone, 50, who had joined the firm in 1985.

Nakasone proposed a major revamping. Inventories would be streamlined and reduced with heavy markdowns to clear out slow-selling goods and overstocks. Some of the problems with inventories were a consequence of TRU stockrooms being a mess. The company averaged less than four inventory turns a year, compared with seven turns at Wal-Mart and eight turns at Target Stores.[7] The following information box shows the importance of high inventory turnover for profitability.

Nakasone also announced that the work force would be slashed by as much as 3,000 or 2.8 percent, and 50 underperforming toy stores, mostly in Germany and France, and nine in the United States, would be closed. Also, 31 of the 214 Kids "Я" Us clothing stores in the United States were to be closed as well as some distribution centers.

Nakasone pinned hopes for the future on TRU's new C-3 stores, with nine stores being tested for the Christmas season in Georgia, Tennessee and North Carolina. In 1999 he planned to upgrade 200 of the 697 U.S. toy stores to this format, with most of the rest in 2000. The conversion would cost about $500,000 per store, considerably less than the $1.5 million of the Concept 2000 redesign. The new concept, as of November 1998, had not been truly tested, only strands of the concept had been in different stores. So much was at stake in these nine test stores. (We would expect company executives to be underfoot in these stores.)

The new C-3 stores included a reduction in the back-room space by 18 percent and a reorganization of the store's layout to feature more departmental display of goods. They were touted as more customer friendly, cost effective, and a concept with a long-term vision.[8]

To enhance shareholder value, the Board of Directors approved a $1 billion share repurchase program.

Following the company announcement of its charges to restructure its store base and reduce inventory levels, credit-rating agency Standard & Poor's on September 16, 1998 placed the debt of the company on a CreditWatch with negative implications for borrowing and interest rates.

Standard & Poor's was also concerned about the company's use of excess cash flow and short-term borrowing to aggressively repurchase shares.[9]

---

[7] Klebnikov, p. 56.

[8] William M. Bulkeley, "Toys 'Я' Us to Take Big Charge, Cut Jobs and Close 59 Stores," *The Wall Street Journal*, Sept. 17, 1998, p. A4; and Laura Liebeck, "Toys 'Я' Us Shakes It Up," *Discount Store News*, October 5, 1998, p. 1.

[9] Bulkeley, p. A4.

INFORMATION BOX

IMPACT OF MERCHANDISE TURNOVER ON PROFITABILITY

Let us compare a Toys "Я" Us store with a Target store of the same sales volume. The TRU store has a turnover of 4, while Target has 8 turns.

Toys "Я" Us:

Sales	$ 12,000,000
Net profit percentage	5%
Net profit dollars	$600,000
Stock turnover	4
Average stock investment	

$$\frac{12,000,000}{4} = \quad \$ 3,000,000$$

Profitability as measured by return on investment, without considering investment in store and fixtures

$$\frac{600,000}{3,000,000} = \quad 20\%$$

Target:

Sales	$ 12,000,000
Net profit percent	5%
Net profit dollars	$600,000
Stock turnover	8
Average stock investment	

$$\frac{12,000,000}{8} = \quad \$ 1,500,000$$

Return on investment

$$\frac{600,000}{1,500,000} = \quad 40\%$$

Therefore, the store with the higher stock turnover will be more profitable; it can also lower prices and still be as profitable (or more so) than its competitor with the lower turnover.

Note: To simplify this example, inventory investment is figured at retail price, rather than cost, which would technically be more correct. However, the significance of increasing turnover is more easily seen here.

Why does a store like Target (or Wal-Mart) have so much higher a merchandise turnover than Toys "Я" Us? What could TRU do to improve its turnover?

ANALYSIS

Disregard for Environmental Changes

Toys "Я" Us never detected significant changes in its environment. This is another example of the unfortunate mindset that success guarantees continued success, that nothing needs to change.

So, for a crucial decade and a half it changed neither its stores nor its way of doing business. Sure, it opened more stores, all the same boxy warehouses. Sure, it diversified into babies and kids apparel stores, again with the same type of store. And it reached for overseas markets, as most firms were wont to do. But its operational strategy remained basically the same.

In particular, it ignored changes in *competition* and *consumer tastes*.

By the 1990s, new competitors were emerging. They were nothing like the small independents or the underfinanced imitators of TRU of the 1970s and 1980s or the department stores for whom toys were only a seasonal sideline. Now TRU faced the might of a Wal-Mart or a Target or warehouse clubs enlarging their toy departments, as well as the creative merchandising of slick toy chains such as Zany Brainy. It had become a victim of its own success. The profits piling up at TRU brought all these rivals salivating to get a piece of the action. And TRU had become flabby and inefficient.

With more attractive shopping alternatives, more and more consumers were becoming dissatisfied with the poor service and the lack of amenities at TRU. In an era of prosperity, greater choice (which TRU still offered, the major competitive advantage it had managed to hold onto) became not as strong a patronage factor as better prices, nicer decor, better service, and excitement/entertainment.

Inability to Be Competitive with Prices

TRU's operating efficiency had worsened over the years. The caliber of employees in its stores was not particularly high, reflecting a misguided cost containment. Undoubtedly, operating procedures and computer technology were not on the cutting edge. As a result, TRU was vulnerable when aggressive and very efficient competitors came on the scene. The inefficiency of TRU was most evident in inventory control and a much lower turnover than these new competitors. Many store stock-rooms were a mess, and control inadequacies led to huge overstocks of some goods and stockouts of others. The efficient inventory control technology of firms like Wal-Mart enabled them to sell profitably at lower prices than TRU could match without straining profit margins.

The Burden of Older Facilities

Half of the TRU toy stores in the United States were built before 1989 (358 of the total of 698 in 1998), and more than half of the Kids "Я" Us stores (112 of the total of 215 in 1998).[10] Many of these were much older than ten years. Its stores were

---

[10] *1998 Toys "Я" Us Annual Report*, p. 2

consequently more dated than most of the newer competitors. In retrospect, we can criticize TRU management for not having established a systematic program for rejuvenating older facilities. But in the eagerness to open ever more new stores, it is easy to understand how older ones were given low priority for attention and funding. Still, this was a crucial flaw in the competitive struggle, and one that brought the need for a major catch-up program, but with it a dilemma in allocating scarce resources.

Defense

TRU instituted a major buyback program for its common stock. The motivation for buybacks of this kind is that profits can be distributed over fewer shares, thus making earnings per share higher to the benefit of investors. However, this is a temporary palliative at best. While it suggests that current stock market valuations of the firm are too low, it also raises the suspicion that management sees less payoff in investing for future growth.

THE ANSWER TO TRU'S PROBLEMS

At this stage in the life cycle of TRU, it appears to face three alternatives if it is to overcome what seems like a pervasive declining trend in market position and profits.

1. *Stronger expansion abroad.* It already has, as of the beginning of 1998, 441 stores overseas or 30 percent of all stores. This is a substantial overseas presence, but these stores have lower operating profits—6 percent versus 8 percent—than the domestic stores, primarily because of labor and other regulations and land expenses. Furthermore, in 2000, the economic situation in many countries remains less promising.

2. *Meet discount stores on price.* Given the relative inefficiencies of TRU compared to Wal-Mart and the other major competitors, it is unlikely that it can achieve this without a revolution in its inventory control and operating procedures. Even if it can do this, TRU will most likely only be matching the efficiency of competitors, and not be gaining a competitive advantage. With major discount competitors using toys as loss leaders, at least during the peak Christmas selling season, a price advantage for TRU can probably never be achieved.

3. *Upscaling.* This option on a large scale would have severe cost consequences. Profits would be drastically affected. But TRU may have no choice but to do some modest scaling up. It must consider getting away from the worst features of the drab warehouse box stores, and the poor service of low-paid employees.

TRU may have to recognize that its category-killer concept was great in its time, but now has become rusty as a vehicle for continued growth in toy retailing. Should this experience be sobering for other category-killer stores?

LATE-BREAKING NEWS

In late August 1999, CEO Robert Nakasone resigned after 18 months on the job, the third departure at TRU by a high-level executive in 1999. Michael Goldstein, his predecessor again took over until a permanent successor could be found. While Naksone had spearheaded renovating most of the company's 700 U.S. stores and reducing a somewhat bloated inventory, operating performance was disappointing. It had lost its number-one position in toy retailing to Wal-Mart, and had stumbled badly trying to establish a competitive online business. Market share had fallen to 16 percent in 1998 from 19 percent three years before, while smaller specialty stores selling education-oriented toys grew to 38 percent from 34 percent during these three years. In an interview, Mr Goldstein said, "There were specific differences of opinion between (the board) and Bob regarding the direction of the company."

Source: Joseph Pereira, "Toys "Я" Us CEO, Nakasone, Resigns," *The Wall Street Journal*, August 27, 1999, p. A3.

WHAT CAN BE LEARNED?

Vulnerability of original masters. We see this time and again. Success does not assure continued success. Boeing and IBM exhibited this in Parts I and II, although IBM eventually made a great comeback. (Perhaps in another edition Toys "Я" Us may also make a great comeback, but it seems doubtful now.) The three C's mindset of conservatism, complacency, and conceit appears to be as operative for Toys "Я" Us as for these other firms.

Now with its aging and unattractive stores, slumping efficiency that results in high overhead and higher prices, as well as poorer service than competitors, for many consumers it is no longer the first choice for toy shopping.

Often, organizational malaise confronts a long-established frontrunner, malaise not only of workers but also of management. It is difficult to detect such letting down, until a competitive position starts to crumble. In the case of Toys "Я" Us, the competitive position worsened rather insidiously. Other toy category-killer chains had been vanquished by the stronger TRU. But the big general merchandise discounters gradually upped their toy assortments, while smaller creative toy chains expanded with nice success. Nothing sudden, nothing traumatic—perhaps this is the worst kind of competitive climate, since it is so lulling to the frontrunner.

How can frontrunners stay sharp? TRU needed to keep in the forefront of the industry in its stores, in technology (primarily computers for information and inventory control), and in procedures for handling operations as efficiently as possible. Stores should have been refurbished and updated on a regular schedule. TRU should have led in the development of inventory control systems and efficient stockroom and warehouse handling and storage of goods to assure lean and adequate stocks. Constant efforts should have been made to assure that procedures were streamlined, that demands on suppliers were reasonable while extracting from them maximum efficiency in providing goods promptly at lowest prices. TRU had the clout to demand the same efficiency from suppliers as it did for itself.

Then there were the employees and management people. Higher caliber, more motivated people were sorely needed. To attract such people was perhaps the most difficult problem of all. Profit-sharing, better advancement opportunities, incentive pay, a specific program to lure higher caliber people—such could have made TRU a more attractive place to work. To the defensive argument that this would cost too much, we know that Wal-Mart and Target have achieved far better employees. At the least it would seem that TRU could have done a much better job of hiring, training, and motivating its people.

Can consumers have too much choice? The premise of category-killer stores is that the more choice offered, the greater the appeal. This may be true for books. But is it true for toys, and everything else? For many consumers, so much choice is confusing, makes decisions difficult, and is time-consuming. For those consumers not altogether thrilled at unlimited choice, the only competitive advantage of Toys "Я" Us is lost.

The Concept of Value

The management guru, Peter Drucker, recently discussed in *Forbes* the need for managers to change their thinking from old assumptions of the past. One of his paradigms concerns the importance of value to a customer, and how this may differ drastically from what management thinks it is.[11]

We can consider what value really is to a mother buying toys. Is a mind-boggling assortment to choose from really the value she is looking for?—especially when checkout lines are four and five deep? or might ease of shopping, good prices, reasonable assortment, and some interactive things for her kids to do in the store while she shops be of far more value?

CONSIDER

Can you think of additional learning insights that could be applicable to other firms in other situations?

QUESTIONS

1. Do you think a consumer can have too much choice in shopping? What might this depend on?

2. Do you think the absolute lowest price for an item is most important for many consumers? What percent would you say comparison shop for the lowest price? What implications, if any, do you see from your estimate?

---

[11] Peter F. Drucker, "Management's New Paradigms," *Forbes,* October 5, 1998, pp. 169–170.

3. Compare the future promise of Borders, the book superstore, and Toys "Я" Us. What in your judgment accounts for the difference in their prospects?

4. "Let's face it. Toys "Я" Us has seen its heyday. It will never come again. It should be content with a smaller share of the market, and not worry so much about Wal-Mart, and making all kinds of drastic and expensive changes." Evaluate this statement from a stockholder's perspective.

5. Would you be content to work as a management trainee at Toys "Я" Us today? If not, what would it take to attract you?

6. In its early decades, Toys "Я" Us ran roughshod over all competitors. Yet today, bigger, with more resources and experience, it is faltering. How do you explain this?

7. In what way does inventory turnover affect profitability? How can inventory turnover be increased?

8. Should the recent experience of TRU be sobering for other category-killer stores? Why or why not?

9. Based on the information presented, do you think Nakasone should have been forced to resign? Discuss.

HANDS-ON EXERCISES

1. It is 1990 and you are a senior assistant to the general merchandise manager of TRU. You sense that the toy environment is changing and you are concerned that TRU is not changing. You have repeatedly told your boss about your concerns, but to no avail. What might you do at this point? Discuss your rationale for whatever decision (or no decision) you take. Also consider the implications.

2. You are a staff assistant to the new CEO, R.C. Nakasone. He has assigned you to develop a proposal to improve the "shopability" of existing TRU stores. He wants you to consider all aspects of this, from some remodeling— but probably not to exceed $500,000 per store—to better customer service, better employees, better layout, as well as whatever other aspects you may come up with. In addition to the recommendations, he wants you to consider the cost/benefit implications. (You may need to make some assumptions on costs.)

TEAM DEBATE EXERCISE

Debate the whole general issue of drastic change versus moderate change for TRU. In arguing the two sides, consider both short-term and long-term aspects. Try to be as specific as you can, including cost consequences, with the less-than-complete information that is available. Be as persuasive in presenting your position as possible, and attack the others' position.

INVITATION TO RESEARCH

1. Try to find out as much about TRU's management development program as you can, such as educational and experiential requirements, starting pay and future expectations, most likely career path, and so on.

2. How is TRU doing today? Has the stock market price come back? How are the newest "C-3 format" stores doing? What has happened to market share?

3. How important has the Internet become for toy retailing? Has TRU been able to establish a competitive online business?

CHAPTER THIRTEEN

Boston Chicken and Planet Hollywood—It Takes More Than Hype

*B*oston Chicken and Planet Hollywood have similar turbulent histories. They both seemed to represent entrepreneurship at its best. Their initial public offerings (IPOs) reflected this as they went public with such market hype that investors frantically bid up the prices. But after a few years it became evident that performances did not match the dreams, and both stocks plummeted. How could investors and an ebullient management have been so wrong?

BOSTON CHICKEN

The Promise

Merrill Lynch took Boston Chicken public in late 1993 with an initial public offering of $20 a share. It made a sizzling debut, with the stock price soaring 143 percent on its opening day, the largest first-day jump of any new issue in 1993, and a year later the stock split 2-for-1. Flush with more than $1 billion from its IPO, the company expanded rapidly. It quickly announced plans to open 300 stores a year with a goal of more than 3,000 by 2003. In December 1996, the share price was $41 (equivalent to $82 before the split), and executives and investors alike basked in the heady optimism of becoming another McDonald's.

The product was rotisserie chicken, sold as a full meal in a style reminiscent of those days when mothers stayed home all day to take care of their families. Boston Chicken executives thought this home meal replacement complete with good food and service should appeal to the busy families of today. The only real competitor was Kenny Rogers Roasters, and since it was doing quite well this seemed to confirm the merits of the concept.

The entrepreneurs believed they had to exploit this market with a tremendous expansion before competitors could jump in. Since they had the means to do so with the money raised by the IPO they decided to capitalize on this and offer their franchisees financing to open stores.

Besides the unique and seemingly attractive concept, investors were also impressed because the chief executive, Scott Beck, had formerly built Blockbuster Video into a major success. In 1994, Beck promised that Boston Chicken sales would reach $3 billion by 1999.[1]

Confusion

Unbelievably, the Boston Chicken concept had not even been proven to work in one store, and now plans were being made for 3,000 stores. Along with its attention given to expansion, the company still groped for the winning food combination. First, it positioned itself as a dinner restaurant; then it experimented with lunch business, introducing Extreme Carver sandwiches that it promoted with coupons. Unfortunately, these discount coupons trimmed profit margins, but worse, the cheaper menu items cannibalized or took sales away from the existing dinner business. (Refer back to chapter 7 for a discussion of cannibalization.)

In a reversal, the company eliminated the Extreme Carver line and went back to the dinner menu but added meatloaf, ham, and other items for additional choices. It also experimented with salad bars, carryout food, and new desserts.

These menu changes, as well as announced stepped-up advertising and cost cutting stimulated Wall Street. Stock analysts were still making buy recommendations in late 1996, when the share price reached its zenith. Overlooked by most was that as early as 1994, credit agencies had rated Boston Chicken's debt as junk, because of doubts about the company's ability to repay its debt.

Some analysts still touting the stock worried about financial figures not being adequately disclosed. Steven Kent, at Goldman Sachs, wrote, "At times, management appears to be elusive with information on this complex story."[2] For example, the company provided no information on same-store sales, and this is rather basic information for how well a chain is doing, since more stores can hide deteriorating sales per store. Furthermore, the reported revenues of Boston Chicken did not represent sales from stores at all, but rather royalties and interest on loans the company had made to franchisees to finance the rapid expansion.

The practice of loaning money to franchisees to open their stores was a significant departure from other franchise operations where franchisees put up their own capital to get into the business. Boston Chicken franchisees needed only a minimum of financial resources; thus, more marginal franchisees were attracted. One critic likened Boston Chicken more to a bank than a restaurant company. In defense, the company saw this as a creative strategy for attaining the most rapid growth.[3]

Red Flags

Abruptly, ominous storm signals shocked investors. In early 1997, the company disclosed that its franchisees had lost about $150 million. This was the first indication

[1] Miriam Hill, "There's Plenty of Blame for All in This Tale of Market Hype," *Cleveland Plain Dealer,* April 27, 1998, p. 40-C.

[2] Hill, p. 4-C.

[3] Ibid.

outsiders had that individual outlets were somehow not doing well. The company finally told Wall Street that its weekly per-store sales, which had been growing at a 3 percent to 6 percent yearly rate, had dropped 20 percent from the previous year. Now the company expected to post losses of $1 a share for 1998.

As a result, Boston Chicken's stock plummeted 82 percent in 1997, making it the worst-performing stock of 1,000 tracked by *The Wall Street Journal.* By April 1998, the price per share was down to $4.50; by August 7, 1998, to $1.125; by October 6, 1998, to 50 cents.

Table 13.1 shows the trend of revenues and income through 1997. Things got worse in 1998.

The Year of Disaster (1998)

Early in 1998, Boston Chicken reported a 1997 loss of $223.9 million. Its top three officers resigned: Saad Nadhir, co-chairman and chief executive; Scott Beck, co-chairman and president; and Mark W. Stephens, chief financial officer and vice chairman.

J. Michael Jenkins, 51 years old, was named chairman, president, and chief executive officer. He brought 37 years of experience in the restaurant business. His most recent position was CEO of Vicorp, a chain of 356 family-type restaurants operating as Village Inn and Bakers Square. Before that he turned around the El Chico chain. In an interview, he announced his intentions of focusing on the company's operations "to get it back rockin' and rollin' and growing." He noted Boston Chicken's strong brand, wide market presence, and positioning in a strong niche for casual dining. "We'll get there," he said.[4]

The company acquired 527 of its franchisee stores, bringing the number of company-owned stores to 936. It put up for sale its 52 percent stake in a bagel

TABLE 13.1. Trend of Revenues and Profits of Boston Chicken, 1992–1997

			(Million $)			
	1992	1993	1994	1995	1996	1997
Revenues	8.3	42.5	96.2	159	265	462
Net Income	–5.8	1.6	16.2	33.6	67.0	–223

Source: Boston Chicken annual reports.

Commentary: Looking at these statistics up to 1997, no one could question that this was truly a growth company. This shows, however, the illusion that can accompany insufficient operating information. Individual stores were losing money, and debt buildup was becoming precarious.

Now let us look at two balance sheet statistics:

Long-term Debt	Nil	Nil	130	130	130	739
Cash Flow	–5.6	3.6	22.2	45.0	89.8	–177

The problems have suddenly surfaced in earnest, and Boston Chicken is forced into bankruptcy.

---

[4] Scott McCartney, "Boston Chicken Officers Resign Top Three Posts," *The Wall Street Journal,* May 4, 1998, p. B10.

chain, and tried to renegotiate hundreds of millions of dollars of debt on facilities. In order to maintain its credit line, it needed an average revenue per week of $17,500 at each of its Boston Market stores, but was barely meeting that figure in the first quarter of 1998.

The loss for the first quarter of 1998 was $312 million. This, compared with a profit of $21.5 million the year before, raised questions about Boston Chicken's survival in the cutthroat fast-food industry. In late May, the company's auditor, Arthur Andersen, warned that Boston Chicken was facing a liquidity crisis.

Troubles mounted. In August, Boston Chicken faced delisting by the Nasdaq Stock Market, which requires that a listed stock maintain a minimum bid price of $5 a share for 30 consecutive days.

For the second quarter, the company reported a loss of $124.5 million, partly reflecting asset writedowns and provision for loan losses, although revenue for the quarter rose 46 percent from the year earlier.

On October 15, five years after going public in a frenzied IPO, Boston Chicken filed for Chapter 11 bankruptcy protection. (Chapter 11 allows a company to hold off its creditors while it tries to put its finances in order.) It initially closed 178 or 15 percent of its stores, and laid off 500 employees and transferred others.

The company had been testing a new prototype store in Charlotte, North Carolina. It claimed that consumer response was positive, but it planned to test the prototype in other markets before a nationwide conversion. This was a partial hope for the future, if enough financing could be obtained.

Boston Chicken wasn't dead yet, even though its stock price at 50 cents was practically off the board.

What Went Wrong?

Such a great success, at the beginning—how could so much early promise change to disaster? Was fraud or misrepresentation involved? There are no allegations of fraud, although perhaps naive stock brokers were swayed by the hype, and contributed to runaway expectations.

A lot of condemnation focused on the financing of the franchises. "You had a group of nonrestaurateurs operating a restaurant as a finance company," said William H. Moore, an industry analyst.[5] But are these criticisms completely justified?

This strategy could be a vehicle for incredibly rapid expansion, provided the money initially was there, as it was from the public offering. Of course, the risk is far greater than if franchisees are putting up most or all of the investment needed. So, maybe it was a crapshoot, a Vegas experience. But did it have to be?

Not if the franchised outlets were profitable.

But the great majority were not profitable, at least after their overhead charges of interest on loans and franchise fees. Still, many of the outlets had good traffic.

---

[5] Alejandro Bodipo-Memba, "Boston Chicken Inc. Files for Chapter 11, Lays off 500 and Shuts 178 Restaurants," *The Wall Street Journal*, October 6, 1998, p. A4.

The Wall Street Journal even reports on the long lines at company restaurants.[6] Another observer, Dennis Amato, chief investment officer with Maxus Investments, said. "The stores I go into are always busy. That's why it seems kind of strange that they're having all these problems."[7]

What was so wrong? Was it poor screening of potential franchisees? Was it poor training and supervision of franchisees and their employees? Maybe. Was it lack of Boston Chicken controls and franchisee guidance and supervision? Probably. Maybe the concept was good, but the execution was abysmal.

Did Boston Chicken expand too far too fast? From May 1992 to 1998, it grew from 34 stores in the Northeast to 1,143 nationwide. Sales jumped from about $21 million in December 1991 to nearly $1.2 billion in 1996, a tremendous growth. One wonders how any central organization could handle all the details and challenges of effectively dealing with and guiding such growth.

Great growth is possible. Witness Wal-Mart, McDonald's, Kmart in its heyday, and many others. But none of these grew as wildly as Boston Chicken. We must have controlled growth. This means growth within the capability of the firm to wisely select its franchisees, give them adequate training, and insist on tight controls over operations, costs, customer service, and locations.

Boston Chicken's problems seem to be not so much emanating from the concepts of family-style restaurants and aggressive financing of franchisees, but in the nitty-gritty of store operations.

Another criticism levied at Boston Chicken was that they had no assured menu and store prototype, that they were still experimenting as they went from 30 stores to more than a thousand. Maybe, but flexibility sometimes is desirable. One would think experimenting with menus and format would lead to better tapping of consumer demand and value satisfaction. Better this than being set in a rigid pattern that allows for no deviations even though some things about the product/service package could be improved.

PLANET HOLLYWOOD

The Vision

Seeking to capitalize on the seemingly universal appeal of celebrities in entertainment and sports—and to blend this with eating out—the restaurant chain, Planet Hollywood, went public in April 1996, and received a stock-market valuation of $3.5 billion that same day. The link with the celebrities, who received stock and options in return for promotional appearances, stimulated strong investor and customer demand, at first.

What was glossed over at the time of the stock offering, and had major implications for successful expansion, was that 43.8 percent of Planet Hollywood's sales came from just four of the company's 14 restaurants in 1995. These four were located in major tourist markets: Las Vegas, Orlando, London, Paris.

---

[6] Hill, p. 4-C.

[7] Miriam Hill, "Boston Chicken Cooks Up New Menu to Boost Profits," *Cleveland Plain Dealer,* April 27, 1998, p. 4-C.

The investor movie stars—Demi Moore, Bruce Willis, Whoopi Goldberg, Arnold Schwarzenegger among others—at grand openings attracted long lines of fans, and raised expectations of an instant global entertainment phenomenon. To tap this potential, the company organized under five operating divisions: consumer products, food and beverage, lodging and gaming, retail and merchandise, and theaters/entertainment. Paul Westra, Salmon Brothers analyst, wrote: "Planet Hollywood may ultimately become four separate $5 billion businesses: theme restaurants, gaming, lodging and other.'" He compared the potential with Starbucks, Disney, and Nike.[8]

In the first few years, most of the concentration was on restaurants. By the end of 1997, the company had grown to 78 Planet Hollywood restaurants, including 46 company-owned and 32 franchised units in 29 countries. Official All Star Cafe, geared to sports celebrities, had nine units in three countries. The company sought to locate in high profile, heavy trafficked areas, thereby being able to attract both destination customers and passers-by.

The company also entered into a number of joint ventures to construct hotels, including casino resort hotels in Las Vegas and Atlantic City. Sales of a broad range of merchandise carrying the company logo also provided revenue. Table 13.2 shows revenue and income figures from 1992 through 1997.

Robert Earl, Co-founder and CEO

British-born Earl, 47, ran the successful Hard Rock Cafe before starting up Planet Hollywood with Keith Barish, a movie producer. With his background, his personality, and his flair for intriguing ideas, he was the consummate promoter/entrepreneur. He easily swayed investors and analysts with grand plans for expanding the company through tantalizing diversifications. Unfortunately, while he also developed a second eating chain, the All Star Cafe that had rather modest success, his other projects fizzled.

TABLE 13.2.   Trend of Revenues and Income, Planet Hollywood, 1992–1997

	(Million $)					
	1992	1993	1994	1995	1996	1997
Revenues	20.4	30.7	126	271	373	475
Net Income	−4.5	−5.3	−9.3	20.7	48.1	8.3

Source: Company annual reports.

Commentary: This company went public in April 1996, with a stock-market valuation of $3.5 billion the same day. Looking at the previous three years of losses, it is difficult to understand such investor exuberance. Of course, it did double revenues in 1995 and also made $20 million in profits. But that surely could not have been fully known in April 1995. The increase in revenues of 1994 over 1993 must have contributed to the enthusiasm, but losses almost doubled from 1993 to 1994. We have to think that hype infected stock brokers and investors alike.

[8] Richard Gibson, "Fame Proves Fleeting at Planet Hollywood as Fans Avoid Reruns," *The Wall Street Journal*, October 7, 1998, p. A1.

Marvel Mania, a theme restaurant idea based on Marvel Comic characters, was touted in the stock prospectus, but didn't work out. Nor did a Planet Hollywood Barbie doll promised for Christmas 1997. Cool Planet, joint venture ice-cream parlors, stagnated at two, and the ice cream never made it into supermarkets. Earl had envisioned using for Cool Planet ice cream such movie knockoff names as "Die-Hard Chocolate" and "Termi-Nutter" sundae, but couldn't get the needed permissions.

Another idea intrigued Wall Street: "Chefs of the World," a merchandising and retailing concept. As conceived, renowned chefs would be used, possibly with a TV show. Cookbooks, cookware and utensils, mail order and licensing agreements would follow, along with yet more theme restaurants. But nothing materialized. Still another idea, a chain of live-music locations called "Sound Republic," produced only one restaurant and no ancillary activities.

If it wasn't for his success with Hard Rock Cafe, some would call Robert Earl a dreamer and not a doer. See the following box for a discussion of dreams versus practicality for entrepreneurs.

Problems

Somehow the celebrity theme had no staying power. What did people expect to see? A real live movie star every time they came to a Planet Hollywood?—hardly, except in their dreams. They could see celebrities on oversize video screens in the darkened halogen-

---

INFORMATION BOX

DREAMS VERSUS PRACTICALITY: WHAT IS THE FORMULA FOR ENTREPRENEURS?

The common notion for success in entrepreneurship is the need for the "great idea." With this great idea, this dream, success is almost guaranteed, some will tell us; without it, one is doomed to mediocrity and failure. Yet, many entrepreneurs dispute such thinking. For example, Nolan Bushnell, founder of Atari, the electronic games company, and several other companies, says that entrepreneurs don't have better ideas than lots of other people, but they have an uncanny ability to translate ideas into practical solutions.[9]

Robert Earl was a consummate idea man, ready to put his dreams to the test. But we can wonder at his ability to tap the practical side of his brain. Can a dreamer make it as a successful entrepreneur? Is perseverance in never giving up dreams a possible substitute for a healthy dose of practicality? Robert Earl may further test the issue.

Many dreamers never escape from their armchair thinking. Earl had no difficulty with this. He was ready to run with his ideas, and also convince other people of their merits. You may want to compare your psyche with his.

---

[9] John Merwin, "Have You Got What It Takes?" *Forbes*, August 5, 1981, p. 60.

spotted interior, but never in person. So they ordered an overpriced appetizer, maybe bought Planet Hollywood T-shirts on the way out, perhaps to remember the experience, and never came back. Would they have come back if the food had been better?

Could you blame the celebrities in not patronizing their own restaurants, in not mingling with the common folk? Even if a few might have wanted to, difficult celebrity schedules would have precluded any consistent appearances, even in New York City and Orlando, much less in Minneapolis, Minnesota, St. Louis, Missouri, and Gurnee Mills, Illinois.

For 1996, the year Planet Hollywood went public, same store sales at all restaurants fell 2 percent. In 1997, same store sales fell 11 percent. For the first two quarters of 1998, sales plunged 13 percent and 17 percent respectively. Total second quarter revenue fell 13.8 percent from the previous year. Not surprisingly, the stock price that was $32.13 the day of the initial offering, plunged to under $4 by October 1998. Westra, the analyst who thought so highly of Planet Hollywood two years before, lamented, "Of all the stocks in my career, I was most wrong with Planet Hollywood."[10]

Now, expansion plans were aborted, with a $44.6 million charge taken to write off some projects. In the summer of 1998, Robert Earl brought in William H. Baumhauer, formerly head of the Fuddruckers hamburger chain, to be president. Baumhauer announced plans to close some restaurants, to reduce employment, to boost pay for restaurant managers to attract better talent, and most important, to fix the food.

Problems worsened. On December 15, 1998, lenders slashed Planet Hollywood's borrowing power and forced the sale of its Orlando, Florida headquarters. A major shareholder, Saudi Prince Alwaleed, sought to sell his 16 percent stake.

What Went Wrong?

We have to wonder at the fickleness of the appeal of celebrities, when the product or service does not match the image or the expectation. Will customers go back to a place in the unreasonable hope that some celebrity might show up, if food compares poorly with other restaurants?

Historical evidence is rather compelling that the use of a celebrity's name without good food is the recipe for failure. Back in the 1960s when fast-food franchises had an early boom, such chains as Minnie Pearl's Chicken, Here's Johnny Restaurants (Johnny Carson), Al Hirt Sandwich Saloon, Broadway Joe's (Joe Namath), Jerry Lucas Beef 'n Shake, and Mickey Mantle's Country Cookin' Restaurants came on the scene with high expectations by investors and franchisees. What soon became apparent, however, was that although the public might pay to see the entertainer or sports figure perform, they would not frequent a fast-food outlet simply because of the famous name, or a picture or poster of the celebrity—unless the food and service warranted their patronage.

[10] Ibid.

Things apparently have not changed over the last thirty years. The lure of Planet Hollywood was the possibility of a celebrity appearance, except this was practically nonexistent after the grand opening. Food was ordinary and unexciting and videos of celebrities were not enough to bring back many customers under such circumstances. So we have the great idea—the attraction of celebrities—but abysmal capitalizing on it.

Could Planet Hollywood have done a better job in luring celebrities? Even if it gave celebrities more than a small stake in a restaurant chain, perhaps through stock or options, would these multimillionaires willingly commit time to such an endeavor? They would likely spend any spare time in far more exciting activities than making a personal appearance at a restaurant or store. Besides, in a chain of close to a hundred restaurants how is one going to schedule appearances of such celebrities to assure that each outlet has its fair and frequent share? For the lesser known, or third-rate celebrities, more appearances could be enticed, but would they be that much draw?

So while the concept was interesting, even intriguing at first view, it was a dud in actuality.

With the benefit of hindsight, we wonder why analysts, investors, and management did not foresee that there would be no parade of celebrities except at grand openings, and that after the first few even these would be poorly attended. How could so many have been so myopic about this flawed concept?

UPDATE

On June 21, 1999, Boston Chicken, struggling to find other ways to sell its products, got bankruptcy court approval for its agreement with H.J. Heinz Company to sell packaged Boston Market foods to grocery stores, for which Heinz would pay royalties. The commitment depended on the results of test marketing to come later in 1999. Boston Chicken was still struggling to recover from losses by closing locations and trimming costs and, of course, was still in bankruptcy.[11]

Planet Hollywood was faring no better, although it had escaped bankruptcy as yet. Its fate seemed to match that of its two most ardent celebrities, actors and spouses Bruce Willis and Demi Moore. Bruce and Demi have split and the stock has fallen to 81 cents a share.[12]

In late June 1999, Planet Hollywood's president, William Baumhauer, who had been recruited less than a year before from Fuddruckers, abruptly resigned, joining two other high-level executives in getting out. The company's auditors expressed uncertainty about the company's ability to continue as a going concern, but founder and chairman Robert Earl, when asked about the possibility of bankruptcy filing, said, "There's nothing contemplated. Everything is part and parcel of the resolution of the bondholders."[13]

[11] "Boston Chicken Deal with Heinz is Cleared by Bankruptcy Court," Reported in *Cleveland Plain Dealer,* June 22, 1999, p. 3C.

[12] Sara Nathan, "Planet Hollywood Falters," *USA Today,* May 4, 1999, p. 3B.

[13] Richard Gibson, "Planet Hollywood's President, Recruited to Help Firm Recover, Resigns Abruptly," *The Wall Street Journal,* June 28, 1999, p. B10.

LATE-BREAKING NEWS

Toward of the close of 1999, both Boston Chicken and Planet Hollywood's problems were getting no better. On October 12, 1999, Planet Hollywood finally filed for Chapter 11 bankruptcy protection after closing nine restaurants in such places as Chicago, Fort Lauderdale, Maui, Miami, and Phoenix. Chapter 11 gives a firm protection from creditors while it reorganizes. Its stock, which had once sold for $28.50, was now at about 20 cents.

Boston Chicken, already in bankruptcy protection since October 5, 1998, now only traded in the Pink Sheets, the realm of penny stocks. But it refused to give up, sinking $40 million in 1999 into advertising brimming with confidence, trying to convince consumers that it offered good homestyle dinners when time was important. It had 1,143 stores when it filed Chapter 11 in 1998; a year later it had 860 stores. While its lower-priced selections still appealed to consumers, the bankruptcy stigma hurt. It seemed unable to reduce its overhead sufficiently to be profitable without substantial volume increases, and now hoped to sell its assets to another party.

So these once-high-flyers barely cling by their fingernails.

Sources: Brian Steinberg, "Boston Chicken, Weighing Sale, Tries Through Ad Campaign to Fly Again," *The Wall Street Journal,* October 25, 1999, p. B23; James P. Miller, "Planet Hollywood Tentatively Agrees to Refinancing Pact," *The Wall Street Journal,* August 18, 1999, p. A4; and "Planet Hollywood Requests Bankruptcy Aid, Closes Sites," *Cleveland Plain Dealer,* October 13, 1999, p. 2-C.

WHAT CAN BE LEARNED?

Beware of being swayed by hype and emotional optimism. Especially for new ideas and ventures it is easy to become caught up by enthusiastic forecasts of entrepreneurs and analysts. It is natural to want to believe and be part of an enterprise with golden prospects, and assume the best and ignore any naysayers.

In both of these cases we saw the drastic consequences of such myopia. Critical questions could have been raised at the time of the IPOs about:

1. With Boston Chicken, the use of the moneys generated, primarily to open more outlets and financing franchisees to get started. The strategy implied sacrificing careful selection of franchisees for great growth. The great growth planned also suggested less attention given to store location, training, and controls.

2. With Planet Hollywood, the great dependence on the presence of celebrities. This was the engine that was to drive the company, not the food. How much could Planet Hollywood count on such public appearances? Any sober analysis should have deduced that the restaurants needed to stand on their own without such dependence.

Evaluate ideas for practicality. So we want to be careful not to be swayed by emotionality and hype. But we must be careful not to go to the other extreme, of ignoring creative ideas of high merit. What to do?

Nothing is for sure. But we can make some suggestions. They have worked for many decision makers, but have sometimes led to discarding promising but uncertain ventures:

1. *Look at the worst scenario.* What is the worst that could happen if we go ahead with this? What would lead to this worst scenario? Could these factors somehow be blunted and overcome? Can we assign probabilities to the various consequences of this decision? Based on our best knowledge, is it worth taking?

2. *Use a devil's advocate.* A devil's advocate is one who takes the opposing position, on the basis of better opening up all sides of a decision. Such a devil's advocate, if well chosen and conscientious, can flesh out the worst scenario and let it stand on its own merits against the proposed action.

Would such techniques have prevented the investor mistakes of Boston Chicken and Planet Hollywood? They might have raised second thoughts to blunt the enthusiasm. Perhaps all would have gained—entrepreneurs and investors alike—from a more sober and objective evaluation of these ideas.

Execution must not be downplayed in the infatuation with euphoric ideas. With proper execution both of these entrepreneurial adventures might have had success. Good execution at Boston Chicken meant satisfactory location research, selecting well-qualified franchisees and training them properly and giving them continuing supervision and control to help achieve profitable enterprises. For Planet Hollywood, it meant making the food service so good and value oriented that people would come back for the food and service, celebrities or no celebrities. Planet Hollywood had a great asset, but it was slipping away: The celebrity theme at first would bring hordes of people to the restaurants during the grand openings. With outstanding food and service they could have been repeat customers. What an opportunity wasted.

Never neglect older operations in the rush to open new ones. The temptation in a strong growth mode is to concentrate most attention and resources on opening new outlets. As a consequence the existing ones are given short shrift in attention and resources needed. The surest indication of such deemphasis is when same store sales decline. Both Boston Chicken and Planet Hollywood faced this, and it led to their comeuppance. Good supervision and controls (i.e., adequate management attention) of older outlets must not be sacrificed in the enthusiasm and rush to open new ones. Yet many firms are guilty of this neglect of their older facilities.

CONSIDER

Can you think of any additional learning insights?

QUESTIONS

1. Do you see any possible way that well-known celebrities can be induced to periodically visit far-flung restaurants or other outlets, except perhaps those in entertainment centers such as New York and Los Angeles?

2. Do you think most well-known celebrities really want to mingle with common folk?

3. Have you eaten in a Boston Chicken (or Boston Market) or Planet Hollywood restaurant? What were your impressions?

4. "The worst thing that could have happened to Boston Chicken was the huge success of their initial public offering." Comment.

5. How do you account for the initial wild investor enthusiasm for both Boston Chicken and Planet Hollywood? Does this mean that all IPOs should be looked at skeptically?

6. Would stronger controls have prevented most of the problems of these two enterprises? How could controls have been more effective?

7. Do you think Boston Chicken can be salvaged?

8. Can Planet Hollywood still be salvaged?

HANDS-ON EXERCISES

Before

1. Design a program for sound growth for Boston Chicken at its beginning, after the IPO.

2. Design a strategy to achieve an enduring customer attraction for Planet Hollywood after the IPO.

After

1. Design a program to salvage Boston Chicken now.

2. Design a program to salvage Planet Hollywood now.

TEAM DEBATE EXERCISE

Debate the two extreme growth orientations: run-with-the-ball versus slow-and-steady-wins-the-race in the Boston Chicken and Planet Hollywood agendas.

INVITATION TO RESEARCH

What is the situation with these two firms today? Have their prospects improved? Have stock prices gone up?

CHAPTER FOURTEEN

Borden—Letting
Brands Wither

Elsie the cow has long been the symbol of Borden, the largest producer of dairy products. But Borden grew well beyond dairy products to become a diversified food processor and marketer. Decades of children cherished its Cracker Jack candied popcorn with a gift in every box; its Creamette pasta was the leading national brand, and it had strong regional brands as well. Lady Borden ice cream, milk, and frozen yogurt were well known, as were other dairy brands, national and regional. Even Elmer's glue belonged to the Borden family. With its well-known brands, Borden experienced solid growth in sales and profits for years and became a $7 billion company. Then in 1991, fortunes took a turn for the worse, and dark days were upon Borden. Top management had somehow allowed its brand franchises—the public recognition and acceptance of its brands—to deteriorate. Regaining lost ground was to prove no easy matter.

PRELUDE TO THE DARK DAYS

Borden was founded in 1857 by Gail Borden, Jr., a former Texas newspaperman. It sold condensed milk during the Civil War and later diversified into chemicals. In the 1960s Borden acquired such food brands as Cracker Jack and ReaLemon. Because of the wide earnings swings of cyclical chemical prices, Eugene J. Sullivan, the CEO, intensified the shift into consumer products in the 1970s.

In November 1991 Anthony S. D'Amato took the helm at Borden. He succeeded Romeo J. Ventres, a good friend, who convinced the board when he retired in 1991 that his protege, D'Amato, was the ideal successor. The two men, however, had sharply different management styles. Ventres was an idea man who had great faith in his top managers and gave them free rein. D'Amato was blunt, profane, and believed in personally becoming deeply involved in operations. D'Amato's different management approach was not well received by some Borden top managers, and the company went downhill fast under D'Amato's chairmanship.

But the seeds of Borden's problems were sowed before D'Amato took the helm. Ventres had dreamed of transforming Borden from a rather unexciting conglomerate into a major food marketer. Between 1986 and 1991, Ventres spent nearly $2 billion on 91 acquisitions. "We were hurriedly buying companies for the sake of buying companies," said one Borden executive. In its rush to move quickly on its acquisition program, the company sometimes spent as little as two weeks researching an acquisition candidate before making a decision.[1]

Some acquisitions turned out to be real losers. For example, in 1987 Borden purchased Laura Scudder potato chips for nearly $100 million. Unfortunately, major union problems led Borden to close all of Laura Scudder's California plants only a year after the purchase. Borden then shifted production to a plant in Salt Lake City, only to encounter high costs and quality control problems it could not correct. In 1993 it sold Laura Scudder for less than $20 million. All told, this fiasco cost Borden nearly $150 million.

Most acquisitions were small and medium-sized regional food and industrial companies. Ventres' strategy was to obtain growth by marketing these regional brands beyond their regular market areas. By consolidating manufacturing and distribution, he thought Borden could become the low-cost producer of a variety of product lines, thereby gaining more clout in the marketplace.

In the late 1980s this strategy seemed to work well. With its acquisitions, company sales grew 54 percent between 1985 and 1988. Earnings climbed even sharper to 61 percent, the most rapid growth in the company's history. (See Table 14.1.) Regional marketing and tailoring products to local tastes seemed a potent strategy.

In 1987, *Fortune* magazine featured Borden as a model of corporate performance. It termed the company "a consumer products brute" and extolled "some 40 acquisitions over two years that have made Borden, already the world's largest dairy company, the nationwide king of pasta and the second-largest seller of snack foods behind PepsiCo's Frito-Lay." The regional brand strategy was praised as motivating regionals to create new products as well as borrow from one another. For example, in just 6 weeks, Snacktime, one of Borden's new regional brands, developed Krunchers!, a kettle-cooked potato chip differentiated from those made the conventional way through continuous frying. The chip became an instant success, generating $17 million in annual sales.[2]

In 1987, the milk business was among the most profitable in the industry. Borden, with its Elsie the cow symbol, was able to charge more than competitors could, which was surprising for a commodity such as milk, which is virtually the same product whatever cow it comes from. The company insisted that its high quality and service standards made the "Borden difference." But when asked exactly what that difference was, a veteran dairyman in a succinct quote said, "About a buck a gallon."[3] Perhaps this was a portent of what was to come.

Premonitions

Flaws in the execution of the strategy were beginning to emerge by the end of the 1980s. In the race to expand the food portfolio, the company had ignored some of the

---

[1] Kathleen Deveny and Suein L. Hwang, "A Defective Strategy of Heated Acquisitions Spoils Borden Name," *The Wall Street Journal,* January 18, 1994, p. A4.

[2] Bill Saporito, "How Borden Milks Packaged Goods," *Fortune,* December 21, 1987, pp. 139–144.

[3] Saporito, p. 142.

TABLE 14.1. Revenues and Net Income, 1983–1989

	Revenues ($millions)	% Change	Net Income ($millions)	% Change
1989	7,593	4.8	(61)	
1988	7,244	11.2	312	16.9
1987	6,514	30.2	267	19.7
1986	5,002	6.1	223	14.9
1985	4,716	3.2	194	1.5
1984	4,568	7.1	191	1.1
1983	4,265	—	189	—

Source: Company reports.

Commentary: Growth was steady during most of these years, but it really accelerated in 1987 and 1988. No wonder the 1987 *Fortune* article spoke in glowing terms about Borden.

well-known and successful brands it already had. For example, it had sold ice cream under the Lady Borden label for decades, but it ignored the golden opportunity in the 1980s to extend the line into superpremium ice cream, which was becoming highly popular. Borden showed the same negligence in not aggressively developing new products for many of its other strongest brand names. (See the following information box for a discussion of the effective brand extension strategy.) And one could wonder how much longer the price premium charged for milk and Lady Borden ice cream could hold up as the company moved into the skeptical 1990s.

INFORMATION BOX

BRAND EXTENSION

Brand extension can be a particularly effective use of branding. It is a strategy of applying an established brand name to new products. As a result, customer acceptance of the new products is more likely because of customer familiarity and satisfaction with the existing products bearing the same name. This reduces the risk of new-product failure. Today about one-half of new consumer products use some form of brand extension, such as the same product in a different form, a companion product, or a different product for the same target market.

The more highly regarded a brand is by customers, the better candidate it is for brand extension—provided that a new product will not hurt its reputation and has some relevance to it. The strong favorable image of the Lady Borden brand made it ideal for such brand extension. A favorable image should be zealously protected from being cheapened or having its perception of good value undermined.

Discuss why brand extension may not always work.

Borden was now finding difficulty in digesting its hodgepodge of acquisitions. (Table 14.2 shows the broad range of food and nonfood products and the business segment contributions to total sales and profits as of 1992.) It continued to operate as a conglomeration of unintegrated businesses and thereby proved to be neither as efficient as major competitors nor as able to amass marketing clout.

By the time D'Amato took over, the company was clearly ailing. By the end of 1991, sales had declined 5 percent from the previous year, and net income had fallen 19 percent. D'Amato quickly tried to consolidate the loosely structured organization, but all his efforts seemed only to make matters worse.

D'AMATO'S FUTILITY

Shortly after becoming CEO, D'Amato tried to better integrate the morass of consumer food businesses. He wanted to tighten up and centralize the widely decentralized company, with its "dozens of independent fiefdoms." Even corporate offices were scattered between New York City and the hub of the company's operations in Columbus, Ohio. Such geographical distance suited the hands-off management style of Ventres, who rarely got involved in day-to-day operations and spent most of his time at Borden's small Park Avenue offices in New York. D'Amato moved to centralize far-flung operations in Columbus. There he involved himself deeply in day-to-day operations. He increasingly saw the need to eliminate or sell many of Borden's small regional businesses while focusing most efforts on building national brands: a reversal of the strategy of Ventres.

TABLE 14.2. Business Segment Contributions to Total Company Sales and Earnings, 1992

	Sales	Operating Profits
Grocery[a]	26%	42%
Snacks and International Consumer[b]	26	18
Dairy[c]	20	5
Packaging and Industrial[d]	28	35

[a] Grocery products include North American pasta and sauces (Creamette, Prince, Dutch Maid, Goodman's, Classico, Aunt Millie's); niche grocery products (Eagle-brand condensed milk, Campfire marshmallows, Cracker Jack candied popcorn); refrigerated products (Borden cheese); and food service operations.

[b] Snacks and International Consumer products include Borden's worldwide sweet and salty snacks (Borden, Wise, Snack Time!); other food products outside the United States and Canada (Weber sweet snacks, KLIM milk powder, Lady Borden ice cream); and films and adhesives in the Far East.

[c] Dairy products, including milk, ice cream, and frozen yogurt, are sold under national and branded labels, which include Borden, Lady Borden, Meadow Gold, Viva, and Eagle.

[d] Packaging and Industrial products include consumer adhesives (Elmer's glue); wallcoverings; plastic films and packaging products (Proponite food packaging film, Resinite and Sealwrap vinyl food-wrap films); and foundry, industrial, and specialty resins.

Source: Company public information.

Analysts initially applauded D'Amato's strategy for turning Borden around, but their praise was short-lived. Results failed to meet expectations and even brought new problems.

D'Amato was especially wedded to the notion that the brand recognition of certain brands should allow the company to charge a premium price. For example, Borden's own research had shown that 97 percent of consumers recognized Borden as a leading milk brand.[4] D'Amato saw this as supporting such a premium price. Then, in early 1992, raw milk prices dropped by about one-third. Borden doggedly held its prices while competitors lowered theirs to reflect the drop in commodity prices. Before long, Borden began losing customers, who were realizing that milk is milk. Good brand recognition did not insulate a national brand from lower priced competition of other national brands and private brands. See the following information box for a discussion of the battle between national and private brands.

INFORMATION BOX

THE BATTLE OF THE BRANDS: PRIVATE VERSUS NATIONAL

Wholesalers and retailers often use their own brands—commonly referred to as private brands—in place of or in addition to the national brands of manufacturers. Private brands usually are offered at lower selling prices than nationally advertised brands, yet they typically give dealers more per-unit profit since they can be bought on more favorable terms, partly reflecting the promotional savings involved. Some firms, such as Sears and Penney, used to stock mostly their own brands. Thus, they had better control over repeat business since satisfied customers could repurchase the brand only through the particular store or chain.

With private brands directly competing with manufacturers' brands, often at a more attractive price, you may ask why manufacturers sell some of their output to retailers under a private brand. A major reason is to minimize idle plant capacity. Manufacturers can always rationalize that if they refuse private-label business, someone else will not, and competition with private brands will continue. Other manufacturers welcome private-brand business because they lack the resources and know-how to enter the marketplace effectively with their own brands.

By the 1990s, more knowledgeable and frugal consumers were realizing that private brands often offered the best value. National consumer brands were being hurt. Recognizing this new intense competition, some manufacturers of branded goods, led by makers of cigarettes and disposable diapers, in 1993 rolled back the price differentials over private brands of their national labels. Borden management had difficulty accepting the idea that the price premiums of its national brands were no longer sustainable if market share was to be maintained.

How do you personally feel about private brands?

---

[4] Elizabeth Lesly, "Why Things Are So Sour At Borden," *Business Week*, November 22, 1993, p. 82.

D'Amato opted to tough out the loss of market share, expecting that higher profit margins would offset somewhat lower sales. Only after almost a year of steadily declining sales did he abandon the premium-pricing policy. By then sales had fallen so drastically that the milk division was operating at a loss.

Another marketing mistake involved misuse of advertising. In his strategy to build up Borden's major brands, D'Amato had boosted marketing efforts for Creamette, the leading national pasta brand. With the sizable promotional expenditures, the brand's sales rose 1.6 percent in 1992. This may have seemed like a significant increase but for the fact that, nationally, pasta sales rose 5.5 percent.

How could the promotional efforts have been so ineffective? Unbelievably, most of the advertising featured recipes aimed at increasing pasta consumption, rather than at building selective demand for the Creamette brand.

Making the marketing efforts for Creamette even more misguided, Borden neglected its regional pasta brands, such as Anthony's in the West and Prince in the Northeast. These sales slumped, so that total division sales were down $600 million in the first 9 months of 1993. D'Amato admitted the mistake: "There was a very strong desire to make Creamette the one bigger brand beyond anything else. That's a great objective, [but] when you do it at the expense of your strong regional brands, maybe it doesn't make any sense."[5]

The snack food division also bedeviled D'Amato. He planned to launch a national Borden brand of chips and pretzels in the expectation that this could replace many of the company's regional snack brands. Combining the regionals' manufacturing and distribution costs under a single brand should enable Borden both to cut costs and also gain marketing muscle. The company tested its new snack line in Michigan, but results were only mediocre. Unfortunately, Borden was going up against PepsiCo's Frito-Lay and Anheuser-Busch's Eagle Snacks—major entrenched national brands. It could not wedge its way in. The company finally refocused its efforts to attempt to build up regional brands such as Jay's and Wise. But they were ineffective or too late.

THE CHANGING OF THE GUARD

D'Amato's sweeping strategy to rejuvenate the ailing Borden left the company worse off than before. Two of its four divisions, dairy and snacks, were operating at losses. Its other two divisions, grocery products and chemicals, could not take up the slack. On October 27, 1993, Standard and Poor downgraded much of Borden's debt. Since the beginning of 1993, Borden's share price had plummeted 43 percent.

In June 1993 D'Amato hired Ervin R. Shames, 53, as president and heir apparent. Whereas D'Amato's background had been in chemical engineering for most of his 30 years with Borden, Shames was an experienced food marketer, having spent 22 years in the industry, holding top positions with General Foods USA

---

[5] Lesly, p. 84.

and Kraft USA. He most recently had been chair, president, and chief executive of Stride Rite Corporation. In making Shames president, D'Amato gave him a compensation package that exceeded those of Borden's other top executives, including himself.

Shames and D'Amato now attempted to correct Borden's problems together. They quickly stopped offering deals to retailers to encourage heavier end-of-quarter shipments. While these deals temporarily boosted sales, they hurt profits and also stole business from the next quarter.

Shames and D'Amato accelerated the examination of Borden's various businesses. Teams of management consultants and financial advisers helped with the evaluation. As a consequence, morale among managers, who feared drastic changes, plummeted almost to the point of paralysis.

In October 1993 the independent directors of the board considered the possibility of selling the entire company. But the efforts proved futile. Hanson PLC and RJR Nabisco briefly appeared interested, but talks broke down. Several other possible buyers, including Nestle SA, also looked over Borden's portfolio of businesses but declined to negotiate. The weak condition of Borden was proving a major hindrance to any buyout. It likely would have to solve its own problems without outside help.

Shames and D'Amato believed that the biggest problem was the fact that the company was spread too thin in too many mediocre businesses. Although it was unlikely that the entire company could be sold at this time, still certain parts should be salable. They had to decide which should be sold if the company was to be streamlined enough to reverse the consequences of its haphazard and even confused former growth mentality. An early recognized candidate for pruning was the $1.4 billion chemical business. This had little relevance with the core food properties, but still it was a major profit generator, as shown in Table 14.2.

D'Amato was not to see the conclusions of his latest efforts to turn around Borden. On December 9, 1993, the board of directors fired him and left Shames in charge. At the same time, D'Amato's predecessor and former supporter, R.J. Ventres, resigned from his board seat. Operating results through 1993 were a disaster, as shown in Table 14.3.

TABLE 14.3. Operating Performance, 1990–1993

| | Revenues | | Net Income | |
	($millions)	% Change	($millions)	% Change
1993	6,600[a]	(7.6)	(593)[a]	
1992	7,143	(1.3)	(253)	
1991	7,235	(5.2)	295	(19.0)
1990	7,633	—	364	—

[a] Estimates.
Source: Borden.

RECOVERY EFFORTS

Shames announced a $567 million restructuring plan on January 5, 1994. It included the sale of the salty snacks division and other niche grocery lines. The dividend was also slashed for the second time in 6 months. In a speech to security analysts, Shames identified four reasons for Borden's problems: lack of focus, insufficient emphasis on brand names, absence of first-rate executives and managers, and a tangled bureaucracy. He vowed to purge weak managers and increase advertising with much greater focus on core lines, notably pasta, the namesake dairy products, and industrial businesses such as adhesives and wallcoverings. For example, he planned to increase advertising for pasta from $2 million to $8 million for 1994 and to focus on the company's faded regional brands. The pasta would also be crossmarketed with Classico, the successful premium pasta sauce.

Shames also pledged to bring Borden from last place among food companies to the top 25 percent. See Table 14.4 for a ranking of Borden with other major competitors as of the beginning of 1994. He began bringing in a new management team, many of them his former colleagues. In a major shake-up, three senior managers announced their early retirement: the chief financial officer, the general counsel, and the former executive vice president in charge of the struggling snack food and international consumer products unit.[6]

Some security analysts were encouraged by Shames' speech. They believed that Borden's bringing in an experienced outsider—at the time, Shames had been with the company for only 7 months—showed that the company was truly committed to the drastic changes needed for a turnaround. Other people were more skeptical. After all, Borden has been "restructuring" for five years. "Who's to say the latest plan will work any better than previous ones?" Joanna Scharf, an analyst with S. G. Warburg & Co., was among such skeptics: "I found some of [Shames] remarks heartening. However, this is not something that is going to turn around in six months." And she maintained she was not going to change her advice to investors to sell the stock.[7]

With so many brands in its portfolio stable, reflecting nearly 100 recent acquisitions, Borden lost focus. Key brands were often not sufficiently championed. Brand extensions, such as one for Lady Borden ice cream, were often overlooked or only half-heartedly attempted. One wonders how many opportunities were ignored by a management team whose attention was caught up in a frenzy for acquisitions.

A Sputtering Recovery

The troubles of Borden did not go away. At a $1 million cash salary plus mouth-watering stock options, Shames was unable to turn things around. His initial efforts were to build sales volume, but this adversely affected the bottom line of profitability. For example, with pasta, Borden held firm on prices despite a recent 75 percent increase

---

[6] Suein L. Hwang, "Borden Aides Leaving as Part of Shake-Up," *The Wall Street Journal*, February 15, 1994, p. A4.

[7] Vindu P. Goel, "Putting Elsie Back on Track," *Cleveland Plain Dealer*, January 23, 1994, pp. 1-E, 5-E.

TABLE 14.4. **Comparison of Borden and Major Competitors, 5-year Average, 1988–1993**

	Return on Equity	Sales Growth	Earnings per Share
General Mills	42.8%	10.0%	10.4%
Kellogg	31.8	10.2	11.6
H. J. Heinz	25.4	5.8	8.6
Quaker Oats	24.6	4.9	12.2
Sara Lee	21.1	6.2	16.1
Hershey Foods	18.4	7.1	8.3
Campbell Soup	16.5	5.3	NM[a]
Dole	11.7	11.7	–5.4
Borden	5.8	1.3	NM

[a] *NM,* not meaningful.

Source: Industry statistics as reported in *Forbes,* January 3, 1994, pp. 152–154.

Commentary: Borden's poor performance compared with that of its major peers is starkly indicated here, with Borden dead last in 5-year average return on equity, sales growth, and earnings per share.

in durum wheat prices, while competitors raised prices. The result: Borden gained less than a point of market share, but lost on the bottom line. So eager was Borden for volume that in November 1993 it paid an Oklahoma City–based supermarket chain $9.5 million for preferential treatment on grocer shelves.[8]

Shames failed to curb costs. Even though he shed 7,000 employees, payroll costs actually rose. Some of this was hardly Shames' fault. The board approved substantial salaries paid to former top executives. For example, D'Amato was paid $750,000 in cash severance, and $900,000 per year for four years plus $65,000 in secretarial and legal fee reimbursements. Borden still maintained a fleet of company jets to fly board members around the country. Country club memberships of executives hardly attested to a firm on the verge of bankruptcy. Consultant and advisory fees numbered in the millions. The fat could not be trimmed, it seemed.

Efforts to sell off some of the units to ease the crushing burden of creditor demands were also less than successful. For example, H. J. Heinz Company bought Borden's $225 million (sales) food service division for only 31 percent of annual revenues, a miserably low price for assets that should have brought $1 for every $1 in revenues.[9]

In late 1994, Borden was bought for $1.9 billion by Kohlberg Kravis Roberts and Co., a low figure for a $6 billion company but then it had been losing money. Robert Kidder, former top executive of Duracell, became CEO. Borden, once a top 20 public firm became the third largest private firm in the U.S. KKR directed hundreds of

---

[8] Matthew Schifrin, "Last Legs," *Forbes,* September 12, 1994, pp. 150ff.

[9] Schifrin, pp. 150ff.

millions of dollars for updating plants, installing new systems, and developing new products. In May 1995, Borden underwent a complete restructuring, with all marketing efforts split into 11 business units, each with its own board of directors, capital structure, and operational control, thus assuring 100 percent accountability.[10] Could Borden be on the verge of a turnaround?

ANALYSIS

Acquiring other businesses is a common growth strategy. Through acquisitions a company can quickly achieve a relatively large size, bypassing the time needed to develop such new ventures internally. By acquiring already proven businesses, the buyer can obtain personnel and management experienced to run such businesses effectively.

Several problems, however, can occur in such buyouts: First, a buying firm may pay too much and be saddled with heavy debt and interest overhead. Second, the acquisition may prove incompatible with the buyer's existing resources and strategy. In such a situation, it may find great difficulty in integrating the new enterprise with existing operations and making it a profit contributor.

In the 1980s Ventres, D'Amato's predecessor, took on $1.9 billion in debt to acquire 91 regional food and industrial companies. He had hoped to build these up to be regional powerhouses and to marry efficiencies of scale in manufacturing with the marketing nimbleness of regional operations. By centralizing production in the most efficient plants, costs should be lowered and profits enhanced. And there was always the potential for a regional brand to take off and be worthy of national distribution. This was the theory behind many of Borden's acquisitions in the 1980s.

Unfortunately, theory and practice did not meld well. The businesses were never integrated and continued to operate autonomously with diverse and often competing brands. Production never achieved the efficiency of most of the large competitors, and Borden still lacked their marketing clout. It also encountered great problems in allocating advertising among the diverse brands: Which should be given strong support, and why? And should the other brands be allowed to languish?

Compounding its problems with unwise and unassimilated acquisitions, Borden management grievously misjudged the mood of the market. It overestimated consumers' willingness to pay premium prices for its most popular brands. Borden's stubbornness in maintaining high prices for Lady Borden milk at the very time when raw milk prices were collapsing simply invited competitors to increase their market share at Borden's expense. Attempts to raise ice cream prices backfired as well.

The early 1990s, a period of recession and considerable unemployment and fear of layoffs, brought a new consumer recognition that many national brands were not much, if any, better than competing private brands. Many national-brand manufacturers, faced with declining sales in the face of strong private-label competition, began price rollbacks. So it was not surprising that Borden found difficulty with a

---

[10] "A New Life for Borden," *Prepared Foods,* July 1995, p. 35; and "Borden's CEO Finds Answers to How It's Been Losing Money," *Cleveland Plain Dealer,* February 13, 1996, p. 5-C.

changed marketing environment. What was surprising was its slowness to adapt to these changing conditions.

WHAT CAN BE LEARNED?

Beware an unfocused strategy. An unfocused strategy often accompanies too much unrelated diversification. A firm has difficulty deciding what it is, other than being a conglomerate. Not many managements cope well with a lot of diversification, although many have tried to. Often such acquisitions become candidates for sale some years later, thus confirming flawed acquisition decisions.

In Borden's case most of the acquisitions were related to its major food business. But there were too many, and they were not integrated into the main corporate structure. Such diffusion of resources and uncoordinated marketing efforts made it difficult indeed to achieve either cost savings or a unified and powerful approach to the marketplace.

How much decentralization? Here we are confronted with the negative consequences of too much decentralization or autonomy. Borden acquisitions' autonomy led to lack of coordination and great inefficiency.

Does this have to be true? Or can decentralization work without causing loss of control and efficiency? Can intrafirm competition among semi-independent units lead to greater performance incentive? The answer is yes, decentralization is often far more desirable than centralization. For example, we saw this in IBM's efforts to move away from its centralized bureaucratic organization toward more decentralization. Still, there are degrees of decentralization. Too much uncontrolled autonomy led to Borden's problems. There has to be some focus and common purpose along with sufficient controls to prevent unpleasant surprises. But in the final analysis, the issue depends on the competence of the managers. If they are highly competent, then an organization will likely thrive under decentralization. If they are incompetent, as appeared to be the case with Borden, then decentralization can be a disaster.

Run with your winners. Although any firm wants to develop new products and bring them to fruition as soon as possible, it must not neglect its older products and brands that are doing well, that are winners. Advertising and other marketing efforts, such as brand extension, should not be curtailed as long as the products are growing and profitable. Marketing commitments should perhaps even be increased for such winners, since favorable growth trends often can continue for a long time. Alas, Borden sometimes exercised the opposite strategy: It cut back on its winners and directed resources to futilely trying to build up weak regional brands.

But we should not completely condemn Borden for ignoring its winners. It threw all its advertising support behind Creamette, the leading national brand of pasta. But Creamette's sales failed to take off. Meantime, Borden's strong regional brands—in particular, Prince in the Northeast and Anthony's in the West—stagnated with no support. D'Amato must have thought "damned if you do and damned if you don't." But there were reasons for the lack of success with the Creamette advertising, as we will examine next.

For mature products, beware using primary-demand advertising. Despite a strong boost in marketing efforts for Creamette in 1992, the brand's sales rose only 1.6 percent. At the same time total U.S. pasta sales rose 5.5 percent.[11] Was this poor showing the fault of the product? Hardly, since it was the leading national pasta brand. Rather, the advertising was at fault. Most of it was built around recipes that did more to promote pasta consumption than to promote the superior qualities of Creamette. In other words, a primary-demand theme was used rather than selective-demand theme stressing the merits of a particular brand. Because primary-demand advertising helps the industry and all competitors, it is best used with new products in a young growth industry. Primary-demand advertising is seldom appropriate in a mature industry. The results of the advertising efforts for Creamette confirm this. Shouldn't Borden managers have been more savvy? They should never have approved such a theme for an advertising campaign.

CONSIDER

Do you see any other learning insights coming from this case?

QUESTIONS

1. Do you think the problems in Borden's acquisition strategy stemmed from a flaw in the basic concept or in the execution? Support your position.

2. Is primary-demand advertising ever advisable for a mature product? If so, under what circumstances?

3. Prince is a strong regional pasta brand in the Northeast. What would it take to convert it into a national brand? Should Borden have attempted this?

4. Should Borden have made a strong effort to create a presence in the private brand market? Why or why not?

5. Critics have decried Borden's lack of focus. What does this mean? How can the criticisms best be resolved?

6. "After firing D'Amato, the board one month later adopted virtually the same restructuring plan he had proposed. What an injustice!" Discuss.

7. How much of a price premium do you think national brands ought to command over private brands? Justify your position.

HANDS-ON EXERCISES

1. It is 1984 and you are the assistant to the president. He has asked you to design a growth plan for the next decade. What are your recommendations? Take care to avoid the pitfalls that actually beset the company.

---

[11] Lesly, p. 84.

2. It is early 1994. You are the assistant to the new CEO, Ervin Shames. The company is in sorry straits. What do you propose to enable your boss to meet his pledge to boost Borden from the bottom of the food company heap to the top 25 percent?

TEAM DEBATE EXERCISE

Debate the issue of growth by acquisitions versus internal growth. Which of the pros and cons do you think are most compelling?

INVITATION TO RESEARCH

Since Borden is now a private company under the stable of Kohlberg Kravis Roberts and Co., it is difficult to find as much information as if it were publicly held. Still, you may be able to find something about the present fortunes of the firm and its brands.

CHAPTER FIFTEEN

Disney—Euro Disney and Other Stumbles

Disney continues to boast of one of the great brands in the world. Its appeal to kids, and to those who are kids at heart, seems everlasting. Yet, in the decade of the 1990s it stumbled, at first in Euro Disney, and then near the end of the millennium, in perhaps too aggressive an expansion program. Adding to the woes was an acrimonious lawsuit between Jeffrey Katzenberg, former studio chief who left the company in 1994, and Disney CEO Michael Eisner, whose compensation of $631 million topped the list of highest-paid executives in 1998.

EURO DISNEY

Prelude

With high expectations Euro Disney opened just outside Paris in April 1992. Success seemed ensured. After all, the Disney parks in Florida, California, and, most recently, Japan, were all spectacular successes. But somehow all the rosy expectations were revealed to be a delusion. The opening results cast even the future continuance of Euro Disney into doubt. How could what seemed so right be so wrong?

Optimism

Perhaps a few early omens should have raised some cautions. Between 1987 and 1991, three $150 million amusement parks had opened in France with great fanfare. All had fallen flat, and by 1991 two were in bankruptcy. Now Walt Disney Company was finalizing its plans to open Europe's first Disneyland early in 1992. This would turn out to be a $4.4 billion enterprise sprawling over 5,000 acres 20 miles east of Paris. Initially it would have six hotels and 5,200 rooms, more rooms than the entire city of Cannes, and lodging was expected to triple in a few years as Disney opened a second theme park to keep visitors at the resort longer.

Disney also expected to develop a growing office complex, one only slightly smaller than France's biggest, La Defense, in Paris. Plans also called for shopping malls, apartments, golf courses, and vacation homes. Euro Disney would tightly control all this ancillary development, designing and building nearly everything itself, and eventually selling off the commercial properties at a huge profit.

Disney executives had no qualms about the huge enterprise, which would cover an area one-fifth the size of Paris itself. They were more worried that the park might not be big enough to handle the crowds:

> "My biggest fear is that we will be too successful." "I don't think it can miss. They are masters of marketing. When the place opens it will be perfect. And they know how to make people smile—even the French."[1]

Company executives initially predicted that 11 million Europeans would visit the extravaganza in the first year alone. After all, Europeans accounted for 2.7 million visits to the U.S. Disney parks and spent $1.6 billion on Disney merchandise. Surely a park closer would draw many thousands more. As Disney executives thought more about it, the forecast of 11 million seemed most conservative. They reasoned that since Disney parks in the United States (population of 250 million) attract 41 million visitors a year, then if Euro Disney attracted visitors in the same proportion, attendance could reach 60 million with Western Europe's 370 million people. Table 15.1 shows the 1990 attendance at the two U.S. Disney parks and the newest Japanese Disneyland, as well as the attendance-population ratios.

Adding fuel to the optimism was the fact that Europeans typically have more vacation time than do U.S. workers. For example, five-week vacations are commonplace for French and German employees, compared with two to three weeks for U.S. workers.

TABLE 15.1. Attendance and Attendance/Population Ratios, Disney Parks, 1990

	Visitors	Population	Ratio
		(millions)	
United States			
Disneyland (Southern California)	12.9	250	5.2%
Disney World/Epcot Center (Florida)	<u>28.5</u>	250	<u>11.4%</u>
Total United States	41.4		16.6%
Japan			
Tokyo Disneyland	16.0	124	13.5%
Euro Disney	?	310[a]	?

[a] Within a two-hour flight.

Source: Euro Disney, *Amusement Business Magazine.*

Commentary: Even if the attendance/population ratio for Euro Disney is only 10 percent, which is far below that of some other theme parks, still 31 million visitors could be expected. Euro Disney "conservatively" predicted 11 million the first year.

[1] Steven Greenhouse, "Playing Disney in the Parisian Fields," *New York Times*, February 17, 1991, Section 3: 1, 6.

The failure of the three earlier French parks was seen as irrelevant. Robert Fitzpatrick, Euro Disneyland's chairman, stated, "We are spending 22 billion French francs before we open the door, while the other places spent 700 million. This means we can pay infinitely more attention to details—to costumes, hotels, shops, trash baskets—to create a fantastic place. There's just too great a response to Disney for us to fail."[2]

Nonetheless, a few scattered signs indicated that not everyone was happy with the coming of Disney. Leftist demonstrators at Euro Disney's stock offering greeted company executives with eggs, ketchup, and "Mickey Go Home" signs. Some French intellectuals decried the pollution of the country's cultural ambiance with the coming of Mickey Mouse and company: They called the park an American cultural abomination. The mainstream press also seemed contrary, describing every Disney setback "with glee." French officials in negotiating with Disney sought less American and more European culture at France's Magic Kingdom. Still, such protests and bad press seemed contrived, unrepresentative, and certainly not predictive. Company officials dismissed the early criticism as "the ravings of an insignificant elite."[3]

The Location Decision

In the search for a site for Euro Disney, Disney executives examined 200 locations in Europe. The other finalist was Barcelona, Spain. Its major attraction was warmer weather, but its transportation system was not as good as that around Paris, and it lacked level tracts of land of sufficient size. The clincher for the Paris decision was its more central location. Table 15.2 shows the number of people within 2 to 6 hours of the Paris site.

The beet fields of the Marne-la-Vallee area was the choice. Being near Paris seemed a major advantage, since Paris was Europe's biggest tourist draw. And France was eager to win the project to help lower its jobless rate and also to enhance its role as the center of tourist activity in Europe. The French government expected the project to create at least 30,000 jobs and to contribute $1 billion a year from foreign visitors.

TABLE 15.2.   Number of People within 2–6 Hours of the Paris Site

Within a 2-hour drive	17 million people
Within a 4-hour drive	41 million people
Within a 6-hour drive	109 million people
Within a 2-hour flight	310 million people

Source: Euro Disney, *Amusement Business Magazine.*
Commentary: The much more densely populated and geographically compact European continent makes access to Euro Disney much more convenient that it is in the United States.

[2] Greenhouse, p. 6.

[3] Peter Gumbel and Richard Turner, "Fans Like Euro Disney But Its Parent's Goofs Weigh the Park Down," *The Wall Street Journal,* March 10, 1994, p. A12.

To entice the project, the French government allowed Disney to buy up huge tracts of land at 1971 prices. It provided $750 million in loans at below-market rates, and it spent hundreds of millions of dollars on subway and other capital improvements for the park. For example, Paris's express subway was extended out to the park; a 35-minute ride from downtown cost about $2.50. A new railroad station for the high-speed Train a Grande Vitesse was built only 150 yards from the entrance gate. This enabled visitors from Brussels to arrive in only 90 minutes. Once the English Channel tunnel opened in 1994, even London would be only 3 hours and 10 minutes away. Actually, Euro Disney was the second largest construction project in Europe, second only to construction of the English Channel tunnel.

Financing

Euro Disney cost $4.4 billion. Table 15.3 shows the sources of financing, in percentages. The Disney Company had a 49 percent stake in the project, which was the most that the French government would allow. For this stake it invested $160 million, while other investors contributed $1.2 billion in equity. The rest was financed by loans from the government, banks, and special partnerships formed to buy properties and lease them back.

The payoff for Disney began after the park opened. The company receives 10 percent of Euro Disney's admission fees and 5 percent of the food and merchandise revenues. This is the same arrangement as Disney has with the Japanese park. But in the Tokyo Disneyland, the company took no ownership interest, opting instead only for the licensing fees and a percentage of the revenues. The reason for the conservative position with Tokyo Disneyland was that Disney money was heavily committed to building the Epcot Center in Florida. Furthermore, Disney had some concerns about the Tokyo enterprise. This was the first non-American and the first cold-weather Disneyland. It seemed prudent to minimize the risks. But this turned out to be a significant blunder of conservatism, because Tokyo became a huge success, as the following information box discusses in more detail.

TABLE 15.3. Sources of Financing for Euro Disney (percent)

Total to Finance: $4.4 billion	100%
Shareholders equity, including $160 million from Walt Disney Company	32
Loan from French government	22
Loan from group of 45 banks	21
Bank loans to Disney hotels	16
Real estate partnerships	9

Source: Euro Disney.

Commentary: The full flavor of the leverage is shown here, with equity comprising only 32 percent of the total expenditure.

INFORMATION BOX

THE TOKYO DISNEYLAND SUCCESS

Tokyo Disneyland opened in 1983 on 201 acres in the eastern suburb of Urazasu. It was arranged that an ownership group, Oriental Land, would build, own, and operate the theme park with advice from Disney. The owners borrowed most of the $650 million needed to bring the project to fruition. Disney invested no money but receives 10 percent of the revenues from admission and rides and 5 percent of sales of food, drink, souvenirs.

Although the start was slow, Japanese soon began flocking to the park in great numbers. By 1990 some 16 million a year passed through the turnstiles, about one-fourth more than visited Disneyland in California. In fiscal year 1990, revenues reached $988 million with profits of $150 million. Indicative of the Japanese preoccupation with things American, the park serves almost no Japanese food, and the live entertainers are mostly American. Japanese management even apologizes for the presence of a single Japanese restaurant inside the park: "A lot of elderly Japanese came here from outlying parts of Japan, and they were not very familiar with hot dogs and hamburgers."[4]

Disney executives were soon to realize the great mistake they made in not taking substantial ownership in Tokyo Disneyland. They did not want to make the same mistake with Euro Disney.

Would you expect the acceptance of the genuine American experience in Tokyo to be indicative of the reaction of the French and Europeans? Why or why not?

---

[4] James Sterngold, "Cinderella Hits Her Stride in Tokyo," *New York Times*, February 17, 1991, p. 6.

Special Modifications

With the experiences of the previous theme parks, and particularly that of the first cold-weather park in Tokyo, Disney construction executives were able to bring state-of-the-art refinements to Euro Disney. Exacting demands were placed on French construction companies, and a higher level of performance and compliance resulted than many thought possible to achieve. The result was a major project on time, if not completely on budget. In contrast, the Channel tunnel was plagued by delays and severe cost overruns.

One of the things learned from the cold-weather project in Japan was that more needed to be done to protect visitors from such weather problems as wind, rain, and cold. Consequently, Euro Disney's ticket booths were protected from the elements, as were the lines waiting for attractions, and even the moving sidewalk from the 12,000-car parking area.

Certain French accents—and British, German, and Italian accents as well—were added to the American flavor. The park has two official languages, English and

French, but multilingual guides are available for Dutch, Spanish, German, and Italian visitors. Discoveryland, based on the science fiction of France's Jules Verne, is a new attraction. A theater with a full 360-degree screen acquaints visitors with a sweep of European history. And, not the least modification for cultural diversity, Snow White speaks German, and the Belle Notte Pizzeria and Pasticceria are right next to Pinocchio.

Disney had foreseen that it might encounter some cultural problems. This was one of the reasons for choosing Robert Fitzpatrick as Euro Disney's president. He is American but speaks French, knows Europe well, and has a French wife. However, he was unable to establish the rapport needed and was replaced in 1993 by a French native. Still, some of his admonitions that France should not be approached as if it were Florida fell on deaf ears.

RESULTS

As the April 1992 opening approached, the company launched a massive communications blitz aimed at publicizing the fact that the fabled Disney experience was now accessible to all Europeans. Some 2,500 people from various print and broadcast media were lavishly entertained while being introduced to the new facilities. Most media people were positively impressed with the inauguration and with the enthusiastic spirit of the staffers. These public relations efforts, however, were criticized by some for being heavy-handed and for not providing access to Disney executives.

As 1992 wound down after the opening, it became clear that revenue projections were, unbelievably, not being met. But the opening turned out to be in the middle of a severe recession in Europe. European visitors, perhaps as a consequence, were far more frugal than their American counterparts. Many packed their own lunches and shunned the Disney hotels. For example, a visitor named Corine from southern France typified the "no spend" attitude of many: "It's a bottomless pit," she said as she, her husband, and their three children toured Euro Disney on a 3-day visit. "Every time we turn around, one of the kids wants to buy something."[5] Perhaps investor expectations, despite the logic and rationale, were simply unrealistic.

Indeed, Disney had initially priced the park and the hotels to meet revenue targets and had assumed demand was there at any price. Park admission was $42.25 for adults—higher than at the American parks. A room at the flagship Disneyland Hotel at the park's entrance cost about $340 a night, the equivalent of a top hotel in Paris. It was soon averaging only a 50 percent occupancy. Guests were not staying as long or spending as much on the fairly high-priced food and merchandise. We can label the initial pricing strategy at Euro Disney as *skimming pricing*. The following information box discusses skimming and its opposite, penetration pricing.

Disney executives soon realized they had made a major miscalculation. Whereas visitors to Florida's Disney World often stayed more than 4 days, Euro Disney—with one theme park compared to Florida's three—was proving to be a 2-day experience

---

[5] "Ailing Euro Disney May Face Closure," *Cleveland Plain Dealer,* January 1, 1994, p. E1.

INFORMATION BOX

SKIMMING AND PENETRATION PRICING

A firm with a new product or service may be in a temporary monopolistic situation. If there is little or no present and potential competition, more latitude in pricing is possible. In such a situation (and, of course, Euro Disney was in this situation), one of two basic and opposite approaches may be taken in the pricing strategy: skimming or penetration.

Skimming is a relatively high-price strategy. It is the most tempting where the product or service is highly differentiated because it yields high per-unit profits. It is compatible with a quality image. But it has limitations. It assumes a rather inelastic demand curve, in which sales will not be appreciably affected by price. And if the product or service is easily imitated (which was hardly the case with Euro Disney), then competitors are encouraged because of the high profit margins.

The penetration strategy of low prices assumes an elastic demand curve, with sales increasing substantially if prices can be lowered. It is compatible with economies of scale, and it discourages competitive entry. The classic example of penetration pricing was the Model T Ford. Henry Ford lowered his prices to make the car within the means of the general public, expanded production into the millions, and in so doing realized new horizons of economies of scale.

Euro Disney correctly saw itself in a monopoly position; it correctly judged that it had a relatively inelastic demand curve with customers flocking to the park regardless of rather high prices. What it did not reckon with was the shrewdness of European visitors: Because of the high prices they shortened their stay, avoided the hotels, brought their own food and drink, and bought only sparingly the Disney merchandise.

What advantages would a lower price penetration strategy have offered Euro Disney? Do you see any drawbacks?

at best. Many visitors arrived early in the morning, rushed to the park, staying late at night, then checked out of the hotel the next morning before heading back to the park for one final exploration.

The problems of Euro Disney were not public acceptance (despite the earlier critics). Europeans loved the place. Since the opening it attracted just under 1 million visitors a month, thus easily achieving the original projections. Such patronage made it Europe's biggest paid tourist attraction. But the large numbers of frugal patrons did not come close to enabling Disney to meet revenue and profit projections and cover a bloated overhead.

Other operational errors and miscalculations, most of these cultural, hurt the enterprise. A policy of serving no alcohol in the park caused consternation in a country where wine is customary for lunch and dinner. (This policy has since been reversed.) Disney thought Monday would be a light day and Friday a heavy one and allocated staff accordingly, but the reverse was true. It found great peaks and valleys in attendance: The number of visitors per day in the high season could be ten times the number in slack times. The need to lay off employees during quiet periods came up against France's inflexible labor schedules.

One unpleasant surprise concerned breakfast. "We were told that Europeans don't take breakfast, so we downsized the restaurants," recalled one executive. "And guess what? Everybody showed up for breakfast. We were trying to serve 2,500 breakfasts at 350-seat restaurants. The lines were horrendous."[6]

Disney failed to anticipate another demand, this time from tour bus drivers. Restrooms were built for 50 drivers, but on peak days 2,000 drivers were seeking the facilities. "From impatient drivers to grumbling bankers, Disney stepped on toe after European toe."[7]

For the fiscal year ending September 30, 1993, the amusement park had lost $960 million, and the future of the park was in doubt. (As of December 31, 1993, the cumulative loss was 6.04 billion francs, or $1.03 billion). Walt Disney made $175 million available to tide Euro Disney over until the next spring. Adding to the problems of the struggling park were heavy interest costs. As depicted in Table 15.3, against a total cost of $4.4 billion, only 32 percent of the project was financed by equity investment. Some $2.9 billion was borrowed primarily from 60 creditor banks, at interest rates running as high as 11 percent. Thus, the enterprise began heavily leveraged, and the hefty interest charges greatly increased the overhead to be covered from operations. Serious negotiations began with the banks to restructure and refinance.

ATTEMPTS TO RECOVER

The $921 million lost in the first fiscal year represented a shortfall of more than $2.5 million a day. The situation was not quite as dire as these statistics would seem to indicate. Actually, the park was generating an operating profit, but nonoperating costs were bringing it deeply into the red.

Still, operations were far from satisfactory although they were becoming better. It had taken 20 months to smooth out the wrinkles and adjust to the miscalculations about demand for hotel rooms and the willingness of Europeans to pay substantial prices for lodging, meals, and merchandise. Operational efficiencies were slowly improving.

By the beginning of 1994, Euro Disney had been made more affordable. Prices of some hotel rooms were cut—for example, at the low end, from $76 per night to $51. Expensive jewelry was replaced by $10 T-shirts and $5 crayon sets. Luxury sit-down restaurants were converted to self-service. Off-season admission prices were reduced from $38 to $30. And operating costs were reduced 7 percent by streamlining operations and eliminating over 900 jobs.

Efficiency and *economy* became the new watchwords. Merchandise in stores was pared from 30,000 items to 17,000, with more of the remaining goods being pure

---

[6] Gumbel and Turner, p. A12.

[7] Ibid.

U.S. Disney products. (The company had thought that European tastes might prefer more subtle items than the garish Mickey and Minnie souvenirs, but this was found not so.) The number of different food items offered by park services was reduced more than 50 percent. New training programs were designed to remotivate the 9,000 full-time permanent employees, to make them more responsive to customers and more flexible in their job assignments. Employees in contact with the public were given crash courses in German and Spanish.

Still, as we have seen, the problem had not been attendance, although the recession and the high prices had reduced it. Still, some 18 million people passed through the turnstiles in the first 20 months of operation. But they were not spending money as people did in the U.S. parks. Furthermore, Disney had alienated some European tour operators with its high prices, and it diligently sought to win them back.

Management had hoped to reduce the heavy interest overhead by selling the hotels to private investors. But the hotels had an occupancy rate of only 55%, making them unattractive to investors. Although the recession was a factor in such low occupancy rates, a significant part of the problem lay in the calculation of lodging demands. With the park just 35 minutes from the center of Paris, many visitors stayed in town. About the same time as the opening, the real estate market in France collapsed, making the hotels unsalable in the short term. This added to the overhead burden and confounded the business plan forecasts.

While some analysts were relegating Euro Disney to the cemetery, few remembered that Orlando's Disney World showed early symptoms of being a disappointment. Costs were heavier than expected, and attendance was below expectations. But Orlando's Disney World turned out to be one of the most profitable resorts in North America.

ANALYSIS

Euro Disney, as we have seen, fell far short of expectations in the first 20 months of its operation, so far short that its continued existence was even questioned. What went wrong?

External Factors

A serious economic recession that affected all of Europe undoubtedly was a major impediment to meeting expectations. As noted before, it adversely affected attendance—although still not all that much—but drastically affected spending patterns. Frugality was the order of the day for many visitors. The recession also affected real estate demand and prices, thus saddling Disney with hotels it had hoped to sell at profitable prices to eager investors to take the strain off its hefty interest payments.

The company assumed that European visitors would not be greatly different from those visitors, foreign and domestic, of U.S. Disney parks. Yet, at least in the first few years of operation, visitors were much more price conscious. This suggested that those within a 2- to 4-hour drive of Euro Disney were considerably different from the ones who traveled overseas, at least in spending ability and willingness.

Internal Factors

Despite the decades of experience with the U.S. Disney parks and the successful experience with the new Japan park, Disney still made serious blunders in its operational planning, such as the demand for breakfasts, the insistence on wine at meals, the severe peaks and valleys in scheduling, and even such mundane things as sufficient restrooms for tour bus drivers. It had problems in motivating and training its French employees in efficiency and customer orientation. Did all these mistakes reflect an intractable French mindset or a deficiency of Disney management? Perhaps both. But Disney management should have researched all cultural differences more thoroughly. Further, the park needed major streamlining of inventories and operations after the opening. The mistakes suggested an arrogant mindset by Disney management: "We were arrogant," concedes one executive. "It was like 'We're building the Taj Mahal and people will come—on our terms.'"[8]

The miscalculations in hotel rooms and in pricing of many products, including food services, showed an insensitivity to the harsh economic conditions. But the greatest mistake was taking on too much debt for the park. The highly leveraged situation burdened Euro Disney with such hefty interest payments and overhead that the breakeven point was impossibly high, and it even threatened the viability of the enterprise. See the following information box for a discussion of the important inputs and implications affecting breakeven, and how these should play a role in strategic planning.

Were such mistakes and miscalculations beyond what we would expect of reasonable executives? Probably not, with the probable exception of the crushing burden of debt. Any new venture is susceptible to surprises and the need to streamline and weed out its inefficiencies. While we would have expected such to have been done faster and more effectively from a well-tried Disney operation, European, and particularly French and Parisian, consumers and employees showed different behavior and attitude patterns than expected.

The worst sin that Disney management and investors could make would be to give up on Euro Disney and not to look ahead 2 to 5 years. A hint of the future promise was Christmas week of 1993. Despite the first year's $920 million in red ink, some 35,000 packed the park most days. A week later on a cold January day, some of the rides still had 40-minute waits.

POSTSCRIPT

On March 15, 1994, an agreement was struck aimed at making Euro Disney profitable by September 30, 1995. The European banks would fund another $500 million and make concessions such as forgiving 18 months' interest and deferring all principal payments for 3 years. In return, Walt Disney Company agreed to spend about $750 million to bail out its Euro Disney affiliate.[9] Thus, the debt would be

---

[8] Gumbel and Turner, p. A12.

[9] Brian Coleman and Thomas R. King, "Euro Disney Rescue Package Wins Approval," *The Wall Street Journal*, March 15, 1994, pp. A3, A5.

INFORMATION BOX

THE BREAKEVEN POINT

A breakeven analysis is a vital tool in making go/no go decisions about new ventures and alternative business strategies. This can be shown graphically as follows:

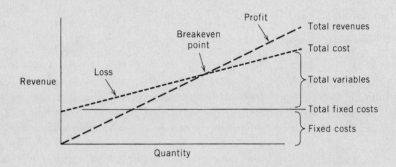

Below the breakeven point, the venture suffers losses; above it, the venture becomes profitable.

Let us make a hypothetical comparison of Euro Disney with its $1.6 billion in high interest loans (some of these as high as 11 percent) from the banks, and what the situation might be with more equity and less borrowed funds.

For this example, let us assume that other fixed costs are $240 million, that the average interest rate on the debt is 10 percent, and that average profit margin (contribution to overhead) from each visitor is $32. Now let us consider two scenarios: (a) the $1.6 billion of debt; and (b) only $0.5 billion of debt.

The number of visitors needed to break even are determined as follows:

$$\text{Breakeven} = \frac{\text{Total fixed costs}}{\text{Contribution to overhead}}$$

Scenario (a): Interest = 10% ($1,600,000,000) = $160,000,000
      Fixed costs = Interest + $240,000,000
                = 160,000,000 + 240,000,000
                = $400,000,000

$$\text{Breakeven} = \frac{\$400,000,000}{\$32} = 12,500,000 \text{ visitors needed to break even}$$

Scenario (b) Interest = 10% (500,000,000) = $50,000,000
      Fixed costs = 50,000,000 + 240,000,000
                = $290,000,000

$$\text{Breakeven} = \frac{\$290,000,000}{\$32} = 9,062,500 \text{ visitors needed to break even}$$

(continues)

THE BREAKEVEN POINT *(continued)*

Because Euro Disney expected 11 million visitors the first year, it obviously was not going to breakeven while servicing $1.6 billion in debt with $160 million in interest charges per year. The average visitor would have to be induced to spend more, thereby increasing the average profit or contribution to overhead.

In making go/no go decisions, many costs can be estimated quite closely. What cannot be determined as surely are the sales figures. Certain things can be done to affect the breakeven point. Obviously it can be lowered if the overhead is reduced, as we saw in scenario b. Higher prices also result in a lower breakeven because of greater per customer profits (but would probably affect total sales quite adversely). Promotion expenses can be either increased or decreased and affect the breakeven point, but they probably also have an impact on sales. Some costs of operation can be reduced, thus lowering the breakeven. But the hefty interest charges act as a lodestone over an enterprise, greatly increasing the overhead and requiring what may be an unattainable breakeven point.

Does a new venture have to break even or make a profit the first year to be worth going into? Why or why not?

halved, with interest payments greatly reduced. Disney also agreed to eliminate for 5 years the lucrative management fees and royalties it received on the sale of tickets and merchandise.

Still, the problems of Euro Disney were not resolved. However, a new source for financing emerged. A member of the Saudi royal family agreed to invest up to $500 million for a 24 percent stake. Prince Alwaleed had invested in troubled enterprises in the past; now his commitment to Euro Disney showed a belief in its ultimate success.

Finally, in the third quarter of 1995, Euro Disney posted its first profit, some $35 million for the period versus a year-earlier loss of $113 million. By now, Euro Disney was only 39 percent owned by Disney. The turnaround was attributed partly to lower prices and the new "Space Mountain" ride that mimicked a trip to the moon. Cheaper transportation to the park also helped, with cross-channel price wars pushing down the costs of traveling to Europe.

In August 1995 news broke of Walt Disney Company's proposed $10 billion acquisition of Capital Cities/ABC Inc. Experts saw this as creating an entertainment behemoth into the next century. Although many growth avenues were now possible, including great international growth in television programming and distribution such as ESPN and the Disney Channel, theme parks were considered very promising. CEO Michael Eisner announced possibilities of new theme parks in South America as well as in Asia.[10]

---

[10] Lisa Bannon, "Expanded Disney to Look Overseas for Fastest Growth," *The Wall Street Journal*, August 2, 1999, p. A3.

In November 1997, *Forbes* magazine updated the situation with Euro Disney—it had been renamed Disneyland Paris—under the provocative title, "Mickey's Last Laugh." The article noted that it had 11.7 million visitors in 1996, up from 8.8 million three years before, and the cash-flow margins even exceeded those of Tokyo Disneyland, the world's most popular park.[11]

Latest Problems for Walt Disney Company

Critical investor attention focused on Walt Disney Company in 1999. In April the firm reported a 41 percent drop in earnings for its fourth consecutive quarter of weak earnings. Analysts were pessimistic about Disney quickly having a turnaround, despite what most recognized as its underlying strength.

Over the previous two years, Disney had invested heavily in new enterprises, most of which were slow in generating any profits, and might even be years away from doing this. For example, there was Disney Cruise Line, an operation that lost $80 million in fiscal 1998, as serious delays were encountered in launching the first ship, the *Disney Magic*. But in 2001, with two ships in service, hopefully this venture would earn a profit.

Disney had started a chain of high-tech arcades called Disney Quest. It had begun a series of ESPN restaurants. It had expanded its Disney Channel and other cable operations. It was constructing a new theme park in Anaheim, California. The company also expanded vigorously on the Internet, both through its Disney Online unit and through the company's 43 percent investment in Infoseek. These all gobbled up funds.

Even some existing businesses were now faltering. Since the acquisition in 1995, Disney had struggled with its ABC network and its low ratings. Now ratings were improving, but Disney had saddled itself with a prodigious $1.1-billion-a-year contract with the National Football League to broadcast its games. Another key business, home videos of Disney animated films and old classics, was not meeting expectations.

The most sensational of Disney's problems involved the legal dispute with Jeffrey Katzenberg over whether he was owed $250 million in bonuses for his work at Disney. Ramifications go beyond the $250 million. Disney and CEO Eisner were accused of underreporting earnings and exaggerating expenses. This could stimulate lawsuits from finance companies, actors, writers, and unions whose pay was tied to a percentage of the take on movies and TV shows. Furthermore, Katzenberg's lucrative contracts with Disney—involving, for example, a $5 million home, $100,000 in home video equipment, private planes, and butler service—could inspire other executives and talents to up their demands. Surprisingly, few criticisms surfaced about Eisner's $631 million in 1998 compensation.[12]

---

[11] "Mickey's Last Laugh," *Forbes*, November 3, 1997, p. 16.

[12] This section has been compiled from various sources, including Keith Alexander, "Disney Case Grows Ominous," *USA Today*, May 4, 1999, p. 3B; Robert McGough and Bruce Orwall, "Disney: Lion King's Roar Stays Hoarse," *The Wall Street Journal*, April 29, 1999, pp. C1 and C2; "Compensation Fit for a King," *Forbes*, May 17, 1999, pp. 202–203.

WHAT CAN BE LEARNED?

Beware the arrogant mindset, especially when dealing with new situations and new cultures. French sensitivities were offended by Disney corporate executives who often turned out to be brash, insensitive, and overbearing. A contentious attitude by Disney personnel alienated people and aggravated planning and operational difficulties. "The answer to doubts or suggestions invariably was, Do as we say, because we know best."

Such a mindset is a natural concomitant with success. It is said that success breeds arrogance, but this inclination must be fought against by those who would spurn the ideas and concerns of others. For a proud and touchy people, the French, this almost contemptuous attitude by the Americans fueled resentment and glee at Disney miscues. It did not foster cooperation, understanding, or the willingness to smooth the process. One might almost speculate that had not the potential economic benefits to France been so great, the Euro Disney project might never have been approved.

Great success may be ephemeral. We often find that great successes are not lasting, that they have no staying power. Somehow the success pattern gets lost or forgotten or is not well rounded. Other times an operation grows beyond the capability of the originators. Hungry competitors are always in the wings, ready to take advantage of any lapse. As we saw with Euro Disney, having a closed mind to new ideas or to needed revisions of an old success pattern—the arrogance of success— makes expansion into different environments more difficult and even risky.

While corporate Disney has continued to have strong success with its other theme parks and its diversifications, competitors are moving in with their own theme parks in the United States and elsewhere. We may question whether this industry is approaching saturation, and we may wonder whether Disney has learned from its mistakes in Europe.

Highly leveraged situations are extremely vulnerable. During most of the 1980s, many managers, including corporate raiders, pursued a strategy of debt financing in contrast to equity (stock ownership) financing. Funds for such borrowing were usually readily available, heavy debt had income tax advantages, and profits could be distributed among fewer shares so that return on equity was enhanced. During this time a few voices decried the overleveraged situations of many companies. They predicted that when the eventual economic downturn came, such firms would find themselves unable to meet the heavy interest burden. Most lenders paid little heed to such lonesome voices and encouraged greater borrowing.

The widely publicized problems of some of the raiders in the late 1980s, such as Robert Campeau, who had acquired major department store corporations only to find himself overextended and unable to continue, suddenly changed some expansionist lending sentiments. The hard reality dawned that these arrangements were often fragile indeed, especially when they rested on optimistic projections for asset sales, for revenues, and for cost savings to cover the interest payments. An economic slowdown hastened the demise of some of these ill-advised speculations.

LATE-BREAKING NEWS

In the fiscal fourth quarter of 1999, Disney net fell 71 percent from the year before, making 1999 the second straight year of negative growth, and Eisner would not predict when growth would be back: "I think it's coming, but it's not coming tomorrow."[13] The company continued to suffer from poor performances in its home-video and consumer-products units, including sales declines in Disney Stores.

Theme parks, however, were showing promise. To the delight of the French government, plans were announced to build a movie theme park, Disney Studios, next to the Magic Kingdom, to open in 2002. It was estimated that this expansion would attract an additional 4.2 million visitors annually, drawing people from further afield in Europe. In 1998, Disneyland Paris had 12.5 million visitors, being France's No. 1 tourist attraction, beating out Notre Dame.

Also late in 1999, Disney and Hong Kong agreed to build a major Disney theme park there, with Disney investing $314 million for 43 percent ownership while Hong Kong contributed nearly $3 billion. Hong Kong's leader expected the new park would generate 16,000 jobs when it opened in 2005, certainly a motivation for the unequal investment contribution.

[13] Bruce Orwall, "Disney Net Fell 71% in Fiscal 4th Quarter," *The Wall Street Journal,* November 5, 1999, p. A3.

Sources: "Hong Kong Betting $3 billion on Success of New Disneyland," *Cleveland Plain Dealer,* November 3, 1999, p. 2-C; Charles Fleming, "Euro Disney to Build Movie Theme Park Outside Paris," *The Wall Street Journal,* September 30, 1999, pp. A18 and A21.

Disney was guilty of the same speculative excesses with Euro Disney, relying far too much on borrowed funds and assuming that assets, such as hotels, could be easily sold off at higher prices to other investors. As we saw in the breakeven box, hefty interest charges from such overleveraged conditions can jeopardize the viability of the enterprise if revenue and profit projections fail to meet the rosy expectations.

Be judicious with the skimming price strategy. Euro Disney faced the classical situation favorable for a skimming price strategy. It was in a monopoly position, with no equivalent competitors likely. It faced a somewhat inelastic demand curve, which indicated that people would come almost regardless of price. So why not price to maximize per-unit profits? Unfortunately for Disney, the wily Europeans circumvented the high prices by frugality. Of course, a severe recession exacerbated the situation.

The learning insight from this example is that a skimming price assumes that customers are willing and able to pay the higher prices and have no lower-priced competitive alternatives. It is a faulty strategy when many customers are unable, or else unwilling, to pay the high prices and can find a way to experience the product or service in a modest way.

CONSIDER

Can you think of other learning insights from this case?

QUESTIONS

1. How could the company have erred so badly in its estimates of the spending patterns of European customers?

2. How could a better reading of the impact of cultural differences on revenues have been achieved?

3. What suggestions do you have for fostering a climate of sensitivity and goodwill in corporate dealings with the French?

4. How do you account for the great success of Tokyo Disneyland and the problems of Euro Disney? What are the key contributory differences?

5. Do you believe that Euro Disney might have done better if located elsewhere in Europe rather than just outside Paris? Why or why not?

6. "Mickey Mouse and the Disney park are an American cultural abomination." Evaluate this critical statement.

7. Consider how a strong marketing approach might be made to both European consumers and agents, such as travel agents, tour guides, even bus drivers.

8. A major Disney stockholder angrily comments upon seeing the latest *Forbes* rankings of executive compensation: "It's an insult to us shareholders to pay Michael Eisner $631 million last year (1998), more than any other executive of any other firm, when Disney profits have been steadily declining under his leadership. I'm selling my Disney stock." Discuss.

HANDS-ON EXERCISES

Before

1. It is three months before the grand opening. As a staff assistant to the president of Euro Disney, you sense that the plans for high price and luxury accommodations are ill advised. What arguments would you marshall to persuade the company to offer lower prices and more moderate accommodations? Be as persuasive as you can.

After

2. It is six months after opening. Revenues are not meeting target, and a number of problems have surfaced and are being worked on. The major problem remains, however, that the venture needs more visitors and/or higher expenditures per visitor. Develop plans to improve the situation.

TEAM DEBATE EXERCISE

It is two years after the opening. Euro Disney is a monumental mistake, profitwise. Two schools of thought are emerging for improving the situation.

One is to pour money into the project, build one or two more theme parks and really make this another Disney World. The other camp believes more investment would be wasted at this time, that the need is to pare expenses to the bone and wait for an eventual upturn. Debate the two positions.

INVITATION TO RESEARCH

Has the recent profitability of Euro Disney continued? Has the declining profitability of the Disney Corporation been turned around? Is the Disney Cruise Line a success? Has the lawsuit by Jeffrey Katzenberg been settled, and if so, who won?

CHAPTER SIXTEEN

Coors—What's Wrong with Being Number Three?

A tragedy occurred in the winter of 1960 that was to have an impact years later on the fortunes of the brewer Adolph Coors Company. On the morning of February 9, Adolph Coors III, 44-year-old chairman of the board, kissed his wife and four children good-bye and drove off for the plant 12 miles away. He was never seen again, alive.

For months, this brought one of the most intensive manhunts in Colorado history. Finally, on September 26, more than seven months later, clothing and bones were accidentally discovered in a desolate, heavily wooded area some 40 miles southeast of Denver. Apparently, after the body had been dumped, the remains were scattered by coyotes or hogs. Dental charts confirmed the identification of Coors.

At the start of the new millennium, forty years later, Coors had forged its way to third-largest U.S. brewer, but still a *distant* third to Anheuser-Busch and Miller Brewing. Therein lay its problems.

HISTORY

The Golden Years

Adolph Coors III had been sharing leadership responsibilities with his father, Adolph Coors II. After the murder, the father again assumed sole leadership until he died in 1970 at the age of 86. The elder of the two surviving sons, William H. Coors, became chairman and chief executive, and the other son, Joseph, president.

Both Bill and Joe (employees called them by their first names) were rugged outdoorsmen. They regarded physical fitness as so important that executives and workers were sent to outdoor survival schools, where they not only had to participate but also compete. "If you can't fight competition, you don't need to survive," Bill asserted.[1]

---

[1] "Colorado's Coors Family Has Built an Empire on One Brand of Beer," *The Wall Street Journal*, October 26, 1973, p. 1.

Sensational Growth

By 1970, the accomplishments of Coors in the brewing industry were awesome—all the more in light of the nonconformity of Coors to existing industry practices. The company produced only one kind of beer, and this in a single brewery, albeit the largest in the world. It sold its beer in only 11 Western States, most of these the most sparsely populated areas of the United States. It refused to build branch plants and had not expanded its territory in 22 years. The one brewery in Golden, Colorado, was not even close to its biggest market, California—indeed, the average barrel of Coors traveled over 900 miles. Finally, its ads featuring rushing mountain streams, and the slogan "Brewed with pure Rocky Mountain spring water," had not been changed in 33 years.

Yet, this little regional brewer had moved up to the big time. With a 19 percent increase in production in 1969 over 1968, it was fourth in the national beer rankings, the only regional brewer to come close to the national brewers. Furthermore, in nine of the 11 states where it was distributed, Coors topped all other brands in sales. Overall demand outstripped supply so much that the company had to ration its product among distributors.

In compiling this performance record, the brothers shunned a *marketing orientation*. (See the following information box for a comparison of the marketing orientation with an internal or production orientation.) Bill Coors stated: "Our top management thrust is on engineering and production.... We're production-oriented. Nobody knows more about production than I do."[2] Emphasis was on making a quality beer in terms of processing and raw materials.

The result was a mild, light-bodied beer, using hops, rice, Rocky Mountain spring water, and a specially developed strain of barley grown by contract farmers. Pasteurization, which would add greatly to the ease of preserving, was shunned, since it would slightly affect the taste. Eliminating pasteurization, however, greatly increased logistical problems since the beer had to be canned at near-freezing temperatures and shipped under refrigeration to refrigerated warehouses. Otherwise, the natural taste could not be maintained. To further ensure perfection of taste, distributors were required to pull Coors off shelves in 30 days lest some flavor be lost.

Coors had become the beer of celebrities, from President Ford, who packed Coors on Air Force One, to Henry Kissinger, and to actors such as Paul Newman (who, in an *Esquire* interview, claimed, "The best domestic beer, bar none, is Coors") and Clint Eastwood. In these years, the famous, as well as the rank and file were all contributing to the Coors "mystique." Some 300,000 Coors fans a year toured the brewery; others made "pilgrimages" to a waterfall near Grand Lake, Colorado, which was supposed to be the one pictured on Coors bottles and cans. T-shirts and sweatshirts emblazoned with "Coors—Breakfast of Champions" were being sold by entrepreneurs hoping to cash in on the Coors mystique. And in the East, where Coors was not directly distributed, it could sell for three times the regular price.

---

[2] "The Brewery That Breaks All the Rules," *Business Week*, August 22, 1970, p. 60.

INFORMATION BOX

INTERNAL VS. EXTERNAL (MARKETING) ORIENTATION

A firm, in planning and executing its strategy, can primarily focus on internal factors, such as technology and cost cutting. The key to attracting customers is thereby seen as improving production and distribution efficiency and lowering costs if possible. Henry Ford pioneered this philosophy in the early 1900s with his Model T. Coors was certainly successful with such an orientation up to about 1976. But then consumer preferences began changing, and competition became keener. The internal or production orientation may succeed for a while where

1. Demand exceeds supply because of attractive uniqueness; new technologies; or scarcity, as in developing countries.
2. Production costs are high, and market expansion depends on reducing costs.

An external, or marketing, orientation recognizes the fallacy of the assumption that products will forever sell themselves. Looking outside the firm to the business environment results in major priority being given to determining customers' needs and wants, how these may be changing as evidenced by shifts in buying patterns, and adapting products and services accordingly. The external focus also permits more responsiveness to other external forces that may be factors, such as major competitive thrusts, changing governmental laws and regulations, and economic conditions. With such a focus, attention can be directed to locating new opportunities, to meeting and even anticipating change rather than being engrossed in internal production and technological advances. So, the marketing orientation is more attuned to the dynamic environment of today.

Do all firms need a marketing orientation? Can you think of any that probably do not and will not?

Besides the product, the company was unique from the rest of the industry in certain other respects. In the heady years of the 1960s and early 1970s, Bill and Joe shunned outside expertise. Advertising and promotion were handled by inside staff, and total expenditures averaged only one-quarter those of major competitors. Construction at the brewery was done by Coors' own construction crews. Company engineers designed machinery for the can plant. Management talent was developed and promoted from within the organization rather than brought in from outside.

The guiding philosophy of the company since it was founded by a German orphan who stowed away on a U.S.-bound ship to avoid conscription into the German army—the first Adolph Coors, in 1873—was to refuse to go to a bank for a loan. Such fiscal conservatism led the company to reject some seemingly attractive expansion possibilities. For example, the company's can-manufacturing subsidiary, Coors Container Company, was instrumental in developing the technical process for making a two-piece aluminum can. Coors, however, sold the process to Continental Can Company and American Can Company: "We could have dominated the industry, but we would have had to borrow from the banks, and Coors doesn't do that."[3] Between 1970 and 1974, in order to keep up with the burgeoning demand for Coors beer, some $276 million was spent on plant expansion. And how was this financed? All of it from cash flow.

How Come the Mystique?

What was the magic of Coors? How durable was this magic or mystique likely to be? Perhaps part of the mystique was accidental and fortuitous: being a Western-made brew at a time when the freedom and environmental purity of the West—emphasized by Coors' slogan, "Pure Rocky Mountain Spring Water"—was seen by many consumers as contrasting sharply with the degradation of the industrial centers of population. But was it a better beer—better tasting, higher quality? There were many who said it was. Whether real or imagined, Coors offered a "unique selling proposition" that distinguished it from other beers. One could claim that coming from a single brewery ensured better quality control and uniformity of ingredients and flavor. The company liked to boast that Coors was the most expensively brewed beer in the world, even though it sold in the popular price range. A plant geneticist was employed full-time to develop improved strains of barley for malting. Most hops were imported from Germany. And, as noted before, great pains were taken to prevent any deterioration of the flavor in shipping and handling.

Undoubtedly, part of the mystique came from the contagion generated by the aficionados, those famous and not so famous. A Western image conveying the out-of-doors and environmental purity, a light-tasting beer... perhaps the timing could not have been better in the 1960s and the early 1970s. (In the cigarette industry, Marlboro rose to become the top seller on a somewhat similar advertising and image thrust: the Marlboro man.)

It hardly seemed to Bill and Joe that the golden image of their beer could in the span of just a few years fade drastically. How could it help but be enduring?

Going Public

For 103 years, ever since the first Adolph Coors opened his brewery on the trail to the Colorado gold camps, the company stayed private—talks of having public or outside shareholders were anathema to the Coors family. And it seemed that the company could indeed finance large-scale capital expenditures internally. Throughout the decade of the 1960s its average rate of growth was over 10 percent, all this without turning to outside stock ownership or borrowing. In 1975, Coors had only $2 million in long-term debt on its books, against $375 million in equity.

But, in 1975, the proud family tradition had to be abandoned. With the death of the parents of Bill and Joe, the Internal Revenue Service presented a bill for $50 mil-

---

[3] "Colorado's Coors Family," p. 27.

lion in inheritance taxes. While many companies would have solved such a problem by going into debt, Bill and Joe decided to go public as the lesser of two evils. In order not to risk relinquishing control of the company to outsiders, they would offer only nonvoting shares. Furthermore, to avoid diluting the equity, no more than 5 percent of net income would be paid as dividends.

The time for such a stock offering was not very propitious. The Dow Jones Industrial Average was then moving between 620 and 690, and many were the investors who thought it would go still lower. Added to a sick stock market, the restrictions placed on this new stock venture were hardly likely to appeal to many investors. Since the shares would be nonvoting, this precluded listing on the New York Stock Exchange, as well as being offered for sale in many states, including California, where Coors' stock could otherwise have had a warm reception. The nonvoting feature would also make the stock offering unattractive to many large institutional investors.

In the end, Coors lucked out. When the offering finally reached the market, the stock market was beginning to rebound. Coors' investment bankers found so much interest in the stock in the last days before the offering that they raised the price to $31 a share. And it was a sellout the first afternoon. Not only was the $50 million raised to pay off the inheritance taxes, but an additional $77 million went into the company coffers. This $127 million offering was the first major new stock issue to come to market since 1973 and the fourth largest offering by industrial companies in the previous 10 years. The mystique of the company and its beer mitigated all the negative factors impinging on demand.

Geographical Expansion

Bill Coors now turned his attention to geographical expansion. The first target was eastern and southern Texas. Prior to this, the only Texas inroads were in the northern part of the state around Dallas and the western part.

Eager to jump on a lucrative bandwagon, potential distributors lined up like beauty queen candidates, vying for selection by Coors. The contest, however, was hardly for the weak or poorly financed, since Coors' distributors had to build refrigerated warehouses so that Coors' unpasteurized beer could be kept under 40 degrees until opened by customers. From 4,000 "panting" contestants, Coors selected 29 distributors for the eastern Texas expansion.

By 1976, Coors was also invading Montana, and looking closely at expanding into Washington state, Arkansas, Nebraska, and Missouri, the latter state being the home base of Anheuser-Busch, the largest brewer. Bill Coors was also laying plans for expanding to the heavily populated Eastern market: "I think we've got a good enough beer—the beer that won the West—to assure ourselves 20 percent to 25 percent of the nationwide market," he told *Forbes'* reporters in the summer of 1976.[4] A bold statement this, with Anheuser holding 24 percent of the total market, whereas Coors had only 8.2 percent. Admittedly, however, this figure was

---

[4] "Off Coors," *Forbes,* June 1, 1976, p. 60.

based on far less than national distribution, in fact on only 20 percent of the total national distribution.

The question of whether expansion could still be handled out of the one brewery in Golden seemed not particularly troublesome to Bill. While the Golden brewery was already at an annual capacity of 12.3 million barrels, about one million barrels of capacity was being added a year, and Bill was aiming for a total of 25 million. "Eventually we might build other breweries," he said. "But if you take a circle up around from where we already ship to in Northern California, you hit Atlanta, Georgia."[5]

The growth and profitability picture—and the highly successful public stock offering—should have been cause for heady optimism and great satisfaction for the Coors brothers. Sales for 1975 were $520 million, up from $350 million just four years before. Operating margin on net sales had reached 28 percent, the highest in the industry. Profit per barrel averaged almost $9, about double that of Anheuser. But there were some ominous clouds on the horizon.

STORM SIGNALS FOR COORS, 1975–1976

While the successful public stock float spurred new ambitions, trouble was brewing in the California market—a key market that accounted for almost 40 percent of all Coors' sales. In a bitter dispute with Coors' Oakland distributor, the California Teamsters called for a statewide boycott of the beer. At the same time, Anheuser was bringing on line a new 3.75 million barrel brewery in northern California. As a result, in this key market, Coors' sales dropped about 10 percent in 1975, while market share fell 4 percent to 36 percent. Anheuser picked up most of this, gaining 3 percent to a 23.2 percent share of the California market. Perhaps another contributor to the market share losses in California was a hefty price hike made in 1974 without first warning retailers.

Several other aggravations were also being encountered. The Federal Trade Commission in January 1975 was upheld by the Supreme Court in its efforts to loosen the tight grip Coors had held on its 167 distributors. Then the Equal Opportunities Commission filed a suit against Coors alleging discrimination against minorities in hiring and in promotions. And the Colorado Health Department charged Coors with polluting Clear Creek, in the very same valley where the "Rocky Mountain spring water" rises.

Finally, brother Joe was embarrassed as the Senate Commerce Committee vetoed his nomination to the board of the Corporation for Public Broadcasting, citing Coors' ownership of a right-wing television news service as a conflict of interest. Joe had long been known locally as an archconservative, but his political views came to national attention in 1975 when the *Washington Post* ran four lengthy stories about his right-wing efforts in allegedly using Television News, Inc., a broadcast news agency subsidiary of the Coors Company, to further his own political views. This pub-

[5] Ibid., p. 61.

licity, as well as the fact that the news subsidiary was losing money, induced the company to close down the TV news service. Whatever negative effect might have emanated from the hardly favorable publicity could not be gauged.

Some dangers could be seen in the decision to push East, even though such a move, if successful, would greatly increase the sales of Coors as well as lessen the risks inherent in relying on only a few markets—such as the California one—for maintenance of growth and even viability. To attempt to enter the Eastern markets would bring Coors face-to-face with entrenched major brewers: Schlitz, Pabst, and Philip Morris's Miller, in addition to Anheuser-Busch. Miller, in particular, looked like a most formidable competitor; it had become the nation's fastest-growing major beer company, and by the beginning of 1976 had risen to third place in the U.S. beer market, moving ahead of Coors in the process. Undoubtedly, Coors' push into the East would necessitate massive additional advertising expenditures. Although sales might be increased by such expansion efforts, more questionable was what effect such would have on profits. Furthermore, despite optimism by Bill Coors about their one brewery being adequate to supply their entire national market, rather serious logistical problems could be expected.

THE END OF THE GOLDEN AGE, 1977–

In 1977, the boom was lowered. Although Tables 16.1 and 16.2 show Coors as faltering considerably less than Schlitz and Pabst in sales and profits, still 1977 marked a serious trend reversal after the heady years of growth. Furthermore, the reversal appeared to be not shortlived but rather symptomatic of serious underlying problems, with the dominance of Anheuser-Busch and Miller becoming ever greater.

In 1977, Coors earned $1.92 a share, down 12 percent from 1976. It shipped 12.8 million barrels of beer, down 5 percent from 1976. It lost market share in many of the 16 Western states where it had the bulk of its distribution. The problems continued into 1978. Only a few years before, Coors had been selling its beer by allocation only; now, suddenly, it had to cut back production.

The Eastern markets no longer beckoned, either. They were heavily saturated with strong, well-entrenched competitors. In fact the big Eastern brewers were mov-

TABLE 16.1. Relative Sales of Top Five U.S. Brewers, 1973–1977

	Sales (millions of dollars)				
	1973	1974	1975	1976	1977
Anheuser-Busch	1109.7	1413.1	1645.0	1441.2	1838.0
Miller	275.9	403.6	658.3	982.8	1327.6
Schlitz	703.0	814.5	923.0	1000.0	937.4
Pabst	355.4	431.3	525.0	600.5	582.9
Coors	378.8	467.8	520.0	593.6	593.1

Source: Company annual reports.

TABLE 16.2.   Relative Profits of Top Five U.S. Brewers, 1973–1977

	Net Profits (millions of dollars)				
	1973	1974	1975	1976	1977
Anheuser-Busch	65.6	64.0	84.7	55.4	91.9
Miller	(2.4)	6.3	28.6	76.1	106.5
Schlitz	55.2	49.0	30.9	50.0	17.8
Pabst	23.8	18.3	20.7	32.4	21.8
Coors	47.5	41.1	59.5	76.5	67.7

Source: Company annual reports.

ing West because of this. Anheuser had built a new plant in California. Miller was building one. Schlitz had expanded its capacity in the West. Coors, with its single plant in the mountains of Colorado, faced exorbitant transportation costs in trying to reach the Eastern markets, all the more so because its beer had to be shipped under refrigeration to maintain quality. Unfortunately, the quality image of the beer had suffered when bootleggers brought it into the East, handled it carelessly, and sold it at black-market prices. As a result, Coors had even been forced to take out newspaper ads in some Eastern cities advising beer drinkers not to drink Coors. But a negative image had been created in the minds of many Eastern beer drinkers.

Labor Problems

Labor problems exacerbated a deteriorating situation. On April 5, 1977, the brewery workers at the Golden, Colorado, plant walked out. A week after the walkout, the AFL–CIO approved a nationwide boycott of the company's beer.

The company was unyielding and now proposed that all prospective employees take lie detector tests. The idea of polygraph testing hearkens back to the kidnapping of Adolph Coors III and fears of the family that this could happen again. Eventually, more than 1,000 of the 1,472 workers who walked out returned, while the rest were replaced. The strike lasted 15 months, and eventually the union was rejected by the employees. But the wrath of labor was incurred in the process, and Coors now ranked with J.P. Stevens Company on union hate lists.

Opinions differ as to the effects the union boycott had on Coors' sales and profits: how much of the decline was due to labor boycotting, and how much was due to intensified competition? Bill Coors blamed most on the union boycott: "It was a shock for us to find that, as far as the union is concerned, anything goes. No lie is too great to tell if it accomplishes their boycott objectives. We view the boycott as a monument to immorality and dishonesty."[6]

The mystique of Coors, the image it had gloried in and which seemed to give it a competitive edge over all other brews, was gone, abruptly, bewilderingly. One won-

---

[6] "Coors Beer: What Hit Us?" *Forbes*, October 16, 1978, p. 71.

ders whether the ultraconservative policies emanated from the tragedy of a brother's kidnapping and murder, over a decade-and-a-half previously, and could have blinded the company to a changing environment.

Competition

As evident from Table 16.1, the aggressive marketing efforts of Anheuser and Miller were having detrimental effects on the other members of the big five, not to mention the smaller regional brewers. The erosion of Coors' market share in California, its biggest market, where previously it had a 40 percent market share, was particularly worrisome, especially as it hinted at a greater erosion to come. In the first six months of 1978, Anheuser took over first place with a 35 percent share, with Coors dropping to 25 percent. Even more alarming was the threat of the surging Miller. While number two nationally, Miller was still a poor third in California, with less than 10 percent of the market. But Miller was building a brewery there, and Coors certainly had to expect that once its production facilities were established at a sufficiently high level, Miller's aggressive marketing efforts would be leveled at California. Coors would be placed in the more vulnerable position in attempting to match the expenditures and the expertise of Miller and Anheuser in a hotly contested market.

COORS FIGHTS BACK

Bill and Joe turned to marketing research to determine where they had gone wrong. The answer was definitive. The beer industry was growing at only 3 percent a year, but almost all the growth was coming from two products: light or low-calorie beer, and superpremium beer. Coors offered neither of these. Furthermore, research revealed that four out of every 10 new light-beer drinkers had switched from Coors.

Bill and Joe finally moved to rectify the product deficiencies of a single-beer strategy, and in the spring of 1978 introduced their first new product in 20 years, Coors Light. They also began developing a superpremium beer, planning market tests in early 1980. Coors' reluctance to expand the product line is understandable, if not commendable: Making different kinds of beer in the same brewery complicates production and is more costly than an unchanging production line.

Coors now increased its expansion efforts, bringing to 17 the number of states in which it was marketing its beer. The Coors brothers had reached the painful conclusion that the company must abandon its comfortable role as a regional brewer and emerge as a national power.

Coors' promotional expenditures had lagged far behind its major competitors and even some of the much smaller regional brewers. (See Table 16.3.) In 1978 the company finally upped advertising to $15 million, a whopping increase. But this produced only a small gain in sales to $624.8 million, while profits declined almost 20 percent to $54.8 million.

The question at this point was whether Coors had waited far too long to adapt to a changing environment. Deeply embedded conservatism and unchanging policies,

TABLE 16.3. Relative Advertising Expenditures for Top Eight Brewers, 1973–1976*

| | *Expenditures (millions of dollars)* | | | |
	1973	1974	1975	1976
Anheuser-Busch	20.5	17.8	27.4	28.5
Jos. Schlitz	19.7	20.9	26.5	34.1
Miller	10.9	13.6	21.3	29.1
Pabst	7.2	8.4	9.6	9.7
Coors	1.4	1.6	1.2	2.0
Olympia	3.3	3.9	5.8	5.7
Stroh's	4.5	4.4	4.0	5.0
F. & M. Schaefer	4.4	4.3	2.7	2.5

* These expenditures are understated, since they do not include the large sums typically spent by brewers on point of purchase materials and other nonmeasured media.
Source: Advertising Age, September 26, 1977, p. 112.

misplaced confidence in the everlasting appeal of one beer and its mystique, and a confrontation policy with union employees—these helped end the golden years.

The 1980s

By 1981, Coors was budgeting $87 million for advertising, nearly double what it had spent two years before, and many times the $1.2 million spent in 1975. Coors Light was running neck and neck with Miller's nationally dominant Lite in the 20 states in which Coors was now selling. But problems remained.

Both barrelage and income were down. Coors' share of the California market had dropped to 20 percent in 1981. Anheuser was invading Coors' stronghold of Texas, and its Bud Light gained 3 percent in one month.

In 1983, however, Coors moved aggressively into the Southeast and captured 11 percent of the market with a good coordination of advertising and dealer incentives. But Western markets continued to erode. In California, its competitive position had fallen to 16.1 percent by 1983. In this state with the highest beer consumption in the nation, market share had been 37.8 percent 10 years before.

By 1984, the company had expanded to 26 states with its Coors Premium and Light brands, and clung to fifth place among all brewers with a 7.6 percent share of the market, exactly the same as in 1978 when it had a much smaller geographic distribution.

Then, on August 19, 1987, the AFL–CIO ended its 10-year boycott, satisfied that the major complaints had been addressed. In the next two months Coors gained more than 1,800 new accounts. Advertising expenditures now totaled $200 million. Coors Light, dubbed the "Silver Bullet," was effectively promoted to the Hispanic market, with the beer described as part of the *pura vida,* the good life.

As Coors moved into the 1990s, it ranked third among U.S. brewers, largely due to strength in Coors Light and Keystone, a new popular-priced beer introduced in 1989. And the firm was in strong financial shape.

COORS FACES THE NEW MILLENNIUM

In 1998, Coors was 125 years old, having been started by Pete's great-grandfather in 1873. The principals had inevitably changed from the glory years of the early 1970s. The president was now W. Leo Kiely III, a hearty extrovert with a beer belly who had come from Frito-Lay in 1993. The CEO was Pete Coors, a lean and taut mountain man, and the chairman was another Bill Coors. The company was still a distant third in its industry, with a domestic market share of only 11 percent. Its 1998 sales of $1.9 billion compared with Anheuser-Busch's $11.2 billion and the Miller division of Philip Morris's $4.1 billion. See Table 16.4 for Coors' revenue, income, and return-on-equity 10-year comparisons with Anheuser.

Coors still remained a target for left-leaning interest groups, with the Internet providing opportunity for unions, neoprohibitionists, and gay rights activists to condemn the Coors family's political conservatism. Pete Coors wearily sighs, "They need a whipping post, and we have been one for a long time."[7]

Life as Number Three in the Industry

Coors was subjected to savage price pressures from its two much larger competitors. These affected its income figures as shown in Table 16.4. In 1998, Coors netted less than 4 cents on every revenue dollar, while Anheuser-Busch netted nearly 11 cents.

Coors was also severely disadvantaged in its advertising and promotion budget. To have more impact, it was forced to concentrate its promotional efforts on certain seasons and activities. It became involved with auto racing, a hot spectator sport in many areas, with two-time Daytona 500 winner Sterling Marlin driving a Coors Light car on the premier NASCAR circuit.

It sought uniqueness with innovative packaging, using some 600 different packages, including baseball-bat-shaped bottles and holographic labels. A "pigskin" bottle was introduced in 1998 having leather grain texture and laces to support football season promotions. The association with the Rocky Mountains was reinforced by adding strong mountain imagery to packaging graphics.

The nonpasteurization was still the most unique aspect of Coors beer, but the better flavor depended on it staying cold all the way to the grocer's cooler, and this had always brought nagging problems. Coors was still having trouble distributing its product nationwide. At first it had tried a logistics system with 27 satellite warehouses to get the beer closer to wholesalers. But this was costly and delivery often took more time than if coming directly from Colorado. Eventually the warehouses were reduced to 12, and more beer was delivered directly by truck.

---

[7] Seth Lubove, "No Fizz in the Profits," *Forbes*, September 7, 1998, p. 74.

TABLE 16.4.   Coors versus Anheuser-Busch, 1989–1998

	1989	1992	1995	1998
Anheuser-Busch:				
Revenues (millions $)	9,481	11,394	10,341	11,245
Net Income (millions $)	767	994	887	1,233
% Net Inc. of Revs.	8.1	8.7	8.6	11.0
% Ret. on Equity	24.8	22.2	20.0	30.0
Coors:				
Revenues (millions $)	1,764	1,551	1,675	1,900
Net Income (millions $)	13	36	43	69
% Net Inc. of Revs.	.7	2.3	2.6	3.6
% Ret. on Equity	1.2	4.0	6.3	9.0

Source: Company reports.

Commentary: Several aspects are notable about these comparative statistics. Over the 10-year period, Anheuser's revenue gain is 18.6 percent, far from outstanding and maybe hardly acceptable. But Coors is only 7.7 percent for this same period. For 10-year net profit gains, the situation differs: Anheuser had a 60.8 percent increase, Coors a 430 percent increase. But Coors' increase reflects a very poor profit performance in 1989.

The net income percentages and the return-on-equity percentages are more revealing. And Coors shows up very poorly on both. Admittedly its situation improved steadily over these 10 years, but the comparison with Anheuser is poor. For example, in 1998, its best year of the decade, Coors achieved 3.6 percent net income to sales and a 9.0 percent return on its equity. But Anheuser had 11.0 percent and 30.0 percent respectively.

So, Coors remained viable as the underdog in a highly competitive market. The likelihood of ever rising above number three seemed unlikely. There are some who question whether any underdog can ever rise above being left in the dust by the number-one player with the greater resources. (See the following information box.) But let us not disregard this 125-year-old firm that once had a glorious mystique, and lost it, but now is a scrappy number three in its industry.

INFORMATION BOX

IS THE WINNER INVINCIBLE?

In a 1995 book, *The Winner Take All Society,* Robert Frank of Cornell University saw the top firms in their industries as becoming so dominant as to be virtually unassailable. These firms were enjoying a huge and widening gap in financial rewards and stock-market valuations, often gaining the means to further consolidate their positions by acquiring rivals.

(continues)

INFORMATION BOX (continued)

The rise of Internet companies appears to support this, with most traffic volume concentrated on a few Web sites. Beyond this, however, the free-agent labor market is hypothesized as inducing the best people to jump to the winners—after all, we all like to be associated with winners, don't we?—to the disadvantage of weaker rivals. Name or brand recognition also supports the theory, as the biggest firms not only can spend more for advertising and distribution, but are increasing this wherewithal much faster than smaller competitors, and can rise above the pack with customers, suppliers, and creditors.

An industry that is a multicompany battleground, such as autos, airlines, banking, and much of the energy sector, however, will not produce such a clear winner, and smaller rivals may not be as much disadvantaged.

In regard to the brewing industry, does this theory presage the dynasty of Anheuser-Busch at the expense of its lesser rivals? Do you see any flaws in this theory? Does it support the merger mania we are seeing today?

Source: Bernard Wysocki Jr., "No. 1 Can Be Runaway Even in a Tight Race," *The Wall Street Journal*, June 28, 1999, p. A1.

WHAT CAN BE LEARNED?

The early decades of the Coors case show a classic disregard for *external factors*—not only present and potential competition, but also changing consumer tastes—at least until great damage was done to market share. In particular, Coors' marketing function had never developed. Of course, this was to change, but decades late.

An internal production orientation is passé in today's competitive environment. Coors' problem was not that the company was not growth-minded; it was–if increasing the production capacity and efficiency of the single brewery and venturing into other geographical regions can be construed as growth-minded. However, this philosophy of growth ignored the externals: changes in the environment that necessitated adjustments in marketing. Sure it is tempting when things are going well, when a product is receiving accolades from ordinary people as well as the famous, to be lulled into complacency. But it is hardly viable in today's market places.

The power of a mystique. We might think of mystique as something bordering on a cult following. Few products are able to gain such a mystique. But Coors certainly had this in the 1960s and early 1970s, when it became the brew of celebrities and the emblem of the purity and freshness of the West. In the tobacco industry, Marlboro rose to become the top seller on a somewhat similar image thrust: the Marlboro man on the range. Perhaps the Ford Mustang had a mystique at one time. And, somehow, the big bikes of Harley Davidson developed a mystique.

How does a firm develop (or acquire) a mystique? There is no simple answer, no guarantee. Certainly the product has to be somewhat different from competitors', even if only psychologically. But this is hardly enough—indeed, many firms strive for and never achieve a mystique. Image-building advertising, focusing on the type of person the firm is targeting, may help some. Even better is image-building advertising using the people customers might wish to emulate, such as Nike has done with athletes, and Marlboro with the rugged cowboy.

Perhaps in the final analysis, acquiring a mystique is more accidental and fortuitous than deliberate. Two lessons, however, can be learned about mystique. First, do not expect it to last forever. Second, run with it as long as you can, and try to expand the reach of the name or logo to other goods, even unrelated ones, perhaps through licensing.

A *"cash cow" philosophy is dangerous for a major product vulnerable to competitive inroads.* In the 1970s, Coors apparently regarded its situation as a "cash cow," from which the profits could be fully milked, while investments in advertising and in new product planning and other expenditures were kept at a minimum. Certainly, as Table 16.3 reveals, Coors' expenditures for advertising were woefully below those of other brewers, even those much smaller than Coors. The following information box shows the cash cow strategy in relation to alternatives. Unfortunately, a cash cow strategy can leave a firm vulnerable, especially when the total market is large, as the beer market was.

A *good image is difficult to achieve, and easy to lose.* Here we see another example of the impermanence of a good image. It is difficult to develop an image of quality and great desirability; even more difficult is the creation of a mystique. Although such an image can be a company's biggest asset while it lasts, it can be fleeting. Coors' image of quality and great taste was lost in the Eastern markets because of bootleggers carrying the beer into these markets illegally and selling it at greatly inflated prices, while maintaining no quality care such as product rotation and adequate refrigeration. But we also see that

---

INFORMATION BOX

BOSTON CONSULTING GROUP'S APPROACH TO STRATEGY IMPLEMENTATION

The Boston Consulting Group, a leading management consulting firm, has boiled down the major strategy decisions a firm faces to only four, depending on a firm's competitive position in a particular industry and the growth of that industry. Accordingly, a firm's major business categories can be classified as Stars, Question Marks, Cash Cows, and Dogs. Figure 16.1 presents a matrix of this concept.

A different strategy implementation is recommended for each of these business categories, as follows:

(continues)

INFORMATION BOX (continued)

Category	Strategy Implementation
Stars	*Build.* In a dominant market position and a rapidly growing industry, more investment and long-term profit goals are recommended, even if they come at the expense of short-term profitability.
Question Marks	*Build or Divest.* The decision as to whether to commit more resources to trying to build such products into leaders or whether to divest and use company resources elsewhere is not clear-cut and easily made. It may depend on the strength of major competitors and how well heeled the company is: for example, it may decide it cannot provide sufficient financing to achieve the growth needed vis-à-vis competition.
Cash Cows	*Harvest.* When in a dominant position in a low-growth industry, the recommended strategy implementation is to reap the harvest of a strong cash flow. Only enough resources should be reinvested to maintain competitive position.
Dogs	*Divest.* There is no use wasting resources on poor competitive positions in low-growth industries. The recommended strategy is to sell or liquidate this business.

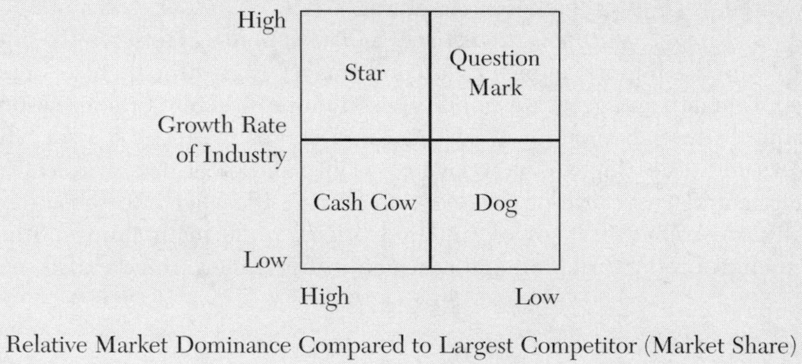

Relative Market Dominance Compared to Largest Competitor (Market Share)

Figure 16.1. Matrix of a firm's major business categories.

Star = Dominant market position in a high-growth industry.
Question Mark = Weak market position in a high-growth industry.
Cash Cow = Dominant market position in a low-growth industry.
Dog = Weak market position in a low-growth industry.

Coors, at the time of this mistake, was obviously in a "cash cow" situation, with high profits but minimum growth prospects facing the industry. It did not want to disrupt the harvesting of this business, but it became greedy in the sense of being reluctant to invest resources that might have resulted in diluting the beautiful cash flow.

Do you see any limitations to the Boston Consulting Group's model?

consumer wants can be fickle and can change drastically: Today's sought-after image may not necessarily be that of next year. The new sought-after image became light or low-calorie beer, and superpremium beer. Coors' brand image was dimmed.

Never underestimate competitors. Management should not beguile itself that it is invincible to present and potential competitors. Yet, we can see how easily such an entrapment could occur: During the heady days of the early 1970s, Coors dominated every market it was in. But the reality soon changed. Without greatly increased marketing expenditures there could be little chance of cracking the Eastern market against powerful competitors. Furthermore, even Coors' captive Western markets—particularly the huge California market—were vulnerable to aggressive competitors. A firm cannot expect the status quo to endure.

CONSIDER

Can you think of other learning insights emerging from this case?

QUESTIONS

1. How do you account for the fact that Coors beer achieved such a success despite the company's lack of advertising, new product development, and national distribution?

2. Discuss why an internal orientation is particularly unsuited for the brewing industry.

3. Do you think Coors' fortunes would have remained strong and growing if advertising expenditures had been doubled or tripled during the late 1960s and early 1970s?

4. Is it likely that Coors' labor disputes had any serious effect on its fortunes?

5. "Coors' insistence on not pasteurizing its beer is its biggest burden. This archaic policy should be abandoned to bring it into the modern day." Discuss this position of a beer industry analyst.

6. Do you think "cute" packaging is that important to beer drinkers today?

7. Have you ever tried one of the Coors brews? If so, how did you like it? Would you buy it again?

HANDS-ON EXERCISES

1. Place yourself in the role of Pete Coors, then (in 1986) the young senior vice president for sales and marketing. How would you attempt to reverse the company's fading performance? Be as specific as you can; also consider and identify any constraints to a marketing strategy that should be recognized. You might also want to consider how a mystique might again be built up for the Coors brand.

2. Place yourself in the role of a staff analyst. You have been asked to evaluate the desirability of opening another brewery in the East—perhaps in Virginia. Consider as many pros and cons as you can. (You will, of course, have to make some assumptions, especially regarding construction costs.) Develop a recommendation for a go/no-go decision, and be prepared to defend it before a top management committee.

3. At the new millennium, Coors is still firmly entrenched in a distant-third position in its industry. As a management consultant, what would you advise for the firm to try to take over the number-two position from Miller? Be as specific as you can, and support your recommendations.

4. How about an exercise in creativity? Situation: Present day; Coors has $100 million to spend for advertising and promotion; its adversaries have ten times as much. What ideas can you come up with for using this $100 million in the most effective way? (If you come up with some really great ideas, maybe Coors will hire you.)

TEAM DEBATE EXERCISE

Take sides in this controversy: Should Coors abandon its nonpasteurization policy for its brews and join competitors in pasteurizing?

INVITATION TO RESEARCH

How is Coors doing today? Is it improving its position, or worsening it? Has it introduced any new brews? Has there been any diversification?

CHAPTER SEVENTEEN

Maytag—Bungling a Promotion in England

The atmosphere at the annual meeting in the little Iowa town of Newton had turned contentious. As Leonard Hadley faced increasingly angry questions from disgruntled shareholders the thought crossed his mind: "I don't deserve this!" After all, he had only been CEO of Maytag Corporation for a few months, and this was his first chairing of an annual meeting. But the earnings of the company had been declining every year since 1988, and in 1992, Maytag had had a $315.4 million loss. No wonder the stockholders in the packed Newton High School auditorium were bitter and critical of their management. But there was more. Just the month before, the company had the public embarrassment and costly atonement resulting from a monumental blunder in the promotional planning of its United Kingdom subsidiary.

Hadley doggedly saw the meeting to its close, and limply concluded: "Hopefully, both sales and earnings will improve this year."[1]

THE FIASCO

In August 1992, Hoover Limited, Maytag's British subsidiary, launched this travel promotion: Anyone in the United Kingdom buying more than 100 U.K. pounds worth of Hoover products (about $150 in American dollars) before the end of January 1993 would get two free round-trip tickets to selected European destinations. For 250 U.K. pounds worth of Hoover products, they would get two free round-trip tickets to New York or Orlando.

A buying frenzy resulted. Consumers had quickly figured out that the value of the tickets easily exceeded the cost of the appliances necessary to be eligible for them. By the tens of thousands, Britishers rushed out to buy just enough Hoover products to qualify. Appliance stores were emptied of vacuum cleaners. The Hoover factory in Cambuslang, Scotland, that had been making vacuum cleaners only three days a week was suddenly placed on a 24-hour, seven days a week production sched-

---

[1] Richard Gibson, "Maytag's CEO Goes Through Wringer at Annual Meeting," *The Wall Street Journal,* April 28, 1993, p. A5.

ule—an overtime bonanza for the workers. What a resounding success for a promotion! Hoover managers, however, were unhappy.

Hoover had never ever expected more than 50,000 people to respond. And of those responding, it expected far less would go through all the steps necessary to qualify for the free trip and really take it. But more than 200,000 not only responded but qualified for the free tickets. The company was overwhelmed. The volume of paperwork created such a bottleneck that by the middle of April only 6,000 people had flown. Thousands of others either never got their tickets, were not able to get the dates requested, or waited for months without hearing the results of their applications. Hoover established a special hot line to process customer complaints, and these were coming in at 2,000 calls a day. But the complaints quickly spread, and the ensuing publicity brought charges of fraud and demands for restitution. This raises the issue of loss leaders—how much should we use loss leaders as a promotional device?—discussed in the following box.

Maytag dispatched a task force to try to resolve the situation without jeopardizing customer relations any further. But it acknowledged that it's "not 100% clear" that all eligible buyers will receive their free flights.[2] The ill-fated promotion

---

ISSUE BOX

SHOULD WE USE LOSS LEADERS?

Leader pricing is a type of promotion with certain items advertised at a very low price—sometimes even below cost, in which case they are known as loss leaders—in order to attract more customers. The rationale for this is that such customers are likely to purchase other regular price items as well with the result that total sales and profits will be increased. If customers do not purchase enough other goods at regular prices to more than cover the losses incurred from the attractively priced bargains, then the loss leader promotion is ill advised. Some critics maintain that the whole idea of using loss leaders is absurd: the firm is just "buying sales" with no regard for profits.

While U.K. Hoover did not think of their promotion as a loss leader, in reality it was: they stood to lose money on every sale if the promotional offer was taken advantage of. Unfortunately for its effectiveness as a loss leader, the likelihood of customers purchasing other Hoover products at regular prices was remote, and the level of acceptance was not capped, so that losses were permitted to multiply. The conclusion has to be that this was an ill-conceived idea from the beginning. It violated these two conditions of loss leaders: they should stimulate sales of other products, and their losses should be limited.

Do you think loss leaders really are desirable under certain circumstances? Why or why not?

---

[2] James P. Miller, "Maytag U.K. Unit Find a Promotion Is Too Successful," *The Wall Street Journal*, March 31, 1993, p. A9.

was a staggering blow to Maytag financially. It took a $30 million charge in the first quarter of 1993 to cover unexpected additional costs linked to the promotion. Final costs were expected to exceed $50 million, which would be 10 percent of UK Hoover's total revenues. This for a subsidiary acquired only four years before that had yet to produce a profit.

Adding to the costs were problems with the two travel agencies involved. The agencies were to obtain low-cost space available tickets, and would earn commissions selling "packages," including hotels, rental cars, and insurance. If consumers bought a package, Hoover would get a cut. However, despite the overwhelming demand for tickets, most consumers declined to purchase the package, thus greatly reducing support money for the promotional venture. So, Hoover greatly underestimated the likely response, and overestimated the amount it would earn from commission payments.

If these cost overruns added greatly to Maytag and Hoover's customer relations and public image, the expenditures would have seemed more palatable. But with all the problems, the best that could be expected would be to lessen the worst of the agitation and charges of deception. And this was proving to be impossible. The media, of course, salivated at the problems and were quick to sensationalize them:

> One disgruntled customer, who took aggressive action on his own, received the widest press coverage, and even became a folk hero. Dave Dixon, claiming he was cheated out of a free vacation by Hoover, seized one of the company's repair vans in retaliation. Police were sympathetic: They took him home, and did not charge him, claiming it was a civil matter.[3]

Heads rolled also. Initially, Maytag fired three UK Hoover executives involved, including the president of Hoover Europe. Mr. Hadley, at the annual meeting, also indicated that others might lose their jobs before the cleanup was complete. He likened the promotion to "a bad accident... and you can't determine what was in the driver's mind."[4]

The issue receiving somewhat less publicity was why corporate headquarters allowed executives of a subsidiary such wide latitude that they could saddle parent Maytag with tens of millions in unexpected costs. Did not top corporate executives have to approve ambitious plans? A company spokesman said that operating divisions were "primarily responsible" for planning promotional expenses. While the parent may review such outlays, "if they're within parameters, it goes through."[5] This raises the issue, discussed in the following box, of how loose a rein foreign subsidiaries should be allowed.

---

[3] "Unhappy Brit Holds Hoover Van Hostage," *Cleveland Plain Dealer,* June 1, 1993, p. D1; and Simon Reeve and John Harlow, "Hoover Is Sued Over Flights Deal," *London Sunday Times,* June 6, 1993.

[4] Gibson, p. A5.

[5] Miller, p. A9.

ISSUE BOX

HOW LOOSE A REIN FOR A FOREIGN SUBSIDIARY?

In a decentralized organization, top management delegates considerable decision-making authority to subordinates. Such decentralization—often called a "loose rein"—tends to be more marked with foreign subsidiaries, such as UK Hoover. Corporate management in the United States understandably feels less familiar with the foreign environment and is more willing to let the native executives operate with less constraints than it might with a domestic subsidiary. In the Maytag/Hoover situation, decision-making authority by British executives was evidently extensive, and corporate Maytag exercised little operational control, being content to judge performance by ultimate results achieved. Major deviations from expected performance goals, or widespread traumatic events—all of which happened to UK Hoover—finally gained corporate management attention.

Major advantages of extensive decentralization or a loose rein are: first, top management effectiveness can be improved since time and attention is freed for presumably more important matters; second, subordinates are permitted more self-management, which should improve their competence and motivation; and third, in foreign environments, native managers presumably better understand their unique problems and opportunities than corporate management, located thousands of miles away, possibly can. But the drawbacks are as we have seen: parameters within which subordinate managers operate can be so wide that serious miscalculations may not be stopped in time. Since top management is ultimately responsible for all performance, including actions of subordinates, it faces greater risks with extensive decentralization and giving a free rein.

"Since the manager is ultimately accountable for whatever is delegated to subordinates, then a free rein reflects great confidence in subordinates." Discuss.

BACKGROUND ON MAYTAG

Maytag is a century-old company. The original business, formed in 1893, manufactured feeder attachments for threshing machines. In 1907, the company moved to Newton, Iowa, a small town thirty miles east of Des Moines, the capital. Manufacturing emphasis turned to home-laundry equipment, and wringer-type washers.

A natural expansion of this emphasis occurred with the commercial laundromat business in the 1930s, when coin meters were attached to Maytag washers. Rapid growth of these coin-operated laundries took place in the U.S. during the late 1950s and early 1960s. The 1970s hurt laundromats with increased competition and soaring energy costs. In 1975, Maytag introduced new energy-efficient machines, and "Home Style" stores that rejuvenated the business.

The Lonely Maytag Repairman

For years Maytag reveled in a marketing coup, with its washers and dryers enjoying a top-quality image, thanks to decades-long ads in which a repairman laments his loneliness because of Maytag's trouble-free products. (The actor who portrayed this repairman died in early 1997.) The result of this dependability and quality image was that Maytag could command a price premium: "Their machines cost the same to make, break down as much as ours—but they get $100 more because of the reputation," grumbled a competitor.[6]

During the 1970s and into the 1980s, Maytag continued to capture 15 percent of the washing machine market, and enjoyed profit margins about twice that of competitors. Table 17.1 shows operating results for the period 1974–1981. Whirlpool was the largest factor in the laundry equipment market, with a 45 percent share, but this was largely because of sales to Sears under the Sears' brand.

Acquisitions

For many years, until his retirement on December 31, 1992, Daniel J. Krumm had influenced Maytag's destinies. He had been CEO for eighteen years and chairman since 1986, and his tenure with the company encompassed 40 years. In that time, the home-appliance business encountered some drastic changes. The most ominous occurred in the late 1980s with the merger mania, in which the threat of takeovers by hostile raiders often motivated heretofore conservative executives to greatly increase corporate indebtedness, thereby decreasing the attractiveness of their firms. Daniel Krumm was one of these running-scared executives, as rumors persisted that the company was a takeover candidate.

Largely as a defensive move, Krumm pushed through a deal for a $1 billion buyout of Chicago Pacific Corporation (CPC), a maker of vacuum cleaners and

TABLE 17.1. Maytag Operating Results, 1974–1981 (in millions)

	Net Sales	Net Income	Percent of Sales
1974	$229	$21.1	9.2%
1975	238	25.9	10.9
1976	275	33.1	12.0
1977	299	34.5	11.5
1978	325	36.7	11.3
1979	369	45.3	12.3
1980	346	35.6	10.2
1981	409	37.4	9.1
Average net income percent of sales: 10.8%			

Source: Company operating statistics.

Commentary: These years show a steady, though not spectacular growth in revenues, and a generally rising net income, except for 1980. Of particular interest is the high net income percentage of sales, with this averaging 10.8 percent over the 8-year period, with a high of 12.3 percent.

[6] Brian Bremmer, "Can Maytag Clean Up Around the World?" *Business Week*, January 30, 1989, p. 89.

other appliances with $1.4 billion in sales. As a result, Maytag was burdened with $500 million in new debt. Krumm defended the acquisition as giving Maytag a strong foothold in a growing overseas market. CPC was best known for the Hoover vacuums it sold in the United States and Europe. Indeed, so dominant was the Hoover brand in England that many people did not vacuum their carpets, but "hoovered the carpet." CPC also made washers, dryers, and other appliances under the Hoover brand, selling them exclusively in Europe and Australia. In addition, it had six furniture companies, but Maytag sold these shortly after the acquisition.

Krumm had been instrumental in transforming Maytag, the number-four U.S. appliance manufacturer—behind General Electric, Whirlpool, and Electrolux—from a niche laundry-equipment maker into a full-line manufacturer. He had led an earlier acquisition spree in which Maytag had expanded into microwave ovens, electric ranges, refrigerators, and freezers. Its brands now included Magic Chef, Jenn-Air, Norge, and Admiral. The last years of Krumm's reign, however, were not marked by great operating results. As shown in Table 17.2, revenues showed no gain in the 1989–1992 period, while income steadily declined.

Trouble

Although the rationale for internationalizing seemed inescapable, especially in view of a recent wave of joint ventures between U.S. and European appliance makers, still the Hoover acquisition was troublesome. While it was a major brand in England and in Australia, Hoover had only a small presence in Europe. Yet, this was where the bulk of the market was, with some 320 million potential appliance buyers.

The probabilities of the Hoover subsidiary being able to capture much of the European market were hardly promising. Whirlpool was strong, having ten plants there in contrast to Hoover's two plants. Furthermore, Maytag faced entrenched European competitors such as Sweden's Electrolux, the world's largest appliance maker; Germany's Bosch-Siemens; and Italy's Merloni Group. General Electric had also entered the market with joint ventures. The fierce loyalty of Europeans to

TABLE 17.2. **Maytag Operating Results, 1989–1992**

	Revenue (000,000)	Net Income	% of Revenue
1989	$3,089	131.0	4.3%
1990	3,057	98.9	3.2
1991	2,971	79.0	2.7
1992	3,041	(315.4)	(10.4)

Source: Company annual reports.

Commentary: Note the steady erosion of profitability, while sales remained virtually static. For a comparison with profit performance of earlier years, see Table 17.1 and the net income to sales percentage of this more "golden" period.

domestic brands raised further questions as to the ability of Maytag's Hoover to penetrate the European market without massive promotional expenditures, and maybe not even then.

Australia was something else. Hoover had a good competitive position there, and its refrigerator plant in Melbourne could easily be expanded to include Maytag's washers and dryers. Unfortunately, the small population of Australia limited the market to only about $250 million for major appliances.

Britain accounted for half of Hoover's European sales. But at the time of the acquisition its major appliance business was only marginally profitable. This was to change: after the acquisition it became downright unprofitable, as shown in Table 17.3 for the years 1990 through 1992, as it struggled to expand in a recession-plagued Europe. The results for 1993, of course, will reflect the huge loss for the promotional debacle. Hardly an acquisition made in heaven.

Maytag's earlier acquisitions also were becoming soured. Its acquisitions of Magic Chef and Admiral were diversifications into lower-priced appliances, and these did not meet expectations. But they left Maytag's balance sheet and its cash flow weakened (see Table 17.4). Perhaps more serious, Maytag's reputation as the nation's premier appliance maker became tarnished. Meanwhile, General Electric and Whirlpool were attacking the top end of its product line. As a result, Maytag found itself in the number-three or -four position in most of its brand lines.

TABLE 17.3. Operating Results of Maytag's Principal Business Components 1990–1992

	Revenue (000,000)	Income[a] (000)
1990		
North American Appliances	$2,212	$221,165
Vending	191	25,018
European Sales	497	(22,863)
1991		
North American Appliances	2,183	186,322
Vending	150	4,498
European Sales	486	(865)
1992		
North American Appliances	2,242	129,680
Vending	165	16,311
European Sales	502	(67,061)

Source: Company annual reports.

Commentary: While these years had not been particularly good for Maytag in growth of revenues and income, the continuing, and even intensifying, losses in the Hoover European operation had to be troublesome. And this is before the ill-fated early 1993 promotional results.

[a] This is operating income, that is, income before depreciation and other adjustments.

TABLE 17.4. **Long-Term Debt as a Percent of Capital from Maytag's Balance Sheets, 1986–1991**

Year	Long-Term Debt/Capital
1986	7.2%
1987	23.3
1988	48.3
1989	46.8
1990	44.1
1991	42.7

Source: Company annual reports.

Commentary: The effect of acquisitions, in particular that of the Chicago Pacific Corporation, can be clearly seen in the buildup of long-term debt: in 1986, Maytag was virtually free of such commitments; two years later its long-term debt ratio had increased almost seven-fold.

ANALYSIS

Flawed Acquisition Decisions

The long decline in profits after 1989 should have triggered strong concern and corrective action. Perhaps it did, but the action was not effectual as the decline continued, culminating in a large deficit in 1992 and serious problems in 1993. As shown in Table 17.2, the acquisitions brought neither revenue gains nor profitability. One suspects that in the rush to fend off potential raiders in the late 1980s, the company bought businesses it might never have under more sober times, and that it also paid too much for these businesses. Further, they cheapened the proud image of quality for Maytag.

Who Can We Blame in the U.K. Promotional Debacle?

Corporate Maytag management was guilty of a common fault in their acquisitions: it gave newly acquired divisions a loose rein, letting them continue to operate independently with few constraints: "After all, these executives should be more knowledgeable about their operations than corporate headquarters would be." Such confidence is sometimes misguided. In the U.K. promotion, Maytag management would seem as derelict as management in England. Planning guidelines or parameters were far too loose and under-controlled. The idea of subsidiary management being able to burden the parent with $50 million of unexpected charges, and to have such erupt with no warning, borders on the absurd.

Finally, the planning of the U.K. executives for this ill-conceived travel production defies all logic. They vastly underestimated the demand for the promotional offer and they greatly overestimated paybacks from travel agencies on the package deals. Yet, it took no brilliant insight to realize that the value of the travel offer exceeded the price of the appliance—indeed, 200,000 customers rapidly arrived at this conclusion—and that such a sweetheart of a deal would be irresistible to many, and that it could prove to be costly in the extreme to the company. A miscalculation, or complete naivete on the part of executives and their staffs who should have known better?

How Could the Promotion Have Avoided the Problem?

The great problem resulting from an offer too good could have been avoided, and this without scrapping the whole idea. A cost-benefit analysis would have provided at least a perspective as to how much the company should spend to achieve certain benefits, such as increased sales, greater consumer interest, and favorable publicity. See the following information box for a more detailed discussion of the important planning tool of a cost-benefit analysis.

A cost-benefit analysis should certainly have alerted management to the possible consequences of various acceptance levels, and of the significant risks of high acceptance. However, the company could have set limits on the number of eligibles: perhaps the first 1,000, or the first 5,000. Doing this would have held or capped the costs to reasonably defined levels, and avoided the greater risks. Or the company could have made the offer less generous, perhaps by upping the requirements, or by lessening the premiums. Such more moderate alternatives would still have made an attractive promotion, but not the major uncontrolled catastrophe that happened.

INFORMATION BOX

COST-BENEFIT ANALYSIS

A cost-benefit analysis is a systematic comparison of the costs and benefits of a proposed action. Only if the benefits exceed the costs would we normally have a "go" decision. The normal way to make such an analysis is to assign dollar values to all costs and benefits, thus providing a common basis for comparison.

Cost-benefit analyses have been widely used by the Defense Department in evaluating alternative weapons systems. In recent years, such analyses have been sporadically applied to environmental regulation and even to workplace safety standards. As an example of the former, a cost-benefit analysis can be used to determine if it is socially worthwhile to spend X million dollars to meet a certain standard of clean air or water.

Many business decisions lend themselves to a cost-benefit analysis. It provides a systematic way of analyzing the inputs and the probable outputs of particular major alternatives. While in the business setting some of the costs and benefits can be very quantitative, they often should be tempered by nonquantitative inputs to reach the broadest perspective. Schermerhorn suggests considering the following criteria in evaluating alternatives:[7]

[7] John R. Schermerhorn, Jr., *Management for Productivity*, 4th ed. (New York: Wiley, 1993), p. 164.

(continues)

INFORMATION BOX (continued)

Benefits: What are the "benefits" of using the alternatives to solve a performance deficiency or take advantage of an opportunity?

Costs: What are the "costs" to implement the alternatives, including direct resource investments as well as any potential negative side effects?

Timeliness: How fast will the benefits occur and a positive impact be achieved?

Acceptability: To what extent will the alternatives be accepted and supported by those who must work with them?

Ethical soundness: How well do the alternatives meet acceptable ethical criteria in the eyes of multiple stakeholders?

What numbers would you assign to a cost-benefit analysis for Maytag Hoover's plan to offer the free airline tickets, under an assumption of 5,000 takers? 20,000 takers? 100,000 takers? 500,000 takers? (Make any assumptions needed as to costs.) What would be your conclusions for these various acceptance rates?

FINAL RESOLUTION?

Maytag's invasion of Europe proved a costly failure. In the summer of 1995, Maytag gave up. It sold its European operations to an Italian appliance maker, recording a $135 million loss.

Even by the end of 1996, the Hoover mess was still not cleaned up. Hoover had spent $72 million flying some 220,000 people and had hoped to end the matter. But the fight continues four years later with disgruntled customers who never flew taking Hoover to court. A Liverpool lawyer chortled: "There's about 365,000 people who haven't flown," said Denis Whalley. "I hope lots of other people who have been cheated by Hoover will come forward."[8] Even though Maytag had sold this troubled division, it still could not escape emerging lawsuits.

Update—Leonard Hadley

In the summer of 1998, Leonard Hadley could look forward and backward with some satisfaction. He would retire the next summer when he turned 65, and he had already picked his successor. Since assuming the top position in Maytag in January 1993, and confronting the mess with the U.K. subsidiary his first few months on the job, he had turned Maytag completely around.

He knew no one expected much change from him, an accountant who had joined Maytag right out of college. He was known as a loyal but unimaginative lieutenant of his boss, Daniel Krumm, who died of cancer shortly after naming Hadley his successor.

---

[8] "Hoover Can't Clean Up Mess from Free Flights," *Cleveland Plain Dealer*, December 12, 1996, p. 1-C; and Dirk Beveridge, "Hoover Loses Two Lawsuits Tied to Promotion," *Gannett Newspapers*, February 21, 1997, p. 4-F.

After all, he reflected, no one thought that major change could come to an organization from someone who had spent his whole life there, who was a clone so to speak, and an accountant to boot. Everyone thought that changemakers had to come from outside, like Al Dunlap of Scott Paper and Sunbeam. Well, he had shown them, and given hope to all number-two executives who resented Wall Street's love affair with outsiders.

Within a few weeks of taking over, he'd fired a bunch of managers, especially those rascals in the U.K. who'd masterminded the great Hoover promotion that cost the company dearly. He determined to get rid of foreign operations, most of them newly acquired and unprofitable. He just did not see that appliances could be profitably made for every corner of the world, because of the variety of regional customs. Still, he knew that many disagreed with him about this, including some of the board members who thought globalization was the only way to go. Still, over the next 18 months he had prevailed.

He chuckled to himself as he reminisced. He had also overturned the decades-long corporate mindset not to be first to market with new technology because they would "rather be right than be first." His "Galaxy Initiative" of nine top-secret new products was a repudiation of this old mindset. One of them, the Neptune, a front-loading washer retailing at $1,100, certainly proved him right. Maytag had increased its production three times and raised its suggested retail price twice, and still it was selling like gangbusters. Perhaps the thing he was proudest of was getting Maytag products in Sears stores, the seller of one-third of all appliances in the United States. Sears' desire to have the Neptune is what swung the deal.

As an accountant, he probably should be focusing first on the numbers. Well, 1997 was certainly a banner year with sales up 10.9 percent over the previous year, while profitability as measured by return on capital was 16.7 percent, both sales and profit gains leading the industry. And 1998 so far was proving to be even better, with sales jumping 31 percent and earnings 88 percent.

He remembered the remarks of Lester Crown, a Maytag director: "Len Hadley has—quietly, softly—done a spectacular job. Obviously, we just lacked the ability to evaluate him [at the beginning]."[9]

Leonard Hadley retired August 12, 1999. He knew he had surprised everybody in the organization by going outside Maytag for his successor. He was Lloyd Ward, 50, Maytag's first black executive, a marketing expert from PepsiCo, and before that Procter & Gamble, who had joined Maytag in 1996 and was currently president and chief operating officer.

WHAT CAN BE LEARNED?

Beware overpaying for an acquisition. Hoping to diversify its product line and gain market share overseas, Maytag paid $1 billion for Chicago Pacific in 1989. As it turned out, this was far too much, and the debt burden was an albatross. Chief

[9] Carl Quintanilla, "Maytag's Top Officer, Expected to Do Little, Surprises His Board," *The Wall Street Journal,* June 23, 1998, pp. A1, A8.

Executive Leonard Hadley conceded as much: "In the long view, it was correct to invest in these businesses. But the timing of the deal, and the price of the deal, made the debt a heavy load to carry."[10]

Zeal to expand, and/or the desire to reduce the attractiveness of a firm's balance sheet and thus fend off potential raiders, do not excuse foolhardy management. The consequences of such bad decisions remain to haunt a company, and the ill-advised purchases often have to be eventually sold off at substantial losses. The analysis of potential acquisition candidates must be soberly and thoroughly done, and rosy projections questioned, even if this means the deal may be soured.

Beware giving too loose a rein, thus sacrificing controls, especially of unproven foreign subsidiaries. Although decentralizing authority down to lower ranks is often desirable and results in better motivation and management development than centralization, it can be overdone. At the extreme, where divisional and subsidiary executives have almost unlimited decision-making authority and can run their operations as virtual dynasties, then corporate management essentially abdicates its authority. Such looseness in an organization endangers cohesiveness; it tends to obscure common standards and objectives; and it can even dilute unified ethical practices.

Such extreme looseness of controls is not uncommon with acquisitions, especially foreign ones. It is easy to make the assumption that these executives were operating successfully before the acquisition and have more firsthand knowledge of the environment than the corporate executives.

Still, there should be limits on how much freedom these executives should be permitted—especially when their operations have not been notably successful. In Maytag's case, the U.K. subsidiary had lost money every year since it was acquired. Accordingly, one would expect prudent corporate management to have condoned less decentralization and insisted on tighter controls than it might otherwise.

In decision planning, consider a worst-case scenario. There are those who preach the desirability of positive thinking, confidence, and optimism, whether it be in personal lives, athletics, or business practices. But expecting and preparing for the worst has much to commend it, since a person or a firm is then better able to cope with adversity, avoid being overwhelmed, and more likely to make prudent rather than rash decisions.

Apparently the avid acceptance of the promotional offer was a complete surprise; no one dreamed of such demand. Yet, was it so unreasonable to think that a very attractive offer would meet wild acceptance?

In using loss leaders, put a cap on potential losses. Loss leaders, as we noted earlier, are items promoted at such attractive prices that the firm loses money on every sale. The expectation, of course, is that the customer traffic generated by such attractive promotions will increase sales of regular profit items so that total profits will be increased.

---

[10] Kenneth Labich, "What Companies Fail," *Fortune,* November 14, 1994, p. 60.

The risks of uncontrolled or uncapped loss leader promotions are vividly shown in this case. For a retailer who uses loss leaders, the loss is ultimately capped as the inventory is sold off. With UK Hoover there was no cap. The solution is clear: Attractive loss leader promotions should be capped, such as the first 100 or the first 1,000 or for one week only. Otherwise, the promotion should be made less attractive.

The power of a cost-benefit analysis. For major decisions, executives have much to gain from a cost-benefit analysis. It forces them to systematically tabulate and analyze the costs and benefits of particular courses of action. They may find that likely benefits are so uncertain as to not be worth the risk. If so, now is the time to realize this, rather than after substantial commitments have already been made.

Without doubt, regular use of cost-benefit analyses for major decisions improves executives' batting averages for good decisions. Even though some numbers may have to be judgmental, especially as to probable benefits, the process of making this analysis forces a careful look at alternatives and most likely consequences. For more important decisions, input from diverse staff people and executives will bring greater power to the analysis.

CONSIDER

What additional learning insights can you add?

QUESTIONS

1. How could the promotion of UK Hoover have been better designed? Be as specific as you can.

2. Given the fiasco that did occur, how do you think Maytag should have responded?

3. "Firing the three top executives of UK Hoover is unconscionable. It smacks of a vendetta against European managers by an American parent. After all, their only 'crime' was a promotion that was too successful." Comment on this statement.

4. Do you think Leonard Hadley, the Maytag CEO for only two months, should be soundly criticized for the U.K. situation? Why or why not?

5. Please speculate: Why do you think this UK Hoover fiasco happened in the first place? What went wrong?

6. Evaluate the decision to acquire Chicago Pacific Corporation (CPC). Do this both for the time of the decision and for now—after the fact—as a postmortem. Defend your overall conclusions.

HANDS-ON EXERCISES

1. You have been placed in charge of a task force sent by headquarters to England to coordinate the fire-fighting efforts in the aftermath of the ill-

fated promotion. There is neither enough productive capacity nor enough airline seats available to handle the demand. How do you propose to handle this situation? Be as specific as you can, and defend your recommendations.

2. As a staff vice president at corporate headquarters, you have been charged to develop companywide policies and procedures that will prevent such a situation from ever occurring again. What do you recommend?

TEAM DEBATE EXERCISE

Two schools of thought are emerging after the promotional debacle. One position advocates repudiating the offer, citing the impossibility of fulfilling all the demand. The other position maintains that the promise must be met at all costs, even if private planes have to be leased. Debate the options.

INVITATION TO RESEARCH

How is Lloyd Ward doing as CEO? Has Maytag entered overseas markets again? How is the Neptune washer doing? Has Maytag brought out any other innovative products?

CHAPTER EIGHTEEN

Rubbermaid—Perils of Not Satisfying a Major Customer

Rubbermaid, manufacturer and marketer of high-volume, branded plastic and rubber consumer products and toys, was a darling of investors and academicians alike. For 10 years in a row, it placed in the *Fortune* survey of "America's Most Admired Corporations," and was number one in both 1993 and 1994. It was ranked as the second-most-powerful brand in a Baylor University study of consumer goodwill, and received the "Thomas Edison Award" for developing products to make people's lives better. Under CEO Stanley Gault, its emphasis on innovation often resulted in a new product every day, thereby helping the stock routinely to return 25 percent annually.

By the middle 1990s Rubbermaid began faltering, partly because of its inability to meet the service demands of its major customer, Wal-Mart. Its stock plummeted 40 percent from the 1992 high, leaving it ripe for a takeover. Newell Company acquired Rubbermaid on March 24, 1999, expecting to turn it around. But then Newell had to wonder…

THE ACQUISITION AND WOLFGANG SCHMITT

Former Rubbermaid CEO Wolfgang Schmitt felt a cloak of apprehension settling over him in May 1999. It was only two months after the merger with Newell had been completed, and things were not going as he had expected.

Schmitt had become CEO a year after the legendary Stanley Gault retired in 1991. Gault had returned in 1980 to his home town of Wooster, Ohio (Rubbermaid headquarters) after more than 31 years with the General Electric Company. During Gault's tenure, Rubbermaid stock split four times to the delight of stockholders. A tough act to follow?

Wolfgang often thought about this, but he was certainly a worthy successor to Gault. He had spent all of his working life with Rubbermaid after graduating in 1966 from Otterbein College in Westerville, Ohio, only about 60 miles from Wooster, with a degree in Economics and Business Administration. A recruiter visiting the campus convinced him to join Rubbermaid, a fast-moving growth company. So he started as a management trainee, and in the space of 27 years worked his way up the corporate ranks to become chairman of the board and chief executive officer in 1993. He was proud of this accomplishment, and he thought his experience must be an inspiration to young people in the company: Any one of them could dream of becoming CEO, with hard work and loyalty. A significant highlight of his professional life came when he was invited back to Otterbein in November 1997 to inaugurate its Distinguished Executive Lecture Series.

During his reign, Rubbermaid reached $2 billion in sales in 1994. When it celebrated its 75-year anniversary a year later, Schmitt set the company's sights on $4 billion in sales for the turn of the century. To do this, he knew it had to become a truly global company, and he instigated four foreign acquisitions that year.

He was an effective CEO, and he knew it. When the Newell Company, a slightly larger multinational firm, expressed an interest in merging, Schmitt thought he owed it to his stockholders, and to himself, to pursue this. After all, its houseware and hardware products and marketing efforts were compatible, and the combination would make a $7-billion-a-year consumer-products giant. Aiding the decision to merge was a nice severance guarantee of $12 million after taxes in addition to his stock options. While John McDonough, CEO of Newell, would assume the CEO position of the merged corporation, Schmitt was to be a vice chairman and would work closely with McDonough to ensure the smooth merger and to help mold the new company.

Now, barely two months later, Schmitt had been shunted aside. He did not have an office at headquarters, his name was not listed in a new report of the seven highest-paid executives, and he was not even included in the list of directors reported to the Securities and Exchange Commission (SEC). He couldn't help but feel betrayed that now he no longer had a role in the operations of the company, after he had been so instrumental in bringing about the merger. At 55 years of age he still had many productive years left. More than this, it was the principle of the thing: This was like a kick in the teeth.

But he was not alone. Three of Rubbermaid's five division presidents—the five divisions were Home Products, Little Tykes, Graco-Century, Curver, and Commercial Products—had already been replaced since the merger. Furthermore, in the Home Products division, only two of the top eight executives were still there.

NEWELL'S ASSESSMENT OF RUBBERMAID

If John McDonough of Newell was so unhappy with current Rubbermaid management and operations, why did he buy Rubbermaid in the first place, and for $6.3 billion dollars, more than two times current sales? At a shareholders' meeting in late May he tried to explain. He told them that Rubbermaid was a troubled company, but that once it's pulled into the revered operations of Newell, it can be great again.[1]

McDonough indeed had specialized in buying out small, marginal firms and bringing them to acceptable performance. In 10 years he had bought 75 such firms and pol-

---

[1] Teresa Dixon Murray, "Newell Details Its Plans for Rubbermaid," *Cleveland Plain Dealer,* May 27, 1999, p. 1-C.

ished them by eliminating poorer products, employees, factories, and customers. This format began to be called "newellizing." Hardly surprising, most of the acquisitions had strong brand names, but poor customer service. Rubbermaid fit this mode, though it was by far the biggest acquisition, and would nearly double Newell's sales.

The shareholders were told that while jobs were being cut, the operations would be stronger in the long run. As a strength, McDonough noted that Rubbermaid commanded 94 percent brand loyalty and generated great customer traffic in stores. But Rubbermaid executives needed to slash unnecessary costs, introduce robotics, and reduce product variety. For example, was it necessary to have dozens of the same type of wastebasket?

Still he saw poor customer service as the biggest deficiency of Rubbermaid, the most unacceptable aspect of its operation, and the one that Newell could most easily correct. After all, Newell had achieved a 98.5 percent on-time delivery rate in dealings with Wal-Mart. He would see that Rubbermaid was brought up to this same performance standard.

Rubbermaid's Customer Service Problems

Perhaps a declining commitment to customer service dated back to the retirement of Gault, though Schmitt would likely dispute that. Customer service can erode without being obvious to top management. While some customers complain, many others simply switch their busines to competitors. Still, Rubbermaid's lapses in customer service should have been obvious for years. After all, Wal-Mart was not tolerant with vendors not meeting its standards. When McDonough's people began digging deeper into Rubbermaid's operations, they found that the company wasn't even measuring customer service. This deficiency is almost the kiss of death when dealing with major retailers.

Up to the mid-1990s, about 15 percent of Rubbermaid's $2 billion-plus revenues came from Wal-Mart (see Chapter 21 for a complete case on Wal-Mart). Rubbermaid had had an impressive earnings growth of at least 15 percent a year to go along with 20 percent operating margins, much of this due to the generous space Wal-Mart gave its plastic and rubber products. This was to change abruptly.

In 1995, Wal-Mart refused to let Rubbermaid pass on much of its higher raw material costs, and began taking shelf space away and giving it to smaller competitors who undersold Rubbermaid. This resulted in a major earnings drop (see Table 18.1) that forced Rubbermaid to shut nine facilities and cut 9 percent of its 14,000 employees. "When you hitch your wagon to a star, you are at the mercy of that star."[2]

Wal-Mart not only complained about poor deliveries but began taking more drastic action. Each day Wal-Mart gives suppliers such as Newell a two-hour time slot in which their trucks can deliver orders placed 24 hours before. Should the supplier miss the deadline it pays Wal-Mart for every dollar of lost margin. Now such a fast replenishment of orders required that factories be tied in with Wal-Mart's comput-

---

[2] Matthew Schifrin, "The Big Squeeze," *Forbes*, March 11, 1996, p. 46.

TABLE 18.1. Rubbermaid Sales and Earnings, 1992–1997

	1992	1993	1994	1995	1996	1997
Sales						
(billions $)	$1.81	$1.96	$2.17	$2.34	$2.35	$2.40
Net earnings						
(millions $)	184	211	228	59	152	143
Percent of sales	10.2%	20.0%	18.9%	4.9%	14.2%	13.8%
Per share	1.15	1.32	1.42	.38	1.01	.95

Source: Company reports.

Commentary: This six-year comparison of sales and the various profit indicators show rather starkly the decline in fortunes of Rubbermaid beginning in 1995. Sales remained practically static from 1995 on, although admittedly they were not growing very robustly in the three years before. The lack of growth occurred during a period of unprecedented prosperity.

The earnings comparisons show up worse. While acceptable earnings growth occurred up to 1995, they greatly worsened beginning in 1995. Not only were net earnings figures drastically reduced, but they showed little sign of recouping, even though there was some improvement from the bottom of 1995. Of course, net earnings as a percent of sales and per share also drastically declined from what they were in 1992–1994. Rubbermaid's major problems with Wal-Mart occurred in 1995.

ers. Rubbermaid began installing software to do this in 1996 and had spent $62 million by 1999, but still was often not even achieving 80 percent on-time delivery service. This was unacceptable to Wal-Mart, and returns and fines for poor service rose to 4.4 percent of sales in 1998.[3] Finally, Wal-Mart purged most of its stores of Rubbermaid's Little Tykes toy line, giving the space to a competitor, Fisher Price. See the following information box for a discussion of the power of a giant retailer and the demands that it can make.

INFORMATION BOX

THE DEMANDS OF A GIANT RETAILER

Giant retailers, especially the big discount houses, stand in a power position today relative to their vendors. Part of this power lies in their providing efficient access to the marketplace—imagine the problems of a large consumer goods manufacturer in trying to deal with thousands of small retailers rather than the few big firms that dominate their markets. These giant firms can account for 50 percent and more of many manufacturers' sales. However, if such a major customer is lost or not completely satisfied, a vendor's viability could be in jeopardy.

(continues)

---

[3] Murray, p. 3-C.

INFORMATION BOX *(continued)*

Retailers like Wal-Mart make full use of their power position. Take paying of invoices, for example. Many vendors give a 2 percent discount if bills are paid within 10 days instead of 30. Wal-Mart routinely pays its bills closer to 30 days and still takes the 2 percent discount. Wal-Mart has also led in "partnering" with its vendors. This "partnering" really means that vendors have to pick up more of the inventory management and merchandising costs associated with Wal-Mart stores, most of these involved in providing fast replenishment so that the stores can maintain lean stocks without lost customer sales through stockouts.

So-called slotting fees are common in the supermarket industry, with manufacturers paying to get things on store shelves. It is estimated that some $9 billion annually changes hands in private, unwritten deals between grocery retailers and food and consumer goods manufacturers.[4]

The following is an example of a slotting fee stipulation of a supermarket chain:

Effective January 1, 1996
Our slotting fee is… $2,500

An item authorized, will remain authorized for a minimum of six months (as long as the basic cost does not go up substantially).
Just as a reminder, many times it is the "slotting fee" that determines whether we authorize an item or not.

With the coercive power of a big retailer, a vendor is practically forced to meet their demands no matter what the cost.

Do you think a big manufacturer, such as Coca-Cola, can be coerced by a big retailer? Why or why not? What might determine the extent of retailer coercion? Can a manufacturer coerce a retailer?

---

[4] John S. Long, "Specialty Items to Drive New Market," *Cleveland Plain Dealer*, October 6, 1999, p. 4-F.

Attesting to the high regard that Wal-Mart had for the customer service of Newell, upon hearing of the impending merger with Newell Wal-Mart again began carrying Little Tykes toys. McDonough vowed to get Rubbermaid's on-time delivery rate of 80 percent up to Newell's 98.5 percent, and he began ripping out Rubbermaid's computer system and writing off the entire $62 million. In addition, McDonough claimed to be able to squeeze $350 million of costs out of Rubbermaid, which would double its operating income.[5]

---

[5] Michelle Conlin, "Newellizing Rubbermaid," *Forbes*, May 31, 1999, p. 118.

AFTER THE MERGER

Did Newell quickly turn around and newellize Rubbermaid? Stockholders had to be disappointed. In a time of rising stock prices, Newell Rubbermaid's shares plunged 20 percent in one day in September 1999 as the now-giant consumer goods firm warned that third-quarter earnings would fall short of expectations. This was only the latest in a string of negatives, and Newell Rubbermaid's stock had lost almost half of its value since the Rubbermaid acquisition in March. It blamed lower-than-expected sales of Rubbermaid's plastic containers and Little Tykes toys. Still, company officials maintained that "the integration process remains on plan."[6]

A month later, coinciding with a Wal-Mart announcement that it was expanding vigorously in Europe, Newell Rubbermaid said it would focus on expanding overseas to serve domestic retailers who are moving abroad. The company had been getting a quarter of its sales outside the United States. "Our customers are going international," McDonough said. "We have the opportunity to follow them. It's a once-in-a-lifetime opportunity."[7]

The company also maintained that it had sharply reduced the number of late shipments of Rubbermaid products and expected to have 98 percent of orders shipped on time either in the present quarter or next.[8]

Was this a wise merger? Did Newell pay too much for a faltering Rubbermaid? It was hardly likely that in the first year of a merger management would admit that maybe it was a mistake. But stockholders are betting with their money. Meantime, Wolfgang Schmitt ponders his exile and the erosion of value of his stock options.

ANALYSIS

This experience emphasizes the risks of dealing with behemoth customers, but also the rewards if you can satisfy their demands. After all, Newell Rubbermaid prepared to follow Wal-Mart to Europe and be a prime supplier of its stores there. But a vendor has to have the commitment and ability to meet stringent requirements. If a 24-hour delivery cycle is demanded, the vendor must somehow achieve this regardless of costs. If selling prices are to be pared to the bone, efficiency must somehow be jacked up and production costs pruned, or else profitability may have to be sacrificed even to the point of extreme concern. Otherwise, the vendor can be replaced.

The alternative? To be content with far less revenues and a host of smaller accounts, or else to have such a brand name as to be partly insulated from price competition. Rubbermaid thought it had this, due to its public accolades of past years. Perhaps this contributed to its apathy regarding its delivery service. But Wal-Mart

---

[6] James P. Miller, "Newell Rubbermaid Shares Fall 20% As an Earnings Short Fall Is Predicted," *The Wall Street Journal*, September 7, 1999, p. A4.

[7] "Newell Rubbermaid to Resume Acquisitions, Expand Overseas," *Cleveland Plain Dealer*, October 6, 1999, p. 2-C.

[8] Ibid.

hardly was impressed with the superiority of this brand's products that cost more than alternative suppliers and could not be delivered on time.

We should note that improving service and shortening replenishment time is not easily or cheaply done. Rubbermaid did spend $62 million on computer technology to enable it to meet Wal-Mart's demands, but this did not do the job. Better control of warehouse inventories and production schedules is essential. The vendor will need to carry more of the inventory burden traditionally assumed by the retailer and incur additional expenses and investment for more manpower and trucks and other equipment.

Perhaps the most damning indictment of Rubbermaid's service deficiencies was how long these continued without being corrected. The problem initially surfaced in 1995, but by 1999 on-time deliveries had still not improved appreciably. What was Rubbermaid top management doing all this time? Wolfgang Schmitt can hardly escape the blame that in almost five years he had not corrected this serious problem with the most important customer.

The eagerness to merge that we saw in this case, both on the part of McDonough of Newell and Schmitt of Rubbermaid, may not always be in the best interests of shareholders, and certainly not of employees. It may even not be in the best interest of the executives involved, as Schmitt realized to his dismay, despite his taking home a sizable severance package. But is this enough to make up for losing the power and prestige of a top management position, and all the perks that go with it?

In this era of merger mania, a more sober appraisal is needed by many firms. Not all mergers are in the best interests of both parties. Too many times a firm pays too much to acquire another firm, as we saw in the previous case where Maytag paid $1 billion for Chicago Pacific, and incurred an albatross and a heavy debt burden. Or else the glowing prospects of synergy do not work out. See the following information box for a discussion of the allure of synergy in a merger.

INFORMATION BOX

SYNERGY

Synergy results from creating a whole that is greater than the sum of its parts, that can accomplish more than the total of the individual contributions. In an acquisition, synergy occurs if the two or more firms, when combined, are more efficient, productive, and profitable than they were as separate operations before the merger. Sometimes this is referred to as $2 + 2 = 5$.

How can such synergy occur? If duplication of efforts can be eliminated, if operations can be streamlined, if economies of scale are possible, if specialization can be enhanced, if greater financial and managerial resources can be tapped—then a synergistic situation is likely to occur. Such an expanded operation should be a stronger force in the market than the individual single units that existed before.

(continues)

INFORMATION BOX (continued)

The concept of synergism is the rationale for mergers and acquisitions. But sometimes combining causes the reverse: negative synergy, where the consequences are worse than the sum of individual efforts. If friction arises between the entities, if organizational missions are incompatible, if the new organizational climate creates fearful, resentful, and frustrated employees, then synergy is unlikely. And if greater managerial and financial resources are not realized—if indeed financial resources are depleted because of the interest overhead due to the acquisition—then synergy becomes negative. The whole, then, is less than the sum of its parts. Furthermore, if because of sheer optimism or an uncontrolled acquisitive drive, more is paid for the acquisition than it is really worth, then we have a grand blunder. Could that have been the case with the Rubbermaid acquisition?

Do you think a typical committee or group has more synergy than the same individuals working alone? Why or why not?

When an acquisition finally turns out to be unwise, especially where too much is paid for the acquired firm, we have to conclude that someone fumbled the homework, that the research and investigation of the firm to be acquired was hasty, biased, or downright incompetent. Admittedly, in some cases several suitors may be bidding for the same acquisition candidate, and this then becomes a contest: Who will make the winning bid? The only beneficiaries in such a situation—besides the consultants, lawyers, and investment bankers—are the shareholders of the firm to be acquired.

WHAT CAN BE LEARNED?

Customer service is vital in dealing with big customers. We saw in this case the consequences of not being able to meet the service demands of Wal-Mart. A firm's very viability may depend on somehow gearing up to meet the service expectations. This should be a top priority if such a customer is not to be lost. Correcting the situation should be a matter of weeks or months, and not years.

The value of a brand name does not always compensate for higher prices or poor service when dealing with big retailers. Generally we think of a well-respected brand name as giving the vendor certain liberties, of insulating the vendor at least somewhat from vicious price competition, and even excusing the vendor from some service standards such as prompt and dependable delivery. After all, a respected brand name gives an image of quality, which lesser brands do not have, and an assured body of loyal customers. Well, Wal-Mart's dealings with Rubbermaid before the merger certainly disproves that notion.

How can this be? It still becomes a matter of power position. Not having Rubbermaid, or Little Tykes toys, was hardly damaging to Wal-Mart with its eager alternative suppliers. But the loss of Wal-Mart, even if only partially through being given less shelf space, was serious for Rubbermaid.

The positive aspects of organizational restructuring for acquisitions are mixed. The idea of restructuring generally means downsizing. Some assets or corporate divisions may be sold off or eliminated, and the remaining organization thereby streamlined. This usually means layoffs, plant closings, and headquarters relocations. In Rubbermaid's case, the small Ohio town of Wooster faced the loss of its headquarters and some 3,000 employees. Of course, management's defense always is that while jobs are being cut, the operations will be stronger in the long run. Perhaps; but not always.

Where an organization has become fat and inefficient with layers of bureaucracy, some pruning of personnel and operations is necessary. But how much is too much, and how much is not enough? Certainly those personnel who are not willing to accept change may have to be let go. Weak persons and operations that show little probability of improvement need to be cut, just as the athlete who can't perform up to expectations can hardly be carried. Still, it is usually better to wait for sufficient information as to the "why" of poor performance before assigning blame for unsatisfactory operational results.

Periodic housecleaning produces competitive health. In order to minimize the buildup of deadwood, all aspects of an organization periodically ought to be objectively appraised. Weak products and operations should be pruned, unless solid justification exists for keeping them. Such justification might include good growth prospects or complementing other products and operations or even providing a desired customer service. In particular, staff and headquarters personnel and functions should be scrutinized, perhaps every five years, with the objective of weeding out the redundant and superfluous. Most important, these evaluations should be done objectively, with decisive actions taken where needed. While some layoffs may result, they might not be necessary if suitable transfers are possible.

Going back to Rubbermaid, the five-years-long tolerance of little improvement in customer service was inexcusable, and one would think that heads should roll (as undoubtedly some did and quickly when Newell took over).

Is there life without Wal-Mart for a big mass market consumer goods manufacturer? Can such a large manufacturer be strong and profitable without selling to the giant retailers? There are certainly other distribution channels available in reaching consumers, such as smaller retailers, different types of retailers, wholesalers, perhaps even the Internet in coming years. For smaller manufacturers some of these are viable alternatives to Wal-Mart, Target, Kmart, and the various large department store corporations. For example, the following information box describes the great success of Beanie Babies, which were primarily marketed to boutiques.

Newell and Rubbermaid's products were diversified but still geared to rather pedestrian household and hardware consumer use, hardly the grist to create a fashion or fad demand similar to Beanie Babies. A limited distribution strategy

INFORMATION BOX

BEANIE BABIES—DISDAIN FOR THE MASS MERCHANTS

Ty Warner has amassed a fortune of $5 billion on Beanie Babies, this placing him at the upper end of the *Forbes 400 Richest Americans* rankings. Dropping out of college, he took a job selling stuffed toys. Then he quit to bum around Italy. Later he designed a line of stuffed Himalayan cats and other toy animals that met some success. His coup was the creation of myriad Beanie Babies: understuffed toy animals. These were afford-ably priced in the $5 to $7 range to appeal to the allowance set. The cute names didn't hurt—Snort the bull, Fleece the lamb. Warner distributed through boutiques rather than mass merchants, a limited distribution but one that had a surprisingly positive effect. In addition to youngsters, it spawned a cult of adult collectors, where prices even reached $12,000 in collectors' circles.[9]

Do you think Ty Warner and his Beanie Babies might have done better with the mass merchandisers such as Wal-Mart? Why or why not?

[9] *Forbes*, October 11, 1999, p. 338.

such as through boutiques would hardly produce the sales volume needed. Only the megaretailers could provide the mass distribution and sales volume needed. Of course, Wal-Mart was not the only large retailer, but it was the biggest. Kmart, Target, and the chain department stores were alternatives. But these tended to be just as demanding as Wal-Mart. This suggests that somehow the demands of the giant retailers had to be catered to, regardless of costs or inclinations for firms like Newell and Rubbermaid.

CONSIDER

Can you find any additional learning insights?

QUESTIONS

1. "Periodic evaluations of personnel and departments aimed at pruning 'deadwood' cause far too much harm to the organization. Such 'axing' evaluations should themselves be pruned." Argue this position as persuasively as you can.

2. Now marshal your most persuasive arguments *for* such "axing" evaluations.

3. How do you account for Rubbermaid's inability to improve its delivery service to Wal-Mart? What factors do you see as contributing to this ongoing deficiency?

4. Do you think Newell acted too hastily in discharging Schmitt and other top executives so soon after the merger? Why or why not?

5. Do you think Wal-Mart and the other large retailers are going too far in their demands on their suppliers? Where would you draw the line?

6. Stanley Gault's strategy of trying to introduce a new product every day was lauded as the mark of a successful firm permeated by innovative thinking. Do you agree with this?

7. Discuss newellizing. Do you think it has any flaws?

8. Is it likely that a decades-old organization, such as Rubbermaid, would be bloated with excessive bureaucracy and overhead? Why or why not?

HANDS-ON EXERCISES

1. You are one of the three divisional presidents fired by McDonough in the first two months of the merger. Describe your feelings and your action plan at this point. (If you want to make some assumptions, state them specifically.)

2. You are a vice president of Rubbermaid, reporting toWolfgang Schmitt in 1995. The first serious complaints have surfaced from Wal-Mart concerning unacceptable delivery problems. Schmitt has ordered you to look into the complaints and prepare a course of action. Be as specific as you can about how you would approach this and what recommendations you would make.

TEAM DEBATE EXERCISE

It is early 1998. The demands of Wal-Mart are intensifying, and Newell is making overtures to acquire Rubbermaid. Debate the following two courses of action this turnabout year for Rubbermaid: (1) We must gear up to meet Wal-Mart's demands, even though estimated costs of complying are $300 million dollars in a new computer network and other capital and operating costs. (2) It is better to sacrifice the increasingly dictatorial Wal-Mart account and seek alternative distribution.

INVITATION TO RESEARCH

What is Wolfgang Schmitt doing after being ousted from an active role with Newell Rubbermaid? Have Rubbermaid's fortunes improved under Newell's management? Has Newell successfully expanded its overseas distribution?

NOTABLE MARKETING SUCCESSES

CHAPTER NINETEEN

Vanguard—Success with Minimal Marketing

Sometime, most likely in only a few years, Vanguard Group will become the largest mutual fund family in the world, besting Fidelity Investments. While Fidelity is still the biggest and increasing its fund assets about 20 percent a year, Vanguard is growing at 33 percent. The giant Fidelity advertises heavily, yet Vanguard does practically no advertising, spending a bare $8 million for a few ads to get people to ask for prospectuses. The Kaufmann Fund, one-hundredth Vanguard's size, spends that much for advertising, and General Mills spent twice as much just to introduce a new cereal, Sunrise.[1]

What is Vanguard's secret? How wise is it with such a consumer product to spurn marketing? The answer lies in the vision and steadfastness of John C. Bogle, the founder and recently retired chairman.

JOHN BOGLE AND THE CREATION OF VANGUARD

In 1950, as a junior at Princeton, Bogle was groping for a topic for his senior thesis. He wanted a topic that no one had written about in any serious academic paper. In December 1949 he read an article in *Fortune* on mutual funds. At that time, all mutual funds were sold with sales commissions often 8 percent of the amount invested, and this was taken off the top as a front end load. (This meant that if you invested $1,000, only $920 would be earning you money. Today we find no funds with a front end load more than 6.5 percent, so there has been some improvement.) In addition these funds had high yearly overheads or expense ratios. As Bogle thought about this, he wondered why funds couldn't be bought without salespeople or brokers and their steep commissions, and if growth could not be maximized by keeping overhead down.

Right after graduation he joined a tiny mutual fund, Wellington Management Company, and moved up rapidly. In 1965, at age 35, he became the chief executive.

---

[1] Thomas Easton, "The Gospel According to Vanguard," *Forbes*, February 8, 1999, p. 115.

Unwisely, he decided to merge with another firm, but the new partners turned out to be active managers, generating high overhead costs. The relationship was incompatible with Bogle's beliefs and in 1974 he was fired as chief executive.

He decided to go his own way and change the "very structure under which mutual funds operated" into a fund distribution company mutually owned by shareholders. The idea came from his Princeton thesis, and included such heresies as "reduction of sales loads and management fees," and "giving investors a fair shake" as the rock on which the new enterprise would be built. He chose the name "Vanguard" for his new company after the great victory of Lord Nelson over Napoleon's fleet with his flagship, HMS Vanguard. Bogle launched the Vanguard Group of Investment Companies on September 26, 1974, and he hoped "that just as Nelson's fleet had come to dominate the seas during the Napoleonic wars, our new flagship would come to dominate the mutual fund sea."[2]

But success was long in coming. Bogle brought out the first index fund the next year, a fund based on Standard & Poor's 500 Stock Price Index, and named it Vanguard 500 Index Fund. It was designed to mirror the market averages, and thus required minimal management decisions and costs. It flopped initially. Analysts publicly derided the idea, arguing that astute management could beat the averages every time, though they ignored the costs of high-priced money managers and frequent trading.

At the new millennium twenty-five years later, this Vanguard flagship fund that tracks the 500 stocks on Standard & Poor's Index had more than $75 billion in assets and had beat 86 percent of all actively managed stock funds in 1998, and an even higher percentage over the past decade. By early 2000 it would overtake Fidelity's famed Magellan Fund as the largest mutual fund of all. The relative growth between Magellan and Vanguard's 500 Index is shown in Table 19.1.

The Vanguard family of funds had become the world's largest no-load mutual fund group, with 12 million shareholders and $442 billion in assets as of the beginning of 1999. Fidelity, partly load and partly no-load, had nearly $700 billion, but the gap was closing fast.

TABLE 19.1. **Relative Growth Comparisons of the Two Largest Mutual Funds**

	Assets (millions $)		5-Year Gain
	6/30/94	6/30/99	(Percent)
Fidelity Magellan	$33,179	$97,594	194.2%
Vanguard 500 Index	8,443	92,644	997.3

Source: Company reports.

Commentary: Especially notable is the tremendous growth of Vanguard's 500 Index Fund in the last five years, growing from $8 billion in assets to over $92 billion.

[2] John C. Bogle, *Common Sense on Mutual Funds* (New York: Wiley, 1999), pp. 402–403.

Bogle, The Messiah

A feature article in *Forbes'* February 8, 1999 issue had this headline:

> The Gospel According to Vanguard
> How do you account for the explosive success of that strange business called Vanguard?
> Maybe it isn't really a business at all. It's a religion.[3]

Bogle's religion was low-cost investing and service to customers. He believed in funds being bought and not sold, thus, no loads or commissions to salespeople or brokers. Customers had to seek out and deal directly with Vanguard. The engine was frugality with the investor-owner's best interests paramount. This was not advertised, not pasted on billboards, but the gospel was preached in thousands of letters to shareholders, editors, Securities and Exchange Commission members, and congressmen. Bogle made many speeches, comments to the news media, and appearances on such TV channels as CNBC, and wrote two best-selling books. With his gaunt face and raspy voice, he became the zealot for low-cost investing, and the major critic of money managers who trade frenetically, in the process running up costs and tax burdens for their investors. As the legions of loyal and enthusiastic clients grew, word-of-mouth from past experiences and favorable mentions in business and consumer periodicals such as *Forbes, The Wall Street Journal, Money,* and numerous daily newspapers, as well as TV stations, brought a groundswell of new and repeat business to Vanguard.

Bogle turned 70 in May 1999, and was forced to retire from Vanguard's board. The new chairman, John J. Brennan, 44, seemed imbued with the Bogle philosophy, and with vision. He said, "We're a small company, and we haven't begun to explore our opportunities, yet." He noted that there's Europe and Asia, to say nothing of the trillions of dollars held in non-Vanguard funds. "It's humbling."[4]

GREAT APPEAL OF VANGUARD

Performance

Each year *Forbes* presents "Mutual Funds Ratings" and "Best Buys." The Ratings lists the hundreds of mutual funds that are open end, that is, can be bought and sold at current net asset prices.[5] The Best Buys are those select few that *Forbes* analysts judged to "invest wisely, spend frugally, and you get what you pay for," and that perform best in shareholder returns over both up and down markets. Vanguard equity and bond funds dominate *Forbes'* Best Buys:

---

[3] Easton, p. 115.

[4] Easton, p. 117.

[5] A far smaller number of mutuals are closed-end funds that have a fixed number of shares and are traded like stocks. These generally have higher annual expenses, yet sell at a discount from net asset value. We will disregard these in this case.

Of 43 U.S. *equity* funds listed in the various categories, 12 are Vanguard funds. Of 70 *bond* funds, 27 are Vanguard funds.[6]

Forbes explains that "the preponderance of Vanguard funds in our Best Buy Tables is a testament to the firm's cost controls... Higher expenses, for most other fund families, are like lead weights. Why carry them?"[7] Table 19.2 shows representative examples of the substantially lower expenses of Vanguard funds relative to others on the Best Buy list.[8]

TABLE 19.2. Comparative Expense Ratios of Representative Mutual Funds

	Annual Expenses per $100
Balanced Equity Funds:	
Vanguard Wellington Fund	0.31
Columbia Balanced Fund	0.67
Janus Balanced Fund	0.93
Ranier Balanced Portfolio	1.19
Index Equity Funds:	
Vanguard 500 Index	.18
T Rowe Price Equity Index 500	.40
Dreyfus S&P 500 Index	.50
Gateway Fund	1.02
Municipal Long-Term Bonds:	
Vanguard High Yield Tax Exempt	.20
Dreyfus Basic Muni Bond	.45
Strong High Yield Muni Bond	.66
High-Yield Corporate Bonds:	
Vanguard High Yield Corp.	.29
Fidelity High Income	.75
Value Line Aggressive Income	.81
Ivesco High Yield	.86

Source: Company records as reported in *Forbes Mutual Fund Guide*, August 23, 1999.

Commentary: The great cost advantage of Vanguard shows up very specifically here. It is not a slightly lower expense ratio, but one that is usually three or four times lower than similar funds. Take, for example, the category of Index Equity Funds, where the goal is to simply track the Index averages, which suggests passive management rather than free-wheeling buying and selling. Yet, Vanguard's costs are far below the other funds; in one case, the Gateway fund is five times higher.

---

[6] *Forbes*, August 23, 1999, pp. 128, 136–137.

[7] Ibid., p. 136.

[8] Ibid., pp. 128, 137.

Looking at total averages, the typical mutual fund has an expense ratio of 1.24 percent of assets annually. The ratio for Vanguard's 101 funds is .28 percent, almost a full percentage point lower.[9]

How does Vanguard achieve such a low expense ratio? We noted before the reluctance to advertise at all; nor does it have any mass sales force. Its commitment has been to pare marketing costs to the absolute minimum. But there have been other economies.

Fidelity and Charles Schwab have opened numerous walk-in sales outposts. Certainly these bring more sales exposure to prospective customers. But are such sales promotion efforts worth the cost? Vanguard decided not. It had one sales outpost in Philadelphia, but closed it to save money.

Vanguard discouraged day traders and other market timers from in-and-out trading of its funds. It even prohibited telephone switching on the Vanguard 500 Index; redemption orders had to come by mail. Why such market timing discouragement? Frequent redemptions run up transaction costs, and a flurry of sell orders might impose trading costs that would have to be borne by other shareholders as some holdings might have to be sold.

Not the least of the economies is what Bogle calls passive investing, tracking the market rather than trying to actively manage the funds by trying to beat the market. The funds with the highest expense ratios are hedge funds and these usually are the most active traders, with heavy buying and selling. Yet, they seldom beat the market but squander a lot of money in the effort and burden shareholders with sizable capital gains taxes because of the flurry of transactions. Still, the common notion prevails that more is better, that the more expensive car or service must be better than its less expensive alternative. See the following information box for another discussion of the price-quality perception.

Another factor also contributes to the great cost advantage of Vanguard. It is a mutual firm, organized as a nonprofit owned by its customers. Almost all other financial institutions, except TIAA-CREF (and we will discuss this shortly), have stock ownership. The insurance industry used to be dominated by mutual firms, but somehow they did not stand out for their low costs and high performance, nor did they serve well their customer-owners. Most insurance firms, especially the large ones, have been demutualizing and in the process drawing up lucrative option packages for their executives. You may remember from the Met Life case that the effort to demutualize was the major incentive to settle all the litigation pending against it.

Customer Service

Many firms espouse a commitment to customer service. It is the popular thing to do, rather like motherhood, apple pie, and the flag. Unfortunately, pious platitudes do not always match reality. Vanguard's commitment to service seems to be more tangible.

---

[9] Easton, p. 116.

INFORMATION BOX

THE PRICE-QUALITY PERCEPTION

We had a similar box in Chapter 9 on Perrier, but the topic is worth further discussion. There we considered whether high-priced bottled water was that much better than regular tap water or lower-priced bottled water, and concluded that it usually was not. The same thing applies to perfume, to beer and liquor, and to many other consumer products. "You get what you pay for," is a common perception, and its corollary is that you judge quality by price: The higher the price, the higher the quality. But this notion leads many consumers to be taken advantage of, and for top-of-the-line brands and products to command a higher profit margin than lower-priced alternatives. Admittedly, sometimes we are led to the more expensive brand or item for the prestige factor.

When it comes to money management, by no means do high fees mean better quality; the reverse is usually true. And prestige should hardly be a factor since we are not inclined to show off our investments like we might a new car. Does a high-overhead index fund deliver better performance than a cheap one, than Vanguard? Not at all. And hedge funds as we noted before seldom even beat the averages despite running up some of the highest expenses in the mutual fund industry. Looking at Table 19.2, which shows typical expense ratios of Vanguard and its competitors, are the other funds doing a better job than Vanguard with their expenses three to five times as high? No, because their high expense ratios take away from any performance advantage, even if frequent trading resulted in somewhat better gains, and that seldom is achieved.

If Vanguard advertised its great expense advantage aggressively to really get the word out, do you think it would win many more customers? Why or why not?

Service to customers is often composed of the simple things, such as just answering the phone promptly and courteously, or responding to mail quickly and completely, or giving complete and unbiased information. Vanguard's 2,000 phone reps are ready to answer the phone by the fourth ring. During a market panic or on April 15 when the tax deadline stimulates many inquiries, CEO John Brennan brings a brigade of executives with him to help answer the phones. Vanguard works to make its monthly statements to investors as complete and easy-to-understand as possible, and it leads the industry in this.

The philosophy of a customer-service commitment was espoused by Bogle: "Our primary goal: to serve, to the best of our ability, the human beings who are our clients. To serve them with candor, with integrity, and with fair dealing. To be the stewards of the assets they have entrusted to us. To treat them as we would like the stewards of our own assets to treat us."

Bogle describes a talk he gave to Harvard Business School in December 1997 on how "our focus on human beings had enabled Vanguard to become what at Harvard is called a 'service breakthrough company.' I challenged the students to find the term *human beings* in any book they had read on corporate strategy. As far as I know, none could meet the challenge. But 'human beingness' has been one of the keys to our development."[10]

Not the least of the consumer best interests has been a commitment to holding down taxable transactions for shareholders. Vanguard has led the industry with tax-managed funds aimed at minimizing the capital gains that confront most mutual fund investors to their dismay at the end of the year.

COMPETITION

Why is Vanguard's low-expense approach not matched by competitors? All the other fund giants that sell primarily to the general public are for-profit companies. Are they willing to sacrifice profits to win back Vanguard converts? Hardly likely. Are they willing to reduce their hefty marketing and advertising expenditures? Again, hardly likely. Why? Because advertising is vital to their visibility and to seeking out customers.

TIAA-CREF

One potential competitor looms, another low-cost fund contender. TIAA-CREF, which manages retirement money for teachers and researchers, in 1997 launched six no-load mutual funds that are now open to all investors. The funds' annual expenses range from 0.29 percent to 0.49 percent, comparable with Vanguard's. A significant potential attraction over Vanguard is that each fund's investment minimum is just $250, compared with Vanguard's usual minimum of $3,000. As of late August 1999, the combined assets of the six TIAA-CREF funds was $1.5 billion, far less, of course, than the near $500 billion of Vanguard.

TIAA-CREF is also run solely for the benefit of its shareholders, being another mutual, with the long-term aim of providing fund-management services at cost. Still, there is some doubt that expense ratios can be kept low, should the new funds fail to attract enough investors.

Is this a gnat up against the giant Vanguard? Perhaps; however, the low investment requirement of only $250 should certainly attract cost-conscious investors who cannot come up with the $3,000 that Vanguard requires on most of its funds. Still, six fund choices versus the more than a hundred of Vanguard is not very attractive yet. Efforts to be as tax-efficient as Vanguard are also unknown.

ANALYSIS

The success of Vanguard with its disavowal of most traditional marketing techniques flies in the face of all that we have come to believe. It suggests that heavy advertising expenditures may at least be questioned as not always desirable—and what a heresy

---

[10] Bogle, pp. 423, 424.

this is. It suggests that relying on word-of-mouth and whatever free publicity can be garnered may sometimes be better than advertising. All you need is a superior product or service. It supports the statement that marketing textbooks like to shoot down: "If you build a better mousetrap, people will come." Marketing wisdom says that without advertising to get the message out, this better mousetrap will fade away from lack of buyer knowledge and interest.

How do we reconcile Vanguard with the conventional thinking that marketing communication is essential to get products and services to customers (except perhaps when selling solely to the government or to a single customer)?

Maybe we should not try to fit Vanguard in with most of our traditional thoughts of marketing. Maybe it is the exception, the anomaly, in its seeming repudiation of marketing. Still, let us not be too hasty in this judgment.

I do not believe that Vanguard contradicts the traditional principles of marketing. Rather, it has opened up rather intriguingly another approach to marketing and the advertising component: the effective use of word-of-mouth publicity. A superior and distinctive product as tangibly demonstrated in relative cost advantages, then effective word-of-mouth enhanced or developed through more formal publicity—from media, public appearances, and publications—can indeed replace the massive advertising expenditures of competitors. But there is a downside to all this.

But first, let us examine the role of word-of-mouth in more detail in the following information box.

INFORMATION BOX

THE POTENTIAL OF WORD-OF-MOUTH AND UNPAID PUBLICITY

Word-of-mouth advertising, by itself, is almost always frowned on by the experts. It is the sign of the marginal firm, one without sufficient resources, so they say, to do what is needed to get established. Such a firm is bound to succumb to competitors who are better managed and better resourced. The best they can say for word-of-mouth advertising is that if the firm can survive for an unknown number of years, and if it really, really has a superior product or service, then it might finally attain some modest success.

Compared to spending for advertising, word-of-mouth takes far longer to have any impact, and most firms do not have the staying power to wait years, so the belief holds. The best strategy would be to have both, with healthy doses of advertising to jumpstart the enterprise, and let favorable word-of-mouth reinforce the advertising.

As we have seen, Bogle and his Vanguard repudiated the accepted strategy, yet became highly successful. But it took time, even decades. If you look at Table 19.1, in 1994 after 16 years the flagship Index 500 fund had reached $8 billion in assets; not bad, but far below the heavily advertised Magellan fund of Fidelity. Its growth has accelerated only in recent years. Would more advertising have shortened the period?

(continues)

In one respect, however, Vanguard illustrates a commendable application of one important marketing principle: the desirability of uniqueness or product differentiation. It differentiated itself from competitors in two respects: (1) its resolve and ability to bring to market a low-priced product and at the same time one of good quality, and (2) its achievement of good customer service despite the low price.

Even today after several decades of competitors seeing this highly effective strategy, Vanguard still is virtually unmatched in its uniqueness, except for one newcomer that is hardly a contender, but could be a factor should Vanguard let down its guard and be tempted to seek more profits.

In part V, we examine remarkably successful firms. In the next two chapters, we will find rather similar product differentiations of an airline and the world's largest retailer.

Prognosis—Can Vanguard Continue As Is?

Is it likely Vanguard can continue its success pattern without increasing advertising and other costs and becoming more like its competitors? Why should it change? It has become a giant with its low-cost strategy. The last decade saw a growing momentum created by favorable word-of-mouth and publicity that made the need for heavy advertising and selling efforts far less than in the early years. It took bravery, or audacity, in those early years not to succumb to the Lorelei beguilement that advertising and commission selling was the only viable strategy. Something would be lost if Vanguard were to change its strategy and uniqueness and become a higher-cost operation just like its competitors.

If Vanguard is so good, why are investors still in large numbers doing business with the higher-cost competitors? We can identify four groups or consumer segments who are noncustomers of Vanguard:

1. Those who have not studied the statistics and editorials of publications like *Forbes* and *The Wall Street Journal,* and are not aware of the Vanguard advantage.

2. Those who are naive in investing and content to let someone else—brokers or bankers—advise them and reap the commissions.

3. Those who are swayed by the massive advertisements of firms like Fidelity, Dreyfus, Rowe Price, and others.

4. Those who put their faith in the price-quality perception: The higher the price the higher the quality.

In addition to continued investments of its ardent customers, Vanguard should find potential in some flaking away or eroding of the commitment of these four consumer groups. Of course, the overseas markets also offer a huge and virtually untapped potential for Vanguard.

WHAT CAN BE LEARNED?

Marketing can be overdone. The success of Vanguard shows that marketing can be overdone. Too much can be spent for advertising, without realizing congruent benefits. Sales expenses and branch office overhead may get out of line. Yet, few firms dare reduce such marketing costs lest they be competitively disadvantaged. For example, it is the brave executive who reduces advertising in the face of increases by competitors, though the results of the advertising may be impossible to measure with any accuracy. (See the first information box in Chapter 2 for a discussion of measuring the effectiveness of advertising.)

Still, despite the success of Vanguard in downplaying marketing, one has to wonder how much faster the growth might have been by budgeting more dollars for marketing at least in the early years.

Can word-of-mouth do the job of advertising by itself? In Vanguard's case, word-of-mouth combined with favorable unpaid publicity from the media brought it to the number-two, going on number-one, largest mutual fund family in the industry. However, the time it took for word-of-mouth, even eventually with good publicity, to build demand has to be a negative. Without such favorable publicity, word-of-mouth in the absence of advertising would have taken far longer.

The benefits of frugality. There is far too much waste in most institutions, business and nonbusiness. Some of the waste comes from undercontrolled costs and from a variety of extravagances, such as lavish expense accounts and entertainment, and expenditures that do little to benefit the bottom line. Other factors may be a top-heavy bureaucratic organization saddled with layers of staff personnel, and/or too many debt payments due to heavy investments in plant and equipment or mergers. Heavy use of advertising, as we saw in Chapter 2, when Coca Cola was outspending Pepsi by $100 million, but was still losing market share may not always pay off enough to justify the expenditures. In money management, trading costs may get far out of line.

Vanguard shows the benefit of austerity in greatly reduced expense ratios for its funds compared to competitors. At last, more and more astute investors are recognizing this unique cost advantage that not only gives a better return on their investment dollars but some of the best customer service in the industry.

The power of differentiation. Firms seek to differentiate themselves, to come up with products or ways of doing business that are unique in some respect from competitors. This is a paramount quest of marketing and accounts for the massive expenditures for advertising. Too often such attempts to find uniqueness are fragile, not very substantial, and easily lost or countered by competitors. Sometimes, though, they can be rather enduring, as for example the quality-image perception perpetrated by advertisements featuring the lonely Maytag repairman. If a firm can effectively differentiate itself from competitors, it gains a powerful advantage and may even be able to charge premium prices.

While Vanguard seemingly disregarded marketing, John Bogle found a powerful and enduring way to differentiate through low-cost quality products and superb customer service. For decades no competitor has been able to match this attractive uniqueness.

Beware placing too much faith in the price-quality relationship. We all are inclined to judge quality by its price relative to other choices. Often this is justified, although the better quality may not always match the higher price. In other words, the luxury item may not be worth the much higher price, except for the significant psychological value that some people see in the prestige of a fine brand name. Unfortunately, there are some products and services where the higher price does not really reflect higher quality, better workmanship, better service, and the like. Then we are taken advantage of with this price-quality perception. Beware of always judging quality by price.

CONSIDER

Can you think of additional learning insights?

QUESTIONS

1. "The success of Vanguard is due to media exploitation of what would otherwise be a very ordinary firm." Discuss.

2. Why do you think people continue to buy front-end load mutual funds with 5–6 percent commission fees when there are numerous no-load funds to be had?

3. Do you think Bogle's shunning advertising was really a success, or was it a mistake?

4. Was Vanguard's failure to open walk-in sales outposts a mistake and an example of misplaced frugality? Why or why not?

5. What are the differences in passive and active fund management? How significant are these?

6. "Vanguard seems too good. There must be a downside." Discuss.

7. What is a service-breakthrough company?

8. Can publicity ever take the place of massive advertising expenditures?

HANDS-ON EXERCISES

1. You are an executive assistant to John Brennan, the new CEO of Vanguard now that Bogle has retired. Brennan is thinking of judiciously adding some marketing and advertising expenditures to the paucity that Bogle had insisted on. He has directed you to draw up a position paper on the merits of adding some advertising and even some walk-in sales outposts such as other big competitors have already done.

2. You are John Brennan, CEO. It is 2005, and TIAA-CREF is turning out to be a formidable competitor and is gaining fast on your first-place position in the industry. What actions would you take, and why? Discuss all ramifications of these actions that you can think of.

TEAM DEBATE EXERCISES

1. You are a member of the board of directors of Vanguard. John Bogle is approaching the retirement age as set forth in the company policies. However, he wants to continue as chairman of the board, even though he is willing to let Brennan assume active management. Debate the issue of whether to force Bogle to step down or bow to his wishes.

2. Debate the no-advertising policy of Bogle.

INVITATION TO RESEARCH

Has Vanguard become number one in the mutual fund industry? Has it increased its advertising expenditures? Has Brennan made any substantial changes?

CHAPTER TWENTY

Southwest Airlines— "Try to Match Our Prices"

*I*n 1992 the airlines lost a combined $2 billion, matching a dismal 1991 and bringing their three-year red ink total to a disastrous $8 billion. Three carriers—TWA, Continental, and America West—were operating under Chapter 11 bankruptcy, and others were lining up to join them. But one airline, Southwest, was profitable as well as rapidly growing—with a 25 percent sales increase in 1992 alone. Interestingly enough, this was a low-price, bare bones operation run by a flamboyant CEO, Herb Kelleher. He had found a niche, a strategic window of opportunity, and oh, how he had milked it! See the following information box for further discussion of a strategic window of opportunity and its desirable accompaniment, a SWOT analysis.

HERBERT D. KELLEHER

Herb Kelleher impresses one as an eccentric. He likes to tell stories, often with himself as the butt of the story, and many involve practical jokes. He admits he sometimes is a little scatterbrained. In his cluttered office, he displays a dozen ceramic wild turkeys as a testimonial to his favorite brand of whiskey. He smokes five packs of cigarettes a day. As an example of his zaniness, he painted one of his 737s to look like a killer whale in celebration of the opening of Sea World in San Antonio. Another time, during a flight he had flight attendants dress up as reindeer and elves, while the pilot sang Christmas carols over the loudspeaker and gently rocked the plane. Kelleher is a "real maniac," said Thomas J. Volz, vice president of marketing at Braniff Airlines. "But who can argue with his success?"[1]

Kelleher grew up in Haddon Heights, New Jersey, the son of a Campbell Soup Company executive. He graduated from Wesleyan University and New York University law school, then moved to San Antonio in 1961, where his father-in-law helped him set up a law firm. In 1968 he and a group of investors put up $560,000 to found Southwest; of this amount, Kelleher contributed $20,000.

---

[1] Kevin Kelly, "Southwest Airlines: Flying High with 'Uncle Herb'," *Business Week*, July 3, 1989, p. 53.

INFORMATION BOX

STRATEGIC WINDOW OF OPPORTUNITY AND SWOT ANALYSIS

A strategic window is an opportunity in the marketplace not presently well served by competitors that fits well with the firm's competencies. Strategic windows often last for only a short time (although Southwest's strategic window has been much more durable) before they are filled by alert competitors.

Strategic windows are usually found by systematically analyzing the environment, examining the threats and opportunities it holds. The competencies of the firm, its physical, financial, and people resources—management and employees and their strengths and weaknesses—should also be assessed. The objective is to determine what actions might or might not be appropriate for that particular enterprise and its orientation. This is commonly known as a SWOT analysis: analyzing the strengths and weaknesses of the firm and assessing the opportunities and threats in the environment.

This analysis may be a formal part of the planning process, or it may also be informal and even intuitive. We suspect that Herb Kelleher instinctively sensed a strategic window in short hauls and lowest prices. Although he must have recognized the danger that his bigger competitors would try to match his prices, he believed that with his simplicity of operation he would be able to make a profit while bigger airlines were racking up losses.

Why do you think the major airlines so badly overlooked the possibilities in short hauls at low prices?

In the early years he was the general counsel and a director of the fledgling enterprise. But in 1978 he was named chairman, despite having no managerial experience, and in 1981 he became CEO. His flamboyance soon made him the most visible aspect of the airline. He starred in most of its TV commercials. A rival airline, America West, charged in ads that Southwest passengers should be embarrassed to fly such a no-frills airline, whereupon Kelleher appeared in a TV spot with a bag over his head. He offered the bag to anyone ashamed to fly Southwest, suggesting it could be used to hold "all the money you'll save flying us."[2]

He knew many of his employees by name, and they called him "Uncle Herb" or "Herbie." He held weekly parties for employees at corporate headquarters, and he encouraged such antics by his flight attendants as organizing trivia contests, delivering instructions in rap, and awarding prizes for the passengers with the largest holes in their socks. But such wackiness had a shrewd purpose: to generate a gung-ho spirit to boost productivity. "Herb's fun is infectious," said Kay Wallace, president of the

---

[2] Kelly, p. 53.

Flight Attendants Union Local 556. "Everyone enjoys what they're doing and realizes they've got to make an extra effort."[3]

THE BEGINNINGS

Southwest was conceived in 1967, folklore tells us, on a napkin. Rollin King, a client of Kelleher, then a lawyer, had an idea for a low-fare, no-frills airline to fly between major Texas cities. He doodled a triangle on the napkin, labeling the points Dallas, Houston, and San Antonio.

The two tried to go ahead with their plans but were stymied for more than three years by litigation, battling Braniff, Texas International, and Continental over the right to fly. In 1971 Southwest won, and it went public in 1975. At that time it had four planes flying between the three cities. Lamar Muse was president and CEO from 1971 until he was fired by Southwest's board in 1978. Then the board of directors tapped Kelleher.

At first Southwest was in the throes of life-and-death low-fare skirmishes with its giant competitors. Kelleher liked to recount how he came home one day "beat, tired, and worn out. So I'm just kind of sagging around the house when my youngest daughter comes up and asks what's wrong. I tell her, 'Well, Ruthie, it's these damned fare wars.' And she cuts me right off and says, 'Oh, Daddy, stop complaining. After all, you started 'em.'"[4]

For most small firms, competing on a price basis with much larger, well-endowed competitors is tantamount to disaster. The small firm simply cannot match the resources and staying power of such competitors. Yet Southwest somehow survived. Not only did it initiate the cut-throat price competition, but it achieved cost savings in its operation that the larger airlines could not. The question then became: How long would the big carriers be content to maintain their money-losing operations and match the low prices of Southwest? The big airlines eventually blinked.

In its early years, Southwest faced other legal battles. Take Dallas, and Love Field. The original airport, Love Field, is close to downtown Dallas, but it could not geographically expand at the very time when air traffic was increasing mightily. So a major new facility, Dallas/Fort Worth International, replaced it in 1974. This boasted state-of-the-art facilities and enough room for foreseeable demand, but it had one major drawback: It was 30 minutes farther from downtown Dallas. Southwest was able to avoid a forced move to the new airport and to continue at Love. But in 1978 competitors pressured Congress to bar flights from Love Field to anywhere outside Texas. Southwest was able to negotiate a compromise, now known as the Wright Amendment, that allowed flights from Love Field to the four states contiguous to Texas. In retrospect the Wright Amendment forced onto Southwest a key ingredient of its later success: the strategy of short flights.[5]

---

[3] Richard Woodbury, "Prince of Midair," *Time*, January 25, 1993, p. 55.

[4] Charles A. Jaffe, "Moving Fast by Standing Still," *Nation's Business*, October 1991, p. 58.

[5] Bridget O'Brian, "Southwest Airlines Is a Rare Air Carrier: It Still Makes Money," *The Wall Street Journal*, October 28, 1992, p. A7.

GROWTH

Southwest grew steadily but not spectacularly through the 1970s. It dominated the Texas market by appealing to passengers who valued price and frequent departures. Its one-way fare between Dallas and Houston, for example, was $59 in 1987 versus $79 for unrestricted coach flights on other airlines.

In the 1980s Southwest's annual passenger traffic count tripled. At the end of 1989, its operating costs per revenue mile—the industry's standard measure of cost-effectiveness—was just under 10 cents, which was about 5 cents per mile below the industry average.[6] Although revenues and profits were rising steadily, especially compared with the other airlines, Kelleher took a conservative approach to expansion, financing it mostly from internal funds rather than taking on debt.

Perhaps the caution stemmed from an ill-fated acquisition in 1986. Kelleher bought a failing long-haul carrier, Muse Air Corporation, for $68 million and renamed it TransStar. (This carrier had been founded by Lamar Muse after he left Southwest.) But by 1987 TransStar was losing $2 million a month, and Kelleher shut down the operation.

By 1993 Southwest had spread to 34 cities in 15 states. It had 141 planes, and these each made 11 trips a day. It used only fuel-thrifty 737s and still concentrated on flying large numbers of passengers on high-frequency, one-hour hops at bargain fares (average $58). Southwest shunned the hub-and-spoke systems of its larger rivals and took its passengers directly from city to city, often to smaller satellite airfields rather than congested major metropolitan fields. With rock-bottom prices and no amenities, it quickly dominated most new markets it entered.

As an example of Southwest's impact on a new market, it came to Cleveland, Ohio, in February 1992, and by the end of the year was offering 11 daily flights. In 1992 Cleveland Hopkins Airport posted record passenger levels, up 9.74 percent from 1991. "A lot of the gain was traffic that Southwest Airlines generated," noted John Osmond, air trade development manager.[7]

In some markets Southwest found itself growing much faster than projected, as competitors either folded or else abandoned directly competing routes. For example, America West Airlines cut back service in Phoenix in order to conserve cash after a Chapter 11 bankruptcy filing. Of course, Southwest picked up the slack, as it did in Chicago when Midway Airlines folded in November 1992. And in California, Southwest's arrival led several large competitors to abandon the Los Angeles–San Francisco route, unable to meet Southwest's $59 one-way fare. Before Southwest's arrival, fares had been as high as $186 one way.[8]

Now cities that Southwest did not serve were petitioning for service. For example, Sacramento, California, sent two county commissioners, the president of the chamber of commerce, and the airport director to Dallas to petition for service. Kelleher consented a few months later. In 1991 the airline received 51 similar requests.[9]

[6] Jaffe, p. 58.

[7] "Passenger Flights Set Hopkins Record," *Cleveland Plain Dealer,* January 30, 1993, p. 3D.

[8] O'Brian, p. A7.

[9] Ibid.

A unique situation was developing. On many routes, Southwest's fares were so low they competed with buses, and even with private cars. By 1991 Kelleher did not even see other airlines as his principal competitors: "We're competing with the automobile, not the airlines. We're pricing ourselves against Ford, Chrysler, GM, Toyota, and Nissan. The traffic is already there, but it's on the ground. We take it off the highway and put it on the airplane."[10]

Following are several tables and graphs that depict various aspects of Southwest's growth and increasingly favorable competitive position. See Tables 20.1, 20.2, and 20.3, and Figure 20.1. Although Southwest's total revenues were still far less than those of the four major airlines in the industry (five if we count Continental, emerging from its second bankruptcy), its growth pattern indicated a major presence, and its profitability was second to none.

Tapping California

The formidable competitive power of Southwest was perhaps never better epitomized than in its 1990 invasion of populous California. By 1992 it had become the second largest player, after United, with 23 percent of intrastate traffic. Southwest achieved this position by pushing fares down as much as 60 percent on some routes. The big carriers, which had tended to surrender the short-haul niche to Southwest in other mar-

TABLE 20.1. Growth of Southwest Airlines; Various Operating Statistics, 1982–1991

Year	Operating Revenues ($ millions)	Net Income ($ millions)	Passengers Carried (thousands)	Passenger Load Factor
1991	$1,314	$26.9	22,670	61.1%
1990	1,187	47.1	19,831	60.7
1989	1,015	71.6	17,958	62.7
1988	860	58.0	14,877	57.7
1987	778	20.2	13,503	58.4
1986	769	50.0	13,638	58.8
1985	680	47.3	12,651	60.4
1984	535	49.7	10,698	58.5
1983	448	40.9	9,511	61.6
1982	331	34.0	7,966	61.6

Source: Company annual reports.

Commentary: Note the steady increase in revenues and in number of passengers carried. While the net income and load factor statistics show no appreciable improvement, these statistics still are in the vanguard of an industry that has suffered badly in recent years. See Table 20.2 for a comparison of revenues and income with the major airlines.

---

[10] Subrata N. Chakravarty, "Hit 'Em Hardest with the Mostest," *Forbes,* September 16, 1991, p. 49.

TABLE 20.2.   Comparison of Southwest's Growth in Revenues and Net Income with Major Competitors, 1987–1991

	1991	1990	1989	1988	1987	% 5-year Gain
Operating Revenue Comparisons ($ millions)						
American	$9,309	$9,203	$8,670	$7,548	$6,369	46.0
Delta	8,268	7,697	7,780	6,684	5,638	46.6
United	7,850	7,946	7,463	7,006	6,500	20.8
Northwest	4,330	4,298	3,944	3,395	3,328	30.1
Southwest	1,314	1,187	1,015	860	778	68.9
Net Income Comparisons ($ millions)						
American	(253)	(40)	412	450	225	
Delta	(216)	(119)	467	286	201	
United	(175)	73	246	426	22	
Northwest	10	(27)	116	49	64	
Southwest	27	47	72	58	20	

Source: Company annual reports.

Commentary: Southwest's revenue gains over these 5 years outstripped those of its largest competitors. While the percentage gains in profitability are hardly useful because of the erratic nature of airline profits during these years, Southwest stands out starkly as the only airline to be profitable each year.

kets, suddenly faced a real quandary in competing in this "Golden State." Now Southwest was being described as a "500 pound cockroach, too big to stamp out."[11]

The California market was indeed enticing. Some 8 million passengers each year fly between the five airports in metropolitan Los Angeles and the three in the San Francisco Bay area, making it the busiest corridor in the United States. It was also one of the pricier routes, as the low fares of AirCal and Pacific Southwest Airlines had been eliminated when these two airlines were acquired by American and USAir.

TABLE 20.3.   Market Share Comparison of Southwest with Its Four Major Competitors, 1987–1991

	1991	1990	1989	1988	1987
Total Revenues (millions):					
American, Delta,					
United, Northwest	$29,757	$29,144	$27,857	$24,633	$21,835
Southwest Revenues:	1,314	1,187	1,015	860	778
Percent of Big Four	4.4	4.1	3.6	3.5	3.6
Increase in Southwest's market share, 1987–1991: 22%					

Source: Company annual reports.

[11] Wendy Zellner, "Striking Gold in the California Skies," *Business Week,* March 30, 1992, p. 48.

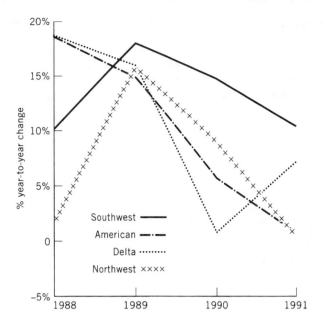

Figure 20.1. Year-to-year percentage changes in revenues, Southwest and its three major competitors, 1988–1991.

Southwest charged into this situation with its low fares and frequent flights. While airfares dropped, total air traffic soared 123 percent in the quarter Southwest entered the market. Competitors suffered: American lost nearly $80 million at its San Jose hub, and USAir still lost money even though it cut service drastically. United, the market leader, quit flying the San Diego–Sacramento and Ontario–Oakland routes where Southwest had rapidly built up service. The quandary of the major airlines was all the greater since this critical market fed traffic into the rest of their systems, especially the lucrative transcontinental and trans-Pacific routes. They could hardly abdicate California to Southwest. American, for one, considered creating its own no-frills shuttle for certain routes.[12] But the question remained: Could anyone stop Southwest, with its formula of lowest prices and lowest costs and frequent schedules? And, oh yes, good service and fun.

INGREDIENTS OF SUCCESS

Although Southwest's operation under Kelleher had a number of rather distinctive characteristics contributing to its success pattern and its seizing of a strategic window of opportunity, the key factors appear to be cost containment, employee commitment, and conservative growth.

[12] Ibid.

Cost Containment

Southwest has been the lowest cost carrier in its markets. Although its larger competitors might try to match its cut-rate prices, they could not do so without incurring sizable losses. Nor did they seem able to trim their costs to match Southwest's. For example, in the first quarter of 1991, Southwest's operating costs per available seat mile (i.e., the number of seats multiplied by the distance flown) were 15 percent lower than America West's, 29 percent lower than Delta's, 32 percent lower than United's, and 39 percent lower than USAir's.[13]

Many aspects of the operation contributed to these lower costs. With a single aircraft type, Boeing 737, for all its planes, costs of training, maintenance, and inventory were low. And since a plane earns revenues only when flying, Southwest was able to achieve a faster turnaround time on the ground than any other airline. Although competitors take upwards of an hour to load and unload passengers and then clean and service the planes, some 70 percent of Southwest's flights have a turnaround time of 15 minutes, and 10 percent have even pared the turnaround time to 10 minutes.

In areas of customer service, Southwest curbed costs as well. It offered peanuts and drinks, but no meals. Boarding passes were reusable plastic cards. Boarding time was minimal because there were no assigned seats. Southwest subscribed to no centralized reservation service. It did not even transfer baggage to other carriers; that was the passengers' responsibility. Admittedly, such customer service frugalities would be less acceptable on longer flights—and this helped to account for the difficulty competing airlines had in cutting their costs to match Southwest's. Still, if the price is right, many passengers might also opt for no frills on longer flights.

Employee Commitment

Kelleher was able to achieve an esprit de corps unmatched by other airlines despite the fact that Southwest employees were unionized. But there was no adversarial relationship with unions like Frank Lorenzo had at Eastern and Continental Airlines. Southwest was able to negotiate flexible work rules, with flight attendants and even pilots helping with plane cleanup. Employee productivity remained very high, permitting the airline to be leanly staffed. Kelleher resisted the inclination to hire extravagantly when times were good, necessitating layoffs during leaner times. This contributed to employee feelings of security and loyalty. The low-key attitude and sense of fun that Kelleher engendered helped, perhaps more than anyone could have foreseen. Kelleher declared, "Fun is a stimulant to people. They enjoy their work more and work more productively."[14]

Conservative Growth Efforts

Not the least of the ingredients of success was Kelleher's conservative approach to growth. He resisted the temptation to expand vigorously—for example, to seek to

---

[13] Chakravarty, p. 50.
[14] Ibid.

fly to Europe or get into head-to-head competition with larger airlines with long-distance routes. Even in its geographical expansion, conservatism prevailed. The philosophy of expansion was to do so only when enough resources could be committed to go into a city with 10 to 12 flights a day, rather than just 1 or 2. Kelleher called this "guerrilla warfare," concentrating efforts against stronger opponents in only a few areas, rather than dissipating strength by trying to compete everywhere.

Even with a conservative approach to expansion, the company showed vigorous but controlled growth. Its debt, at 49 percent of equity, was the lowest among U.S. carriers. Southwest also had the airline industry's highest Standard & Poor's credit rating, A minus.

GALLOPING TOWARD THE NEW MILLENNIUM

In its May 2, 1994 edition, prestigious *Fortune* magazine devoted its cover story to Herb Kelleher and Southwest Airlines. It raised an intriguing question: "Is Herb Kelleher America's best CEO?" It called him a "people-wise manager who wins where others can't."[15] The operational effectiveness of Southwest continued to surpass all rivals, for example, in such productivity ratios as cost per available seat mile, passengers per employee, and employees per aircraft. Only Southwest remained consistently profitable among the big airlines, by the end of 1998 having been profitable for 26 consecutive years. Operating revenue had grown to $4.2 billion (it was $1.3 billion in 1991—see Table 20.2), and net income was $433 million, up from $27 million in 1991.

In 1999, Herb Kelleher was named CEO of the Year by *Chief Executive* magazine.

Geographical Expansion

Late in October 1996, Southwest launched a carefully planned battle for East Coast passengers that would drive down air fares and pressure competitors to back away from some lucrative markets. It chose Providence, Rhode Island, just 60 miles from Boston's Logan Airport, thus tapping the Boston–Washington corridor. The Providence airport escaped the congested New York and Boston air-traffic-control areas, and from the Boston suburbs was hardly a longer trip than to Logan Airport. Experience had shown that air travelers would drive considerable distance to fly with Southwest's cheaper fares.

As Southwest entered new markets, most competitors refused any longer to try to compete pricewise: They simply could not cut costs enough to compete. Their alternative then was either to pull out of these short-haul markets, or be content to let Southwest have its market share while they tried to hold on to other customers by stressing first-class seating, frequent-flyer programs, and other in-flight amenities.

---

[15] Kenneth Labich, "Is Herb Kelleher America's Best CEO?" *Fortune*, May 2, 1994, pp. 45–52.

In April 1997, Southwest quietly entered the transcontinental market. From its major connecting point of Nashville, Tennessee, it began nonstops both to Oakland, California and to Los Angeles. With Nashville's direct connections with Chicago, Detroit, Cleveland, Providence, and Baltimore–Washington, as well as points south, this afforded *one-stop*, coast-to-coast service, with fares about half as much as the other major airlines.

Two other significant moves were announced in late 1998. One was an experiment. On Thanksgiving Day, a Southwest 737–700 flew *nonstop* from Oakland, California to the Baltimore–Washington Airport, and back again. It provided its customary no-frills service, but a $99 one-way fare, the lowest in the business. The test was designed to see how pilots, flight attendants, and passengers would feel about spending five hours in a 737, with only peanuts and drinks served in flight. The older 737s lacked the fuel capacity to fly coast-to-coast nonstop, but with Boeing's new 737–700 series this was no problem. The Thanksgiving Day test was a precursor of more nonstop flights as Southwest had firm orders for 129 of the new planes to be delivered over the next seven years. This would enable it to compete with the major carriers on their moneymaking transcontinental flights.

In November 1998, plans were also announced for starting service to MacArthur Airport at Islip, Long Island, which would enable Southwest to tap into the New York City market. By late 1999 it was flying to 54 cities in 29 states. Table 20.4 lists these cities.

TABLE 20.4. Cities Served by Southwest, October 1999

Albuquerque	Ft. Lauderdale	Midland/Odessa	Rio Grande Valley (South Padre Island/Harlingen)
Amarillo	Hartford, CT°	Nashville	
Austin	Houston (Hobby & Bush Intercontinental)	New Orleans	Sacramento
Baltimore/Washington		Oakland	St. Louis
Birmingham	Indianapolis	Oklahoma City	Salt Lake City
Boise	Islip (Long Island)	Omaha	San Antonio
Burbank	Jackson, MS	Ontario, CA	San Diego
Chicago (Midway)	Jacksonville	Orange County	San Francisco
Cleveland	Kansas City	Orlando	San Jose
Columbus	Little Rock	Phoenix	Seattle
Corpus Christi	Los Angeles (LAX)	Portland	Spokane
Dallas (Love Field)	Louisville	Providence, RI	Tampa
Detroit (Metro)	Lubbock	Raleigh–Durham	Tucson
El Paso	Manchester, NH	Reno/Tahoe	Tulsa

° Service to Hartford, Connecticut began October 31, 1999.

LATE-BREAKING NEWS

On September 23, 1999, Southwest announced it would add 10 new nonstop flights, three one-stop flights, and several special Saturday-only nonstop flights, all of these new nonstops with introductory fares of $99 or less.

Examples of the new nonstop flights included Hartford/Springfield and Las Vegas; Orlando and Chicago; Phoenix and Providence; and Detroit and Phoenix.

WHAT CAN BE LEARNED?

The power of low prices and simplicity of operation. If a firm can maintain prices below those of its competitors, and do so profitably and without sacrificing expected quality of service, then it has a powerful advantage. We noted in the previous chapter the great advantage Vanguard had with its lowest expense ratio in the mutual fund industry. Here, Southwest also achieved this with its simplicity of operation and no-frills, but dependable service. Competition on the basis of price is seldom used in most mature industries (although the airline industry has been an exception), primarily because competitors can quickly match prices with no lasting advantage to anyone. As profits are destroyed, only customers benefit, and then only in the short run before the industry realizes the futility of price competition. (With new and rapidly changing industries, price competition is effective as productivity and technology improve and marginal competitors are driven from the market.)

The effectiveness of the cost controls of Southwest, however, shows the true competitive importance of low prices. Customers love the lowest price *if* the provider does not sacrifice too much quality, comfort, and service. While there was some sacrifice of service and amenities with Southwest, most customers found this acceptable because of the short-haul situation; friendly, dependable, and reasonable service was still maintained. Apparently the same no-frills service was found acceptable on longer flights too, as Southwest expanded these to meet demand.

An intriguing factor regarding the relationship of customer satisfaction and price is explored in the following information box.

The power of a niche strategy. Directing efforts toward a particular customer segment or niche can provide a powerful competitive advantage. Especially is this true if no competitor is catering directly to such a niche, and if it is fairly sizable. Such an untapped niche then becomes a strategic window of opportunity.

Kelleher revealed the niche strategy of Southwest: While other airlines set up hub-and-spoke systems in which passengers are shunted to a few major hubs from which they are transferred to other planes going to their destination, "we wound

---

INFORMATION BOX

THE KEY TO CUSTOMER SATISFACTION: MEETING CUSTOMER EXPECTATIONS

Southwest consistently earns high ratings for its customer satisfaction, higher than those of its giant competitors. Yet, these major airlines all offer more than Southwest's food service; they also provide advance seat assignments, in-flight entertainment on longer flights, the opportunity to upgrade, and a comprehensive frequent-flyer program. Yet Southwest gets the highest points for customer satisfaction.

Could something else be involved here?

Let's call this *expectations*. If a customer has high expectations, perhaps because of a high price and/or the advertising promising high-quality, luxury accommodations, dependable service, or whatever, then if product or service does not live up to these expectations, customer satisfaction dives. Turning to the airlines, customers are not disappointed in the service of Southwest because they don't expect luxury; Southwest does not advertise this. They expect no frills, but pleasant and courteous treatment by employees, dependable and safe flights, and the low price. On the other hand, expectations are higher for the bigger carriers with their higher prices. This is well and good for the first- or business-class service. But for the many who fly coach...?

Do you think there is a point where a low-price/no-frills strategy would be detrimental to customer satisfaction? What might it depend on?

Source: This idea of expectations affecting customer satisfaction was suggested by Ed Perkins for Tribune Media Services and reported in "Hotels Must Live Up to Promises," *Cleveland Plain Dealer,* November 1, 1998, p. 11-K.

---

up with a unique market niche: we are the world's only short-haul, high-frequency, low-fare, point-to-point carrier.... We wound up with a market segment that is peculiarly ours, and everything about the airline has been adapted to serving that market segment in the most efficient and economical way possible."[16] The following information box discusses the criteria needed for a successful niche or segmentation strategy.

Southwest has been undeviating in its pursuit of its niche. Although others have tried to copy it, none has fully duplicated it. Southwest still remains the nation's only high-frequency, short-distance, low-fare airline. As an example of its strong position, Southwest accounts for more than two-thirds of the passengers flying within Texas, and Texas is the second-largest market outside the West Coast. When Southwest invaded California, some San Jose residents drove an hour north to board Southwest's Oakland flights, skipping the local airport where American

---

[16] Jaffe, p. 58.

INFORMATION BOX

CRITERIA FOR SELECTING NICHES OR SEGMENTS

In deciding what specific niches to seek, these criteria should be considered:

1. *Identifiability.* Is the particular niche identifiable so that the persons who constitute it can be isolated and recognized? It was not difficult to identify the short-route travelers, and while their numbers may not have been readily estimated, this was soon to change as demand burgeoned for Southwest's short-haul services.

2. *Size.* The segment must be of sufficient size to be worth the efforts to tap. And again, the size factor proved to be significant: Southwest soon offered 83 flights daily between Dallas and Houston.

3. *Accessibility.* For a niche strategy to be practical, promotional media must be able to reach the segments without much wasted coverage. Southwest had little difficulty in reaching its target market through billboards and newspapers.

4. *Growth potential.* A niche is more attractive if it shows some growth characteristics. The growth potential of short-haul flyers proved to be considerably greater than for airline customers in general. Partly the growth reflected customers won from other higher cost and less convenient airlines. And some of the emerging growth reflected customers' willingness to give up their cars to take a flight that was almost as economical and certainly more comfortable.

5. *Absence of vulnerability to competition.* Competition, both present and potential, must certainly be considered in making specific niche decisions. By quickly becoming the low-cost operator in its early routes, and gradually expanding without diluting its cost advantage, Southwest became virtually unassailable in its niche. The bigger airlines with their greater overhead and less flexible operations could not match Southwest prices without going deeply into the red. And the more Southwest became entrenched in its markets, the more difficult it was to pry it loose.

Assume you are to give a lecture to your class on the desirability of a niche strategy, and you cite Southwest as a classic example. But suppose a classmate asks, "If a niche strategy is so great, why didn't the other airlines practice it?" How will you respond?

had a hub. In Georgia, so many people were bypassing Delta's huge hub in Atlanta and driving 150 miles to Birmingham, Alabama to fly Southwest that an entrepreneur started a van service between the two airports.[17]

[17] O'Brian, A7.

Unlike many firms, Southwest did not permit success to dislodge its niche strategy. It has not attempted to fly to Europe or South America, or match the big carriers in offering amenities in coast-to-coast flights. In curbing such temptations it has not had to sacrifice growth potential: Its strategy still has many U.S. cities to embrace.

Seek dedicated employees. Stimulating employees to move beyond their individual concerns to a higher level of performance, a truly team approach, was by no means the least of Kelleher's accomplishments. Such an esprit de corps enabled planes to be turned around in 15 minutes instead of the hour or more of competitors; it brought a dedication to service far beyond what could ever have been expected of a bare-bones, cut-price operation; it brought a contagious excitement to the job obvious to customers and employees alike.

The nurturing of such dedicated employees was not due solely to Kelleher's extroverted, zany, and down-home personality—although this certainly helped. So did a legendary ability to remember employee names, and company parties, and a sincere interest in the employees. Flying in the face of conventional wisdom, which says an adversarial relationship between management and labor is inevitable with the presence of a union, Southwest achieved its great teamwork while being 90 percent unionized. It helped, though, that Kelleher started the first profit-sharing plan in the U.S. airline industry in 1974. Now, employees own 13 percent of the company stock.

Whether such worker dedication can pass the test of time, and the test of increasing size, is uncertain. Kelleher himself was 68 in 1999, and his retirement looms. A successor will be a different personality. Yet here is a model for an organization growing to large size and still maintaining employee commitment.

The attainment of dedicated employees is partly a product of the firm itself, and how it is growing. A rapidly growing firm—especially when such growth starts from humble beginnings, with the firm as an underdog—promotes a contagious excitement. Opportunities and advancements depend on growth. Where employees can acquire stock in the company and see the value of their shares rising, potential financial rewards seem almost infinite. Success tends to create a momentum that generates continued success.

CONSIDER

Can you identify additional learning insights that could be applicable to other firms in other situations?

QUESTIONS

1. In what ways might airline customers be segmented? Which segments or niches would you consider to be Southwest's prime targets? Which segments probably would not be?

2. Do you think the employee dedication to Southwest will quickly fade when Kelleher leaves? Why or why not?

3. Discuss the pros and cons for expansion of Southwest beyond short hauls. Which arguments do you see as most compelling?

4. Evaluate the effectiveness of Southwest's unions.

5. On August 18, 1993, a fare war erupted. To initiate its new service between Cleveland and Baltimore, Southwest announced a $49 fare (a sizable reduction from the then-standard rate of $300). Its rivals, Continental and USAir, retaliated. Before long the price was $19, not much more than the tank of gas it would take to drive between the two cities—and the airlines also supplied a free soft drink. Evaluate the implications of such a price war for the three airlines.

6. A price cut is the most easily matched marketing strategy, and it usually provides no lasting advantage to any competitor. Identify the circumstances where you see it as desirable to initiate a price cut and a potential price war.

7. Do you think it likely that Southwest's position will continue to remain unassailable by competitors? Why or why not?

8. In Chapter 6 we described another airline, Continental, and its employee-oriented leader, Gordon Bethune. Compare Bethune and Kelleher on as many traits as you can. Which do you think is the greater leader, and why?

HANDS-ON EXERCISES

1. Herb Kelleher has just retired, and you are his successor. Unfortunately, your personality is far different from his. You are an introvert and far from flamboyant, and your memory for names is not good. What is your course of action to try to preserve the great employee dedication of the Kelleher era? How successful do you think you will be? Did the board make a mistake in choosing you?

2. Herb Kelleher has not retired. He is going to continue beyond age 70. Somehow, his appetite for growth has increased as he has grown older, and he has charged you with developing plans for expanding into longer hauls— maybe to South and Central America, maybe even to Europe. Be as specific as you can in developing such expansion plans.

   Kelleher has also asked for your evaluation of these plans. Be as persuasive as you can in presenting this evaluation.

3. How would you feel personally about a five-hour transcontinental flight with only a few peanuts, and no other food or movies? Would you be willing to pay quite a bit more to have more amenities?

TEAM DEBATE EXERCISE

The Thanksgiving Day nonstop transcontinental experiment went fairly well, although customers and even flight attendants expressed some concern about the long, five-hour flight with no food and no entertainment. No one complained about the price.

Debate the two alternatives of going ahead slowly with the transcontinental plan with no frills, or adding a few amenities, such as some food, reading material, or whatever else might make the flight less tedious. You might even want to debate the third alternative of dropping this idea entirely at this time.

INVITATION TO RESEARCH

What is Southwest's current situation? What is its market share in the airline industry? Is it still maintaining a high growth rate? Has the decision been made to expand the nonstop transcontinental service, and have any changes been made in the no-frills service for this? How about international flights? Has Kelleher retired, and if so, what sort of person has succeeded him?

CHAPTER TWENTY-ONE

Wal-Mart—The Unstoppable

*I*n March 1992, Sam Walton passed away after a two-year battle with bone cancer. Perhaps the most admired businessman of his era, he had founded Wal-Mart Stores with the concept of discount stores in small towns, and had brought it to the lofty stature of the biggest retailer in the United States—ahead of the decades-long leader, Sears, ahead of another great discount-store success, Kmart, and ahead of a charging J.C. Penney Company.

His successors continued well his legacy. For 1998, Wal-Mart's sales of $117.9 billion made it one of the largest corporations in the world, and within two years very likely to become the largest of all.

THE EARLY YEARS OF SAM WALTON

Samuel Moore Walton was born in Kingfisher, Oklahoma, on March 29, 1917. He and his brother, James, born three years later, were reared in a family that valued hard work and thrift. They grew up in Missouri in the depths of the Great Depression.

By the time Sam had entered eighth grade in Shebina, Oklahoma, he was already exhibiting the character traits that would dominate his future life: quiet and soft spoken, but a natural leader who became class president and captain of the football team. He even became the first Eagle Scout in Shebina's history.

At the University of Missouri, Sam excelled in academics and athletics. He worked his way through college by delivering newspapers, working in a five-and-dime store, lifeguarding, and waiting tables at the university.

After his graduation in 1940, Sam went to the J.C. Penney Company and became a management trainee at the Des Moines, Iowa store. There he applied his work ethic, competed to become Penney's most promising new man, and became imbued with the Penney philosophy of catering to smaller towns and having "associates" instead of employees or clerks. He also met J.C. Penney himself and was intrigued with his habit of strolling around stores and personally meeting and observing customers and salespeople. After eighteen months Walton left Penney's to enter the U.S. army, but what he had learned in the Penney store in Des Moines was to shape his future ideas.

GROWTH OF WAL-MART

Sam Walton was discharged from the army in August 1945. By chance he stumbled on an opportunity to buy a Ben Franklin variety store franchise in Newport, Arkansas, and he opened it a month later. The lease arrangement with the building's owner did not work out, so he eventually relocated in Bentonville, Arkansas, in 1950. During the 1950s and early 1960s, Walton increased the number of Ben Franklin franchises to 15. In the winter of 1962 he proposed at a Ben Franklin board meeting that the company should aggressively turn its efforts to discounting, citing the great potential of discount stores. The company refused to consider such an innovative idea, so Sam and his brother went ahead anyway and opened a Discount City in Rogers, Arkansas, in 1962; they opened a second store in Harrison, Arkansas, in 1964. The company was incorporated as Wal-Mart Stores on October 31, 1969, and became a publicly held company a year later. In 1970 Walton also opened his first distribution center and general office: a 72,000-square-foot complex in Bentonville, Arkansas. In 1972 Wal-Mart was listed on the New York Stock Exchange.

In 1976 Walton severed ties with Ben Franklin in order to concentrate on the expansion of Wal-Mart. His operations had extended to small towns in Arkansas, Missouri, Kansas, and Oklahoma.

The essence of Walton's management philosophy during these building years was that of an old-fashioned entrepreneur; Walton personally roamed through his own stores, as well as those of competitors, always looking for new ideas in mass-merchandising (i.e., maximizing sales at attractive prices).

But rather than confronting the major retailers—department stores, chains such as Penney's and Sears, and the strong discounters such as Kmart—he confined his efforts to the smaller cities, ones deemed to have insufficient market potential by the major retailers. He saw these towns as a strategic window of opportunity, untapped by competitors. (Review the Southwest Airlines case for a similar seizing of a strategic window.)

Growth accelerated. By the end of 1975 Walton had 104 stores with nearly 6,000 employees and annual sales of $236 million, which generated $6 million net profit. The next year, the number of stores had increased to 125, employees to 7,500, and sales to $340 million, with $11.5 million in profit.

Table 21.1 compares the growth of sales and number of stores of Wal-Mart with that of Kmart, its major competitor, from 1980 to 1990, the decade in which Wal-Mart forged ahead to become the biggest retailer. By the end of fiscal 1991, Wal-Mart had 1,573 stores in 35 states.

Some of these new stores were Wal-Mart SuperCenters, considerably larger than the regular Wal-Marts, having a warehouse-style food outlet under the same roof as the discount store. While such food stores carried items comparable to products in a regular urban supermarket, the assortment and service were superior to those in most direct competitors in the smaller cities. And the key motivation for adding food stores to the general merchandise discount store was the greater frequency of customer shopping: Customers shop weekly for groceries, and such patronage exposes them to the other merchandise in the discount store far more frequently than would otherwise be the case.

TABLE 21.1.   Comparison of Growth in Sales and Number of Stores, Wal-Mart and Kmart, 1980–1990

	Kmart		Wal-Mart	
	Sales (millions)	Number of Stores	Sales (millions)	Number of Stores
1980	$14,204	1,772	$1,643	330
1981	16,527	2,055	2,445	491
1982	16,772	2,117	3,376	551
1983	18,597	2,160	4,667	642
1984	20,762	2,173	6,401	745
1985	22,035	2,332	8,451	859
1986	23,035	2,342	11,909	980
1987	25,627	2,273	15,959	1,114
1988	27,301	2,307	20,649	1,259
1989	29,533	2,361	25,810	1,402
1990	32,070	2,350	32,602	1,573

Source: Company annual reports.

Commentary: Several of these statistics are of particular interest. First, the comparison of the sales from 1980 to 1990, slightly more than one decade, of Wal-Mart and Kmart, show the tremendous growth rate of Wal-Mart, starting at little more than 10 percent of Kmart sales figures to forge ahead by 1990. And Kmart was no slouch during this period.

Second, Wal-Mart achieved its leadership in total sales with almost 800 fewer stores than Kmart had. This means that Wal-Mart's stores were achieving much higher sales volume than Kmart's, a fact that is further borne out by the statistics in Table 21.3.

Wal-Mart by now was also opening another category of stores: Sam's Wholesale, also known as Sam's Clubs. First introduced in 1984, by 1991 there were 148. This wholesale club concept came about as regular discount stores seemed to be reaching saturation in some locations. The wholesale warehouse went a step further in discounting.

Sam's Club stores are large, ranging up to 135,000 square feet. Each store is a membership-only operation, with qualified members including businesses and individuals who are members of certain groups, such as government employees and credit union members. Although the stores are huge, they carry less than 5 percent of the items carried by regular discount stores. Assortments are limited to fast-moving home goods and apparel, generally name brands, with prices 8 to 10 percent over cost but well under those of discount stores and department and specialty stores. Sam's Clubs provided the initial entry for Wal-Mart into the big metropolitan markets that it had avoided in most of its great growth.

In December 1987 Wal-Mart opened its newest merchandising concept, Hypermart USA, in Garland, Texas, a suburb of Dallas. The hypermart offers a combination of groceries and general merchandise in over 200,000 square feet of selling space. The stores also include a variety of fast-food and service shops, such as a beauty shop, shoe repair, and dry cleaners. Thus, a mall atmosphere is created to achieve one-stop shopping.

In spite of optimistic beginnings, the hypermarket idea was not as successful as expected. A scaled-down version was the SuperCenter. Plans were suspended for building more hypermarkets in favor of the super-center concept.

For a comparison of sales and profitability of Wal-Mart with Kmart, Sears, and Penney, see Table 21.2. Note that profitability comparisons include operating profit as a percentage of sales and the more valid measure of profitability, the return on equity (i.e., the return on the money invested in the enterprise). From this table we see that the growth of Wal-Mart in sales and profitability compared with its nearest competitors is awesome. Table 21.3 shows another operational comparison, this time in the average sales per store for Wal-Mart and Kmart. And again, the comparison shows the great growth performance of Wal-Mart.

The Future

Sam Walton received the Medal of Freedom from President Bush on March 17, 1992. Unfortunately, he did not live long to enjoy this high honor bestowed on him (among many honors, such as Man of the Year, Horatio Alger Award in 1984, and Retailer of the Decade in 1989); he died of cancer nine days later, on March 26, 1992.

David Glass, 53 years old, assumed the role of president and chief executive officer. Glass was known for his hard-driving managerial style. He had gained his retail experience at a small supermarket chain in Springfield, Missouri, and had joined Wal-Mart as executive vice president for finance in 1976. He had been named president and chief operating officer in 1984, while Sam Walton had kept the position of chief executive officer. About the transition of executives, Glass had said

> There's no transition to make, because other principles and basic values he (Walton) used in founding this company were so sound and so universally accepted... We'll be fine as long as we never lose our responsiveness to the customer.[1]

AFTER SAM WALTON

The behemoth that Sam Walton created rolled irresistibly ahead without him. He had indeed built an enduring concept and organization. Table 21.4 shows operating results for 1993–95. Particularly to be noted is the amazing sales growth in these years, up well over 20 percent each year to more than $82 billion by 1995. The company in its 1995 annual report confidently projected 1996 sales would be approximately $96 billion. Only three Fortune 500 companies have higher sales: General Motors, Ford Motor, and Exxon. And Exxon's sales of $97 billion in 1994 are within striking distance.

Major accomplishments in fiscal 1995 included:

---

[1] Susan Caminiti, "What Ails Retailing," *Fortune*, January 30, 1989, p. 61.

TABLE 21.2.   10-Year Comparison of Gross Revenues, Percentage of Operating Margin, and Return on Equity for Wal-Mart and its Competitors[a]

Year	Wal-Mart % Operating			Kmart % Operating			Sears % Operating			J.C. Penney % Operating		
	Gross Revenue	Profit Margin	Equity Return %	Gross Revenue	Profit Margin	Equity Return %	Gross Revenue	Profit Margin	Equity Return %	Gross Revenue	Profit Margin	Equity Return %
1981	$2,445.0	5.6	25.6	$16,527.0	2.2	9.0	$27,357	7.2	8.2	$11,860	7.5	13.2
1982	3,376.3	7.8	25.4	17,040.0	4.3	10.1	30,020	8.8	10.1	11,414	8.3	13.3
1983	4,666.9	8.3	26.6	18,878.9	6.0	16.7	35,883	9.7	14.4	12,078	8.7	13.1
1984	6,400.9	8.5	27.5	21,095.9	6.7	15.4	38,828	10.5	14.1	13,451	7.8	11.4
1985	8,451.5	7.2	25.6	22,420.0	6.2	14.4	40,715	9.5	11.5	13,747	7.7	9.8
1986	11,909.1	7.1	26.6	23,812.1	5.7	14.5	44,282	9.1	10.4	15,151	8.6	11.0
1987	15,959.3	6.8	27.8	25,626.6	5.8	15.7	48,439	8.5	12.1	15,747	9.1	14.6
1988	20,649.0	6.4	27.8	27,301.4	6.5	16.0	50,251	9.2	3.0	15,296	8.3	20.4
1989	25,810.7	6.5	27.1	29,532.7	5.8	6.5	53,794	9.2	10.6	16,405	9.2	18.4
1990	32,601.6	6.0	24.1	32,070.0	5.4	14.0	55,971	7.4	7.0	16,365	2.4	15.6

[a] Gross revenue is in $ billions.

Source: Company annual reports.

Commentary: The comparison with major competitors shows Wal-Mart far exceeding its rivals in revenue growth. The operating profit percentage exceeds Kmart's for most years, but Sears and Penney look better here. However, the true measure of profitability is return on equity, and here Wal-Mart shines: It indeed is a very profitable operation, while offering consumers attractive prices.

TABLE 21.3.   Average Sales per Store,
Wal-Mart and Kmart, 1980–1990

	Kmart	Wal-Mart
1980	$8,015,801	$4,978,788
1981	8,042,338	4,979,633
1982	7,922,532	6,127,042
1983	8,609,722	7,269,470
1984	9,554,533	8,591,946
1985	9,448,970	9,838,184
1986	9,835,611	12,152,040
1987	11,274,527	14,325,852
1988	11,833,983	16,401,111
1989	12,508,682	18,409,415
1990	13,646,808	20,726,001

Source: Computed from Table 21.1

Commentary: The great increase in sales per store for
Wal-Mart is particularly noteworthy. In 1980 Wal-Mart's
average store's sales was hardly one-half that of an average
Kmart. By 1990 the average Wal-Mart store was generating more than 50% more sales than an average Kmart.

TABLE 21.4.   Operating Performance, 1993–1995, Wal-Mart

(Dollar amounts in millions except per share data.)	1995	1994	1993
Operating Results			
Net sales	$82,494	$67,344	$55,484
Net sales increase	22%	21%	26%
Comparative store sales increase	7%	6%	11%
Other income—net	918	641	501
Cost of sales	65,586	53,444	44,175
Operating, selling, and general and administrative expenses	12,858	10,333	8,321
Interest costs:			
Debt	520	331	143
Capital leases	186	186	180
Provision for federal and state income taxes	1,581	1,358	1,171
Net income	2,681	2,333	1,995
Per share of common stock:			
Net income	1.17	1.02	.87
Dividends	.17	.13	.11

Source: 1995 Wal-Mart Annual Report.

- Opening 111 new Wal-Mart discount stores and relocating or expanding 60 additional stores
- Entering the Canadian market through the purchase of 122 Woolco stores
- Opening 75 SuperCenters, more than doubling the total to 143
- Expanding 75 selectively into international markets, including 24 stores in Mexico and 3 in Hong Kong

INGREDIENTS OF SUCCESS

Management Style and Employee Orientation

Sam Walton cultivated a management style that emphasized individual initiative and autonomy over close supervision. He constantly reminded employees that they were vital to the success of the company, that they were essentially "running their own business," that they were "associates" or "partners" in the business, rather than simply employees.

In such employee relations philosophy, he borrowed from James Cash Penney, the founder of the J.C. Penney Company, and his formulation of the "Penney idea" in 1913. This Penney idea also stressed the desirability of constantly improving the human factor, of rewarding associates through participation in what the business produces, and of appraising every policy and action as to whether it squares with what is right and just.

Walton emphasized bottom-up communication, thereby providing a free flow of ideas from throughout the company. For example, the "people greeter" concept (described in the following information box) was implemented in 1983 as a result of a suggestion received from an employee in a store in Louisiana. This idea proved so successful that it has since been adopted by Kmart, some department stores, and even shopping malls.

Another example of listening to employees' ideas came when an assistant manager in an Alabama store ordered too many marshmallow sandwiches, or Moon Pies. The store manager told him to use his imagination to sell the excess, so John Love came up with an idea to create the first World Championship Moon Pie Eating Contest. It was held in the store's parking lot. The event was so successful that it is now held every year, drawing spectators not only from the community but from all over Alabama and surrounding states.[2]

Wal-Mart has a profit-sharing plan dating back to 1972 in which all associates share in a portion of the company's yearly profits. As one celebrated example of the benefits of such profit sharing, Shirley Cox had worked as an office cashier earning $7.10 an hour. When she decided to retire after 24 years, the amount of her profit

---

[2] Example described in Don Longo, "Associate Involvement Spurs Gains (Wal-Mart Employees Are Encouraged to Suggest Ideas for Promotions)," *Discount Store News*, December 18, 1989, p. 83.

INFORMATION BOX

GREETERS

All customers entering Wal-Mart stores encounter a store employee assigned to welcome them, give advice on where to find things, and to help with exchanges or refunds. These "greeters" also thank people exiting from the store, while unobtrusively observing any indications of shoplifting.

Staffing exits and entrances is not uncommon by retailers; what makes Wal-Mart's greeters unique is their friendliness and patience. Wal-Mart has found that retirees supplementing pensions usually make the best greeters and are most appreciated by customers. As noted earlier, the greeter idea originated as a suggestion from an employee (associate): Sam Walton liked the idea, and it became a company-wide practice.

Do you personally like the idea of having a store employee greet you as you enter and leave an establishment? On balance, do you think the greeter idea is a plus or a minus? Explain.

sharing in 1988 was $220,127.[3] In addition, associates may participate in the payroll stock purchase plan in which Wal-Mart contributes part of the cost.

The Sam Walton philosophy of business and management was to create a friendly, "down-home" family atmosphere in his stores. He described it as a "whistle while you work philosophy," one that, as he saw it, stressed the importance of having fun while working because you can work better if you enjoy yourself.[4] He was concerned about losing this attitude or atmosphere: "The bigger Wal-Mart gets, the more essential it is that we think small. Because that's exactly how we have become a huge corporation—by not acting like one."[5]

Another incentive is given to all employees in stores that manage to reduce shrinkage (that is, the loss of merchandise due to shoplifting, carelessness, and employee theft). Employees are given $200 each a year if shrinkage limits are met. This causes associates to become detectives by watching shoppers and each other. In 1989 Wal-Mart had a shrinkage rate of 1 percent of sales, below the industry rate of 2 percent.[6]

A rather unusual way of making employees feel vital to the Wal-Mart operation is information sharing, which amplifies the idea that employees are associates of the business. Management shares the good news and the bad news about the company's

---

[3] Example cited in Vance H. Trimble, *Sam Walton: The Inside Story of America's Richest Man* (New York: Dutton, 1990), p. 233.

[4] Ibid., p. 105.

[5] Ibid., p. 104.

[6] Charles Bernstein, "How to Win Employee and Customer Friends," *Nation's Restaurant News*, January 30, 1989, p. F3.

performance. In each store managers share operating statistics with employees, including profits, purchases, sales, and markdowns. Every person, from assistant managers to part-time clerks, sees this information on a regular basis. The result: Employees tend to think of Wal-Mart as truly their own company.

Not the least of the open and people-oriented management practices fostered by Sam Walton is what he called MBWA, Management By Walking Around. Managers, from store level to headquarters, walk around the stores to stay familiar with what is going on, to talk to the associates, and to encourage associates to share their ideas and concerns. Such interactions permit a personal touch usually lacking in large firms but so far still dominant as Wal-Mart grows large.

And how have unions fared in such an environment? Not surprisingly, they have had no success. Walton argued that in his "family environment," associates had better wages, benefits, and bonuses than any union could get for them. In addition, the bonuses and profit sharing were inducements far better than those a union could negotiate. As partners in a business operation, how could employees turn to a union?

State-of-the-Art Technology

Sam Walton's decentralized management style led to a team approach to decision making. But this approach would have been difficult to achieve without a heavy commitment to supporting technology. A huge telecommunications system permits Wal-Mart executives to broadcast and communicate to store managers. In addition, home-office management teams, using the company's 11 turboprop planes, fly to various stores to assess their operations. Coming back to headquarters for Friday and Saturday meetings, they assess any problems and coordinate needed merchandise transfers among stores. Through the use of a six-channel satellite, messages can be broadcast to all stores, and a master computer tracks the company's complex distribution system.

Small Town Invasion Strategy

Adopting a strategy similar to that of the J.C. Penney Company of more than half a century before, Wal-Mart shunned big cities and directed its store openings to smaller towns where competition consisted only of local merchants and small outlets of a few chains, such as Woolworth, Gamble, and Penney.

These merchants typically offered only limited assortments of merchandise, had no Sunday or evening hours, and charged substantially higher prices than they would charge in the more competitive environments of larger cities. Other larger retailers, especially discounters, had shunned such small towns as not offering enough potential to support the high sales volume needed for the low-price strategy.

But Wal-Mart found potential in abundance in these small-town markets, as customers flocked from all the surrounding towns and rural areas for the variety of goods and the prices. (In the process of captivating small town and rural consumers, Wal-Mart wreaked havoc on the existing small-town merchants. See the issue box for a discussion of the sociological impact of Wal-Mart on small-town

ISSUE BOX

IMPACT OF WAL-MART ON SMALL TOWNS

In most of its growth years, Wal-Mart pursued a policy of opening stores on the outskirts of small rural towns, usually with populations between 25,000 and 50,000. Attractive both in prices and assortment of goods, its stores often became beacons in drawing customers from miles around. Wal-Mart also was likely to be the biggest employer in the town, with 200 to 300 local employees.

But the dominating presence of Wal-Mart was a mixed blessing for many communities. Small-town merchants were often devastated and unable to compete. Downtowns in many of these small towns became decaying vestiges of what perhaps a few months previously had been prosperous centers. But consumers benefited.

Wal-Mart brought tradeoffs and controversy: Was rural America better or worse off with the arrival of Wal-Mart? On balance, most experts saw the economic development brought on by Wal-Mart as more than offsetting the business destruction it causes. But few could dispute the sociological trauma.[7]

What is your assessment of the desirability of Wal-Mart coming into a rural small town? How might your assessment differ depending on your particular position or status in that community?

---

[7] For more discussion of the impact of Wal-Mart, see Karen Blumenthal, "Arrival of Discounter Tears the Civic Fabric of Small Town Life," *The Wall Street Journal*, April 14, 1987, p. 1 ff; Hank Gilman, "Rural Retailing Chains Prosper by Combining Service, Sophistication," *The Wall Street Journal*, July 2, 1984, p. 1 ff.

America.) The company honed its skills in such small towns, isolated from aggressive competitors, and found enough business to become the world's largest retail enterprise. Then, flexing its muscles, it began moving confidently into the big cities, whose competitors were as fearful of Wal-Mart as had been the thousands of small-town merchants.

Controlling Costs

Sam Walton was a stickler for holding costs to a minimum in the quest to offer customers the lowest prices. Cost control started with Wal-Mart vendors. Wal-Mart has gained a reputation of being hard to please, of constantly pressuring its suppliers to give additional price breaks and cooperative advertising.[8] In further efforts to buy goods at the lowest possible prices, Wal-Mart has attempted to bypass middlemen and sales reps and buy all goods direct from the manufacturer. In so doing, a factory presumably would save money on sales representatives' commissions of 2 to 6 per-

---

[8] Toni Apgar, "The Cash Machine," *Marketing and Media Decisions*, March 1987, p. 82.

cent of the purchase order and thus be able to pass this savings on to Wal-Mart. Understandably, this has aroused a heated controversy by groups representing sales representatives.

Wal-Mart has been able to achieve great savings in distribution. Its sophisticated use of distribution centers and its own fleet of trucks enable it to negotiate lower prices when it buys in bulk directly from suppliers. More than three-fourths of the merchandise sold in a Wal-Mart store is processed through one of the company's 16 distribution centers. Each center serves 150 to 200 stores with daily delivery. For example, the distribution center in Cullman, Alabama, is situated on 28 acres with 1.2 million square feet. Some 1,042 employees load 150 outbound Wal-Mart trailers a day and unload 180. On a heavy day, laser scanners will route 190,000 cases of goods on an 11-mile conveyor.[9]

Each warehouse uses the latest in optical scanning devices, automated materials-handling equipment, bar coding, and computerized inventory. With all of the stores using the satellite network, messages can be quickly flashed between stores, distribution centers, and corporate headquarters in Bentonville, Arkansas. Hand-held computers assist store employees in ordering merchandise. The result is a distribution system that provides stores with on-time delivery at the lowest possible cost. By using the most advanced technologies, Wal-Mart's distribution expenses are only 3 percent of total sales, which is about one-half that of most chains.[10]

Wal-Mart has previously been able to achieve great savings in advertising costs compared with major competitors. Although discount chains typically spend 2 to 3 percent of sales for advertising, Wal-Mart has been able to hold advertising to less than 1 percent of sales. Much of this difference reflects low media rates in most of its markets, the smaller towns. As Wal-Mart moves into larger metropolitan markets, the advertising cost advantage may diminish.

Finally, Wal-Mart's operating and administrative costs reflect a spartan operation that is rigidly enforced. A lean headquarters organization and a minimum of staff assistants compared with most other retailers completes the cost-control philosophy and reflects the frugal thinking of Sam Walton that dates back to his early days.

"Buy American" and Environmental Programs

As foreign manufacturers increasingly began taking market share away from American producers—and in the process, destroying some American jobs—sentiment began mounting for import restrictions to save jobs. And as the amount of imports grew, so did the trade deficit, with consequences not fully understood by most people but generally understood to be something very bad. However, the idea of restricting free world trade is highly controversial: Many experts question whether tariffs, quotas, and other restrictions are in the general best interest. Some say the

---

[9] John Huey, "America's Most Successful Merchant," *Fortune*, September 23, 1991, p. 54.

[10] *Facts about Wal-Mart Stores,* Company publication (Bentonville, Arkansas, n.d.), p. 4.

best scenario is to induce American consumers to "buy American," or at least to give preferential treatment to products produced in this country by American workers; such a policy would eliminate import restrictions but enhance consumer support of American workers and factories.

In March 1985 Sam Walton became very concerned with what seemed to him to be a serious national situation. He sent a message to his buyers to find products that American manufacturers have stopped producing because they couldn't compete with foreign imports. This was the beginning of Walton's "Buy American" program, which had the long-range objective of strengthening the free enterprise system. The program is essentially a cooperative effort between retailers and domestic manufacturers to reestablish the competitive position of American-made goods in price and quality.

This program showcased the power of the huge retailer. Magic Chef, 3M, Farris Fashions, and many other manufacturers joined Walton's crusade, as Wal-Mart pledged to support domestic production for items ranging from film to microwave ovens to flannel shirts and other apparel.

Wal-Mart has been a leader in challenging manufacturers to improve their products and packaging in order to protect the environment. As a result, manufacturers have made great improvements in eliminating excessive packaging, converting to recyclable materials, and eliminating toxic inks and dyes.

The company participates in Earth Day events, with tree plantings, information booths and videos to show customers how to improve the environment. It has also been active in fund raising for local environmental groups, and in "adopt-a-highway" programs, in which store personnel volunteer at least one day every month to collect trash and clean up local highways and beaches.

UPDATE

As now the biggest retailer by far, Wal-Mart is looking for expansion opportunities beyond the United States. As of April 1998, it operated stores in Germany (21 units), Argentina (11), Brazil (9), and China (3). In North America, Wal-Mart operated 1,908 Wal-Mart stores, 456 SuperCenters, and 444 Sam's Clubs in the United States and 404 in Mexico and 14 in Puerto Rico. Revenues for 1998 reached $117.9 billion, with net income $3.5 billion. The tremendous growth can be compared with its closest competitors left in the dust:

Sears, Roebuck had sales of $40.4 billion and net income of $1.2 billion.

Kmart, the closest discount competitor and one-time biggest retailer, had sales of $32.1 billion and a net loss of $101 million.

J.C. Penney was next in size, with sales of $29.2 billion and net profit of $565 million.

As we saw in the Toys "R" Us case in Chapter 12, the irresistible force of Wal-Mart was even destroying the supreme category-killer retailer in toys.

LATE-BREAKING NEWS

As it approached the new millennium, and was only a short step away from becoming the world's largest firm, Wal-Mart turned to other growth opportunities. It bought Asda Group PLC, a large British supermarket chain, thus greatly expanding its international presence. In the United States it accelerated building discount-grocery SuperCenters, but also began a speedy expansion of its smallish, 40,000 square foot Wal-Mart Neighborhood Markets that were designed to fill the gaps between convenience stores and Wal-Mart's mammoth SuperCenters. Wal-Mart also bought a small savings bank in Oklahoma that could pave the way for bringing to banking its low-prices for such services as check cashing, credit cards, and loans.

The overseas expansion created the most waves. European merchants and labor unions ran scared, while consumers stood to benefit enormously: "Its low-pricing policies and customer-friendly attitude is likely to change the face of British retailing and its reputation for high prices and surly service," one scribe wrote.[11]

Wal-Mart's threat led two rival French retailers to merge in a $16-billion-dollar deal, though the combined company would still be only half as big as Wal-Mart. The battle was perhaps most fierce in Germany, where Wal-Mart had 95 stores. Competitive firms began opening longer hours and attempted to upgrade customer courtesy. However, regulators in Germany closely monitored whether prices were too low, while powerful trade unions worried that price wars would result in store closures and job losses.

In efforts to reduce costs, Wal-Mart began buying globally, negotiating one price for stores worldwide. In so doing, it made an organizational change to combine some domestic and international operations including buying, new store planning, and marketing.

---

[11] Ernest Beck, "The Wal-Mart Is Coming! And Shopping for the British May Never Be the Same," *The Wall Street Journal,* June 16, 1999, p. A23.

Sources: Emily Nelson, "Wal-Mart Revamps International Unit to Decrease Costs," *The Wall Street Journal,* August 10, 1999. p. A6; David Woodruff and John Carreyrou, "French Retailers Create New Wal-Mart Rival," *The Wall Street Journal,* August 31, 1999, p. A 14; Ernest Beck and Emily Nelson, "As Wal-Mart Invades Europe, Rivals Rush to Match Its Formula," *The Wall Street Journal,* August 6, 1999, pp. A1 and A6; "European Retailers Brace for Wal-Mart, *Cleveland Plain Dealer,* August 31, 1999, pp. 1-C and 3-C.

WHAT CAN BE LEARNED?

Take good care of people. Sam Walton was concerned with two groups of people: his employees and his customers. By motivating and even inspiring his employees, he found that customers were also well served. Somehow in the exigencies of business, especially big business, this emphasis on people tends to be pushed aside. Walton made caring for people common practice.

By listening to his employees, by involving them, by exhorting them, and by giving them a real share of the business—all the while stressing friendliness and concern for customers—Walton fostered a business climate unique in almost any large organization. In addition to providing customers with the friendliest of employees, his stores also offered honest values and great assortments and catered to the concerns of many middle-income Americans for the environment and American jobs.

Go for the strategic window of opportunity. Strategic windows of opportunity sometimes come in strange guises. They always represent areas of overlooked or untapped potential business by existing firms. But in the formative and early growth years of Wal-Mart, no window could ever have seemed less promising than the one Sam Walton milked to perfection and to great growth. Small towns and cities in many parts of rural America were losing population and economic strength, partly because of the decline in family farms and the accompanying infrastructure of small businesses. It was therefore not surprising that the major discount chains focused their growth efforts on large metropolitan areas. Although many small cities had Penney's and Sears outlets as well as such other chains as Woolworth, Gamble, and Coast to Coast stores, these were usually small stores, often old, marginal, and rather in the backstream of corporate consciousness. This retail environment was one of small stores with limited assortments of merchandise and relatively high prices.

In this environment Sam Walton seized his opportunity. He saw something that no other merchants had: that the limited total market potential meant a dearth of competition. He also saw that the potential was far greater than the population of the small town and its immediate surrounding population. Indeed, a large Wal-Mart store in a rather isolated rural community could draw customers from many miles away.

Do such windows of opportunity still exist today? You bet they do for the entrepreneur with vision, an ability to look beyond the customary, and the courage to follow up on his or her vision.

The marriage of old-fashioned ideas and modern technology can be a potent strategy. Sam Walton embraced this strategy with more success than any other entrepreneur in modern business, and he made it work throughout his organization, despite its growth to great size. In the forefront of retailers in the use of communications technology and computerized distribution, he still was able to motivate his employees to offer friendly and helpful customer services to a degree that few large retailers have been able consistently to achieve.

Other firms can benefit from the example of Wal-Mart in cultivating homespun friendliness with awesome technology, and competitors are trying to emulate. The particular difficulty that many are finding, however, is in achieving consistency.

Showing environmental concern can pay dividends. Today, as perhaps never before, many people are concerned about the environment, and it seems high time that we have such concern, while much of the environment can still be salvaged and protected from the abuses of a modern industrial age. Given such sentiment, the firm that takes a leadership position for environmental protection stands to benefit from improving customer relations and, not the least, from positive media attention.

Another issue important to many Americans involves foreign inroads to the detriment of many U.S. manufacturers and jobs. Regardless of the great controversy over the desirability of free trade, many middle-class Americans have applauded the leadership of Wal-Mart in its widely publicized "Buy American" policy.

What is the moral for other businesses? Be alert to the increasing concerns of the public, and where possible, act on them to achieve a leadership role.

CONSIDER

Can you identify additional learning insights that could be applicable to firms in other situations?

QUESTIONS

1. How might you attempt to compete with Wal-Mart if you were
   a. a small hardware merchant?
   b. a small clothing store for men?
   c. a Woolworth?

2. Do you think Wal-Mart is vulnerable today, and if so, in what way? If you do not think it is vulnerable, do you see any limits to its growth?

3. Why do you think the hypermarket idea failed to meet expectations? Was Wal-Mart too quick to table expansion plans for its hypermarkets?

4. What weaknesses do you see Wal-Mart as either having now or potentially? How can the company overcome them?

5. Wal-Mart is now entering urban areas. What new challenges does this present? Will Wal-Mart need to change? Can "the Wal-Mart way" work only in rural and exurban areas?

6. Can discounting go on forever? What are the limits to growth by price competition?

7. Discuss Wal-Mart's business practice (especially in regard to unions, invading small towns, and supplier relations) in terms of their ethical ramifications for the industry and for society. Should students be encouraged to emulate these practices?

HANDS-ON EXERCISES

1. You are an ambitious Wal-Mart store manager. Describe how you might design your career path to achieve a high executive position with this growing company. Be as creative as you can.

2. You are the principal adviser to David Glass, who has replaced Sam Walton as chief executive. He is very interested in making greater inroads in international markets. He challenges you to design a strategy to successfully invade these markets. What do you advise, and why?

TEAM DEBATE EXERCISES

1. Debate the notion of Wal-Mart aggressively seeking to enter small communities, such as in rural New England, where many people oppose this. Should Wal-Mart bow to the public pressure (which the company deems to be from a small minority of vehement agitators), or should it carry on with "right on its side."

2. Can the great growth of Wal-Mart continue indefinitely? Debate the pros and cons of this.

INVITATION TO RESEARCH

Investigate the continued onslaught of Wal-Mart. Are there any dangers on the horizon?

PART
SIX

ETHICAL MISTAKES

CHAPTER TWENTY-TWO

ADM—Price Fixing and Political Cronyism

In June 1995, a whistleblower informed federal investigators of the scheme of a giant multinational conglomerate, Archer-Daniels-Midland, to control sales of a widely demanded food additive and thus keep prices high worldwide. For three years, he had been secretly recording meetings of the firm's senior executives with Asian and European competitors. The whistleblower, Mark E. Whitacre, was revealed by an attorney who was supposedly conferring with him as a possible client.

Repercussions quickly followed. The company charged him with stealing from the firm and fired him. The plot became more complicated. But overhanging all was the role of the corporation and its 77-year-old top executive: Did they truly act unethically and illegally, or were the allegations ballooned out of all proportions?

THE WHISTLEBLOWER, MARK E. WHITACRE

Mark Whitacre joined Archer-Daniels in 1989, and spent about half his career there helping antitrust investigators. He was a rising star, recruited to head the fledgling BioProducts division, where he rose to become a corporate vice-president and a leading candidate to become the company's next president while still in his thirties.

He had been recruited from Degussa AG, a German chemical company where he was manager in organic chemicals and feed additives. However, his resume inflated his credentials with the title executive vice-president; he was only a vice-president.

While at ADM, he earned a business degree from a home-study school in California. Later ADM issued biographical material crediting him with an MBA from Northwestern University and the prestigious J.L. Kellogg School of Management. In an interview, Whitacre admitted the claims about his MBA were inflated to impress Wall Street analysts, but he blamed ADM: "I feel bad about it. I, along with other executives that speak at analysts' meetings, cooperated... it's a common practice."[1]

---

[1] "ADM Informant Faces Widening Allegations; He Attempts Suicide," *The Wall Street Journal*, August 14, 1995, p. A4.

His ambition was to become president of ADM, which he claimed was promised him repeatedly.[2] How becoming a governmental informer would help him with this ambition seems murky.

Over three years he secretly helped investigators obtain videotapes revealing two senior executives meeting with Asian and European competitors in various places around the world. The executives were vice-chairman Michael D. Andreas, son and heir apparent of the 77-year-old Dwayne Andreas, chairman and chief executive; and vice-president Terrence Wilson, head of the corn-processing division. Sometimes Whitacre would wear a hidden microphone to obtain the incriminating evidence of price fixing. The following information box discusses whistleblowing in general, but the travails of Whitacre graphically portray a worse scenario.

INFORMATION BOX

WHISTLEBLOWING

A whistleblower is an insider in an organization who publicizes alleged corporate misconduct. Such misconduct may involve unethical practices of all kinds, such as fraud, restraint of trade, price fixing, bribes, coercion, unsafe products and facilities, and violations of other laws and regulations. Presumably, the whistle blower has exhausted the possibilities for changing the questionable practices within the normal organizational channels and, as a last resort, has taken the matter to government officials and/or the press.

Since whistleblowing may result in contract cancellations, corporate fines, and lost jobs, those who become whistleblowers may be vilified by their fellow workers and fired and even framed by their firms. This makes whistleblowing a course of action only for the truly courageous, whose concern for societal best interest outweighs their concern for themselves.

However, there is somtimes a thin line between an employee who truly believes the public interest is jeoparidzed and the individual who has a gripe or is a fanatic. There are some who believe management is condoning misconduct when in fact such misconduct is isolated and without management awareness or acceptance. And some see whistleblowing as a means of furthering their own interests, such as gaining fame or even advancing their careers.

Ralph Nader, in a 1972 book on whistleblowing, suggested that corporate employees have a primary duty to protect society that exists over and above secondary obligations to the corporation. He gives examples of whistleblowing heroes, as well as a course of action for other would-be whistleblowers.[3]

Do you think you could ever be a whistleblower? Under what circumstances?

---

[3] Ralph Nader, Peter Petkas, and Nate Blackwell, *Whistleblowing* (New York: Bantam Books, 1972).

---

[2] Ibid.

FBI agents on the night of June 27 entered the headquarters of the huge grain-processing company in Decatur, Illinois. They carted off files and delivered grand jury subpoenas seeking evidence of price collusion of ADM and competitors. Whitacre was one of the executives subpoenaed, and met with an attorney recommended by the company's general counsel office, a common practice when companies face governmental inquiries.

Shortly after this meeting, the attorney disclosed to ADM that Whitacre was the federal informant in their midst, thus imperiling Whitacre's position in the company. This seemed a clear ethical violation of the confidentiality of lawyer/client relations. But the attorney, John M. Dowd of a prominent law firm doing business with ADM, claimed that Whitacre authorized him to do so. Whitacre and his new attorney angrily denied any such authorization.

In any case, now the company had the knowledge to retaliate. They fired him, accused him of stealing $2.5 million, and reported these findings to the Justice Department. Later, the company increased the amount it claimed Whitacre had stolen to $9 million. They charged that he had been embezzling money by submitting phony invoices for capital expenditures, then channeling the payments into offshore bank accounts.

The Justice Department saw the credibility of their key witness being weakened by such allegations, especially since Whitacre acknowledged that he had indeed participated in the bogus invoice schemes, although he said the payments were made with the full knowledge and encouragement of company higher-ups. Nevertheless, he and as many as 12 other ADM executives came under criminal investigation for evading taxes. The Justice Department's criminal fraud section further examined allegations that the off-the-books payments were approved by top management.[4]

A few days later, Whitacre tried to kill himself. At dawn, he drove his car into the garage of his new home, closed the door, and left the engine running. On this morning he was supposed to fly to Washington to meet with federal authorities. He had arranged for the gardener to come to work late that morning, but the gardener arrived shortly after seven and found Whitacre unconscious in his car.

Shortly before the suicide attempt, Whitacre had written a letter to *The Wall Street Journal*, acknowledging that he had received money from ADM through unusual means: "Regarding overseas accounts and kickbacks; and overseas payments to some employees, Dig Deep. It's there! They give it; then use it against you when you are their enemy."[5]

On September 13, 1995, F. Ross Johnson, an ADM board member, in a talk at Emory University's Goizueta Business School commented on Whitacre's suicide attempt: "You know, he tried to commit suicide. But he did it in a six-car garage, which, I think, if you're going to do it, that's the place to do it. [The audience laughed.] And the gardener just happened to come by. So now he is bouncing around."[6]

---

[4] Ronald Henkoff, "Checks, Lies and Videotape," *Fortune,* October 30, 1995, p. 110.

[5] "ADM Informant Faces…", p. A1.

[6] "ADM and the FBI 'Scumbags'," *Fortune,* October 30, 1995, p. 116.

Whether the suicide attempt was genuine or contrived, Whitacre apparently faced a traumatic period in his life. He wound up in a suburban Chicago hospital with no job and no place to live. He had money problems, being unable to touch any of the funds in his overseas accounts. He and his wife had moved out of their $1.25 million estate near Decatur, Illinois, after contracting to buy a house near Nashville for $925,000. After the suicide attempt, they attempted to back out of the deal, only to be sued for breach of contract.

With all this, somehow Whitacre seemed to have landed on his feet by early October. True, he and his family were living in a rented house in the Chicago area, but he had become chief executive of Future Health Technologies, a startup biotechnology firm, at a six-figure salary comparable to what he earned legally at ADM.

THE ALLEGATIONS AGAINST THE COMPANY

By fall 1995, three grand juries were investigating whether ADM and some of its competitors conspired to fix prices. Three major product lines of ADM were allegedly involved: lysine, high-fructose corn syrup, and citric acid. Lysine is an amino-acid mixed with feed for hogs and chickens to hasten the growth of lean muscles in the animals. High-fructose corn syrup is a caloric sweetener used in soft drinks. Citric acid, like lysine, is a corn-derived product used in the detergent, food, and beverage industries.

The importance of these products in the total product mix of ADM is indisputable. For example, while lysine is virtually unknown to the public, it is a key ingredient in the feed industry. About 500 million pounds are produced annually. Prices since 1961 have been averaging more than $1 a pound. So millions of dollars are at stake to manufacturers. With modern facilities at its sprawling complex in Decatur, Illinois, ADM can produce about half the world's purchases of lysine annually. And this is one of the company's highest profit products.

The sweetener, high-fructose corn syrup, is a major product for ADM, with a $3 billion-a-year market worldwide. Soft drinks account for more than 75 percent of annual production.

ADM entered the citric-acid business in 1991 when it acquired a unit of Pfizer. Today it is the primary U.S. maker of this additive. One of the largest customers is Procter & Gamble, which uses it for detergents.

As one example of the seemingly incriminating evidence of price fixing uncovered in videotapes, Michael Andreas is shown during a meeting he attended with lysine competitors at the Hyatt Regency Hotel at Los Angeles International Airport. There the participants discussed sales targets for each company as a means of limiting supply. This would destroy the free supply/demand machinations of the market and would permit prices to be kept artificially high, thus increasing the profits of the participants.[7]

---

[7] Reported in "Investigators Suspect a Global Conspiracy In Archer-Daniels Case," *The Wall Street Journal*, July 28, 1995, pp. A1 and A5.

With the charges and countercharges of Whitacre and the company, investigations went beyond price fixing to tax evasion for high-level executives sanctioned by top management. Whitacre was the tip of the iceberg. The criminal-fraud division of the Justice Department began investigating whether the company illegally paid millions of dollars in off-the-books compensation to an array of company executives through foreign bank accounts.

It is worth noting the severity of the penalties if suits successfully come to pass. Fines for price fixing can range into the hundreds of millions of dollars, and some executives could even be given jail sentences. Furthermore, class-action suits by shareholders and customers can result in heavy damage awards. See the following information box for a discussion of the famous price-fixing conspiracy of 1959 that set the precedent for jail sentences for executives involved.

ADM AND DWAYNE ANDREAS

The story of Archer-Daniels-Midland Co. is really the story of its chairman, Dwayne O. Andreas. In 1947, ADM chairman, Shreve Archer, died after choking on a chicken bone. Dwayne Andreas was a vice-president at Cargill, a rival firm. For the next 18

INFORMATION BOX

THE FAMOUS PRICE-FIXING CONSPIRACY OF 1959

In 1959, the biggest conspiracy of its kind in U.S. business history impacted the nation's thinking regarding business ethics.

Twenty-nine companies, including such giants as General Electric, Westinghouse, and Allis-Chalmers, were found guilty of conspiring to fix prices in deals involving about $7 billion of electrical equipment. The products involved in the conspiracy included power transformers, power switchgear assemblies, turbine generators, industrial control equipment, and circuit breakers. The companies were fined $1,924,500. Of particular note in this case, 52 executives (none of these top executives) were prosecuted and fined about $140,000. Even more startling, seven of the defendants received jail sentences. This was a first under federal antitrust laws.

On top of all that, almost 2,000 private-action, treble-damage cases were brought as a result of the court findings. In one of these alone, damages of $28,800,000 were awarded.

Incentives for the illegal actions stemmed from several sources. Without doubt, top management was exerting strong pressure on lower executives to improve their performance. Collusion with executives in other firms seemed to be a practical way to do this, especially in an environment rather blasé toward antitrust collusion. This attitude changed with the harsh penalties imposed by Judge J. Cullen Ganey.

Those executives who lost their jobs and went to jail were readily offered equivalent jobs in other corporations. The business community accepted them with open arms. Do you think they deserved such acceptance?

years he advanced steadily in the industry and became wealthy, while Archer-Daniels showed little growth. In 1966, at age 47, Andreas was asked to become a director at ADM. The founding families sold him a sizable amount of stock and proposed to groom him for the top spot. Four years later, he was named chief executive officer.

In 1995, Andreas was still firmly in command and running the publicly traded company almost as a personal dynasty. In 25 years he had built up the firm into the nation's biggest farm-commodity processor, with $12.7 billion in annual revenue. Table 22.1 shows the steady growth of revenues since 1986, while Table 22.2 shows the growth of earnings, not quite as steady but still almost two and a half times greater than in 1986.

POLITICAL MANUEVERING

Although company headquarters were at Decatur, Illinois, Andreas's influence in Washington was probably unparalleled by any other business leader. ADM led corporate America in political contributions; it contributed hundreds of thousands of dollars to both parties. Furthermore, Andreas supported Jimmy Carter's campaign— ADM even bought his struggling peanut farm in 1981. But Andreas also contributed generously to Ronald Reagan and George Bush. During the Reagan years, when U.S. firms were entering the Soviet market, ADM was in the vanguard. Andreas became close to then-Soviet president, Mikhail Gorbachev. But as a hedge, he also courted Boris Yeltsin, Gorbachev's emerging rival.

Perhaps his greatest political supporter became Senator Robert Dole, who is from the farm state of Kansas. When Dole's wife, Elizabeth, took over administration of the American Red Cross, Andreas donated $1 million to the cause. Dole also was given use of an ADM corporate plane, for which he paid the equivalent of a first-class ticket. An added factor in the friendship and rapport was the proximity of their vacation homes: Dole and his wife own a unit in Sea View, Florida, as do David Brinkley, a

TABLE 22.1.   ADM Revenues, 1986–1995

Year Ending June 30	Sales (millions)	Year-to-Year Percent Increase
1986	$5,336	
1987	5,775	10.8%
1988	6,798	11.8
1989	7,929	11.6
1990	7,751	(2.2)
1991	8,468	9.3
1992	9,232	9.0
1993	9,811	6.5
1994	11,374	15.9
1995	12,672	11.4
Gain since 1986		137.5%

Source: Adapted from *1995 ADM Annual Report.*

TABLE 22.2. ADM Net Earnings 1986–1995

Year Ending June 30	Earnings (millions)	Year-to-Year Percent Increase
1986	$230	
1987	265	15.2%
1988	353	33.2
1989	425	20.3
1990	484	13.9
1991	467	(3.5)
1992	504	7.9
1993	568	12.7
1994	484	(14.8)
1995	796	64.5
Gain since 1986		246.1%

Source: Adapted from *1995 ADM Annual Report.*

renowned TV newsman, and Robert Strauss, an ADM board member, and, of course, Dwayne Andreas.[8] Interestingly, President Clinton also regards Andreas as an ally.

Such political presence has brought great rewards to the company. ADM is a major beneficiary of federal price supports for sugar. Because such supports have kept sugar prices artificially high, ADM's sweetener, high-fructose corn syrup, has been attractive for giant companies such as Coca-Cola. Estimates are that fructose generates about 40 percent of ADM's earnings.[9]

Archer-Daniels also benefits from the 54-cent-a-gallon excise-tax break on ethanol, being the major producer of this corn-based fuel additive. Indeed, it is doubtful if the ethanol industry would exist without this tax break, and Bob Dole has been its most ardent congressional supporter.

Despite all the campaign contributions and personal rapport with the seats of power in Washington, Andreas and ADM have done little direct lobbying. Rather, such efforts have been done indirectly through various commodity and trade associations. For example, the American Peanut Sellers Association, with ADM support, handles the lobbying on peanut price supports.[10]

The Board of Directors

The investigations and the charges and countercharges drew fire from some of the major institutional holders of ADM stock. For example, the California Public Employees Retirement System—Calpers, as it is known, and owner of 3.6 million

---

[8] Reported in "How Dwayne Andreas Rules Archer-Daniels By Hedging His Bets," *The Wall Street Journal,* October 27, 1995, p. A8.

[9] Ibid.

[10] Ibid.

shares of Archer-Daniels—complained, charging that the board was too closely tied to Chairman and CEO Dwayne Andreas. "The ADM board is dominated by insiders, many of whom happen to be related to the CEO," Calpers complained. Calpers also criticized the ADM board for approving a 14 percent pay raise for Andreas, "rather than demand the CEO's resignation."[11] Other institutional investors also joined the criticisms: for example, the United Brotherhood of Carpenters, the Teamsters Union, and New York's major pension funds.

Shareholders had several other major criticisms of the board. It was supposed to authorize all capital expenditures above $250,000. The alleged claims for offshore pay were disguised as requests for spending on plant and equipment, and these the board passed with no hesitation. As to the charges of price-fixing and the allegations against major executives, the board was conspicuously uncritical, and finally made some token efforts to look further into the charges.

Brian Mulroney, former prime minister of Canada, co-chaired the special committee charged with coordinating the company's response to the federal investigations. One would think that part of his job was to safeguard the interests of shareholders. But major institutional shareholders doubted his objectivity, and noted his very close relations to Dwayne Andreas. Critics contended that what was needed was not a rubber-stamp special committee but "a team of experts to lead a full-blown, independent investigation."[12]

Regarding the composition of the board, critics seemed to have a case: The board was hardly objective and unbiased toward company top management; rather, it was highly supportive and dominated by insiders, many of whom were related to the CEO. For example, four of Archer-Daniels 17 directors were members of the Andreas family. An additional six directors were retired executives or relatives of senior managers. The outside directors also had close connections to Andreas, such as Robert S. Strauss, the Washington lawyer whose firm represented ADM, and Mulroney, who was also with a law firm used by the company. Even Harvard University professor Ray Goldberg, a member of the board, had strong ties with Andreas, dating back to his dissertation.

While close bonds of boards with management are not unusual with many companies, such cozy relations can be detrimental to shareholders' best interests.

ANALYSIS

ADM's Conduct

ADM was found guilty of unethical conduct, and even illegalities regarding price fixing. Certain other activities of this giant company also posed ethical controversies even if they were not illegal—for example, packing the board with cronies dedicated to preserving the establishment at the expense of stockholders; the great quest for

---

[11] Joann S. Lublin, "Archer-Daniels-Midland Is Drawing Fire From Some Institutional Holders," *The Wall Street Journal,* October 11, 1995, p. A8.

[12] Henkoff, p. 110.

preferential treatment in the highest corridors of power; and just perhaps, the setting up of Whitacre. Let us examine these ethical issues.

Packing the board so that it is exceptionally supportive of the entrenched management may be condemned as not truly representing the rights of stockholders. But with Andreas at the helm, ADM's stock value rose at an annual average rate of 17 percent over the last decade. Few stockholders could dispute Andreas's contribution to the firm, even though they might fume at his riding roughshod over his critics—especially institutions holding large amounts of stock.

Some would maintain that the courting of favoritism and special treatment from high-level Washington politicians may have gone too far. But should not any organization have the right to do its best to push for beneficial legislation and regulation? Of course, some will be more effective than others in doing so. Is this so much different than competition in the marketplace?

Whitacre's Role

Why did Whitacre choose to be a government mole? As of this writing, nothing has been written about this. Still in his thirties, Whitacre had advanced to high position in the company, with corresponding substantial compensation (enough to afford an estate valued at more than a million dollars), and was at least one of the top candidates for the presidency of the firm. Yet he had been secretly taping supposedly illegal discussions. Why? What did he have to gain? There was so much to lose.

Added to this, he must have been a very capable executive, yet he was naive enough to leave himself vulnerable by accepting, and maybe even initiating, illegal scams through false invoices and overseas bank accounts. Then he apparently naively confessed to a company lawyer his involvement as an informant for the FBI, not just recently but for three years. It doesn't make much sense, does it?

UPDATE

In October 1996, ADM pleaded guilty to criminal price-fixing charges and paid a record $100 million fine and nearly that amount again to settle lawsuits by customers and investors. But ADM's troubles were not over.

Early in December 1996, a federal grand jury charged Michael Andreas, earning $1.3 million annually as the number-two executive at ADM and heir apparent to his father to run the company, and Terrance Wilson, former head of ADM's corn-processing division, with conspiring with Asian makers of lysine to rig the price of the livestock feed additive. Andreas took a leave of absence with full pay, and Wilson retired. It was thought that any conviction or guilty plea by Michael Andreas would destroy his chances of continuing his family's three-decades-long reign over ADM. However, Dwayne Andreas could yet preserve the patrimony: His nephew, G. Allen Andreas, a 53-year-old lawyer, was one of three executives named to share Dwayne Andreas's responsibility in a newly formed office of chief executive.

In a surprising twist to the case, Mark Whitacre, the whistleblower, was also indicted.

The Verdict

The verdicts came in late 1998. After a week of deliberation in a two-month trial, the jury found Andreas, Wilson, and Whitacre guilty in a landmark price-fixing case, thereby giving the Justice Department its biggest convictions in a push against illegal global cartels. The federal prosecutors had been thwarted in how to rebuild the case after their mole, Whitacre, had been convicted of embezzlement and was already serving a nine-year prison sentence. The problem was solved by wringing confessions from Asian executives who were also involved in the conspiracy.

The bizarre behavior of Whitacre, after initially providing documentation of the birth of a price-fixing scheme, was unexpected and almost disastrous, and hard to explain even given that he was a big spender who openly pined to become president of ADM.

WHAT CAN BE LEARNED?

Price fixing is one of the easiest cases to prosecute. Conspiracies to fix prices are direct violations of the Sherman Act. The government does not need to prove that competition was injured or that trade was restrained. All that needs to be proven is that a meeting took place with agreements to fix prices, bids, or allocate market share.

The penalties for price conspiracies have greatly increased since the celebrated electrical equipment industry conspiracy of 1959. Given the ease of prosecution, one would think that no prudent executive would ever take such a risk. Yet, there have been sporadic instances of price-fixing since then, and we have it here with Michael Andreas, the son of Dwayne. Is there no learning experience?

Is political patronage necessary? We know that ADM sought political patronage and preferential treatment to an extraordinary degree—perhaps more than any other firm. Is this so bad?

Purists argue that this distorts the objectivity of our governmental institutions. Others say it is part of the democratic process in a pluralistic society. It might be so vital to our type of government that it cannot be eliminated—at best, can only be curbed.

On the other hand, it simply adds one more dimension to the competitive environment. Other firms can be encouraged to flex their muscles in the halls of government.

But when it comes to violations of the law, which supposedly reflects the wishes of society, then no firm is immune to the consequences. Even if its political patronage has been assiduously cultivated, it cannot escape the consequences of its illegal actions. The press, and the legal establishment, see to that.

Beware the "shareholder be damned" attitude. Some shareholders of ADM suspect that ADM had this attitude. As a consequence, the company faced at least two dozen shareholder lawsuits. As it approached the 1995 October annual meeting, nine big institutional investors announced plans to vote against reelecting

ADM directors. But the move was largely symbolic, since their combined shares represented only 4.9 percent of the 505 million outstanding shares.[13] And their views received little attention in the meeting. Nor, apparently did those of other shareholders. *The Wall Street Journal* reported that at the meeting Andreas squelched criticisms of the issue of the antitrust probe and other allegations as he "summarily cut off a critic by turning off his microphone: 'I'm chairman. I'll make the rules as I go along,' Mr. Andreas said."[14]

A cozy relationship with the board encourages such attitudes. And when operating performance is continually improving, such shareholder criticisms may be seen as merely gnats striving for attention, and thus worthy of being ignored. If the top executive is inclined to be autocratic, then the environment is supportive.

But is this wise? Should adversity set in, sometime in the future, then such attitudes toward investors can be self-destructive, even with a supportive board. If performance deteriorates, no board can maintain its sheeplike support for incumbent management, not in the face of vehement shareholders (especially large institutional investors) or major creditors.

But does adversity have to come? Only the profoundest optimist can think that success is forever. In ADM's case, adversity is here and now.

An organization's ethical tone is set by top management. If top management is unconcerned about ethical conduct, or if it is an active participant in less than desirable practices, this sets the tone throughout the organization. It promotes erosion of acceptable moral conduct in many areas of the operation. It becomes contagious as even those inclined to be more morally scrupulous join their colleagues. Then we have the "follow-the-leader" mindset.

In such an unhealthy environment, a few whistleblowers may arise and attempt to right the situation, often unsuccessfully and at great personal risk. Others who cannot tolerate the decline in moral standards, but don't have the courage to be whistleblowers, will leave the company. Almost inevitably, the misconduct will come to light, and repercussions of the severest kind result. Perhaps top management can escape the blame, though lower-level executives will be sacrificed. Occasionally, top management also comes under fire, and is forced to resign. Unfortunately, too often with healthy retirement benefits.

CONSIDER

Can you think of other learning insights?

QUESTIONS

1. What is your position regarding top management's culpability for the misdeeds of their subordinates?

---

[13] "Probe Tears Veil of Secrecy at Archer-Daniels-Midland," *Cleveland Plain Dealer,* October 18, 1995, p. 3C.

[14] "How Dwayne Andreas Rules," p. A1.

2. Do you think ADM's efforts at gaining political favoritism went too far? Why or why not?

3. "If Dwayne's son is found guilty of price-fixing, there's no way that the big man himself cannot be found guilty." Evaluate this statement.

4. "With all the false invoices and persons involved in these millions of dollars of payouts off-the-books, there's no way the company could not have known what was going on." Evaluate.

5. Speculate on what would lead Whitacre to "betray" his company. If a number of possibilities are mentioned, which do you think is most compelling?

6. With the severe penalties and ease of prosecution of price-fixing cases, why would any firm or any executive attempt it today?

7. Why do you suppose, with all its efforts to gain preferential treatment through courting the mighty in government, ADM has not resorted to direct lobbying? Has it missed a golden opportunity to further its causes?

HAND-ON EXERCISES

Before

1. Assume that Dwayne Andreas wants to maintain high ethical standards in his organization. Describe how he should go about this.

After

2. Assume that several key executives have been found guilty of price-fixing; assume further that there are also indictments of illegal payments to certain executives. Further, the Senate ethics committee is investigating whether there have been improprieties in dealings with some members of Congress. How would you as CEO attempt damage control?

TEAM DEBATE EXERCISE

Debate the ethics of aggressively courting prominent politicians and government administrators. The two extreme positions would be: (1) going as far as you can short of being charged with outright bribery; (2) limiting relationship building to a few token contributions to trade association lobbying efforts.

INVITATION TO RESEARCH

Has ADM's public image been badly tarnished by all this publicity, or can you determine this? Has the firm continued to grow and prosper? Is the Andreas family still in control?

CHAPTER TWENTY-THREE

Tobacco—An Industry Beleaguered

Cigarettes are among the world's most profitable consumer products. A cigarette "costs a penny to make, sell it for a dollar, it's addictive, and there's fantastic brand loyalty." So said master investor Warren Buffett as he unsuccessfully sought to take over RJR Nabisco, the tobacco conglomerate.[1] Perhaps because of its profitability, the morality of the business has long been suspect.

Criticisms have accelerated in recent years and bans widely imposed. Still, the tobacco industry remained stubbornly focused on its own best interests. That most critics saw tobacco's best interests as diametrically opposed to society's best interests mattered little to the industry as it aggressively struck back at critics.

In November 1998, a tobacco deal was agreed upon between the industry and 46 states to settle state lawsuits filed to recover Medicaid money spent treating diseases related to smoking. Some said the industry got off far too easy as this seemingly ended the largest-ever legal and financial threat to the industry.

CONTROVERSIAL STRATEGIES IN A SHRINKING MARKET

Targeting Minorities

Uptown

This new cigarette was packaged in a showy black-and-gold box and was the first cigarette aimed specifically at African-American smokers. It followed the new strategy of tobacco companies to introduce new brands directed to specific groups, such as women. Now, using careful research and design, everything about Uptown was tailored to black consumers. The results were a surprise.

A storm of protests quickly ensued. Critics maintained that the marketing of Uptown represented a cold-blooded targeting of blacks, who already suffered a lung cancer rate 58 percent higher than whites. The protests even reached the office of

---

[1] "The Tobacco Trade: The Search for El Dorado," *Economist*, May 16, 1992, p. 21.

Louis Sullivan, the Secretary of Health and Human Services. He quickly sided with the critics: "Uptown's message is more disease, more suffering and more death for a group already bearing more than its share of smoking-related illness and mortality." He condemned "the attempts of tobacco merchants to earn profits at the expense of the health and well-being of our poor and minority citizens."[2]

Given the virulence of the protests, R.J. Reynolds abandoned the brand, bitterly decrying the negative attention being focused on it "by a few zealots." The critics had won, this time.

Dakota

Another new cigarette, also targeted to a specific group, was beset with controversy. Dakota was aimed at "virile females." Critics of tobacco's relationship with lung cancer and heart disease were quick to attack this as a nefarious appeal to women.[3]

Another group was especially upset. In some Native American languages, *dakota* means friend. Yet, to a group that already had high rates of smoking addiction, such a brand name seemed a betrayal.

Controversies Over Tobacco Company Sponsorships

Due to the 1971 federal ban on cigarette advertising on TV and radio, tobacco companies desperately sought other media in which to place their hundreds of millions of advertising dollars. By the early 1990s serious questions were raised about their use of certain media, such as billboards promoting smoking and alcohol in African-American neighborhoods.

Advertising support of black media by tobacco companies also came under fire, even though few other major firms were advertising in black media. Many small minority publications would have folded without the advertising dollars of tobacco companies.

Tobacco company support for minority organizations also began to be questioned. The National Association of Black Journalists turned down a Philip Morris donation: "We couldn't take money from an organization deliberately targeting minority populations with a substance that clearly causes cancer," said the group's president.[4]

The tobacco industry also liberally provided money to women's sports at a time when other money sources were virtually nonexistent. For example, Virginia Slims' funding brought women's tennis into prominence. The controversy concerning this is discussed in the following issue box.

The Old Joe Camel Controversy

In 1988 R.J. Reynolds stumbled upon a promotional theme for its slumping Camel brand. Using a sunglasses-clad, bulbous-nosed cartoon camel that it called Joe, it

---

2 Ben Wildavsky, "Tilting at Billboards," *New Republic*, August 20, 1990, p. 19.

3 Paul Cotton, "Tobacco Foes Attack Ads That Target Women, Minorities, Teens and the Poor," *Journal of the American Medical Association*, September 26, 1990, p. 1505.

4 Ibid., p. 1506.

ISSUE BOX

TOBACCO COMPANY SPONSORSHIP OF ATHLETIC EVENTS

Is it right to allow tobacco companies to sponsor certain athletic events? What seems like a simple question becomes far more complex when we consider tennis tournaments such as Virginia Slims'. There is no longer any doubt that smoking causes serious damage to heart and lungs, yet tennis requires top physical fitness and aerobic capacity.

Such sponsorship had particular advantages from the tobacco industry's perspective. It created the false association of smoking with vitality and good health, and it directly targeted women. Philip Morris essentially was taking advantage of the inadequate funding of women's sports by making itself a strong presence in this sector.

So we have an unhealthy product sponsoring a prestigious athletic event for women, an event that at least in the early days would probably not have been able to get started without such funding. Do we refuse this funding? Do we ban all cigarette promotions that appear to have some tie-in with health and fitness? Does the evil outweigh the good?

You are a feminist leader with convictions that women's athletic events should be promoted more strongly. The major funding for tennis and golf tournaments has been the tobacco industry, with no alternative major sponsors likely in the near future. Discuss your position regarding accepting such tobacco company sponsorships. Present your rationale as persuasively as you can.

---

instituted a $75-million-a-year advertising campaign. It featured Joe in an array of macho gear and targeted the campaign to appeal to younger male smokers who had been deserting the Camel brand in droves.

The campaign was an outstanding success. In only three years, Camel's share of sales among the 18- to 24-year age group almost doubled, from 4.4 percent to 7.9 percent.

But the appeal of Old Joe went far beyond the target age group. It was found to be highly effective in reaching children under 13, who were enamored with the character. Six-year-olds in the United States recognized Joe Camel at a rate nearly equal to their recognition of Mickey Mouse. Children as young as three could even identify the cartoon character with cigarettes. Of even more concern to critics, Camel's share of the market of underage children who smoke was nearly 33 percent, up from less than 1 percent before the Old Joe campaign. See Table 23.1 for other results of the survey.

Controversies Over Billboard Advertising

Critics of Uptown initially focused on its billboard advertising in African-American neighborhoods. They soon expanded their protests to cigarettes in general and to

TABLE 23.1. Survey Results of Knowledge and Attitudes Regarding Camel's Old Joe Advertisements

	Students	Adults
Have seen Old Joe	97.7%	72.2%
Know the product	97.5	67.0
Think ads look cool	58.0	39.9
Like Joe as friend	35.0	14.4
Smokers who identify Camel as favorite brand	33.0	8.7

Source: Data from the *Journal of the American Medical Assn.*, as presented in Walecia Konrad, "I'd Toddle a Mile for a Camel," *Business Week*, December 23, 1991, p. 34. The results are based on a survey of 1055 students, ages 12 to 19 years, and 345 adults, aged 21 to 87 years.

alcohol, and began whitewashing offending billboards. Their only recourse, they argued, was to use civil disobedience to attract attention to their cause.

Reverend Calvin O. Butts III, fiery pastor of Harlem's Abyssinian Baptist Church, led his flock to paint signs with black paint to denote their Afrocentric perspective. Agitation against billboards spread beyond Harlem. In Dallas, County Commissioner John Wiley Price led a group that whitewashed 25 billboards and were arrested on misdemeanor charges. And Chicago priest Michael Pfleger was also arrested for painting billboards. Antismoking and antibillboard activists were having a field day.

Business began heeding the mounting pressure. In June 1990, the Outdoor Advertising Association of America, representing 80 percent of billboard companies, recommended voluntary limits on the number of billboards advertising cigarettes and alcohol near schools, places of worship, and minority neighborhoods.

Targeting Foreign Markets

With increasing restraints on cigarette advertising in the United States and diminishing per capita consumption of cigarettes, the industry turned to foreign markets. But criticisms and restraints surfaced there also.

At least as early as 1984, the Royal College of Physicians in the United Kingdom harshly denounced tobacco usage, stating that smoking killed 100,000 people a year in the U.K. alone. But the Royal College particularly condemned the lack of availability of low-tar cigarettes, "which are practically unknown in the Third World. Developed countries bear a heavy responsibility for the worldwide epidemic of smoking."[5] Most of Europe imposed some bans on advertising by 1991.

With Western Europe's mounting inhospitality to the industry, U.S. tobacco firms eagerly pushed into Asia, Africa, Eastern Europe, and the former Soviet Union.

---

[5] "Developing Countries: Governments Should Take Action Against Cigarettes before Too Many People Acquire the Potentially Lethal Habit," *New Scientist*, December 1, 1983, p. 42.

These were big markets and local cigarette makers were thought vulnerable to the aggressive efforts of U.S. firms.

Countries in the expanding sales area had few marketing or health labeling controls. In Hungary, for example, Marlboro cigarettes were even handed out to young fans at pop music concerts.[6]

ASSESSING THE CONTROVERSIES

Targeting Minorities

Was R.J. Reynolds, with its new Uptown brand, an ogre, as critics claimed? Without question, inner-city African-Americans had higher usage rates of tobacco and alcohol than their suburban counterparts. There was little doubt that the tobacco firms thought they had developed an effective targeting strategy with brands like Uptown. The dispute hinged on this: Are certain minority groups particularly susceptible to advertising so that they need to be protected from potentially unsafe products?

Although proponents of controls argued that certain groups, such as young blacks, needed such protection, others saw that protection as paternalism. Even some black leaders decried the billboard whitewashing and the contentious preaching of certain ministers. Certainly, tempting people was hardly the same as oppressing them. After all, no one had to buy cigarettes and alcohol.

Regardless of the pro and con arguments concerning the susceptibility of inner-city youth to advertisements for unhealthy products, there was more validity to the claims of susceptibility when we consider the vulnerability of children to the attractive models found in most of these commercials and advertisements.

Finally, if legislation should be enacted to ban certain products from billboards, as was done with radio and TV advertising over two decades ago, where should the line be drawn? Should promotions in minority neighborhoods be banned for products that are economically extravagant, such as expensive athletic shoes? Or should promotions be banned for high-cholesterol foods that might cause high blood pressure, or for "muscle" cars?

Assessing Joe Camel

Not surprisingly, criticism abounded after the American Medical Association's disclosure of the study that found Joe Camel so appealing to children. The basis for the concern, of course, was that the popular ads would encourage children to start smoking.

RJR would not yield. It denied that the ads were effective with children: "Just because children can identify our logo doesn't mean they will use the product." It stoutly maintained its right to freedom of speech.[7]

Some advertising people believed RJR's stubbornness was misguided: "By placing Old Joe as a freedom-of-speech issue instead of an unintentional marketing overshoot, [it] risks goading Congress into bans and restrictions on all tobacco

[6] "The Tobacco Trade," p. 23.
[7] "Old Joe Must Go," *Advertising Age*, January 13, 1992.

advertising... which would shift responsibility for tobacco products to the Food and Drug Administration [which] could regulate the tobacco industry into oblivion."[8]

In 1997, without fanfare, RJR quit using the character.

See the following issue box for identification of more cigarette issues.

Assessment of Tobacco's Push Overseas

A firm seems entitled to make all the profit it can. If certain markets are being severely constrained, should the firm not have the right to aggressively develop other markets? This is what the tobacco firms are doing.

The issue is clouded because while smoking is generally conceded to be hazardous to health, the consequences are a long time in coming. As long as many people are willing to take the risk, should the industry be so negatively judged?

When sophisticated and aggressive promotional efforts are directed to countries where consumers are more easily swayed and far more vulnerable to promotional blandishments, does our perception of what is ethical and what is undesirable change? Should it change?

THE SIEGE INTENSIFIES

Allegations of Rigging Nicotine Levels

A new threat arose to severely test the complacency of the tobacco industry: charges of long-time rigging of nicotine levels to assure that smokers stay hooked. Adding fuel to such allegations were Brown & Williamson (B&W) Tobacco Corp. internal documents, including a 54-page handbook, obtained by *The Wall Street Journal*, that indicated the tobacco companies had been adding ammonia-based compounds to their cigarettes. Such compounds essentially increase the potency of the nicotine a smoker actually inhales. The B&W documents asserted that Philip Morris's Marlboro, the top brand with a 30 percent share of the U.S. market at the time, may have been the first to use such ammonia technology. Regardless of who was the trailblazer, the practice seemingly had been widely emulated within the tobacco industry.[9]

Nicotine was viewed by most scientists as the active ingredient that caused cigarettes to be addictive. Anything that enhanced the delivery of this into the bloodstream, then, would increase the addictive potential. The industry would not admit this. It maintained that nicotine simply provided better flavor: "The primary purpose for using DAP [an ammonia additive] is to increase taste and flavor, reduce irritation, and to improve body." While admitting that this also increased nicotine delivery, a B&W spokesperson called this "an incidental effect."[10] And tobacco companies at

---

[8] Craig Stoltz, "RJR Appears Intent on Sticking with Old Joe to the Bitter End," *Adweek Eastern Edition*, March 23, 1992, p. 18.

[9] Alix M. Freedman, "Tobacco Firm Shows How Ammonia Spurs Delivery of Nicotine," *The Wall Street Journal*, October 18, 1995, pp. A1 and A6.

[10] Ibid., p. A6.

ISSUE BOX

CONTROVERSIES ABOUT SMOKING

The controversies concerning cigarettes go beyond those detailed in this chapter. For example:

- Should smoking be restricted in the workplace? in restaurants? on airplanes?
- What about some firms not allowing employees to smoke even when they are not at work?
- Should the tobacco industry pay for employee suits concerning their "right to smoke"?
- Should nonsmokers be protected from passive smoke?
- In general, are the rights of smokers being violated?

Discuss and debate these questions and any other smoking issues you come up with.

that time still doggedly denied any links between cigarette smoking and heart disease, cancer, or other ailments.

But in 1996, newly disclosed documents suggested that Philip Morris, the nation's foremost tobacco company, had in place as far back as the 1970s a system to hide and destroy potentially damaging data about smoking and health because of liability suits: "These documents appear to be further evidence of the industry's extraordinary effort to keep information secret. These are just the tip of the iceberg of evidence of document destruction."[11]

Repercussions

The industry was already under heavy fire before the latest revelations regarding the ammonia component. The increasing pressure, spearheaded by David Kessler, the Food and Drug Administration's (FDA) commissioner, showed a sharp contrast to the situation when he assumed office in 1990. Then, a few health coalitions were complaining about smoking, but this had been going on for decades. Few people in government paid any attention, mostly because the tobacco industry seemed invulnerable: It had the support of powerful southern congressmen and it also had great monetary resources to provide for the finest legal arsenal and lobbying efforts.

[11] Alix M. Freedman and Milo Geyelin, "Philip Morris Allegedly Hid Tobacco Data," *The Wall Street Journal*, September 18, 1996, p. B11.

Though perhaps not obvious to tobacco executives, the climate was subtly changing. In 1985, both Aspen and Vail, Colorado ski resorts, banned smoking in restaurants. Other scattered bans followed. The slow trend abruptly accelerated in 1993 when the Environmental Protection Agency declared smoke a carcinogen. By the end of that year, 436 cities had smoking restrictions. Smoking came to be banned from all domestic air flights regardless of length.

Even the courts were now joining the act. In addition to criminal investigations by the Justice Department in New York and Washington, thirteen other states were seeking reimbursement from the industry for the costs of treating smoking-related illnesses. Moreover, the industry was facing eight class-action suits, filed by smokers claiming they became hooked while the industry concealed the addictive nature of its product. Dr. Kessler also added the resources of the FDA to take up the struggle against cigarettes.

Previous defense strategies of the industry had always been that it was a smoker's free choice to smoke despite an "unproven" risk of lung cancer, so how dare the government interfere? Now Dr. Kessler, given the newest revelations about the ability of the industry to control nicotine with its powerful addictive hold, had a new strategy to present to Capitol Hill. Former Surgeon General C. Everett Koop exhorted him, "Do anything you can" to regulate tobacco. "The country is going to be behind you."[12]

On August 10, 1995, in the White House, President Clinton, with Dr. Kessler standing nearby, unveiled tough proposed regulations on cigarette marketing and sales. This marked the new FDA role against tobacco and one of the most aggressive federal moves ever against the industry.

Even the seemingly fertile overseas markets were rising against tobacco. An aggressive European ad campaign by Philip Morris backfired and had to be abandoned amid a barrage of lawsuits, complaints to regulators, and government criticism. The campaign cited scientific studies to claim that second-hand smoke wasn't a meaningful health risk to nonsmokers. It even suggested that inhaling secondary smoke was less dangerous than eating cookies or drinking milk.[13]

The stakes were high, with Philip Morris's $11.4 billion in European tobacco sales in 1995. But resentment against the tobacco industry was rising by governments struggling to contain burgeoning health-care costs.

Joe Camel was doing somewhat better in Argentina, despite intense criticism by antismoking activists. The first such advertising campaign in Latin America saw sales of the formerly marginal Camel brand shooting up 50 percent, a gain perhaps reflecting that Argentina had no national cigarette age limit.[14]

---

[12] Laurie McGinley and Timothy Noah, "Long FDA Campaign and Bit of Serendipity Led to Tobacco Move," *The Wall Street Journal*, August 22, 1995, p. A4.

[13] Martin Du Dois and Tara Parker-Pope, "Philip Morris Campaign Stirs Uproar in Europe," *The Wall Street Journal*, July 1, 1996, p. B1.

[14] Jonathan Friedland, "Under Siege in the U.S., Joe Camel Pops Up Alive, Well in Argentina," *The Wall Street Journal*, September 10, 1996, p. B1.

THE INDUSTRY FIGHTS BACK

The fight was on. Tobacco firms as well as the advertising industry attacked with lawsuits against the FDA, while tobacco-state legislators desperately worked to replace the proposed regulations with friendlier laws. In the first half of 1996, more than $15 million was spent for lobbying. More millions went to campaign donations to influence lawmakers, and additional millions to defend against lawsuits.[15]

The tobacco industry had been notorious for defending its position aggressively and being confrontational. For example, the professor in Georgia whose study found that Joe Camel was almost as recognizable as Disney characters, thereby calling into question the tobacco industry's claims that their ads were not targeting children, became a target himself. The industry pressured the school administration to fire him. "The only protection he really had was tenure."[16] This saved his job.

Philip Morris has been the most aggressive player in attacking critics. In 1994 it sued the city of San Francisco, trying to overturn one of the nation's toughest antismoking ordinances. The ordinance had banned smoking in offices and would shortly also ban it in restaurants. Philip Morris sought to have the court declare the ordinance invalid and unenforceable.

Geoffrey Bible, chairman of Philip Morris, declared an all-out war on tobacco's enemies, with legal attacks and newspaper ads. "We are not going to be anybody's punching bag," he said. "When you are right and you fight, you win."[17] Bible had spend his career pushing Philip Morris around the world, and he practiced what he preached: smoking cigarettes and attacking all critics.

Those struggling to preserve the tobacco industry and its efforts to avoid regulation were by no means limited to cigarette producers. Tobacco was so ingrained in many sectors of our economy that many would suffer were it curbed—for example, local distributors, truckers, people who own and/or replenish vending machines, those involved with billboard ads for cigarettes, and the hundreds of thousands of vendors who saw cigarette sales as a major part of their total business, not to mention those tobacco growers in the southern states who could not countenance switching their crops to lower-yielding alternatives. Against the arguments that alternative employment would replace cigarette dependence, many looked back over decades of such dependence and cringed at the thought of losing it.

Results

Hopes that campaigns against smoking were becoming more effective were dispelled by a study published in the November 1998 *Journal of the American Medical Association*. The research, carried out at 116 four-year colleges, found 28 percent of

---

[15] "Tobacco Lobbyists Spend Millions," *Cleveland Plain Dealer,* September 9, 1996, p. 8A.

[16] Example cited in Maureen Smith, "Tenure," *University of Minnesota Update,* November 1995, p. 4.

[17] Suein L. Hwang, "Philip Morris's Passion to Market Cigarettes Helps It Outsell RJR," *The Wall Street Journal,* October 30, 1995, p. A1.

college students smoking in 1997, up from 23 percent in 1994. The report concluded that this is a cause for national concern.[18]

In 1998, Philip Morris's share of the U.S. cigarette market passed 50 percent for the first time ever. In addition to its aggressive use of the Marlboro Man on billboards and magazine ads, it had a sales-incentive program called Retail Masters that rewarded retailers with payouts based on sales and display of Philip Morris cigarettes. This program was particularly effective with the rapidly expanding cigarette outlet stores, numbering some 5,800 by 1998, that sold nothing but cigarettes at 10 to 15 percent less than convenience stores because of generous manufacturer rebates and display fees. Other tobacco firms also had incentive programs but they were outmuscled by Philip Morris.

Overseas, Philip Morris captured nearly a quarter of the cigarette market in Turkey. It did this by enlisting help of influential people and lobbying heavily to eliminate the government's control of tobacco prices and distribution. Its prime bargaining chip was the promise that it would invest millions of dollars in the country. True to its word, Philip Morris opened a factory there in 1993, and expanded it into a $230 million facility. Now it could engineer cigarettes to appeal to Turkish tastes but with a stronger kick than local brands. Its salesmen, dressed as cowboys, spread across the country to 130,000 stores with a lavish in-store promotional and incentive plan. Of course, it advertised the Marlboro Man heavily, with cowboy scenes and panoramic vistas. In late 1996, pressured by antitobacco groups, Turkey's Parliament passed one of the strictest cigarette advertising bans in the world. Philip Morris got around this by omitting the word "Marlboro" in its ads and displays, but leaving the easily identifiable red chevron. The company also shrewdly noted that the ban did not cover all nontobacco products and events, and so its Marlboro jeans and other paraphernalia became best sellers and potent promoters of the brand.

Tobacco companies found a new target market for future smokers in women in developing countries. To woo this potential market, they sponsored sporting and entertainment events geared to female audiences; they offered cigarettes with free crystal, designer scarves, and silk camisoles; they sent sample cigarettes as congratulatory gifts to new female college graduates. In the Philippines, a devoutly Catholic nation, calendars were even distributed featuring the Virgin Mary and other women saints praying over cigarette packs.[19]

THE TOBACCO DEAL

In spring 1997, new developments portended monumental changes for the tobacco industry in the United States. In late March, the solidarity of the industry was shaken

---

[18] H. Wechsler et al., "Increased Levels of Cigarette Use Among College Students: A Cause for National Concern," *Journal of the American Medical Association*, Vol. 280, No. 19, November 18, 1998, pp. 1673–1678.

[19] Information for this section has been compiled from a number of sources, including Yumiko Ono, "For Philip Morris, Every Store Is a Battlefield," *The Wall Street Journal*, June 29, 1998, B1 and B4; Suein L. Hwang, "How Philip Morris Got Turkey Hooked on American Tobacco," *The Wall Street Journal*, September 11, 1998, pp. A1 and A8; and Stephanie Stapleton, "Tobacco Targeting Third-World Women," *Cleveland Plain Dealer*, November 10, 1998, p. 3-F.

as Liggett Group settled a lawsuit with 22 states, and in the process, finally admitted that smoking was addictive and caused cancer. Further information from Liggett showed that children were targeted for tobacco sales.

In the middle of April 1997, Philip Morris and RJR Nabisco began talks with attorneys general for 25 states suing to recover billions of dollars in public health-care costs for sick smokers. The industry sought protection from all current and future litigation and was willing to contribute an amazing $300 billion over a 25-year period to a settlement fund as well as making certain other concessions. When Congress took up ratifying the agreement in early 1998, it raised the price to $516 billion and ciga-

LATE-BREAKING NEWS

As of August 1999, despite a stack of lawsuits and other actions filed against it, Philip Morris was still a very profitable company, bullying its competitors and outselling its nearest one, RJR, by 2-to-1. Despite a 70-cents-a-pack price hike to pay off 46 states and their lawyers, demand was almost as big as ever. Not even a partial injunction granted in a lawsuit filed against Philip Morris by its competitors alleging antitrust violations in its Retail Leaders sales-incentive program could phase Philip Morris. It confidently planned to appeal the injunction. Meanwhile, with tens of millions of smokers on its computers, its "relationship marketing programs" were geared to keeping these dedicated smokers in the Philip Morris camp.

The situation was not as good for U.S. tobacco companies in international markets as the new millennium neared. Not even in Asia, home to half of the billion smokers in the world, was the situation encouraging. In China, for example, the state-owned China National Tobacco Corp. had a virtual monopoly with a 200 percent import duty on cigarettes to go along with major distribution restrictions. Elsewhere in Asia, import duties and restraints brought slumping market shares to foreign firms, with their tobacco products not only hard to find and difficult to advertise and promote but priced out of reach of most consumers. For Philip Morris, international tobacco sales were expected to decline 4 percent in 1999.

In the United States, suddenly the industry found that the legal battle was not over. On September 22, 1999, the Justice Department reopened it by filing a massive lawsuit claiming that 45 years of industry deception about the dangers of cigarettes had contributed to the federal government's spending more than $20 billion a year to treat ill smokers.

On October 13, 1999, Philip Morris announced that it would spend about $100 million a year, or about 5 percent of its total ad budget, on a new TV campaign aimed at presenting a "friendlier public face." Antitobacco groups promptly criticized this as an attempt "to win court cases and stave off political change."

Sources: Gordon Fairclough, "Philip Morris TV Ad Campaign Seeks to Repair Cigarette Maker's Image, *The Wall Street Journal,* October 13, 1999, p. B16; David S. Cloud and Gordon Fairclough, "U.S. Sues Tobacco Makers in Massive Case," *The Wall Street Journal,* September 23, 1999, pp. A3 and A8; Seth Lubove, "Brand Power," *Forbes,* August 9, 1999, pp. 98–104; Andrew Tanzer, "Where There's Smoke...," *Forbes,* March 22, 1999, pp. 84–86.

rette makers were denied the legal immunity they sought in return. Not surprisingly, the industry did not accept this.

In November 1998, a milder deal was negotiated, amounting to $206 billion spread over 25 years. Undoubtedly tobacco's position was bolstered by a major victory that Reynolds scored in a Florida state court on May 5, 1997, where a jury found that the firm wasn't responsible for the death of a three-pack-a-day smoker who died of lung cancer at age 49. The trial had been closely watched as a bellwether for future litigation against the industry.

Forty-six states accepted the new deal. Four other states had already settled their individual suits for a total of $40 billion. The deal seemingly put an end to antismoking groups' hopes for a broader agreement that would combat teenage smoking and bring the industry under federal regulation.

WHAT CAN BE LEARNED?

Is it ethically right to vigorously promote a product seen by many as unsafe and even deadly? This issue gets to the heart of the whole matter of tobacco production and marketing. Considered by practically all health experts as dangerous and, in the long term, life threatening, tobacco had been protected by powerful governmental interests, even if such support was eroding.

Even though the industry at last stubbornly admitted some health charges, it refused to soften its aggressiveness in promoting its products. Worse was its aggressive invasion of third-world countries, even though these efforts were now facing major obstacles in many countries.

The industry is huge with stakeholders: tobacco growers, processors, retailers, tax collectors, influential people in the halls of government, even the lowly paster of billboard ads. Not the least of the supporters of the industry are the users themselves—even though this declines a little from year to year, except on college campuses. Loyal users tend to discount the health dangers as being both far in the future and affecting only a minority of users ("And never me!").

What about morality? It is easy for stakeholders to rationalize that any bad consequences are uncertain at best, that the good outweighs any bad possibilities. Still, we wonder if the profit motive is not the overriding consideration, far ahead of societal health risks.

Too many times, what is ethical lies in the eyes of the beholder.

Does a militant minority represent acceptable behavior in promoting its own self-interest? In a pluralistic society, minorities are encouraged to present their positions. The issue becomes one of degree. What level of critical behavior—no matter how justified many might see such criticisms—is acceptable? Is whitewashing billboards acceptable behavior? What about destroying offending billboards or firebombing the stores of opportunistic shopowners? Where do we draw the line? Furthermore, who is to be the judge of what is acceptable and unacceptable: a firebrand preacher, a government agency, the police department, the courts?

Is it not perfectly right for any firm, or industry, to pursue its own best interests, as long as it stays within the present law? Ah, this is the rationale that supports tobacco efforts, whether it's Joe Camel, targeting naive consumers, foreign markets, or nicotine enhancement in pursuit of addiction: These actions formerly were considered entirely legal. Do not laws reflect the majority views on what is moral and ethical? Many would say that they do not reflect prevailing majority views, that they rather reflect the positions of powerful minority interests. Many would see tobacco regulations—or lack thereof—as such.

Perhaps the real issue is whether a firm's best interests should take precedence over those of its customers and of society. Either position can be argued. On the one hand, should not a firm seek to foster a better corporate image and benefit both society and itself? On the other, should not a firm seek to maximize its profitability to the benefit of stockholders, creditors, suppliers, employees and the like, regardless of outside critics?

Is a firm's public image of little consequence as long as it has a loyal body of customers who support it? This is the position taken by the tobacco industry: defiant of critics; secure in the loyalty of a sizable group of addicted customers; aided and abetted by powerful political interests whose constituents have an economic stake in the viability of the industry. For decades this mindset of disregard for public image has successfully prevailed, despite the cries of critics, including most of the medical profession.

Now, finally, could it be that the cigarette makers—and especially Geoffrey Bible of Philip Morris, the industry's most ardent defender—have miscalculated and that they are mistakenly assuming that the past will ever dictate the future and that attitudes and power positions will remain unchanged?

Perhaps it is high time they seek to develop a less dangerous cigarette, even if this lessens the addiction and alienates diehards who demand their nicotine cocktail. At the least, one would think the prudent action in the face of ever-mounting concern and criticism would be to lower the decibels of their protests and their advertising and promotions and maybe to embrace some social responsibility before such actions are forced upon them. The late-breaking news that Philip Morris is starting image-building advertising suggests that it is finally recognizing the importance of public relations, if nothing else, to keep juries from being so negative toward it.

In today's litigious environment, callousness regarding society's growing concerns may be courting disaster. The tobacco industry proudly boasted that it had never lost a lawsuit accusing it of responsibility for lung cancer and other physical ills and deaths. The industry had always successfully defended itself on the grounds that charges of cigarette smoking contributing to such health hazards were unproven, and also on the grounds of individual choice and individual freedom. Now this defense has crumbled. Some at least would see that the industry has capitulated to accept the $206 billion tobacco deal. Others would say that it is the state attorneys general who have capitulated in accepting a deal far milder than the 1997 one. Still, perhaps our litigious environment is on the verge of doing what lawmakers in a pluralistic society with many diverse agendas have been unable to do: Bring the tobacco industry to heel.

In these learning insights we have raised more questions than answers or caveats. But the questions raised ought to be of concern to tobacco executives—and executives of other firms whose products and ways of doing business may not be in the best interests of the general public. A reckoning may be lurking in the wings.

CONSIDER

Can you propose other learning insights or ethical issues?

QUESTIONS

1. Do you actually think Joe Camel leads youngsters to become smokers when they get older? Why or why not?

2. Do you have any problems with the idea of militant ministers leading their followers to whitewash offensive billboards? If not, is tearing down such billboards acceptable? Please discuss as objectively as possible.

3. Do you consider the proof adequate that cigarettes pose a substantial health threat and should be banned or tightly constrained? If you accept this position, should tobacco growers be allowed to continue growing such "unsafe" harvests without restraints?

4. Playing the devil's advocate (one who adopts an opposing position for the sake of argument), what arguments would you offer that the cigarette manufacturers should be permitted complete freedom in targeting developing countries?

5. How do you assess the relative merits of the tangible financial contributions that the tobacco industry has made to various minority groups and media, against the negative health consequences of smoking?

6. What is the ethical difference between promoting cigarettes and promoting fatty, cholesterol-laden foods?

7. Do you agree with banning cigarettes from public buildings, workplaces, restaurants, airplanes, and so on? Why or why not?

8. Are the rights of nonsmokers being too highly emphasized? Do smokers have any rights?

HANDS-ON EXERCISES

1. You are the public relations spokesperson for Philip Morris. You have been ordered by Geoffrey Bible to plan a public relations campaign to overturn some of the banning of cigarettes. Be as specific and creative as you can. How successful do you think such efforts would be?

2. You are an articulate young African-American woman who uses Uptown cigarettes and likes them. At a church outing, your minister denounces Uptowns and the company that makes them. Describe how you might respond to such a tirade against your favorite brand.

3. You have been asked by the executive committee of a major tobacco firm to draw up plans for changing the negative public image of the tobacco industry. The hope thereby is to defuse the probability of upcoming federal legislation that would be detrimental. What do you propose? Be as specific as possible.

TEAM DEBATE EXERCISES

1. A great controversy is brewing in the executive offices of Philip Morris. One group led by CEO Bible is strongly in favor of aggressively attacking all critics and defending cigarettes with no holds barred. Still, there is another group supported by some prominent board members who believe the company and the industry should soften its stance. Debate the two sides of this issue.

2. Debate the issue: The rights of nonsmokers are being emphasized too much. Smokers have rights, too.

3. Debate the great $206 billion deal of the tobacco industry. Who won? Should the attorneys general have held stronger against the industry? (You may need to research the provisions of the final agreement versus what might have been.)

INVITATION TO RESEARCH

1. What is the current situation regarding overseas incursions by U.S. tobacco companies?

2. Has the tobacco industry encountered any new criticisms?

3. Has the Tobacco Deal been advantageous to the industry or not?

4. Has smoking by college students changed since the *JAMA* report of 1998?

5. Is Geoffrey Bible still alive, or has he died of lung cancer?

CHAPTER TWENTY-FOUR

Conclusions—What Can Be Learned?

*I*n considering mistakes, three things are worth noting:

1. Even the most successful organizations make mistakes but survive as long as they maintain a good "batting average."
2. Mistakes should be effective teaching tools for avoiding similar errors in the future.
3. Firms can bounce back from adversity and turn around.

We can make a number of generalizations from these mistakes and successes. Of course we recognize that marketing is a discipline that does not lend itself to laws or axioms. Examples of exceptions to every principle or generalization can be found. However, the decision maker does well to heed the following insights. For the most part they are based on specific corporate and entrepreneurial experiences and should be transferable to other situations and other times.

INSIGHTS REGARDING OVERALL ENTERPRISE PERSPECTIVES

Importance of Public Image

The impact, good or bad, of an organization's public image was a common thread through a number of cases—for example, Nike, Continental, Southwest Airlines, Vanguard, Johnson & Johnson, Coors, Disney, Maytag, Perrier, United Way, and the tobacco industry.

Nike shows the power of an image that was compatible with the product and attractive to the target market. The carefully nurtured association with some of the most esteemed athletes in the world, men and women, whom many of its customers were eager to emulate, if only in their dreams, propelled Nike and its swoosh logo to dominance in the athletic apparel industry. Still, we saw a positive image become tarnished for Nike.

344

Continental Airlines is a case for hope. It shows that a reputation in the pits, not only with employees but with the general public, can be resurrected and revitalized, even over a short period of time, but it takes inspired leadership to do so—and this Gordon Bethune, its new CEO supplied.

Southwest's image of friendliness, great efficiency, and unbeatable prices propelled it to an unassailable position among short-haul airlines. Now it seeks to expand its image to longer hauls. Vanguard has also used its image of frugality and great customer service in the mutual fund industry to propel it to the top with virtually no advertising.

Coors lost its mystique and was never quite the same. Disney found its image did not travel well to Paris, nor did Maytag's quality image to Great Britain.

The positive way Johnson & Johnson responded to a catastrophe back in 1982 still endows the firm with the best corporate reputation in America. Perrier, on the other hand, responded aggressively to a lesser problem with a major product recall, but lost its image of quality.

The nonprofit, United Way, was brought to its knees by revelations about the excesses of its long-time chief executive, William Aramony. Donations dwindled and local chapters withheld funds from the national organization as the reputation of the largest charitable organization was sullied.

As for the tobacco industry, it seems to be forever putting its foot in its mouth in its undeviating quest to maximize profits at any cost.

The importance of a firm's public image is undeniable, yet some continue to disregard this and either act in ways detrimental to image or else ignore the constraints and opportunities that a reputation affords.

Power of the Media

We have seen or suspected the power of the media in a number of cases. Nike, Coca-Cola, United Way, IBM, the tobacco industry, and Vanguard are obvious examples. This power is often used critically—to hurt a firm's public image. The media can fan a problem or exacerbate an embarrassing or imprudent action. In particular, this media focus can trigger the herd instinct, in which increasing numbers of people join in protests and public criticism. And the media in their zeal can sometimes cross the line, as in singling out Nike for all the employment abuses of third-world countries.

We can make these five generalizations regarding image and its relationship with the media:

1. It is desirable to maintain a stable, clear-cut image and undeviating objectives.
2. It is difficult and time-consuming to upgrade an image.
3. An episode of poor quality has a lasting stigma.
4. A good image can be quickly lost if a firm relaxes in an environment of aggressive competition.
5. Well-known firms, and not-for-profit firms dependent on voluntary contributions, are especially vulnerable to critical public scrutiny and must use great care in safeguarding their reputations.

Need for Growth Orientation—But Not Reckless Growth

The opposite of a growth commitment is a status-quo mindset, uninterested in expansion and the problems and work involved. Harley Davidson's downfall in the 1950s was its contentment with the status quo. (We described this in the seventh edition.) Coors came closest to this in this edition, as it tried to coast on its mystique and ignore marketing only to find its advantage fading before aggressive competitors.

In general, how tenable is a low-growth or no-growth philosophy? Although at first glance it seems workable, it usually sows the seeds of its own destruction. Almost four decades ago the following caution was made:

> Vitality is required even for survival; but vitality is difficult to maintain without growth, at least in the American business climate. The vitality of a firm depends on the vigor and ambition of its members. The prospect of growth is one of the principal means by which a firm can attract able and vigorous recruits.[1]

Consequently, if a firm is obviously not growth-minded, its ability to attract able people diminishes. Customers see a growing firm as reliable, eager to please, and constantly improving. Suppliers and creditors tend to give preferential treatment to a growing firm because they hope to retain it as a customer when it reaches large size.

In other cases firms had strong growth commitments, but somehow their growth in bureaucratic overhead let competitiveness slip and they fell back, sometimes after decades of market dominance. IBM readily comes to mind here, before its great comeback. So does Borden, as it now reaps the consequences of reckless growth and unwise diversifications. Boston Chicken and Planet Hollywood expanded too fast and before their formats were well tested, and now even face extinction. And we have the bungled growth efforts of Maytag's Hoover Division in the United Kingdom. Good financial judgment must not be sacrificed to the siren call of growth.

Therefore, an emphasis on growth can be carried too far. Somehow the growth must be kept within the abilities of the firm to handle it. Several examples, such as Southwest Airlines, Wal-Mart, and McDonald's showed how firms can grow rapidly without losing control.

We can make seven generalizations about the most desirable growth perspectives:

1. Growth targets should not exceed the abilities and resources of the organization. Growth at any cost—especially at the expense of profits and financial stability—must be shunned. In particular, tight controls over inventories and expenses should be established, and performance should be monitored closely.

2. The most prudent approach to growth is to keep the organization and operation as simple and uniform as possible, to be flexible in case sales do not meet expectations, and to keep the breakeven point as low as possible, especially for new and untried ventures.

---

[1] Wroe Alderson, *Marketing Behavior and Executive Action* (Homewood, IL: Irwin, 1957), p. 59.

3. Concentrating maximum efforts on the expansion opportunity is like an army exploiting a breakthrough. The concentration strategy—such as that of Southwest Airlines and McDonald's—usually wins out over more timid competitors who diffuse efforts and resources. But such concentration is more risky than spreading efforts.

4. Rapidly expanding markets pose dangers from both too conservative and overly optimistic sales forecasts. The latter may overextend resources and jeopardize viability should demand contract; the former opens the door to more aggressive competitors. There is no right answer to this dilemma, but management should be aware of the risks and the rewards of both extremes.

5. A strategy emphasizing rapid growth should not neglect other aspects of the operation. For example, older stores should not be ignored in the quest to open new outlets, as Toys " Я " Us was guilty of doing.

6. Decentralized management is more compatible with rapid growth than centralized, because it puts less strain on home office executives. However, delegation must have well-defined standards and controls as well as competent subordinants. Otherwise, the Maytag Hoover fiasco may be repeated.

7. The integrity of the product and firm's reputation must not be sacrificed in pursuit of rapid growth. This is especially important when customers' health and safety may be jeopardized.

Strategic Windows of Opportunity

Several of the great successes we examined resulted from exploiting strategic windows of opportunity. Southwest found its opportunity by being so cost effective that it could offer both cut-rate fares and highly dependable short-haul service that no other airline could match. Similarly Vanguard found its strategic niche with the lowest expense ratios and overhead in the mutual fund industry, as did Wal-Mart in retailing.

We can make four generalizations regarding opportunities and strategic windows:

1. Opportunities often exist when a traditional way of doing business has prevailed in the industry for a long time—maybe the climate is ripe for a change.

2. Opportunities often exist when existing firms are not entirely satisfying customers' needs.

3. Innovations are not limited to products but can involve customer services as well as methods of distribution.

4. For industries with rapidly changing technologies—usually new industries—heavy research and development expenditures are usually required if a firm is to avoid falling behind its competitors. But heavy R&D expenditures do not guarantee being in the vanguard, as shown by the tribulations of IBM despite its huge expenditures.

Power of Judicious Imitation

Some firms are reluctant to copy successful practices of their competitors; they want to be leaders, not followers. But successful practices or innovations may need to be copied if a firm is not to be left behind. Sometimes the imitator outdoes the innovator. Success can lie in doing the ordinary better than competitors.

Nike achieved its initial success by imitating many of the successful practices of the entrenched German competitor, Adidas. Somehow the competitors of McDonald's for decades were unable to imitate its undeviating insistence on rigorous standards and controls over all aspects of the operation. We can make this generalization:

> It makes sense for a company to identify the characteristics of successful competitors (and even similar but noncompeting firms) that contributed to their success, and then adopt these characteristics if they are compatible with the imitator's resources. Let someone else do the experimenting and risk taking. The imitator faces some risk in waiting too long, but this usually is far less than the risk of being an innovator.

The Need for Prudent Crisis Management

Crises are unexpected happenings that pose threats, ranging from moderate to catastrophic, to the organization's well-being. We described four cases in Part III: Met Life, Perrier, United Way, Johnson & Johnson. Other cases that involved some crises were Boeing, Continental, Euro Disney, Coca-Cola, Maytag, ADM, Toys " Я " Us, Boston Chicken, Planet Hollywood, and Rubbermaid. Some handled their crisis reasonably well, such as United Way, Coca-Cola, and Euro Disney, although we can question how such crises were allowed to happen in the first place. However, Maytag, ADM, Perrier, and Met Life either overreacted or else failed badly in salvaging the situation. Then there is the paragon of all the best in crisis management, Johnson & Johnson.

Most crises can be minimized if a company takes precautions, is alert to changing conditions, has contingency plans, and practices risk avoidance. For example, it is prudent to prohibit key executives from traveling on the same air flight; it is prudent to insure key executives so that their incapacity will not endanger the organization; and it is prudent to set up contingency plans for a strike, an equipment failure or plant shutdown, the loss of a major distributor, unexpected economic conditions, or a serious lawsuit. Some risks, of course, can be covered by insurance, but others probably cannot. The mettle of any organization may be severely tested by an unexpected crisis. Such crises need not cause the demise of the company, however, if alternatives are weighed and actions taken only after calm deliberation.

Crises may necessitate some changes in the organization and the way of doing business. Firms should avoid making hasty or disruptive changes or, on the other extreme, making too few changes too late and too grudgingly. The middle ground is usually best. Advanced planning can help a company minimize trauma and enact effective solutions.

Vulnerability to Competition and the Three C's

Competitive advantage can be shortlived, success does not guarantee continued success, and innovators as well as long-dominant firms can be overtaken and surpassed. With Toys " Я " Us, IBM, Boeing, Disney, and even United Way, we saw the three C's syndrome of complacency, conservatism, and conceit that often blankets the mindset of leading organizations in their industries. We suggest that a constructive attitude of never underestimating competitors be fostered by:

- Bringing fresh blood into the organization for new ideas and different perspectives
- Establishing a strong and continuing commitment to customer service and satisfaction
- Periodically conducting a corporate self-analysis designed to detect weaknesses as well as opportunities in their early stages
- Continually monitoring the environment and being alert to any changes

The environment is dynamic, often with subtle and hardly recognizable changes. Still, these may eventually have profound impact on ways of doing business and a firm must constantly be alert to protect its position as well as seize opportunities.

Environmental Monitoring

The dynamic business environment may involve changes in customer preferences and needs, in competition, in the economy, and even in international events such as nationalism in Canada, NAFTA, OPEC machinations, changes in Eastern Europe and South Africa, and advances in Pacific Rim countries in productivity and quality control. IBM and Toys " Я " Us failed to detect and act upon significant changes in their industries. Borden and Coors misjudged the dynamics of their industries. Pepsi in South America failed to realize the intricacies of penetrating and protecting its several markets there.

How can a firm stay alert to subtle and insidious or more obvious changes? It needs *sensors* to constantly monitor the environment. A marketing or economic research department may provide such sensors, but in many instances a formal organizational entity is not really necessary to provide primary monitoring. Executive alertness is essential. Most changes do not occur suddenly and without warning. Information can come from: feedback from customers, sales representatives, and suppliers; news of relevant changes and projections in business journals; and even simple observations of what is happening in stores, advertising, prices, and new technologies. Unfortunately, in the urgency of dealing with current operating problems, executives can overlook or disregard changing environmental factors that may affect present and future business.

The following seven generalizations regard vulnerability to competition:

1. Initial market advantage tends to be rather quickly countered by competitors.
2. Countering by competitors is more likely to occur when an innovation is involved than when the advantage comes from more commonplace effective management and marketing techniques, such as superb customer service.
3. An easy-entry industry is particularly vulnerable to new and aggressive competition, especially if the market is expanding. In new industries, severe price competition usually weeds out marginal firms.

4. Long-dominant firms become vulnerable to upstart competitors because of their complacency, conservatism, and even conceit. They frequently are resistant to change, and myopic about the environment.

5. Careful monitoring of performance at strategic control points and comparing similar operating units and their trends in various performance categories can detect weakening positions needing corrective action before situations become serious. (This will be discussed further in the next section.)

6. In expanding markets, increases in sales may hide a deteriorating competitive situation. Market share data is more important.

7. A no-growth policy, or a temporary absence from the marketplace, even if fully justified by extraordinary circumstances, invites competitive inroads.

Effective Organization

From our cases we can identify several organizational attributes that can help or hinder effectiveness:

Management by Exception

With diverse and far-flung operations, it becomes difficult to closely supervise all aspects. Successful managers therefore focus their attention on performances that deviate significantly from the expected at *strategic control points*. Subordinates can be left to handle ordinary operations and less significant deviations. Thereby the manager is not overburdened with details.

Management by exception failed, however, with Maytag and its overseas Hoover division. The flaw lay in loose controls and failing to monitor faulty promotional plans. By the time results came in, it was too late.

The Deadly Parallel

As an enterprise becomes larger, a particularly effective organizational structure is to establish operating units of comparable characteristics. Sales, expenses, and profits can then be readily compared, with both strong and weak performances identified so that appropriate action can be taken. Besides providing control and performance evaluation, this *deadly parallel* fosters intrafirm competition that can stimulate best efforts. For the deadly parallel to be used effectively, operating units must be fairly equalized, perhaps through quotas or similar categories of sales potential. This is not difficult to achieve with retail units, since departments and stores can be divided into various sales volume categories—often designated as A, B, and C units—and operating results within the same volume category can be compared. While the deadly parallel is particularly effective for chain-store organizations, it can also be used with sales territories and certain other operating units where sales and applicable expenses and ratios can be directly measured and compared with similar units.

Lean and Mean

A new climate is sweeping our country's major corporations. In one sense it is good: It enhances their competitiveness. But it can be destructive. Vanguard, Southwest

Airlines, and Wal-Mart have been in the forefront of the lean-and-mean movement; IBM has moved to it, but the downsizing had to be extreme and disruptive. Lean-and-mean firms develop flat organizations with few management layers, thus keeping overhead low, improving communication, involving employees in greater self-management, and fostering an innovative mindset.

In contrast, we saw the organizational bloat of Borden and such behemoths as IBM before its turnaround, with their many management levels, entrenched bureaucracies, and massive overhead. A virtual cause-and-effect relationship exists between the proportion of total overhead committed to administration/staff and the ability to cope with change and innovate. It is like trying to maneuver a huge ship: Bureaucratic weight slows the response time.

The problem with the lemming-like pursuit of the lean-and-mean structure is knowing how far to downsize without cutting into bone and muscle. As thousands of managers and staff specialists can attest, productivity gains have not always been worth the loss of jobs, the destruction of career paths, and the possible sacrifice of long-term potential.

Resistance to Change

People as well as organizations do not embrace change well. Change is disruptive; it destroys accepted ways of doing things and muddles familiar authority and responsibility patterns. Previously important positions may be downgraded or even eliminated, and people who view themselves as highly competent in a particular job may be forced to assume unfamiliar duties amid the fear that they cannot master the new assignments. When the change involves wholesale terminations in a major downsizing, as with IBM, Borden, and Euro Disney, the resistance and fear of change can become so great that efficiency is seriously jeopardized.

Normal resistance to change can be eased by good communication with participants about forthcoming changes, thus dampening rumors and fears. Acceptance of change is helped if employees are involved as fully as possible in planning the changes, if their participation is solicited and welcomed, and if assurances can be given that positions will not be impaired, only changed. Gradual rather than abrupt changes also make a transition smoother.

In the final analysis, however, making needed changes and embracing new opportunities should not be delayed or canceled because of possible negative repercussions on the organization. If change is desirable, as it often is with long-established bureaucratic organizations, then it should be done without delay. Individuals and organizations can adapt to change—it just takes some time.

SPECIFIC MARKETING STRATEGY INSIGHTS

Strengths and Limitations of Advertising

The cases provide several insights regarding the effectiveness of advertising, but they also present unanswered questions and contradictions. At the time of Coca-Cola's blunder with its new Coke it was spending $100 million more for advertising than Pepsi, and all the while was losing market share. Vanguard has become the darling of the mutual fund industry with virtual no advertising, unlike almost all its competitors, relying instead on word-of-mouth and free publicity. Such outcomes cast doubts about the power of advertising.

However, the right theme can bring success, as witness Nike's great success with celebrity endorsements in creating an image irresistible to many of its customers. Maytag Hoover's promotional campaign certainly created great attention and interest, miguided though the plan was. How can we forget the success of the Joe Camel theme, despite public protests? The slow erosion of the glorious mystique of Coors in the late 1970s can be at least partly blamed on lack of advertising and marketing efforts.

Thus we see the great challenge of advertising. One never knows for sure how much should be spent to reach the planned objectives of perhaps increasing sales by a certain percentage or possibly gaining market share. However, despite the inability to measure directly the effectiveness of advertising, it is the brave—or foolhardy— executive who stands pat in the face of increased promotional efforts by competitors. We draw these conclusions:

> There is no assured correlation between expenditures for advertising and sales success. But the right theme or message can be powerful. In most cases, advertising can gener- ate initial trial. But if the other elements of the marketing strategy are relatively unat- tractive, customers will not be won or retained.

Limitations of Marketing Research

Marketing research is usually touted as the key to better decision making and the mark of sophisticated professional management. It is commonly thought that the more money spent for marketing research, the less chance for a bad decision. But heavy use of marketing research does not guarantee the best decision, as we saw with Coca-Cola.

At best, marketing research increases the "batting average" of correct deci- sions—maybe only by a little, sometimes by quite a bit. To be effective, research must be current and unbiased. Marketplace attitudes can change radically if months elapse between the research and the product introduction. The several million dollars spent in taste-test research for Coca-Cola hardly reassures us about the validity of even cur- rent marketing research. Admittedly, results of taste tests are difficult to rely on, sim- ply because of the subjective nature of taste preferences. Still, the Coca-Cola research did not even uncover the latent and powerful loyalty toward tradition, and it gave a false "go" signal for the new flavor.

We do not imply that marketing research has little value. Most flawed studies would have been invaluable with better design and planning. One wonders whether better market research would not have enabled Disney to structure its pricing and other strate- gies more realistically to the market conditions facing its Euro Disney project.

Surprisingly, we see that many successful new ventures initially used little formal research. Vanguard, Southwest Airlines, Wal-Mart, even McDonald's and Nike in their early days, apparently relied on entrepreneurial hunch rather than sophisticated research. Why have we not seen more extensive use of marketing research for new ventures? Consider the following major reasons:

- Most of the founding entrepreneurs did not have marketing backgrounds and therefore were not familiar and confident with such research.

- Available tools and techniques are not always appropriate to handle some problems and opportunities. There may be too many variables to ascertain their full impact, and some of these will be intangible and incapable of precise measurement. Much research consists of collecting past and present data that, although helpful in predicting a stable future, are of little help in charting revolutionary new ventures. If the risks are higher without marketing research, these are often offset by the potential for great rewards.

The Importance of Price as an Offensive Weapon

We generally think of price promotions as the most aggressive marketing strategy and the one most desirable from the point of view of society. We have seen three notable marketing successes that geared their major strategy on having lower prices than competitors: Vanguard, Southwest Airlines, and Wal-Mart. We saw another case where high prices were a real detriment in meeting performance goals: Euro Disney. And we saw low-price competition cutting into the profits of McDonald's. Still, in another case, Perrier, a high-price strategy was a key factor in its marketing success before the crisis, as consumers perceived the high price as indicative of high quality.

The major disadvantage of low prices as an offensive weapon is that other firms in the industry are almost forced to meet the price-cutter's prices—in other words, such a marketing strategy is easy to match. Consequently, when prices for an entire industry fall, no firm may have any particular advantage and all suffer the effects in diminished profits. Thus, in many situations competitive advantage is therefore seldom won by price-cutting. But the three major successes with their greater operating efficiencies and lower overhead cost structures could realize good profits while most competitors did not even attempt to meet their prices.

In general, other marketing strategies are more successful for most firms—strategies such as better quality, better product and brand image, better service, and improved warranties, all aspects of nonprice rather than price competition.

At the same time, we have to recognize that in new industries, ones characterized by rapid technological change and production efficiencies, severe price competition is the rule, and weeds out marginal operations that hoped to cash in on a rapidly growing market. Even a substantial position in such an industry may not insulate a firm from price competition that can jeopardize its viability.

Analytical Tools for Marketing

We identified several of the most useful analytical tools for marketing decision making. In Disney we discussed breakeven analysis, a highly useful tool for making go/no-go decisions about new ventures and alternative business strategies. In Maytag, cost-benefit analysis was described, which might have prevented the bungled promotion in England. And we encountered the SWOT analysis in the Southwest Airlines case. While these analyses do not guarantee the best decisions, they do bring order and systematic thinking into the art of marketing decision making.

Franchising

An important mode for great growth in opening more outlets is franchising. This was discussed more fully in the McDonald's and Burger King case, as well as for Planet Hollywood and Boston Chicken. The great growth comes from the release of the financial burden of company-owned outlets; rather, independent franchisees put up the capital for new outlets. However, franchisee relations can present problems, as McDonald's recently found.

A Kinder, Gentler Stance?

In several cases, we could identify an arrogant mindset as leading to difficulties. The French did not appreciate this arrogance by Disney, and the Euro Disney project was almost a disaster. Arrogance also eventually caught up with Aramony of United Way.

At the other extreme, is there room in today's competitive environment for a kinder, gentler stance by a business firm? While a firm normally comes into contact with a number of different parties, let us consider this question with regard to these: suppliers and distributors, customers, and employees.

Relations with Suppliers and Distributors

With the movement toward just-in-time deliveries in the search for more efficiency and cost containment, manufacturers and retailers are placing greater demands on suppliers. Those who cannot meet these demands will usually lose out to competitors able to do so. The big manufacturer or retailer can demand ever more from smaller suppliers, since it is in the power position and the loss of its business could be overwhelming. We saw the problems of Rubbermaid in being unable to meet the service demands of Wal-Mart. At the least, the big customer deserves priority attention since its business is so important to any supplier. Reebok's callousness in disregarding the new-product concerns of Foot Locker led to its being supplanted by a hard-charging Nike in the sneaker wars of the early 1990s.

Some of the big retailers today, such as Wal-Mart and Kmart as well as supermarket chains, impose "slotting fees." A slotting fee essentially is a toll charged by the retailer for the use of its space; suppliers pay this up front if they wish to be represented in the retailer's stores. Other demands include driving costs down to rock bottom even if this destroys the supplier's profits, and insisting that the supplier take responsibility for inventory control, provide special promotional support, and the like.

While the Wal-Marts and others argue that such use of clout leads to greater marketing efficiencies and lower consumer prices, it can be carried too far. The term *symbiotic relationship* describes the relationship between the various channel-of-distribution members: All benefit from the success of the product and it should be to their mutual advantage to work together. The manufacturer and the distributor thus should represent a valued partnership.

The same idea applies for the dealers or distributors of a powerful manufacturer. They are on the same side; they are not in competition with one another. Yet, we have seen several instances where a manufacturer created soured distributor/dealer relations. Pepsi was not closely attuned to the concerns of its longtime Venezuela bottler and lost distribution in that entire country. And McDonald's callously disregarded concerns of its domestic franchisees in its eager quest to open more and more outlets. Would a kinder, gentler approach to the other members of the channel-of-distribution team have prevented or resolved these problems?

Relations with Customers

Most firms pay lip service to customer satisfaction. Some go much further in this regard than others. Few have gone as far as Vanguard in creating a loyal and enthusiastic body of customers. A symbiotic relationship can also be seen as applying to manufacturer/customer relations: They both stand to win from highly satisfied customers. And again, isn't a kinder, gentler relationship a positive?

Giving Employees a Sense of Pride and a Caring Management

The great turnaround of Continental from the confrontational days of Frank Lorenzo has to be mainly attributed to the people-oriented environment fostered by Bethune. The marvel is how quickly it was done, starting with such a simple thing as an open-door policy to the executive suite, and encouragement of full communication with employees.

Still, Continental was not unique in this enlisting of employees to the team. Kelleher of Southwest Airlines certainly developed this esprit de corps, and this helps account for the great cost advantage Southwest has. Ray Kroc of McDonald's fostered this as McDonald's began its great charge, although relationships with franchisees dimmed somewhat in recent years.

On the other hand, Boeing's problems with its peaks and valleys of layoffs and hiring destroyed any hope of widespread pride and esprit de corps of its employees, except perhaps for a nucleus. A sense of pride was certainly latent with such a national symbol, but management did not cultivate it.

ETHICAL CONSIDERATIONS

A firm tempted to walk the low road in search of greater short-run profits may eventually find that the risks far outweigh the rewards. This holds for industries, too; the tobacco industry has been grudgingly confronting wave after wave of attacks and an eager media quick to publicize them.

We have examined more than a few cases dealing with ethical controversies, for example, ADM's indictment for price fixing and its more subtle efforts to gain special influence in the halls of government. Then there was Met Life's indictment for deceptive sales practices, and the exposés of undesirable practices by United Way.

While we cannot delve very deeply into social and ethical issues,[2] these insights are worth noting:

- A firm can no longer disavow itself from the possibility of critical ethical scrutiny. Activist groups often publicize alleged misdeeds long before governmental regulators will. Legal actions may follow.
- Public protests may take a colorful path, with marches, picketing, billboard whitewashing, and the like, and may enlist public and media support for their cause.

Should a firm attempt to resist and defend itself? The overwhelming evidence is to the contrary. The bad press, the continued adversarial relations, and the effect on public image are hardly worth such a confrontation. The better course of action may be to back down as quietly as possible, repugnant though such may be to a management convinced of the reasonableness of its position.

Johnson & Johnson's secret for gaining rapport with the media was corporate openness and cooperation. After the Tylenol catastrophe, it sought good two-way communication with media furnishing information from the field while J&J gave full and honest disclosure of its own investigation and actions. To promote good rapport, company officials were readily available to the press.

Unfortunately, J&J's openness with the media and concern for customers seems to have eroded in recent years, with publicity of overpricing of a vital cancer drug, and reluctance to make full disclosure of the risks of Tylenol overdosing.

GENERAL INSIGHTS

Impact of One Person

In many of the cases one person had a powerful impact on the organization. Sam Walton of Wal-Mart is perhaps the most outstanding example, but we also have Ray Kroc of McDonald's, who converted a small hamburger stand into the world's largest restaurant operation; Herb Kelleher of Southwest Airlines, tormentor of the mighty airlines; Phil Knight of Nike, who could never break the four-minute mile in college, but went on to bring Nike world leadership in running and other athletic gear. Let us not forget John Bogle, the founder and crusader of the Vanguard Fund Family, and his gospel of frugality.

For turnaround accomplishments, Gordon Bethune, who turned around a demoralized Continental Airlines, stands tall, as does Lou Gerstner of IBM. Virtually and undeservingly unknown is Leonard Hadly, who quietly turned around Maytag after the disaster with its United Kingdom subsidiary.

One person can also have a negative impact on an organization. William Aramony almost destroyed United Way by his high living and arrogance. Less well-known is

---

[2] For more depth of coverage, see R. F. Hartley, *Business Ethics* (New York: Wiley, 1993).

Dwayne Andreas, the long-time CEO of ADM, who set the climate for illegalities both embarrassing and reprehensible. Frank Lorenzo with his confrontational labor relations almost destroyed Continental. And there is Geoffrey Bible of Philip Morris, the industry's most aggressive defender. The impact of one person, for good or ill, is one of the recurring marvels of history, whether business history or world history.

Prevalence of Opportunities for Entrepreneurship Today

Despite the maturing of our economy and the growing size and power of many firms in many industries, opportunities for entrepreneurship are more abundant than ever. Opportunities exist not only for the changemaker or innovator, but also for the person who only seeks to do things a little better than existing, and complacent, competition.

Most entrepreneurial successes are unheralded, although dozens have been widely publicized, such as Bill Gates of Microsoft. Wal-Mart and Southwest Airlines, and even McDonald's and Vanguard, are not so many years away from their beginnings. Opportunities are there for the dedicated. Venture capital to support promising new businesses has helped many fledgling enterprises. As a new business shows early promise, initial public offerings (IPOs) (i.e., new stock issues) become important sources of capital, as we saw with Boston Chicken and Planet Hollywood.

But entrepreneurship is not for everyone. The great venture capitalists look at the person, not the idea. Typically they distribute their seed money to resourceful people who are courageous enough to give up security for the unknown consequences of their embryonic ventures, who have great self-confidence, and who demonstrate a tremendous will to win.

CONCLUSION

We learn from mistakes and from successes, although every marketing problem and opportunity seems cast in a unique setting. One author has likened marketing strategy to military strategy:

> Strategies which are flexible rather than static embrace optimum use and offer the greatest number of alternative objectives. A good commander knows that he cannot control his environment to suit a prescribed strategy. Natural phenomena pose their own restraints to strategic planning, whether physical, geographic, regional, or psychological and sociological.[3]

He later adds:

> Planning leadership recognizes the unpleasant fact that, despite every effort, the war may be lost. Therefore, the aim is to retain the maximum number of facilities and the basic organization. Indicators of a deteriorating and unsalvageable total situation are,

---

[3] Myron S. Heidingsfield, *Changing Patterns in Marketing* (Boston: Allyn & Bacon, 1968), p. 11.

therefore, mandatory… No possible combination of strategies and tactics, no mobilization of resources… can supply a magic formula which guarantees victory; it is possible only to increase the probability of victory.[4]

Thus, we can pull two concepts from military strategy to help guide marketing strategy: the desirability of flexibility in an unknown or changing environment and the idea that a basic core should be maintained in crises. The first suggests that the firm should be prepared for adjustments in strategy as conditions warrant. The second suggests that there is a basic core of a firm's business that should be unchanging; it should be the final bastion to fall back on for regrouping if necessary. IBM had a solid core that it was able to maintain and from which it could mount a resurgence. Whether Toys "Я" Us has such a solid core remains to be seen. Boston Chicken and Planet Hollywood probably have not had time to develop solid core positions.

In regard to the basic core of a firm, every viable firm has some distinctive function or "ecological niche" in the business environment:

Every business firm occupies a position which is in some respects unique. Its location, the product it sells, its operating methods, or the customers it serves tend to set it off in some degree from every other firm. Each firm competes by making the most of its individuality and its special character.[5]

Woe to the firm that loses its ecological niche.

QUESTIONS

1. Design a program aimed at mistake avoidance. Be as specific, as creative, and as complete as possible.
2. Would you advise a firm to be an imitator or an innovator? Why?
3. "There is no such thing as a sustainable competitive advantage." Discuss.
4. How would you build controls into an organization to ensure that similar mistakes do not happen in the future?
5. Array as many pros and cons of entrepreneurship as you can. Which do you see as most compelling?
6. Do you agree with the thought expressed in this chapter that a firm confronted with strong criticism should abandon the product or the way of doing business? Why or why not?
7. We have suggested that the learning insights discussed in this chapter and elsewhere in the book are transferable to other firms and other times. Do you completely agree with this? Why or why not?

[4] Ibid.
[5] Alderson, p. 101.

8. Do you agree or disagree with the author's contention that a kinder, gentler stance toward channel members would be desirable and profitable? Why or why not?

HANDS-ON EXERCISE

Your firm has had a history of reacting to rather than anticipating changes in the industry. As the staff assistant to the CEO, you have been assigned the responsibility of developing adequate sensors of the marketplace. How will you go about developing such sensors?

TEAM DEBATE EXERCISE

Debate the extremes of forecasting for an innovative new product: conservative versus aggressive.